FAITH
HOPE AND WORSHIP

ASPECTS OF RELIGIOUS MENTALITY
IN THE ANCIENT WORLD

STUDIES
IN GREEK AND ROMAN
RELIGION

EDITED BY H. S. VERSNEL

IN CO-OPERATION WITH F. T. VAN STRATEN

VOLUME 2

LEIDEN / E. J. BRILL / 1981

FAITH
HOPE AND WORSHIP

ASPECTS OF RELIGIOUS MENTALITY
IN THE ANCIENT WORLD

EDITED BY

H. S. VERSNEL

LEIDEN / E. J. BRILL / 1981

ISBN   90 04 06425 7

To W. den Boer

CONTENTS

Plates: F. T. van Straten, Gifts for the gods, Figures 1-64.

INTRODUCTION

This is a book on men and gods in the Ancient World. As the title reveals it concentrates above all on the human side of this relationship. The emphasis is on the religious attitude of ancient man, his ways of making contact with the divine world, his responses to divine actions, negative or positive, his tokens of piety or impiety, of belief and disbelief. The papers published in this book originated as lectures delivered during a summer-course for Dutch classical teachers in August 1977. This may explain an occasional colloquialism, and, above all, the distinctly informative nature of the contributions: we considered it our task to provide a picture of ancient religious mentality, rather thàn to embark upon theoretical speculations digestible to specialists only.

Naturally the picture is not complete, selection being unavoidable. Yet we believe that the subjects treated are of central relevance to the religious mentality of the Ancient World. It will soon be apparent to the reader that aspects of both continuity and discontinuity have received due attention.

The original publication of the lectures in the Dutch periodical *Lampas* 12 (1979) 5-151, provoked a number of sympathetic but none the less unequivocal reactions by non-Dutch colleagues wondering whether the authors actually *believed* that anybody outside their borders was able, or willing, to decode their uncouth lingo. The authors did not, and these reactions have been the principal incentive to have the texts translated and to present them to a larger public. This, however, required adaptations, and the result of a great deal of rephrasing, modification and addition has yielded a book that differs in many respects from the original collection of papers. It may serve the purpose of an introduction to sketch briefly the contents of the contributions and to note where they differ from the papers as printed in *Lampas*.

Generally there are two ways of making contact with the gods: the way of the word (oracular question, prayer) and the way of the action (sacrifice, offering, votive gifts). These two aspects form the subjects of the first two contributions. In his discussion of the religious mentality of ancient prayer H. S. Versnel concentrates on elements characteristic of total Antiquity, and investigates, among other things, what ancient man asked for, how he tried to make gods listen (including the problem concerning loud and silent prayer), how he acted when gods did not listen and how he reacted when they did. The latter issue raises questions in connection with the prayer of gratitude: why was it so rare? This section has been totally revised and considerably enlarged.

F. T. van Straten treats the gifts for the gods with special emphasis on the votive gifts as archaeology has brought them to light. He concentrates on the archaic and classical periods of the Greek world, but also traces obvious connections between the ancient and the modern evidence with regard both to the motifs of what is presented and the motivations that induced people to honour the gods in this particular way. New is the appendix with a full collection of the Greek votive offerings representing parts of the human body, as far as they have been published.

In the third essay H. W. Pleket makes an enquiry into an intriguing—and perhaps the most important—process of change in the ancient religious attitude: when and where did the idea originate that the human believer is the subordinate or even the slave of the majestic and despotic god? Against the orthodox opinion that this ideology was introduced *in toto* under the influence of Oriental autocracy both human and divine, it is argued that traces of such feelings of dependency can already be found, albeit incidentally, in pre-Hellenistic Greece. It was only in Hellenistic and Imperial times that this attitude acquired a more structural status. One specific element of the new ideology, the consciousness of guilt and the idea of penance, does not appear to have been anticipated in classical Greece. In this context the new section on εὐλογία is particularly relevant.

In these first three papers it is mainly the uneducated and simple believer who is asked for information. His language may be poor and his artefacts clumsy. But he is human and often much more representative of real life in Antiquity than poets and philosophers. It would, however, be excessive to deny the latter categories the epithet 'human' for the mere reason that they were capable of either versification or reflection or even both. We can in fact discover, in their elevated expressions, sentiments of faith, doubt and hope similar to the ones we meet in inscriptions, popular prayer and votive reliefs.

J. M. Bremer deals with the Greek hymns, describes their conventional structure and typology and shows how they were performed in the ambiance of the religious cult. There is also a survey of the remaining texts of the archaic and classical periods and interpretations of a few specimens.

Finally, P. A. Meijer discusses various aspects of the philosophic and intellectual attitudes towards religion. In his first section he tackles the question of where atheism originated and why it was never accepted or assimilated by Greek philosophy in the classical period. In the next sections—which originally appeared in a later fascicle of *Lampas* 13 (1980) 235-260—he discusses the philosophers' attitude towards prayer and sacrifice respectively, and he concludes with a discussion of the concept of *deisidaimonia* in Theophrastus and Plutarch.

To conclude: the authors have dedicated their work to W. den Boer. Most of them have been his pupils, all have benefited from his works. The fact that the subject of this book belongs to a field that has always attracted his special interest may be regarded as a divine *fiat. Omen accepimus.*

H. S. Versnel

H. S. VERSNEL

RELIGIOUS MENTALITY IN ANCIENT PRAYER*

I. *Introduction*

One of the most moving books I happen to know is *Prières secrètes des Français d'aujourd'hui*, a collection of prayers gathered by S. Bonnet[1] in French churches and places of pilgrimage. Whoever wants to know what and how the average believer in present-day Catholic France believes should not consult a missal or attend a religious service: what he must do is read this book or set out in search himself of these highly personal, frequently ingenuous, but always disarming proofs of individual devotion. Some are strikingly naive.[2] One believer writes (the mistakes are not misprints): 'Sainte Vierge ta grande grace et protection pour voyage en avion pour la Hongrie 15 avril—départ 11 h. 50. petit fils et belle fille et mon fils 27 avril 10 h. 10—arr. 13 h. 35 retour 14 mai 15 h. 50—18 h. 40 merci de tout cœur d'une maman...' The Virgin Mary is obviously expected to keep up with the times. We may hardly be able to suppress a smile at the supplication 'Guérissez ma chièvre', but the smile dies on our lips when we read the next line: 'C'est mon seul moyen de vivre'. We might chuckle at the prayer 'Pour la conversion de Giscard et de tout notre gouvernement', but there is nothing to laugh about in the following petition: 'Maman. Ne nous abandonnez pas je vous en supplie Me voilà avec une tumeur du sein, avec un mauvais pronostic un mari qui a déjà été veuf avec 3 enfants Maintenant ceux-ci sont élevés ou presque, mais il reste mes 2 petits (10 et 6 ans)—ils ont besoin de moi et notre situation financière sera précaire si je ne travaille pas! Demain je viendrai avec mes petits'.

---

* Since the subject of this paper is not prayer but rather the mentality of and in prayer I hope I am excused for not giving a full bibliography of ancient prayer. The interested reader will find an extensive, albeit far from complete list in the article 'Gebet' in *Reallexikon für Antike und Christentum*.

[1] Editions du Cerf (Paris 1976).

[2] In Antiquity, too, people would smile at naive votive inscriptions: Plin. *Ep.* 8, 8, 7, *leges multa multorum omnibus columnis, omnibus parietibus inscripta, quibus fons ille deusque celebratur. Plura laudabis, nonnulla ridebis....*

This is real prayer, prayer in the hour of need and distress. And just as need is a constant feature of world history, so, too, is the prayer born of need. We therefore find striking correspondences between what the prayers deposited in these chapels represent for modern France, or for modern devotion in general,[3] and the votive inscriptions, oracular tablets, magical lead plates and literary texts of Antiquity which reflect similar personal expressions of prayer. For, as we see from the great frequency and repetition of so many prayers, wishes or supplications, Antiquity was already far from 'den alten Zeiten, wo das Wünschen noch geholfen hat', as the Grimm brothers put it.

If this paper is an attempt to give the reader an impression of certain aspects of ancient prayer, the attitude towards prayer and the mentality which emerges from it, I am restricting myself deliberately. No man can describe the whole of prayer, as Origen[4] reminds us: ἓν τῶν ἀδυνάτων ὅσον ἐπὶ τῇ ἀσθενείᾳ ἡμῶν πείθομαι τυγχάνειν τρανῶσαι τὸν περὶ τῆς εὐχῆς ἀκριβῶς καὶ θεοπρεπῶς πάντα λόγον, and this is far from being my object.

Let us, for the sake of convenience, recall C. Ausfeld's formal division of prayer into *invocatio* (invocation by means of the name, surname, epithets and descriptive predicates), the *pars epica* (in which the suppliant explains why he is calling on this particular god for help, what his relationship with the deity is, and why he thinks he can count on his assistance) and the actual *preces* (the content of the wish). In what follows I shall discuss the first and the last of these headings, but will be leaving out the second one altogether since, together with components of the *invocatio*, it leads to the sphere of the hymn and, as such, will be included, together with other more formal and literary aspects, in J. M. Bremer's paper, where it is rightly labelled 'argument'. In reaction against the prevailing formal approach which can be discerned in the vast amount of literature on the subject of prayer, I have decided to opt, within the broader context of 'ancient religiosity', for an elucidation of the prayers of the common man. This choice has also conditioned a large part of the material selected: Artemidorus rather than Plato, Babrius rather than Homer, a personal inscription or a magical papyrus rather than a literary prayer bound to

---

[3] Of course, letters to (God and) the Saints are very common as Lourdes, the Santo Bambino of the Aracoeli and so many other holy places prove. A very able, scientific discussion can be found in W. Heim, *Briefe zum Himmel. Die Grabbriefe an Mutter M. Theresia Scherer in Ingenbohl* (Schriften der Schweiz. Ges. f. Volkskunde 40, Basel 1961).

[4] Origen. Περὶ εὐχῆς (Koetschau, Leipzig 1899) I, II, 1.

stylistic rules, although these extremes influenced each other far more than is generally supposed,[5] and although I shall not go out of my way to avoid more elevated literature.

From Homer to the magical papyri: such, roughly speaking, are the limits of Antiquity. Can we really speak of *the* mentality of prayer in Antiquity? If, for the sake of brevity, I answer in the affirmative and lay aside all subtle distinctions, I feel that I can appeal in the first place to F. Heiler's extensive study, *Das Gebet*, which was written with the perfectly justifiable conviction that it is possible to describe a phenomenology of prayer in general. If this is so, it must be permissible to do as much for Antiquity. I believe, moreover, that Antiquity must be regarded, first and foremost, as a social, psychological and religious unit in which considerable changes can indeed be perceived, but in which a number of fundamental elements and structures can nevertheless be regarded as constant. We are, of course, only entitled to regard those phenomena as characteristic of all Antiquity which are attested at very different moments, even if it is not always possible to quote every single reference. Whenever an important change of mentality can be demonstrated—one of the most remarkable is discussed by H. W. Pleket—and if it affects the domain of prayer, I shall always give a rough chronological indication, for the sake of relativity. Finally, the knowledge that many characteristics of ancient prayer are still part of the religious baggage of present-day believers, particularly in the Mediterranean, justifies a more general approach.

This leads us to another preliminary observation. By and large we can focus our attention either on the elements which Antiquity and the present-day have in common or on those which differentiate one from the other. Of these two categories the second is more likely to surprise us, and consequently to raise questions, than the first. It will be seen that in the present paper—and this is the direct result of our subject—the common elements will be more frequently represented than the discriminatory ones. This, I hope, can serve as an excuse for the prevalently descriptive character of this article, mainly due, in its turn, to the deliberate object of introducing the reader to a type of material which he may not encounter every day. Such material, moreover, must speak for itself: a musty smell

---

[5] This is illustrated by A. Cameron, *HTR* 32 (1939) 1 ff. Cf. also A. J. Festugière, 'Vraisemblance psychologique et forme littéraire chez les anciens', in *Études de religion grecque et hellénistique* (Paris 1972) 249-270.

of 'antiquarianism' here and there is the price that reader and writer will
have to pay. The proud boast made by A. von Harnack in the foreword to
the fourth edition of his epoch-making *Mission und Ausbreitung des Christen-
tums* when he wrote: 'Nachruhmen darf ich dem Werk, dass es so gut wie
keine Hypothesen enthält, sondern Tatsachen zusammenstellt', is unlikely to be made by anyone nowadays: there is no study, however positivistic,
which does not contain opinions and conceal hypotheses. The reader
wishing for *explicit* questions and an hypothetical answer must turn to section VII, where I try to provide a tentative explanation of a really striking
discrepancy between past and present, viz. the virtual absence, in Antiquity, of prayers of gratitude, against the background of the mentality
of an ancient society.

But if ancient prayer accords little space to true gratitude, it accords a
great deal to questions. We can go still further: there are hardly any
prayers—with the exception of a few hymns—in which a question or a
wish is not expressed in one form or another. *What* was asked and of *whom*?
These are the two elements (*invocatio* and *preces*) which will prevail
throughout this paper, and which are nowhere to be found so well ex-
emplified—*at least in combination*—as in a specific form of conversation with
the god: the question to the oracle. Although I am well aware of the differences between prayer and oracle question what I have just said entitles
me, I believe, to open a first tentative section with a number of concrete
attestations of this genre. These will then lead us straight *in medias res* both
with regard to 'what' and to 'whom'.

II. *Prayers expressing wishes: direct and indirect objects*

Whoever wishes to know with what daily cares the common man was
beset in Antiquity has only to follow him to the spot where a god lent his
ear to the mortal more frequently and more certainly than anywhere else:
the oracular shrine. The first that comes to mind, Delphi, is too exalted in
all senses of the word. The questions which survive often have a mythical
or legendary character and, in so far as they have come down to us, were
mainly recorded from the mouths of kings and statesmen. In the collection
of Parke and Wormell[6] the common man hardly ever has a say (although
he visited the Apolline oracle just as frequently as the great of the land).
For direct attestations of popular belief we must descend to the wide plain

---

[6] H. W. Parke and D. E. W. Wormell, *The Delphic Oracle* (Oxford 1956).

of Dodona where Zeus Naios and his spouse Dione ruled and where numerous lead labels with questions have come to light.[7] Here private questions far exceed public ones. One example of the latter category (P. 260 n° 3) Θεόν. τ[ύ]χαν [ἀ]γαθ[άν]. ἐπικοινῶνται τοὶ Κ[ο]ρκυρα[ῖοι τῶι Δὶ] Νάωι καὶ τᾶι Δ[ι]ώναι τίνι κα [θ]εῶν ἢ ἡρώων θύον[τ]ες καὶ εὐχ[ό]μενοι ὁμονοῖεν ἐ[π]ὶ τὠγαθόν. 'God. Good Fortune. The Corcyreans ask Zeus Naios and Dione to which of the gods or heroes they must sacrifice and pray in order to succeed in obtaining concord'. A significant question if we think that it was made at the end of the 5th century B. C. and if we read Thucydides as a background to it. Individuals had other problems. One of the commonest formulas is (SEG XV, 395) [Τ]ίνι κα θεῶι εὐχόμενος καὶ θύων βέλτιον πράσσοι; and n° 405 ibidem adds a bit more concretely καὶ χρημάτων κτῆσις ἀγαθὴ ἔσται. The author of SEG XV n° 386 is cautious about publicising his wish: Τίνι κα θεὸν εὐξάμενος πρᾶξαι hὰ ἐπὶ νόοι ἔχε; As we shall see, he may have wished for something perfectly horrid or he may have been in love. Usually, however, the questions were more concrete and there were few things with which men dared not pester Zeus. There are numerous questions about how one can get 'better', 'better' usually meaning to be 'healed': (P. 267 n° 14) Θρασύβουλος τίνι κα θεῶν θύσα[ς] καὶ hιλαξάμενος τὸς ὀπτίλ[ος] ὑγιέστερος γένοιτο; 'Th. wants to know which of the gods he must propitiate with sacrifices in order for his eyes to be healed'. But there was no objection to financial 'improvement' either: (P. 268 n° 17) ἐρουτᾶι Κλεούται τὸν Δία καὶ τὰν Διώναν, αἴ ἐστι αὐτῶι προβατεύοντι ὄναιον καὶ ὠφέλιμον ('whether it is advantageous and profitable for him to keep sheep'). The editor adds: 'The enquirer was not accustomed to writing'. It would appear that the questions were (sometimes?) written by the suppliant himself—questions which usually revolved round the themes: should I buy a house in town? should I build a workshop? should I acquire a pond? should I take over my father's business? should I embark on a sea voyage? should I stay at home or go away? Unlike Apollo of Delphi, the inspirer of so many colonial expeditions, Zeus appears as a more conservative spirit, as we see from various answers of the following type: (P. 270 n° 23) αὐτεῖ οἰκεῖν καὶ ἐξέχεσθαι 'remain where you are and persevere'. The god was also called in to assist a not altogether effective

---

[7] There is a collection in H. W. Parke, *The Oracles of Zeus* (Oxford 1967). The testimonies taken from this book are indicated with P. More extensive material: *SEG* XV, n° 385-409; XIX, n° 426-432; XXIII, n° 473; XXIV, n° 454. Some beautiful examples in J. et L. Robert, *BE* 1939, n° 153; 1959, n° 231; 1961; n° 171.

detective service: (P. 273 n° 29) ἔκλεφε Δορχίλος τὸ λᾶκος; 'Did D. steal the gown?' and elsewhere 'Did Thopion steal the money?' 'Has so and so kidnapped my slave?' Questions about wife and child were also important (P. 265 n° 6) Θεός· Γηριότον Δία ἐπερωτῆι περὶ γυναικὸς ἢ βέλτιον λαβόντι; 'Is it better to take a wife?' And there always remained the question of whether a wife should have children: ἢ ἔσται μοι γενεὰ ἀπὸ τᾶς Νίκης τῆς γυναικὸς ἧς ἔχει; (P. 265 n° 8). But these men were merely at the beginning of their worries: the truly agonising questions come later: (P. 266 n° 11) ἐρωτῆι Λυσανίας Δία Νάιον καὶ Δηώναν ἦ οὐκ ἐστι ἐξ αὐτοῦ τὸ παιδάριον ὁ Ἀννύλα κύει;

The oracular technique became really professional in the imperial period in Egypt, where numerous fragments of collections of questions have come to light. These include questions ascribed to a legendary magician, Astrampsychos, and known by the name of *Sortes Astrampsychi*.[8] To each of the 92 questions 10 possible answers were formulated which were drawn by way of a sort of lottery. Whoever reads the questions can get an excellent idea of the fears and needs of ancient man: will I receive my wages? will I be sold as a slave? will I get money? will I sign a contract? will I be successful? will I escape? will I become *bouleutès*? shall I divorce my wife? have I been poisoned? shall I inherit? etc.[9] We encounter many of these questions in completely different contexts. The Egyptian oracle question εἰ ζῆ ὁ ἀπόδημος; describes more or less the same situation as we find in a recently published votive inscription by a priest of Cybele.[10] The priest made a vow to the goddess Cybele concerning his friend who had been captured in a ship during the war. He then heard from the goddess in a dream that his friend had indeed been captured, but would be rescued. The dedication was correct, for the interpreter of dreams Artemidorus (*Dream Book* IV, 2) also recommended that after a similar prophetic dream you 'should sacrifice and express your gratitude' (μετὰ δὲ τὸ ἰδεῖν καὶ θῦε καὶ εὐχαρίστει). The same Artemidorus (*ibid.* IV, 2), however, warned against pestering the gods with questions like 'If this is what I must do to get my wish' and 'If this will occur for me' or 'If it is advantageous and profitable

---

[8] G. M. Browne, 'The Composition of the Sortes Astrampsychi', *BICS* 17 (1970) 95 ff.; idem, *The Papyri of the Sortes Astrampsychi* (Meisenheim 1974); J. Hengst, *Griechische Papyri aus Aegypten* (Tusculum 1978) 162 ff.

[9] All this confirms what Plutarch, *Mor.* 408 C quotes as the most representative individual questions: εἰ γαμητέον, εἰ πλευστέον, εἰ δανειστέον, περὶ ὠνῆς ἀνδραπόδου, περὶ ἐργασίας and as representative of state delegations: φορᾶς καρπῶν πέρι καὶ βοτῶν ἐπιγονῆς καὶ σωμάτων ὑγίειας.

[10] E. Schwertheim, in *Festschrift F. K. Dörner* II (Leiden 1978) 811.

to me, I would take something; otherwise I would give it away'. Nor should too much trust be placed in oracular answers given in dreams, as we see from V, 92: 'A sick man implored Serapis to shake his right hand at him in a dream if he was going to live, but, if not, to shake his left hand. And, indeed, he dreamt that he went into the temple of Serapis and that Cerberus shook his right hand at him. Naturally the man died on the following day. For Cerberus, who is considered the personification of death, indicated by raising his right hand, his readiness to receive the man'.[11]

Questions; requests for certainty and for advice. But the wish, which forms the link with the prayer of supplication, is always in the background, usually implicit, but sometimes explicit, as Empedocles discovered, who,[12] 'whenever he visited flourishing cities, was honoured by men and women':

οἱ δ'ἅμ' ἕπονται
μυρίοι ἐξερέοντες, ὅπηι πρὸς κέρδος ἀταρπός,
οἱ μὲν μαντοσυνέων κεχρημένοι, οἱ δ'ἐπὶ νούσων
παντοίων ἐπυθόντο κλυεῖν εὐηκέα βάξιν,
δηρὸν δὴ χαλεπῆισι πεπαρμένοι......

Indeed, the oracle question and the prayer of supplication are close to each other, as we see from the following example, defined by Parke as 'an exceptionally emotional address in the form of a prayer' (P. 263 n° 2), [Θεός. τύχη] ἀγα[θή.] δέσποτα ἄναξ Ζεῦ Νάϊε καὶ Διώνη καὶ Δωδοναῖοι, αἰτεῖ ὑμᾶς καὶ ἱκετεύει Διόγνητος Ἀριστομήδου Ἀθηναῖος δοῦναι αὐτῶι καὶ τοῖς ἑαυτοῦ εὔνοις ἅπασιν καὶ τεῖ μητρὶ Κλεαρέτει καὶ....

This is a prayer emphatically expressing the wish of the suppliant that Zeus should give to himself, to all those who are well-disposed towards him and to his mother... (fortune? health? all the best?). Here we see clearly how asking for *knowledge* and asking for *help* are frequently two sides of the same thing.[13] What was the purpose of the numerous treasuries of Delphi if not to persuade Apollo to give a favourable answer or, after he had done

---

[11] Several other examples: *ibid.* V, 71-72; 91-94.

[12] Fragment 112 (D).

[13] This is also strikingly illustrated by a special type of prayers in Babylonia. People do not pray for various kinds of blessings but for dreams or portents which foretell these blessings: G. Widengren, *The Accadian and Hebrew Psalms of Lamentation as Religious Documents* (Uppsala 1936) 263 f.

so, to thank him for it? Does the anxious question of 'whether my son will recover from consumption' (P. 267 n° 13) not imply the unspoken prayer that the reply be favourable?

So the above examples from the domain of oracles pave the way for true prayers of supplication, the content of which we know usually not from the prayer itself but from the votive formula after the prayer had been granted. There are thousands of such examples and the similarity with modern expressions is obvious. What did ancient man ask for? For everything. He asked for recovery and good health for himself, his wife and his child (separately: ὑπὲρ ζωῆς πελλόμενος τέκνοιο,[14] or combined: εὐξάμενος ὑπὲρ γυνέκος καὶ τέκ[νων] καὶ συγγενῶν ἀνέθ[η]κεν;[15] we find endless repetitions of the formulas pro se et suis; pro salute sua et suorum; ὑπὲρ τῶν ἰδίων) and the emperor. Prayers were made for crops: εὐξάμενοι περὶ τῶν ἰδίων πάντων σωτηρίας καὶ καρπῶν θελεσποπορίας.[16] People would pray for their own horse or donkey ('Ελπὶς 'Ανδρονίκου εὐξαμένη ὑπὲρ τοῦ ἡμιόνου εὐχήν)[17] and also that the horse of their rival might break its legs (frequent in magical defixiones). People prayed without reserve for fortune, honour, wealth ('Ερμῆ δίκαιε κέρδος 'Εκτίκῳ [δί]δου[18]). They prayed for pregnancy, to conceive children and to keep them (τιμῶσα Εὐλοχίαν ῎Αρτεμιν ἀντὶ τέκνων) and they asked to be finally redeemed from pregnancy ('Αρτέμιδι 'Ιλιθύαι Μενέπολις 'Επίνου παυσιτοκεῖα ἀνέθηκε),[19] the latter in a not entirely clear formula. This occurs frequently: we are by no means

[14] From Thrace. Read παλλόμενος 'tremblant pour la vie de son enfant': L. Robert, BE 1952, n° 97, correcting G. Mihailov, REG (1951) 104 ff.

[15] Baalbek: AE 1961, n° 233.

[16] Th. Drew-Bear, Nouvelles Inscriptions de Phrygie (Zutphen 1978) 38, n° 3. On prayer for τελεσφορία τῶν καρπῶν see BE 1956, n° 294.

[17] From Maeonia in Lydia: L. Robert, Hellenica VI, 107. See on prayers for livestock and domestic animals ibid. VII, 158 n. 4; X, 35 f.; BE index s.v. troupeaux.

[18] A graffito in Ostia: R. Meiggs, Roman Ostia (Oxford 1960) 231. Reflection of a literary example, which might glimmer through in Ovid Fasti 5, 689, da modo lucra mihi? Thus R. J. Littlewood, Latom. 34 (1975) 673. I have accepted the corrected version by H. Solin, 'Analecta epigraphica XIII', Arctos 7 (1972) 194.

[19] The latter inscriptions are from Gonnoi: B. Helly, Gonnoi II. Les inscriptions (Amsterdam 1973) n° 173 and 175 bis. Of the several possible interpretations Helly prefers to take παυσιτοκεῖα as neutr. plur: 'M. a consacré ce qui met fin à ses couches, ce qui en marque le terme de sa délivrance', and he is followed by L. Robert, BE 1973, n° 247. I wonder whether the miracles of Asclepius do not provide more relevant parallels. E.g. R. Herzog, Die Wunderheilungen von Epidauros (Philol. Suppl. XXII, 1931) n° I, where a woman has been pregnant for five years, but finally is 'delivered' by the god, and n° II, a three years pregnancy, containing the term τόκος, 'birth'. Cf. further the remarks by H. W. Pleket and F. T. van Straten in Mnemos. 29 (1976) 327.

always sure what the author of the prayer or the votive text really meant. Take the following dedication: Θεῶι Ἵρωι Κανζηρηνῷ εὐχαριστήριον περὶ κυνὸς μενομένου.[20] What does this mean? Was the man thanking the god for curing his dog of rabies or for having escaped from a dog with rabies? The latter solution seems more plausible, even from a medical point of view, especially when we consider that escape from all sorts of danger is one of the commonest themes in prayers of supplication and votive formulas. We find numerous inscriptions with the general εὔπλοια—formula[21] (for a good voyage) or dedications *pro (itu et) reditu*. It is also quite frequent to find texts like the following: *Genio pr[ovinciae] (...) sac(rum), rebus prospe[re gestis in] desperatissim[am turb]am et factionem (...) v.l.s;*[22] or *In honorem d(omus) d(ivinae) bonis Cassibus* (Germanic gods) *eo quod pos[t] summersam bon(a)e salu[ti] sit reddițu[s] et sui(s) L. Licinius Divixtus negotiato[r] ex voto posu(it);*[23] Διὶ Σωτῆρι Ἀσκληπιῶ Αἰμ. Σαβεῖνος καὶ Ἐρεννιανὸς ἀπὸ τῆς ἔξω θαλάσσης καὶ τῶν ἐκεῖ βαρβάρων σωθέντες ὑπ' αὐτοῦ,[24] but danger can sometimes come from an unexpected quarter: Δωρίων τέκτων τῶν μετ' Εὐμήδου ἀναζεύξας ἐπὶ τὴν θήραν τῶν ἐλεφάντων καὶ ἐσώθην εἰς Αἴγυπτον[25] and mad dogs are perhaps more suitable companions for wild elephants. I know of no prayer for a better memory from Antiquity, although the pupil who asked the Muses for εὐμαθία gets quite close to it.[26] I myself would nevertheless be particularly grateful for divine assistance in this respect: I am almost sure of having seen a Latin *iussu*—dedication, the author of which had escaped from a mad dog, but I can no longer trace it.[27] We can

---

[20] From Thrace: L. Robert, *Hellenica* X, 32 n. 6; *BE* 1952, n° 81, hesitates but deems the escape 'moins vraisemblablement'. Cf. below note 27.

[21] N. Sandberg, *Euploia* (Göteborg 1954); D. Wachsmuth, *Pompimos ho Daimon* (Berlin 1974) *passim*; L. Robert, *Stud. Clas.* 16 (1974) 83 n. 26.

[22] From Africa: *AE* 1966, n° 597.

[23] From Germania: *AE* 1969-70, n° 436.

[24] Chr. Habicht, *Altertümer von Pergamon VIII, 3. Die Inschriften des Asklepieions*, n° 63.

[25] A. Bernand, *Le Paneion d'El-Kanaïs. Les inscriptions* (Leiden 1972) n° 9, with a drawing of an elephant. Egypt, 3rd century B.C.

[26] The *eumathia*- text in the *Greek Anthology* VI, 310. Prayers for a good memory did occur in the Middle Ages as my teacher N. van der Blom instructs me, referring to his *Grepen uit de Geschiedenis van het Erasmiaans Gymnasium 1328-1978* (Rotterdam 1978), 76, 'Gunt my Uwe genade.... om hetgeen my van myn Meester voorgehouden werd ... getrouwelijk te onthouden'. I understand now why Apollonius of Tyana (Philostr. *Vita Apoll.* I, 14) every morning sang a hymn to Mnemosyne, 'Memory', and why he says (*ibid.* III, 16): Μνημοσύνης ἦν ἡμεῖς μάλιστα θεῶν ἀγαπῶμεν.

[27] There is a story about a person healed from the bite of a mad dog in Philostr. *Vita Apoll.* VI, 43.

never be sure, however, just as we must guess the cause of the gratitude in
the posthumous ex-votos from Cyprus with texts such as Θεῷ Ὑψίστῳ
᾿Αριστοχράτης εὐ[ξ]άμενος.[28] At any rate no banal wishes here, and we also
come across nobler prayers elsewhere in Antiquity: for friendship, virtue,
concord, happiness and peace,[29] but these are to be found mainly in more
literary, if not actually philosophical, texts. Prayers for forgiveness, on the
other hand, also appear, somewhat surprisingly perhaps, in normal life.[30]

In short, it is hard to perceive a sharp distinction between Greek and
Roman attitudes to prayer or between ancient and modern ones, either
from a thematic or an emotional point of view. Social discrepancies can of
course account for specific differences: the numerous *servus vovit, liber
posuit*—dedications[31] are only conceivable in Antiquity, but, as we can see
from a formula familiar to all those who have done their military service
(*quod miles vovit, veteranus solvit*),[32] there are numerous direct lines running
from Antiquity to the present day which are conditioned psychically rather
than historically and which can perhaps best be illustrated in the age-old
church prayer *A peste, fame, belloque libera nos, Domine*.

Against this connecting element we can also place an aspect of discontinuity. This too is exemplarily embodied in the oracle questions with
which we started. It will take us from the direct object to the indirect one.

Generations of students have chuckled over Xenophon's *pia fraus*[33]
which induced him to ask Apollo which gods he should sacrifice to in order
to have a good journey and not, as Socrates desired, whether it was better
to go or to remain. In our amusement, however, we risk losing sight of the
fact that this was a perfectly customary formula in oracle questions. We
saw certain examples above, and we find many more in the oracle collec-

---

[28] T. B. Mitford, *The Inscriptions of Kourion* (Philadelphia 1971) n° 160-161, and see his
suggestions on p. 304 f. We are here in syncretistic-Jewish, possibly, but not probably, even
in Christian sphere, where one can imagine the function of gratitude for the blessings given
by the Highest God during life, or perhaps after death.

[29] Examples in C. Ausfeld, 'De Graecorum precationibus quaestiones', *Jahrb. class. Philol.
Suppl.* 28 (1903) 540 ff.

[30] Philostr. *Vita Apoll.* 6, 40; Xen. *Memor.* 2, 2; Herod. 6, 86; Aristoph. *Nub.* 1478 f.; *Vesp.*
1001. W. Horn, *Gebet und Gebetsparodie in den Komödien des Aristophanes* (Nürnberg 1970) 60,
rightly ranges these prayers among the 'echte Gebete', particularly the 'spontane
Privatgebete'. Cf. also K. J. Dover, *Greek Popular Morality* (Berkeley-Los Angeles 1974) 261.
Latin *veniam peto* has a different origin but develops in the same direction.

[31] A collection in P. Veyne, 'Epigraphica', *Latom.* 23 (1964) 32-35.

[32] *AE* 1926, n° 72.

[33] Xen. *Anab.* 3, 1, 5.

tions. Apparently, this was a problem for the Greeks, a problem naturally inherent in polytheism. It is still more regrettable here than in the preceding section that we can only touch on a couple of aspects of this topic, since no subject is more fascinating than the functioning of polytheism and the problems (particularly the psychological ones) connected with it: an enormous field of research.

Prudentius, *Apoth.* 453, mockingly describes Julian the Apostate as *amans ter centum milia divum*, whereat E. Bickerman,[34] with his customary precision, remarked 'The apologist exaggerates. Hesiod (*Op.* 251) counted only 30,000 gods'. For us even thirty thousand gods are enough, or rather, too many, just as they were for the Greeks and the Romans. Would that it were true that each god had one specific function or area of activity, as the simplest booklets on mythology will have us believe and as the least complex Roman *indigitamenta*-deities would seem to attest—but this was far from being the case. Just as a certain herb was believed to be of use in improving a meal and combating sleeplessness and diseases of the gall-bladder, but of no use against a sore throat, so the deities functioned in various domains, and the greater they were the more varied were their qualities. The situation is further complicated by the fact that one god in his many surnames sometimes contained completely different, even conflicting, qualities, a phenomenon that characterises the whole of Antiquity. The Olympic god of the heavens, Zeus, was substantially different from the chthonic Zeus, who manifests himself, under the name of Meilichios, as a snake. The contrast Juppiter-Veiovis is similar. In his *Dream Book*, II, 37 Artemidorus following Plato, mentions an opposition between Aphrodite Pandemos and Aphrodite Uranius, and this is how we can interpret the series, so puzzling at first sight, which we find in prayers and votive inscriptions like: Διὶ Ἀποτροπαίωι, Διὶ Μειλιχίωι, Ἀρτέμιδι Προθυραίαι καὶ Ἀρτέμιδι [.....].[35]

I know of no plurality of Zeus in similar formulas,[36] but people did not hesitate to adapt such simplifications. There are dedications to the

---

[34] *AJP* (1974) 369 n. 31. The same scholar refers to an observation by Petronius that the city of Cumae has more immortal than mortal inhabitants: 'Anonymous Gods', *Journ. Wardburg Inst.* 1 (1937-8) 187.

[35] In a *lex sacra* from Pergamon discussed by M. Wörle, in Chr. Habicht, *op. cit.* (above note 24) 167 ff. The second epithet of Artemis has disappeared thrice in this inscription.

[36] Apollo occurs once in a plural form: *IG* II², 1945 (Athens) on which cf. L. Robert, *Hellenica* XI-XII, 177 ff., to whom I owe the following examples. On the phenomenon of the multiplication of deities cf. *idem, La Carie* II (Paris 1954) 143 f. Two Apollones on a relief: *idem, Hellenica* X, 126.

Νεμέσεις, to the Ἀφροδείται and a curse with the τρὶς θ[εοὺς] Μῆνας, the latter being explained by comparing Μῆνας τόν τε οὐράνιον καὶ τοὺς καταχθονίους[37] in another inscription, whereas matters are complicated still further by the appearance of a Μὴν Ἰταλικός.[38] Suchlike developments can be found primarily in Asia Minor in the imperial period, where indeed we come across the most unlikely phenomena. It is here that people *outside the circles of philosophers* first put into practice the idea that all gods were in fact one, as Aelius Aristides, *Hier. Log.* II, 18, shows when he writes of a god who appeared to him: 'He was both Asclepius and Apollo, that of Claros and the one called Callitechnos at Pergamon'. We find all-embracing henotheistic gods like Ὅσιος καὶ Δίκαιος[39] or τὸ Θεῖον (τὸ μέγα Θεῖον)[40] or ὁ Πάνθεος[41] or ὁ Εἷς καὶ Μόνος Θεός, but polytheism did not admit defeat since we come across paradoxical associations in priests' titles and votive formulas, as in a dedication to Θείῳ καὶ Ἀπόλλωνι,[42] a priest in Phrygia Θεόφιλος Θεοφίλου ἱε[ρ]εὺς Διονύσου κ(αὶ) Πανθέου ἀν[έθηκεν][43] or, to give an extreme example: τοῦ Ἑνὸς καὶ Μόνου Θεοῦ ἱερεὺς καὶ τοῦ Ὁσίου καὶ Δικαίου.[44] In a mystery oath from the cult of Isis[45] the adept swears by the one and unique deity who has separated heaven and earth, etc., etc., but none the less adds ἐπόμνυμαι δὲ καὶ οὓς προσκυνῶ θεούς, 'and I swear furthermore by the gods I adore'. Henotheistic tendencies in a polytheistic world must inevitably give rise to inconsistencies, to problems which a priest, Asclepiades, from Pergamon, can be said to have at least skirted with his unique dedication Θεοῖς τοῖς πανταχοῦ.[46]

---

[37] Both inscriptions in W. M. Ramsay, *Studies in the History and Art of the Eastern Provinces* (Aberdeen 1906) p. 160 and 164. Cf. E. Peterson, *Eis Theos* (Göttingen 1926) 270; J. Keil, *Denkmäler aus Lykaonien, Pamphylien und Isaurien* (1953) 18; E. N. Lane, *Corpus Monumentorum Religionis Dei Menis* I, n°'s 155 and 156. Cf. n° 154.

[38] Lane *CMRDM* I, n° 93.

[39] Recent literature and new testimonies in P. Herrmann, 'Das Testament des Epikrates', *Sitz. Ber. Oesterr. Ak. Phil. Hist. Kl.* 265 (1970) 50 ff.; Th. Drew-Bear, 'Local Cults in Phrygia', *GRBS* 17 (1976) 263.

[40] P. Herrmann, *op. cit.* (preceding note) 53 f. and above all L. Robert, *Anatolia* (1958) 113 ff.

[41] K. Ziegler, 'Pantheion', *RE* (1949), 697 ff.; F. Jacobi, *Pantes Theoi* (Diss. Halle 1930) 121 ff.

[42] A. Körte, *Athen. Mitt.* (1900) 431 n. 54, from Phrygia.

[43] *BCH* 11 (1887), 64 n. 39. More examples in F. Jacobi, *op. cit.* (above note 41) 121 n. 4.

[44] P. Herrmann, *op. cit.* (above note 39) 51 f.

[45] Discussed by R. Merkelbach, *ZPE* 1 (1967) 72-3.

[46] Habicht, *op. cit.* (above note 24) n° 133 and a splendid discussion on p. 12 ff.

We get the definite impression that the believers of later Antiquity did not know *exactly* what they meant with their acclamations Εἷς Ζεύς, Εἷς Σέραπις, Εἷς "Ηλιος, and that they were 'in a position in which they never allow themselves to ask just what they mean by what they are doing' (A. D. Nock). At all events we can now understand why, as from the second century A.D., 'the age of anxiety', ever more desperate questions were being put τί ὁ θεός; to get answers like 'Born of himself, wise in himself, without a mother, immovable, having no name, with many names, living in the fire: that is god...',[47] a final, existential offshoot of the age old question: 'to which god should I pray, to which should I sacrifice?' We now also see why in the period before pantheism or henotheism had their chance, the oracular answer to the latter question seldom contained a single god but usually recommended sacrificing to various gods. In official prayers and sacrificial inscriptions we find series of gods mentioned, and even then it was regarded as advisable to add καὶ τοὺς λοιποὺς θεούς[48] or καὶ τοὺς ἄλλους θεοὺς πάντας καὶ πάσας (in common use since the 5th century B.C.), just as the Romans added *di deaeque omnes* or *ceteri di deaeque.*[49] It was better to be too extensive than to risk forgetting one god as Oineus (*Iliad* IX, 534 ff.) discovered when he omitted Artemis at a sacrifice: ἢ λάθετ' ἢ οὐκ ἐνόησεν. We already find sacrifices and prayers to 'All the Gods' in Mycenean texts from Cnossos,[50] a total of 15 dedications *pasiteoi*, sometimes beside individual gods, but we only come across the earliest example from the private sphere in Menander fragm. 1 *Kolax* (Athen. XIV, 659 d), after which the custom swiftly increased.

Yet the more personal singular was constantly breaking through the all too vague plural. Someone prays πρὸς πάντας τοὺς θεοὺς μάλιστα δὲ πρὸς τὸν Διόνυσον.[51] In a dedication[52] *Iovi O.M. depulsori et diis deabusque omnibus* the author cannot help adding *et Genio loci* (frequently the most familiar,

---

[47] This inscription was found in recent times at the city-gate of Oenoanda. It received a royal treatment by L. Robert, *CRAI* (1971) 597-619 and one by M. Guarducci, *Rend. Acc. Linc.* 27 (1972) 335-347 ('nous n'entendons pas parfaitement cet exposé et ces considérations', *BE* 1974, n° 555).

[48] E.g. *AE* 1948, n° 41; many parallels.

[49] An early instance from the third century B.C. in Degrassi, *ILLRP* I, no. 27: *Apoline Minervia Ive Librtati Victorie Dis Deabus.*

[50] M. Gérard-Rousseau, *Les mentions religieuses dans les tablettes mycéniennes* (Rome 1968) 170 ff. with discussion. Cf. W. Burkert, *Griechische Religion der archaischen und klassischen Epoche* (Stuttgart-Köln-Mainz 1977) 83 and 88.

[51] Ph. Le Bas-W. H. Waddington, *Voyage archéologique en Grèce et Asie Mineure* III, 75, 80.

[52] *ILS* 3022 = *CIL* XIII, 1745 (Lyon).

because local, deity), and in an inscription from Selinus[53] (mid 5th century B.C.) the inhabitants give thanks for their victory to Zeus, Phobos, Heracles, Apollo, Poseidon, the Tyndarides, Athena, Malaphoros, Pasicrateia and the other gods, *but most of all to Zeus* 'and they therefore put his name first'.

One god or one category of gods was often more familiar, and therefore more reliable, then many gods or all gods. Dedications to gods with the function of guardian angel of a family or an individual (*Iovi conservatori possessionum Rosciorum; Iuppiter Purpurion*—of the Purpuris family; *Herculi defensori Papirii; Silvanus Flaviorum;*[54] then also the first uses of *meus* and *suus* with the name of a god) are typical of the imperial period,[55] but they find their formal adumbration in Hellenism, and, as far as mentality is concerned, the phenomenon is as old as Odysseus and his protectress Athena.

Prayers to many gods: that is one expression of polytheism. Prayers to one god, prevalent in the archaic and classical periods of Greece and Rome, raised problems of their own within such a system. Arnobius, *Adv. Haer.* III, 42 sums up the matter concisely: *omnis enim qui quaerit alicuius numinis impetrare responsum debeat necessario scire cui supplicat.* In the first place one had to know the name of the god in order to formulate an invocation, and precision could be increased by way of defining predicates. It is perfectly possible that this was one of the manners in which the series of epithets in epic poetry denoting place and function originated; at the same time we can discern a glorifying function which, together with the list of former favours and genealogical data, was to flourish in the hymns. There were also occasions on which the god could not be named with absolute certainty. We all know Aesch. *Agam.* 160: Ζεύς, ὅστις ποτ' ἐστίν, εἰ τόδ' αὐτῷ φίλον κεκλημένῳ, τοῦτο νιν προσεννέπω, and we tend to discern a philosophical influence. Yet the phenomenon also appears in more primitive mentalities. People knew more or less what sort of deity they needed, but they left it up to him to decide whether the chosen name (or which of the chosen names) was best. Numerous εἴτε ... εἴτε, or *sive ... sive*

---

[53] *SIG* 1122.

[54] *ILS* n° 3018, 3040, 3466, 3537 respectively. On this phenomenon: A. D. Nock, *Essays on Religion and the Ancient World* I (Oxford 1972) 41 and 156.

[55] Cf. also the unique(?) curse ἐχέτω τοὺς δήμου Ῥωμαίων θε[οὺς κεχολ]ωμένους πάντας καὶ πάσας, probably written by a Roman citizen from Lydia, besides frequent imprecations of the type θεῶν Πισιδικ[ῶν] κεχολωμένων τύχοιτο. The former in Keil-Premerstein, *Denkschr. Ak. Wien* 54 (1911) 99; F. Jacobi, *op. cit.* (above note 41) 27 n° 9A. An instance of the latter type *ibid.* n° 10.

formulas are the result.[56] This was obviously a general custom in Greece since Plato, *Krat.* 400 E, says that it was customary in prayers to use the formula οἵτινές τε καὶ ὁπόθεν χαίρουσιν ὀνομαζόμενοι. The Romans made a still more fundamental use of this possibility, at any rate in official prayers. There the pontifices prayed: *Iuppiter O.M. sive quo alio nomine te appellari volueris*, a formula which already appears in the extremely ancient *carmen evocationis* (Macrob. *Sat.* III, 9, 9): *Dis pater, Veiovis, Manes, sive quo alio nomine fas est nominare.*

The uncertainty was frequently a result of the syncretism of various gods in one great deity, as we see exemplarily in the Isis figure. Even in the earliest testimonies however, we can perceive a kindred phenomenon of a far more primitive nature: it happened frequently that, especially in spontaneous divine manifestations, people had no idea which deity was in action. In magic it was perfectly normal for the practitioner not to know which demon he had called to his assistance and he therefore said δαῖμον ὅστις ποτ' εἶ, *demon quicumque es*.[57] But even Odysseus, praying to the god who stirs up the sea, has to say κλῦθι, ἄναξ, ὅτις ἐσσί (*Od.* V, 445) and Telemachus appeals to ὃ χθιζὸς θεὸς ἤλυθες (*Od.* II, 262). The Romans often had so much difficulty in defining the identity of a particular deity that they either gave the god a name *ad hoc*, Aius Locutius being the best known, or they left the matter open. Thus there developed a typically Roman custom of addressing a deity as *sive deus sive dea* or *sive mas sive femina*. Cato *Agric.* 139: *Lucum conlucare Romano more sic oportet. Porco piaculo facito, sic verba concipito: 'Si deus, si dea es, quoium illud sacrum est, ...'* We have a series of *cippi* dedicated to a god who is only called *sei deus sei dea*[58] and a list of sacrifices in the records of the Fratres Arvales[59] makes a definitely

---

[56] Illustrations and discussion of these phenomena in E. Norden, *Agnostos Theos*⁴ (1956) 144 ff.; Ausfeld, *op. cit.* (above note 29) 518; G. Appel, *De Romanorum precationibus* (Giessen 1909) 76 ff.; J. Pépin, 'Ueber das Gebet', in *Frühschriften des Aristoteles* (Darmstadt 1975) 328; Y. Grandjean, *Une nouvelle arétalogie d'Isis à Maronée* (Leiden 1975) 68 n. 153 and literature cited there. This may be the background of the advices given by Apollonius of Tyana who teaches how θυσιῶν τε ἥπτοντο καὶ κλήσεων, αἷς θεοὶ χαίρουσι, (Philostr. *Vita Apoll.* III, 41). He also wrote a book περὶ θυσιῶν καὶ ὡς ἄν τις ἑκάστῳ θεῷ προσφόρως τε καὶ κεχαρισμένως θύοι. Cf. *ibid.* IV, 19 and IV, 40.

[57] A. Audollent, *Defixionum Tabellae* (Paris 1904) n° 242 and 286.

[58] Degrassi, *ILLRP* I, 291-293, with commentary. Cf. Macrobius, *Sat.* III, 9, 2-3, and a very interesting new inscription from Isaura, translated by R. E. A. Palmer, *Roman Religion and Roman Empire* (Philadelphia 1974) 236 n. 318 '....the imperator Servilius, son of Gaius, kept his vow if god, if goddess be in whose care was the town of old Isaura', and which is discussed by J. Le Gall, in *Mélanges J. Heurgon*, I (Paris-Rome 1976) 519-524.

[59] Henzen, p. 144.

astonishing impression: *Deae Diae boves feminas, Iano patri arietes, Iovi berbeces, Marti arietes, Iunoni Deae Diae oves, Sive Deo Sive Deae oves*...

Although the Greeks with their altar ἀγνώστῳ θεῷ did not know exactly how to get round such problems either we can here perceive a difference between the early Roman and the early Greek concept of god. If we consult the textbooks about the characteristic differences between these two religions, one of the standard answers is that the gods of the early Romans, unlike those of the early Greeks, were never actually visualised and individualised. Deprived of individual personality their identity was primarily defined by their function; they rarely possessed 'shapes' either in a plastic or in a psychological sense. Although there is room for a more differentiated approach anyone who compares the bloodless Ceres (power of growth) with the hot-blooded and suffering Demeter, or the original neuter Venus with the anything but neuter Aphrodite, can see what is meant. Greek gods 'live', Roman gods 'work', i.e. function, sometimes for a very short time, in their own domain, but never step outside it. This would explain the greater hesitation of the Romans, to which we have already alluded, concerning the identity of a god, even in prayer, and might also be connected with the fact that the Roman attached a particular value to the correct formulation of prayer and votive sayings, which appears to have given these *carmina* a sort of autarkic effect. I cannot go into this any further here, but we can cautiously suggest that where gods have so few human traits the formula necessarily acquires a greater emphasis and a certain autonomous value.

I started this brief section with the assumption that, in ancient polytheism, we can observe a phenomenon which differs radically from modern concepts. This is certainly true if we limit ourselves, as far as Antiquity is concerned, to the cultic practices of private and public religion (and thus leave out the philosophers), and, as far as the present is concerned, if we take as our object of comparison Reformed Christianity. Yet this view is too simple, for, if we compare modern cultic practices of Catholic believers, especially of those who have not yet felt the need to be more Protestant than the Protestants, the result is completely different. I therefore hasten to qualify my observation about discontinuity in this sense with a few modern examples.

It will not have escaped anybody's attention that specialised saints have taken over the task of the heathen specialists. Here too we see that the saint of one particular spot is not necessarily the same as the same saint of another spot. R. and E. Blum[60] give various examples from modern Greece. 'The St. George we have is not the same saint as comes from Cappadocia. Ours is from right here' (p. 46). About a St. Paraskevi chapel: 'I'm not sure if the bones belong to the same St. Paraskevi as people usually talk about, or whether this is a different Saint...' (p. 93). But even on a higher level theology has not yet succeeded in turning the scales. The Panagia of one convent is certainly not the same as that of another, and the competition, especially where miracles are concerned, is fierce. This gives rise to interesting utterances. In a work by Thomas More[61] we read: 'Of all Our Ladies I love best Our Lady of Walsingham'. 'And I Our Lady of Ipswich'. In the Spanish civil war there was a veritable iconoclasm in the churches of the villages in communist hands, but in one village the image of the Virgin Mary was saved by the inhabitants who claimed: '*Our Virgin is a communist*'.[62] The *sive mas sive femina* theme also occurs sporadically. 'I'm not sure whether the devil is a he or a she, I guess a he' (Blum, p. 99). Finally, the unrivalled J. C. Lawson[63] personally witnessed a rainmaker on Santorini praying to τὸν ἄνω θεὸ καὶ τὸν κάτω θεό, and who had forgotten, to her distress, the name of the third god in charge of thunder—by no means so odd at a time when there was a current saying in Athens which ran: νὰ σ'ἀξιώσῃ ὁ Θεὸς νὰ εὐχαριστήσῃς θεοὺς καὶ ἀνθρώπους 'May God reward you and make you pleasing to gods and men'.

Even in areas where Antiquity and the present seem, at first sight, to have lost all contact, historical and psychic correspondences still appear to be both strong and numerous. We shall keep this in mind when treating certain aspects of the mentality of prayer.

III. '*Gebetsegoismus*'

Somewhere or other Stendhal tells us that he remembered a motto which he saw on a banner in his youth in Grenoble: 'Vive le roi, ma femme et moi'.[64] When expressing wishes the first person who comes to the mind is the *ego*—and 'first' must here be taken literally. For, although

---

[60] R. and E. Blum, *The Dangerous Hour* (London 1970).

[61] Quoted by K. Thomas, *Religion and the Decline of Magic* (Penguin 1973) 29, in a passage on saints and their specialisms.

[62] W. A. Christian Jr., 'The Spanish Shrine', *Numen* 24 (1977) 77.

[63] J. C. Lawson, *Modern Greek Folklore and Ancient Greek Religion. A Study of Survivals* (Cambridge 1910) 48 ff.

[64] I owe this information to H. van Galen Last in the *Nieuwe Rotterdamse Courant*, 19-4-1978.

we do indeed come across wishes and prayers in Antiquity, as we did in
Grenoble, of the type ὑπὲρ τῆς πόλεως καὶ τῆς ἑαυτῶν ὑγιείας[65] or εὐξάμενοι
ὑπὲρ ὑγιείας τοῦ κυρίου (in this case Commodus) καὶ ἑαυτῶν[66] or, better still,
ὑπὲρ δεσποτῶν (his own masters) καὶ θρεμάτων (small live stock) καὶ τῶν
κυνῶν,[67] we saw in the oracle prayer of Diognetos that the I-figure occupied the first place, and we do not have to look very far to see that this
sequence (e.g. ὑπὲρ ἑαυτοῦ καὶ τῶν δεσποτῶν; *pro se et pro patronis*) was preferred in Antiquity. The psychological explanation of such a phenomenon
is so obvious that it is superfluous to say that the term 'Gebetsegoismus',
in common use for such phenomena, is purely descriptive and is not intended as a value judgement, let alone as a condemnation. In Roman
prayers 'I' always comes first, both in private prayers (Cato, *agr.* 144, 3
duis bonam salutem ... mihi domo familiaeque nostrae) and in public ones (Liv.
29, 27, 1 *uti...ea mihi, populo plebique Romanae, sociis nominique Latino... bene
verruncent*). This, of course, corresponds directly with common parlance,[68]
as anyone will know who has told his children never to say 'I and Johnny'
and then comes up against so much lack of understanding and opposition
that he wonders to what extent hypocrisy can dictate laws of language.

Egoism,[69] the request for health, happiness, and wealth, is not
necessarily negative or damaging, human as it is. Nevertheless, there are
also certain truly aggressive forms of 'Gebetsegoismus'. O. Weinreich has
written an extensive study[70] on it which shows that this aggressivity is
often unintentional, and still more often inevitable. This can be explained

---

[65] An arbitrary example taken from B. Latyschev, *Inscriptiones Antiquae Orae Septentrion.
Ponti Euxini* I, 1885, n° 80, 83, 86, 88, 89.

[66] In a votive inscription by a certain Diogenes and his wife from Syria: *BE* 1974, n° 632,
after J.-P. Rey-Coquais, *Mélanges Beyrouth* 47 (1972) 87-105.

[67] L. Robert, *Hellenica* X, 28-35, where the next example can also be found.

[68] This phenomenon has been discussed by J. Wackernagel, 'Zur Wortfolge, besonders
bei den Zahlwörtern', in: *Festschrift G. Binz* (Basel 1935) 33-54, especially 52 ff., with many
examples. Cf. Appel, o.c. (*supra* note 56) 144. It was, in Antiquity, so customary to say ἐγὼ
καί ..... that it strikes St. Augustine as odd when Luke 2, 48 writes ὁ πατήρ σου κἀγώ (*Sermo*
LI, II, no 18. *PL* XXXVIII, 343), discussed by H. J. de Jonge, 'Sonship, Wisdom, Infancy.
Luke II, 41-51a', *New Test. Stud.* 24 (1977) espec. 330 ff.

[69] The prayer for the loved one is egoistic in an indirect way. On prayer for the fellow-
human being see O. Michel, 'Fürbitte', *RAC* 9, 1 ff. The prayer for the enemies, though not
restricted to Christendom (see Heiler, 44, and W. Havers, *op. cit.* (next note), 160), can be
left out of account.

[70] O. Weinreich, 'Primitiver Gebetsegoismus', reprinted in: *idem, Religionsgeschichtliche
Studien* (Darmstadt 1968) 7-44. Additional material in W. Havers, 'Zum primitiven
Gebetsegoismus', in *Hommages à M. Niedermann* (Coll. Latomus XXIII, 1956) 159-163.

as follows: prayers for the recovery from illness or misfortune are numerous—we have only to think of the famous prayer in Cato, *agr.* 141: *uti tu morbos visos invisosque, viduertatem vastitudinemque, calamitates intemperiasque prohibessis defendas averruncesque*... Now, however, we are faced with the fact that, according to the Ancients, illness or evil were not merely abstract concepts, but rather semi-concrete, even physical, entities which sometimes turned into demons, monsters or spirits (e.g. *Phthonos*). In suchlike cases defence alone is not enough. In order to guarantee *permanent* elimination the evil must be directed somewhere else,[71] preferably far away: into the sea or overseas, 1000 miles away, to the mountains where the cock does not crow and the dog does not bark (that is very far away indeed) or as far away as the heavens are removed from the earth. Εἰς ὄρος ἢ εἰς κῦμα is a standard expression. In *Oedip. Rex*, 190 f. Athena must banish the horrible Ares 'far from the fatherland, to the great nuptial room of Amphitrite or to the inhospitable Thracian gulf'. Even in our times the unfortunate Thracians get it in the neck because, in the Breviar. Rom. 30 jan. S. Martinae Virg. et Mart. Hymn. I, 4, we read: *Armorum strepitus et fera proelia in fines age Thracios*, a prayer which, from a purely historical point of view, has been satisfactorily granted. There were no hostile designs behind such a prayer, of course, any more, I should imagine, than behind the prayer of the little girl who, in order to ensure her own safety, expressed the wish that a thunder-storm would burst over Zoetermeer, where she was not, rather than over the Hague, where she was.[72] This is obviously how the human mind works: farmers in Baden pray or prayed: 'Es steht ein Gewitter über der Erd, wenn 's nur in's Württembergische fährt',[73] and in the South of Germany people pray (or prayed): 'O heiliger Sankt Florian, verschon dies Haus, zünd andre an'.[74] When Catullus 63,

---

[71] I have collected some instances and literature in my 'Polycrates and his Ring', *Studi Storico Religiosi* 1 (1977) 41-42, where I also try to explain the throwing away of the ring against this background.

[72] Oral communication by Mrs. Van Veen on her granddaughter.

[73] Weinreich, *op. cit.* (above note 70) 31.

[74] *Ibidem*, 29. More examples in Havers, *op. cit.* (above note 70). My colleague J. C. H. Lebram informs me of his doubts concerning the real intentions behind both German prayers. In the text with Skt. Florian he discerns a satirical trait perhaps dating from the period of the Enlightenment. This, I think, may be very well possible. About the *exsecratio* against Württemberg, Weinreich wrote: 'als Württemberger .... muss ich es missbilligen, als Liebhaber der Volkskunde hab ich meine Freude daran' (p. 31). Lebram, however, thinks that this is a sample of the propaganda by the democrats of 1848 against the 'Kleinstaaterei'. Again, I do not venture to decide, but I do wish to underline the universali-

92-3 prays *procul a mea tuos sit furor omnis, era, domo. Alios age incitatos, alios age rabidos*, he is displaying the same mentality which caused a disappointed lover, in a recently discovered Archilochus fragment,[75] to say Νεοβούλη [ν μὲν ὦν] [ἄ]λλος ἀνὴρ ἐχέτω, after which there follows directly [ἐς] κόρακας ἄπεχε. Away with evil, if necessary to the neighbours, even to one's nearest and dearest: 'Do it to Julia! Not me! Julia! I don't care what you do to her... Not me! Julia! Not me!' screams the hero in Orwell's *Nineteen Eighty-Four*, and tries to place his beloved, '*one* person to whom he could transfer his punishment', between himself and 'the worst thing in the world'. And he had not even read the Alcestis! Here, in its most dispiriting form, we have the violent contrast with, and the complement of, the *in meum caput (reiiciatur)*[76] of which man is evidently also capable.

What a great step forward is the idea not only of removing evil from one's *own* sphere, but also of visiting one's *enemy* with it in his home— a two-edged sword, drawn on countless occasions! Εἰς ἐχθρῶν κεφαλάς was what people proverbially wished to evil,[77] and the Roman Catholics, to whom nothing Roman is alien, still pray: Missale Rom. Introit. 9th Sunday after Pentecost, *averte mala inimicis*. This may not be very nice, but it is certainly practical: people already wished their enemies ill, so why not transfer one's own misfortunes to them? Of the numerous examples I shall simply give one: Liv. 5, 18, 22 *precibus ab dis petitum ut exitium ab urbis tectis templisque ac moenibus Romanis arcerent Veiosque* (here neighbour = enemy)

---

ty of prayers that try to avert the evil to other fields or countries. Here is another example quoted by J. Grimm, *Deutsche Mythologie* I⁴, 146, an Esthonian prayer to the thunder (17th cent.): 'Liebe Donner, wir opfern dir einen Ochsen, der zwei Hörner und vier Klauen hat und wollen dich bitten um unser Pflügen und Säen, dass unser Stroh kupferrot, unser Getreide goldgelb werde. Stoss anderswohin alle schwarzen, dicken Wolken, über grosse Sümpfe, hohe Wälder, breite Wüsten. Uns Pflügern und Säern gib aber fruchtbare Zeit und süssen Regen. Heilige Donner, bewahre unseren Acker, dass er trage gut Stroh unterwärts, gute Aehren überwärts und gut Korn innenwärts'. Perfect indeed is what Lebram tells me about an aged aunt of his who once during a thunder-storm said: 'Wir müssen beten, dass es weitergeht' and when told that this would not be very fair to other people, replied: 'Die müssen es dann auch weiterschicken'.

[75] R. Merkelbach-M. L. West, *ZPE* 14 (1974) 97-113. See on this text J. M. Bremer, *Het gemaskerde ik* (Rede Amsterdam 1978) 8 ff. and notes 5 ff.

[76] This is of course in the first place a curse against the own person, but there is more to it. Cf. e.g. Val. Max. 2, 4, 5, where parents pray *ut puerorum periculum in suum caput transferrent*. Instances of similar vicarious sacrifices in H. S. Versnel, 'Two Types of Roman Devotio', *Mnemosyne* 29 (1976) 390 ff. and *idem*, 'Self-sacrifice', in *Le sacrifice dans l'antiquité* (Entretiens Hardt 1981).

[77] Weinreich, *op. cit.* (above note 70) 15 ff.; H. S. Versnel, 'Two Types' (above note 76) 389 f.

eum averterent timorem. The Romans, who were more efficient than the Greeks in this respect, have attained perfection. Not only did they see the chance of afflicting their enemies with plague, ruin, fear, panic, death and destruction, but also of drawing their enemy's gods to Rome by pointing out how undesirable it is to remain in so distressed an area. This combination of *devotio* and *evocatio*[78] is just as characteristic of Roman religious imperialism as the true two-edged sword is of the secular one.

This, of course, is all very nasty, but it would be wrong not to point out that enemies, even neighbours, can be very nasty as well. Some 40 years ago many Christians prayed to God to let a certain Hitler die a ghastly death as soon as possible, and they were right. We saw above that an anonymous person asked the oracle whether 'Dorkilos had stolen his gown'. What if the answer was yes? Did the suppliant then return home satisfied with the awareness that he now at least knew who the guilty party was? Did he go with the answer to the police? No. Unless Dorkilos, as in a case described below, had undertaken to respect the oracle, all the man who had been robbed could do was to remain in the sanctuary and, in justifiable fury, to implore the god—or another god—to shower every conceivable horror onto the head of the thief, possibly until the object stolen was returned. And right he was. When the state apparatus is either lacking or incapable of enforcing the law, or when there is no such thing as a concrete proof, the god must assist. This particular circumstance has yielded us some splendid examples of 'juridical' or 'revenge' prayers, especially from the Hellenistic and imperial periods when 'great gods' frequently assumed the character of avenging and all-seeing judges. They provide us with unique glimpses into the heart and the hatred of the believers.

IV. *Offensive, indecent and improper prayers*

Some particularly interesting prayers of revenge have survived from Cnidos in Asia Minor.[79] They are written on lead and were placed near, on or under the image of Demeter. An example: Ἀνιεροῖ Ἀρτεμεὶς Δάματρι Κούρα[ι θεο]ῖς παρὰ Δάματρι πᾶσι ὅστις τὰ ὑπ' ἐμοῦ καταλιφθέντα ἱμάτια καὶ ἔν-

---

[78] On their relation and the term *vicarii*, indicating that the enemies are indeed the substitutes of the Romans in catching the evil: H. S. Versnel, 'Two Types', (above note 76).

[79] A. Audollent, *Defixionum Tabellae* (Paris 1904) n°'s 1-13, and n° 212 from Bruttium; F. S. Steinleitner, *Die Beicht im Zusammenhange mit der sakralen Rechtspflege in der Antike* (Diss. München 1913) n°'s 34-47. On this type of curse: G. Björck, *Der Fluch des Christen Sabinus* (Uppsala 1938) 121 ff. Related *defixiones* were found in recent times. See H. S. Versnel, 'Two Types' (above note 76) 397 n. 88.

δυμα καὶ ἀνάκω[λ]ον, ἐμοῦ ἀπαιτ[ησά]σας οὐκ ἀπέδ[ωκέ] μοι. ἀνενέγκα[ι] αὐτὸς
παρὰ Δ[άμ]ατρα καὶ εἴ τι[ς ἄλλος] τἀμὰ ἔχ[ει πεπρη]μένος ἐξ[αγορεύ]ων. ἐμο[ὶ
δὲ ὅσια κ]αὶ ἐλεύ[θερα..........] καὶ συμπιεῖν καὶ συμφαγεῖν καὶ ἐπ[ὶ τὸ α]ὐτὸ
στέγος ἐ[λθ]εῖν. ἀδίκημαι γὰρ Δέσπο[ι]να Δάματερ...... 'Artemis (not the
goddess!) dedicates (accurses) to Demeter, Kore and all the gods together
with Demeter, the person who will not return to me the articles of clothing
I left with him although I asked for them. May he himself bring them back
to Demeter, and if someone else now has my possessions, may he, consumed by fire (?),[80] confess it publicly. But let me not infringe any divine
law in this and may I be free... to drink and eat and consort under the
same roof (with the accursed). For I have suffered wrong, oh Ruler
Demeter...'.

In a section on the dangerous and negative aspects of prayer, what concerns us particularly are the last phrases of this prayer of revenge, phrases
which display some fairly standard characteristics. In Antiquity it was
regarded as undesirable to consort with or to live under the same roof as
someone tarnished by sacrilege, murder, etc., and the attempt was made
to anticipate this through prayer.[81] In the situation in question the chances
were high that the accuser might land herself in difficulties. By her cursing
(ἀνιερόω, ἀνιαρίζω, ἀνατίθημι) the anonymous thief the latter inevitably
found himself in a taboo situation which could be dangerous for table companions or members of the household. And perhaps it *was* a member of her
household, or a close friend who was guilty. Hence the addition[82] and the
apologetic-sounding apostrophe ἀδίκημαι γὰρ Δέσποινα Δάματερ, which was
a commonly used term in the Ptolemaic-Egyptian *enteuxeis* on which our
prayer was undoubtedly based.[83] In a magical *defixio* from the Agora of
Athens[84] the *defigens* appears to be apologising almost explicitly for an act
which he obviously did not regard as altogether proper. After the curse

[80] I do not go into the vexed question of the meaning of the word πεπρημένος.

[81] K. Latte, 'Schuld und Sünde in der griechischen Religion', in *idem*, *Kleine Schriften*
(München 1968) 9 with relevant texts in note 12.

[82] On these ἐμοὶ δὲ ὁσίη formula's: Björck, *op. cit.* (above note 79) 122 ff.; 124 note 1; 132;
K. Latte, *op. cit.* (preceding note) and *Heiliges Recht* (Tübingen 1920) 64-5; 75 note 40 and
Nachträge.

[83] W. Schulze, *Kleine Schriften* (1933) 160-189 and A. Cameron, *HThR* 32 (1939) 10-11,
already point out the relation between these prayers and the Egyptian petitions. Cf. the collection in O. Guéraud. ΕΝΤΕΥΞΕΙΣ (Kairo 1931).

[84] A. Elderkin, 'Two Curse Inscriptions', *Hesperia* 6 (1937) 383 ff.; n° 3 p. 390 f., to
which Björck, *op. cit.* (above note 79) 137 n. 1 adds: Wünsch 100 a 13 [σῴζετε(?) τὸ]ν μολυβ-
δοκόπον, for various reasons an exceptional text.

formula, which has been lost, he proceeds... ΕΣ σέβου (?) με τὸν καταγράφοντα καὶ τὸν ἀπολέσαντα ὅτι οὐκ ἑκὼν ἀλλὰ ἀναγκαζόμενος διὰ τοὺς κλέπτας τοῦ ·· ποιεῖ. Transition from the first to the third person is no problem, and alt᾽ ough the first verbal form *is* enigmatic, what concerns us here is the apologetic tone: the man had no choice but to take his unsympathetic measures. The best example which I know, of the caution which had generally to be observed towards prayer is a revenge text from Pessinus composed by a mother whose son had died—in the case of wasting diseases in Antiquity people rapidly concluded that magic, witchcraft or poison was at play[85]—and who addressed Helios with the prayer: ὃς ἂν ἐνεχίρησε Μηνοδώρῳ χωρὶς θεοῦ βίας, ῞Ηλι Κύρι, μή σ᾽ ἀρέσι..... 'that the deed of the ensnarer of Menodorus, unless it was performed by the power of a god, be displeasing to you, Helios Kurios...'—a remark which makes the editor, P. Lambrechts, think of a 'dieu jaloux du jeune homme'.[86]

People were never sure, particularly regarding the question whether their prayer was righteous. This question, coupled with the ethical problem of whether one could ask a god for everything, was one of the most recurrent topics of discussion amongst philosophers and moralists from the late archaic period onwards. Since this aspect will be treated elsewhere by P. A. Meijer I shall restrict myself here to a few examples of less exalted, but by no means less tormented, spirits and the problems facing them where prayer was concerned. The safest thing to do was to leave it up to the god himself to decide what was for the best or what the possibilities were: Demosth. *c. Leptin.* 25, 'for I ask the gods in the first place that we can obtain a great deal of property, but if that is not possible that we can retain a reputation for reliability and integrity'.[87] Unfortunately there were some difficulties which not even a god could solve, as is illustrated by Aesop (96 Hunger = 166 Halm): a father visits one of his daughters married to a market-gardener who prays for rain, and shortly afterwards he meets his other daughter married to a potter, who prays for sun and dry weather. The conflict is inevitable: ἐὰν σὺ μὲν εὐδίαν ἐπιζητῇς, ἡ δὲ ἀδελφή σου χειμῶνα, ποτέρᾳ ὑμῶν συνεύξωμαι; The advantage of the one is

---

[85] See e.g. J. Zingerle, 'Heiliges Recht', *Oest. Jahresh.* 23 (1926) 18-19. Very interesting on this idea in various civilizations: K. Meuli, 'lateinisch *morior-* deutsch *morden*' in *idem*, *Gesammelte Schriften* I (Basel-Stuttgart 1975) 439-444.

[86] P. Lambrechts et R. Bogaert, *Hommage à M. Renard* II (Coll. Latomus 1969) 404-414; L. Robert, *BE* 1968, 535 and 1970, 600 hesitates to give an interpretation.

[87] A less noble variant: Apul. *Metam.* 9, 29.

the disadvantage of the other, and that was far from being the only problem.[88] Here we have another: who can tell for sure whether what he now regards as desirable will still appear profitable after his prayer has been granted? In his 23rd fable Babrius tells of a cowherd who has lost a bull and promises the gods a reward if he finds the thief. He does find him but the thief turns out to be a lion, so that the cowherd, put to flight, promises the gods an additional bull if he can escape with his life. Moral:

ἐντεῦθεν ἡμᾶς τοῦτ' ἔοικε γινώσκειν·
ἄβουλον εὐχὴν τοῖς θεοῖσι μὴ πέμπειν
ἐκ τῆς πρὸς ὥραν ἐκφορουμένης λύπης.

We must not leap to the conclusion that the authors of these fables ultimately derived their philosophy from true philosophers. It is far more likely that we are here faced with true popular wisdom, as we shall see from the following example, which is also connected with the problem of prayer. In Babrius' 20th fable a cowherd whose waggon has slipped into a trench prays to Heracles for help, but receives the advice to tackle the problem himself and urge on his oxen: τοῖς θεοῖς δ'εὔχου ὅταν τι ποιῇς χαὐτός, ἢ μάτην εὔξῃ. It is more than probable that this is simply the 'romanticisation' of a well-known proverb σὺν 'Αθηνᾷ καὶ χεῖρα κίνει,[89] which is still used in Greece in a Christian variant. Ernestine Friedl[90] gives a good example of the practical attitude of present day Greek farmers when she tries to demonstrate that 'an appeal to fate or God is never an excuse for neglecting actions which are humanly possible...'. For example, one farmer, at a time of unseasonable drought, remarked as he looked at his tobacco fields: 'I won't make the sign of the cross, I'll bring my pump over here and irrigate the field'. Indeed, the Christians understood at an

---

[88] A different aspect is that one can promise one god more than another to get what one wants: Justin. 20, 3, 1 tells us that the inhabitants of Croton promise Apollo one tenth of the booty and the inhabitants of Locri one ninth in reaction to an oracle *responsum prius votis hostes quam armis vincendos* (Parke-Wormell, n° 76).

[89] Ps. Plut. *De proverbiis Alexandrinorum* ed. O. Crusius (Tübingen 1887) and comm. (1895) n° 36 in *Paroemiogr. Graec. Suppl.*; Aesop. Halm n° 300 = n° 30 (Hunger). Cf. Plut. *Moral.* 239 A, and an oracle text found in Syedra (Cilicia), where much good advice is being given but also: σὺν δὲ καὶ ὑμέες ἅπτεσθαι κρατεροῖο [π]όν[οι]ο: F. Sokolowski, 'Sur l'oracle de Claros destiné à la ville de Syedra', *BCH* 92 (1968) 519-522. The Roman soldiers in Livy 32, 30, 10, had understood this, when their commander had pronounced a vow and they shouted *compotem voti consulem se facturos*. Cf. also Philostr. *Vita Apoll.* 2, 21, where king Poros refuses to sacrifice to the river Hyphasis in order to prevent Alexander from crossing with the words: οὐκ ἔστιν τῶν ὅπλα ἐχόντων τὸ καταρᾶσθαι.

[90] E. Friedl, *Vasilika. A Village in Modern Greece* (New York 1962) 75.

early stage that not everything was sent from above, as we see in a realistic mosaic inscription from Galilee:[91] Θεοῦ δυνάμι, Χ(ριστο)ῦ βοηθίᾳ, Ἁγίου Πνεύματος εὐδοκίᾳ καὶ τ[ῶν κωμητῶν?] πόνο[ις] ἐγένετο τὸ ἔρ[γον]. Nor did they distinguish themselves from heathens in this particular domain, as is shown by an inscription from Thasos: Εὐχαριστοῦμεν Θεοῖς Σώζουσιν καὶ ἐνπόρῳ Οὐλπίῳ 'We give thanks to the Rescuing Gods and merchant Ulpius'.[92]

When all is said and done praying looks more difficult than one might have thought. It was not only the wiseman who knew this, but also the simple believer who, as Artemidorus V, 9 tells us, vows to Asclepius that, if he remains in health for a year, he will sacrifice a cock, and who makes another vow the next day that he will sacrifice another cock if he does not go blind. When Asclepius appears in a dream at night and says: εἷς μοι ἀλεκτρυὼν ἀρκεῖ he is applying a criticism of prayer (and with the most horrible effect) which was normally reserved for philosophers. Their criticisms have been collected by H. Schmidt, *Veteres philosophi quomodo iudicaverint de precibus*,[93] from which we can learn, positively, that we must pray to the gods for τὰ καλὰ ἐπὶ τοῖς ἀγαθοῖς and leave it up to them to decide what that is[94] and, negatively, that every other sort of prayer disregards divine providence and undermines morality. Epicurus puts it as follows: 'if God were to grant all wishes and prayers, mankind would soon disappear from the face of the earth, so much evil are men for ever wishing on one another'.[95] A glance at *defixio* magic and prayers of revenge confirms the accuracy of this statement.

This leads us finally to a curious formal difference between praying out loud and praying in silence, a difference about which the last word has yet to be said.[96] One of the few things that are supposedly certain about

---

[91] B. Lifshitz, *ZPE* 6 (1970) 63. Whatever the conjecture, it must imply human help.

[92] P. Bernard et F. Salviat, *BCH* (1962) 609-611.

[93] *RVV* IV (Giessen 1907).

[94] See for instance Xenoph. *Mem.* I, 3, 2; Ps. Plato, *Alk.* 2, 141a ff., espec. 148b-149e; Plut. *Mor.* 239a; Diod. 10, 9, 7 f.

[95] H. Usener, *Epicurea* (Leipzig 1887) n° 388 p. 259.

[96] In this connection S. Sudhaus, 'Lautes und leises Beten', *ARW* 9 (1906) 185-200, is always referred to, but the additions given by H. Schmidt, *op. cit.* (above note 93) 55-71, are actually much more important, particularly because he also deals with the positive side of silent prayer. Cf. also J. Bidez-F. Cumont, *Les mages hellénisés* II (Paris 1933) 285 n. 3; J. Festugière, 'Initiée par l'époux', *Monum. Piot* 53 (1963) 135-146, espec. 142. H. Wagenvoort makes some observations on the subject in two articles collected in H. Wagenvoort, *Pietas* (Leiden 1980) 206 ff. and 210 ff.

ancient prayer is that it was basically uttered out loud—and indeed, there
are numerous attestations of such a phenomenon.[97] Now, there is nothing
very attractive about wishing out loud in a temple *magna stante corona* that
neighbour, rival or emperor should die as soon as possible. Yet this was a
normal component of the various wishes expressed and in *such* cases it was
customary to murmur the prayer between one's lips, or to say it in complete silence, so that the connection between silent prayer and evil became
a *topos* in literature. Martial I, 39, 5 f. *Si quis erit recti custos mirator honesti, et
nihil arcano qui roget ore deos* has his distant precursor in the Pythagorean injunction: μετὰ φωνῆς εὔχεσθαι ...... ὅτι δικαίας ἐβούλοντο εἶναι τὰς εὐχάς, ἃς
οὐκ ἄν τις αἰδεσθείη ποιεῖσθαι πολλῶν συνειδότων.[98] We find splendid examples of *murmur humilesque susurros* and prayers in which a man only *labra
movet* in satire (e.g. Horace *epist.* I, 16, 59; Pers. II, 3 ff.) and Seneca,
Epist. 10, 5 exclaims: *Tunc scito esse te omnibus cupiditatibus solutum cum eo
perveneris ut nihil deum roges nisi quod rogare possis palam. Nunc enim quanta
dementia est hominum! Turpissima vota dis insusurrant. Si quis admoverit aurem,
conticiscent, et quod scire hominem nolunt deo narrant.*

It will come as no surprise, therefore, to find that in malicious magic we
constantly come across instructions to pronounce the formulas softly or
between one's lips.[99] This, in its turn, leads to a certain automatism:
whoever prays softly is undoubtedly practising magic: Apul. *Apol.* 54,
tacitas preces in templo dis allegasti: igitur magus es, and a lex Cornelia in the *Institut.* IV 18,5 condemns those *qui susurris magicis homines occiderunt*. These
phenomena give an additionally tragic aspect to a late defender of dying
paganism, Libanius, when he says somewhat ironically that the pagan can
no longer pray to his gods πλὴν ἢ σιγῇ καὶ λανθάνων.[100]

V. *Hearing gods*

And yet... the silent prayer can also express a completely different
attitude, one of intimacy, familiarity and trust in the deity. It was not only
evil desires that were whispered to the god. Seneca himself suggests this

---

[97] See for instance S. Pease, *ad* Cicero *Div.* 1, 129; Sudhaus, *op. cit.* (preceding note) 187,
and cf. P. Veyne, *Le pain et le cirque* (Paris 1976) 350 n. 255; F. J. Dölger, *Sol Salutis*[2], 308 n.
2; P. J. T. Beckmann, *Das Gebet bei Homer* (Diss. Würzburg 1932) 72 f.

[98] *Apud* Clemens Al., *Strom.* 4, 26 (172, 1). The injunction is pythagorean, the interpretation of Clemens.

[99] Sudhaus, *op. cit.* (above note 96) 197 ff. Many examples in Schmidt *op. cit.* (above
note 96) 59 ff.

[100] Libanius, 30, 52.

elsewhere (*Epist.* 41, 1): *Non sunt ad caelum elevandae manus nec exorandus aedituus ut nos ad aurem simulacri quasi magis exaudiri possimus, admittat: prope est a te deus, tecum est, intus est.* Here, of course, against the background of Stoic reservations about the current practice of prayer,[101] a strong impression of intimacy is aroused in the scene criticised: the suppliant whispers his deepest secrets into the ear of the god. At another point (*De benef.* II, 1, 4) Seneca seems to imply that this sort of silent prayer was not uncommon and Cicero confirms as much, *Div.* I, 129: *Ex quo fit ut homines etiam cum tacite optent quid aut voveant, non dubitent quin di illud exaudiant.* It is above all where love is concerned that man, even ancient man, confided his secrets to a god but not to his neighbour. Ps. Tibullus gives some good examples. In IV, 5, 17f. Sulpicia says that while she prays for her friend: *optat idem iuvenis quod nos, sed tectius optat: nam pudet haec illum dicere verba palam,* and in IV, 6, 15f., when her mother is conducting the prayer, we read *Praecipit en natae mater studiosa, quod optet. Illa aliud tacita clam sibi mente rogat...* The wishes of lovers were not noised abroad,[102] as Aristaenetus 16 shows with the example of a bashful lover πλὴν οὐ τεθάρρηκα τὸν πόθον ἐκφῆναι, ἐντὸς δὲ μόλις τῶν χειλῶν ὑποστένω· 'σὺ τοίνυν, ὦ Ἔρως, δύνασαι γὰρ, αὐτὴν παρασκεύασον πρώτην αἰτῆσαι'. Such wishes and prayers were pronounced *tacito labello* (Catull. 64, 104) and this accounts for the existence—beside a Heros Psithuros at Lindos[103] and a Hermes Psithuros,[104] who really belongs to the previous section—of an Aphrodite Psithuros,[105] 'the whisperer', since it was customary to whisper prayers in her ear. An epigram from Pergamon[106] shows a person who wished to remain anonymous and to conceal his wish even after it had been granted:

Οἶσθα μὲν ἀντὶ τίνος χρυσέαν, Κύπρι, φημί σε τεύξειν,
οἶσθα δὲ καὶ τίς ὁ θεὶς καὶ τίνος οἶδα χάριν.

[101] Cf. W. J. Richards, *Het gebed bij Seneca die Stoisijn* (Diss. Utrecht 1964). On this passage p. 112.

[102] Cf. also Tibull. 2, 1, 83 ff., where it is stated that the aim is that the bystanders do not hear the prayer. Parallels from the sphere of love in Schmidt o.c. (above note 96) 58 ff.

[103] Mentioned by Sudhaus, *op. cit.* (above note 96) 189.

[104] He is of course the god of thieves: Weinreich, Θεοὶ Ἐπήκοοι, *Athen. Mitt.* 37 (1912) 56 n. 2; H. Usener, *Götternamen* (1928³) 267 n. 52 (reference by J. M. Bremer). In Rome people prayed in silence to the goddess Laverna: schol. Hor. *Ep.* 1, 16, 59.

[105] Eustathius *in Od.* 20, 8 says precisely why the goddess had this epithet: ἐκαλεῖτο δέ, φασί, Ψίθυρος διὰ τὸ τὰς εὐχομένας αὐτῇ πρὸς τὸ οὖς λέγειν.

[106] Chr. Habicht, *op. cit.* (above note 24) n° 129. Here, too, there are modern parallels. S. Bonnet, *op. cit.* (above note 1) 23: 'Merci de tout mon cœur à Notre Dame. Elle sait bien pourquoi'; 33: 'Oh. Notre Dame. Vous savez bien'.

I know of no example from pagan Antiquity which bears a greater
resemblance to the well known anonymous Christian votive formulas such
as: οὗ τὸ ὄνομα ὁ Κύριος γινώσκει εὐξάμενος ὑπὲρ σωτηρίας αὐτοῦ.[107] But this
exudes a different mentality.

For the time being we can conclude by pointing out that prayers were
often, if not primarily, said out loud, but that various circumstances made
a silent prayer preferable. The circumstances were not necessarily limited
to hate or love. People can hardly have felt an urgent need to publicise
private matters in their prayers and it depended furthermore on the emotional degree of the situation whether prayers were uttered aloud, whether
they were murmured between one's lips, or whether they were exclusively
mental. What present-day visitor of a Mediterranean church can draw a
precise distinction?

At the same time the extremely plastic scene of the suppliant whispering
in the ear of a deity raises further questions: could a god hear the suppliant
in all circumstances? Cicero and Seneca thought he could, but when they
wrote that they were in a philosophical mood. Did a god always listen?
What must/could one do in order to attract the god's attention? Which
were the available means of communication? In what follows I can only
deal with a few aspects of the situation.

Already in the Iliad 16,515 we find a man praying to the deity: δύνασαι
δέ σὺ πάντοσ' ἀκούειν and there are frequent allusions to the capacity of the
gods to hear men everywhere and in all circumstances (ὃς πάντ' ἐφορᾷς καὶ
πάντ' ἐπακούεις, not, of course, said mainly about Helios by chance). The
oracular god Apollo says (Herod. I, 47) Καὶ κωφοῦ συνίημι καὶ οὐ φωνεῦντος
ἀκούω,[108] but the very emphasis of such utterances leads us to suppose that
ancient man did not regard this divine capacity as a matter of course and
that what we are really dealing with is 'Zwecksoptimismus'. This, for example, is evident from the fact that some gods are more emphatically (all-)
hearing gods than others.[109] Does the epithet *exaudientissimus* not imply

---

[107] The inscription in the text is from *MAMA* II, 107 and is discussed by C. Foss, *ZPE* 25
(1977) 282 ff., who rightly rejects former interpretations. His suggestion is that 'it referred to
the different name which God would give to the elect in Paradise' (?? H.S.V.) .... and later
became 'a sign of modesty'. Cf. G. Pugliese-Carratelli, 'Cuius nomen Deus scit', *Studi
Medio-latini e volgari* 1 (1953) 193-196; P. Devambez, *Le sanctuaire de Sinuri près de Mylasa* II
(Paris 1959) 45. Two recent finds: L. Robert, *BE* 1974, 298; 1976, 271.

[108] On the divine capacities of hearing silent prayer see K. J. Dover, *Greek Popular Morality*
(Berkeley-Los Angeles 1974) 257-258, and Sudhaus, *op. cit.* (above note 96) 190 f.

[109] In a recently found oracle-inscription of Apollo Kareios, the god even says that he does
not know everything and that one god should not consider himself more clever than other

trust *and* distrust? And is the same not true of the recently discovered unique dedication to εὐχοδότῃ Διί?[110] For if this Zeus is the 'hearer of prayers' *par excellence*, what about the other (Zeus) gods? The deepest cause of uncertainty is, of course, the fact that the philosophical vision constantly clashes with the simple believer's more anthropomorphic concept of god. If, even in Homer, Poseidon, in distant Ethiopia, cannot hear the conversation on Olympus, we can hardly be surprised at the following fable, again by Babrius (n° 2): a farmer suspects his neighbours of having stolen his pick-axe, but they deny it. He then takes the suspects to the town where, in contrast to the country, gods can be found who are genuine and see everything (ἀληθεῖς καὶ τὰ πάντ' ἐποπτεύειν).[111] Before he can ask the deity who the thief is, a *kèrux* comes out and says that anyone who can give information about a recent temple robbery will get a reward. Thereupon the farmer decides against taking any further action κλέπτας γὰρ ἄλλους πῶς ὁ θεὸς ἂν εἰδείη ὃς τοὺς ἑαυτοῦ φῶρας οὐχὶ γινώσκει;[112] Thus the desire that the gods should see everything (or at least one's own good deeds and the evil deeds of others) clashed again and again with the realistic awareness that this was obviously and regrettably not always the case. This being so, it was necessary to try to attract the god's attention.

Prayer after prayer contains the words κλῦθι, ἄκουε, ἄκουσον, *audi, exaudi*.[113] It was necessary to ἐπικαλεῖσθαι, προσκαλεῖν, *invocare, advocare* the deity, and this usually meant more than merely invoking him. The god had frequently to be persuaded to come nearer so that he could really hear the voice of the suppliant: hence the ὕμνοι κλητικοί,[114] hence the frequent call ἐλθέ, ἴθι, φάνηθι and also βλέφον πρὸς ἡμᾶς (Eurip. *Helen*. 1442 for example), *veni, adsis, ades* and also *aspice nos, converte voltus ad meas clades, pater*.

---

gods (M. L. West, 'Oracles of Apollo Kareios. A Revised Text', *ZPE* 1 (1967) 183-187, especially 187). But this modesty is characteristic of a time when various gods lose their self-conceit.

[110] Th. Drew-Bear, *Nouvelles Inscriptions de Phrygie* (Zutphen 1978) 48, n° 24. Reference of H. W. Pleket.

[111] This is a significant phrase. The two divine qualities of greatness and the capacity to see and control everything (espec. juridically) are also combined in the well-known *lex sacra* of Philadelphia where one reads in line 33 θεοὶ γὰρ ἐν αὐτῶι ἵδρυνται μεγάλοι καὶ τ[αῦτα ἐπισκοποῦ]σιν ......, commented upon by O. Weinreich, *Sitz. Ber. Heidelb. Ak. Wiss. Phil.-Hist. Kl.* (1919) 60 ff., with parallels.

[112] A similar case in Aesop. 286 (Halm) = 170 (Hunger), and cf. Aesop. 312 (Halm).

[113] Full information in Ausfeld, *op. cit.* (above note 29) 516-7; Appel, *op. cit.* (above note 56) 115-119; Cf. E. Norden, *Agnostos Theos* (1926²) 148.

[114] Examples: Diod. Sic. 3, 4; Anacreon 2, 6; Soph. *Antig.* 1140 ff.; Eurip. *Bacch.* 1017 ff. And cf. J. M. Bremer below p. 194.

We perceive the wish that the god should, for an instant, turn his exalted attention to the mortal. Mere attention often suffices: 'to attend' is to 'assist', *ad-esse* is *adesse*, παρίστασθαι also means 'to help'.[115]

Central, however, is the act of listening: ἀκούω becomes ἐπακούομαι; 'hearing' becomes 'granting'. Thus we come to the paradoxical conclusion that in certain circumstances whispering could have exactly the same function as shouting out loud. The whispering in the ear of the image of the god in Seneca can indeed be explained as he suggests: 'in the illusion that we will thus be heard all the better'.[116] But the same object can of course also be achieved by raising one's voice, shouts and emotional outbursts, of which tears can be one. *Domine, quas tuorum preces exaudis, si has non exaudis?* exclaims St. Augustine (*Civ. Dei*, 22, 8) in a particularly emotional prayer. 'Weeping was prescribed during prayer', wrote Engelmann,[117] not without a touch of exaggeration. But it is quite true that tears are often mentioned as a sign of true feeling, and not only in the more personal emotions of the Isis and Serapis cults.

In the whole of Antiquity, but especially in the later period, we can perceive the attempt to attain the proximity of the god by way of his image. A telling example can be found in Seneca (*apud* Augustine *Civ. Dei* 6, 10)[118] who is referring to 'adepts' in the temple of the Trias Capitolina: *Alius nomina subicit, alius horas Iovi nuntiat, alius lector est, alius unctor qui vano*

---

[115] Examples where παρεστάναι or παραστατεῖν have the meaning of βοηθεῖν in L. Robert, *Hellenica* VI, 109-111.

[116] A remarkable consequence is that people sometimes pray to the ears of the god which are fixed at the walls of the temple: O. Weinreich, *op. cit.* (above note 104) 57.

[117] H. Engelmann, *The Delian Aretalogy of Sarapis* (Leiden 1975) 49 *ad* line 72. Cf. also Appel, *op. cit.* (above note 56) 208; Schmidt, *op. cit.* (above note 96) 71 n. 1. It depends on the universality of weeping during prayer whether Apul. *Met.* 11, 1 contains a corruption: see Gwyn Griffiths *ad loc.* Philostr. *Vita Apoll.* 6, 43 seems to regard weeping as belonging to a certain category of suppliants when he says of a person ὥσπερ οἱ βώμιοι τῶν ἱκετῶν κλαίων. Jews and Christians wept with even more enthusiasm: E. von Severus, 'Gebet', *RAC* 8, 1163. Here sometimes weeping is prescribed: K. Meuli, *Gesammelte Schriften* I, (Basel-Stuttgart 1976) 374-380.

[118] Nobody seems to know exactly in what period and in what religious climate this scene must be placed. Wissowa, *RuK*², 423 n. 3, connects it with the *epulum Iovis*. P. Veyne, *Le pain et le cirque* (Paris 1976) 499 n. 58 hesitates but promises to return to the problem (*Ann. Coll. de France* 76, 1976, 578). Cf. K. Latte, *RRG*, 328, and J. Le Gall, *La religion romaine* etc. (Paris 1975) 202, connecting it with Egyptian rites. I wonder if we should not connect it with Degrassi, *ILLRP* no 301 (republican): *Paul(la) Toutia M.f. et consuplicatrices*, which may reflect the atmosphere of οἱ συνελθόντες θρησκευταὶ ἐπὶ θεοῦ Διὸς Ὑψίστου (J. M. R. Cormack, *Mélanges Helléniques G. Daux*, 51-55). Cf. also the material presented by H. W. Pleket, below p. 159 ff.

motu bracchiorum imitatur... Sunt quae Iunoni ac Minervae capillos disponant, sunt quae speculum teneant, sunt qui libellos offerant et illos causam suam doceant... Sedent quaedam in Capitolio quae se a Iove amari putant. But the addressing of prayers directly to the image of the god is of course a familiar phenomenon throughout Antiquity. In Euripides' *Andromache*, 1117 we read: χῶ μὲν κατ' ὄμμα στὰς προσεύχεται θεῷ, and there are various other attestations.[119] One of the problems was to have access to the image in the temple—and this was not always easy.[120] If I say that the longing for the proximity of the god was more intensive in the imperial period, I have in mind above all the more personal devotions expressed, for example, in contemplation in the presence of the image, as in the cult of Isis: Apul. *Met.* XI, 24, 5 *inexplicabili voluptate simulacri divini perfruebar... provolutus denique ante conspectum deae,*[121] (this makes me wonder whether Heubner, in his commentary, is not underestimating Tac. *Hist.* IV, 82, 1, *Vespasianus... numini intentus,* i.e. before the Serapis image in the temple of Alexandria, by translating it 'der Gottheit zugewandt')'or in the kissing of the foot or knee of an image, like the gigantic statue of Serapis in Alexandria, a pagan Peter.[122] Nor, indeed, is this the only similarity with the image of Peter, whose toes show evident signs of wear. This is also said of images in Antiquity: Lucret. *Rer. nat.* I, 316:

> *tum portas propter aëna*
> *signa manus dextras ostendunt adtenuari*
> *saepe salutantum tactu praeterque meantum*

and Cic. *in Verrem*, act II, IV, 94: *Ibi ex aere simulacrum ipsius Herculis quo non facile dixerim quicquam me vidisse pulchrius, tametsi non tam multum in istis rebus intellego, quam multa vidi, usque eo, iudices, ut rictum eius ac mentum paulo sit at-*

---

[119] See e.g. Herod. I, 31, 4; 5, 72; 6, 61.

[120] See e.g. the very interesting passages in Philostr. *Vita Apoll.* 4, 40 and Pausan. 10, 32, 13. Generally on this subject: J. W. Hewitt, 'The Major Restrictions of Access to Greek Temples', *TAPA* 40 (1909) 83-92. Pleket refers me to L. Robert, *Études anatoliennes* (Paris 1937) 32 and P. E. Corbett, 'Greek Temples and Greek Worshippers', *BICS* 17 (1970) 149-158.

[121] See commentary Gwyn Griffiths *ad loc.*; H. Engelmann, *op. cit.* (above note 117) *ad* lines 12 and 13. Generally: F. Festugière, *Personal Religion among the Greeks* (Berkeley 1954) 68-84. Cf. P. Veyne, *Ann. Coll. de France* 76 (1976) 578.

[122] A. Henrichs, 'Vespasian's Visit to Alexandria', *ZPE,* 3 (1968) 51-80, espec. 70 ff., who mentions also Heliod. *Aeth.* 7, 8, 7, and Chariton 1, 7; 2, 2, 7. M. Guarducci, 'Le impronte del Quo vadis', *Rend. Pont. Ac. Arch.* 19 (1942-3) 305-344, espec. 322. Cf. also Appel, *op. cit.* (above note 56) 193 f., 197 f.

tritius, quod in precibus et gratulationibus non solum id venerari sed etiam osculari solent.

In order to prevent the god from forgetting the prayer in Antiquity, as indeed nowadays, the supplication was frequently attached to the image on a wax tablet, or even written on the image. We have many indirect testimonies of this,[123] since most of the direct ones have unfortunately disappeared with the images themselves. Not all, however: from the confession-inscriptions of the second and third centuries A.D. we are acquainted with the custom, in the case of an unproven crime, of presenting a πιττάκιον to the god in which he might be asked to force the culprit to confess by way of a miraculous punishment. Certain examples of this type, engraved in lead (a feature which they share with the *defixio*), have come down to us.[124] They are among the most personal attestations which we possess. We can hear the author of this tablet from Amorgos[125] grinding his teeth: Κυρία Δημήτηρ βασίλισσα, ἱκέτης σου προσπίπτω .... ἐπὶ σὲ καταφεύγω σοῦ εὐιλάτου τυχεῖν καὶ ποιῆσαί με τοῦ δικαίου τυχεῖν. μὴ παιδὶν κλαύσαιτο μὴ τράπεζαν ἱλαρὰν θεῖτο, μὴ κύων ὑλακτήσαιτο, μὴ ἀλέκτωρ κοκκύσαιτο, σπείρας μὴ θερίσαιτο. μὴ γῆ μὴ θάλασσα καρπὸν ἐνέγκαιτο. ἀπόλοιτο, καὶ τὰ παρ' αὐτοῦ πάντα. κυρία Δημήτηρ, λιτανεύω σε παθὼν ἄδικα. ἐπάκουσον, θεά, καὶ κρῖναι τὸ δίκαιον ... βασίλισσα, ἐπάκουσον ἡμῖν παθοῦσι, κόλασαι τοὺς ἡμᾶς τοιούτους ἡδέως βλέποντας. 'Ruler Demeter, queen, I fall as a suppliant at your feet... I seek my refuge in you to ask your mercy; grant that justice be done to me... (may what follows afflict my enemy): that no child will ever cry to him, that he never set up a successful sacrificial table, that no dog bark at him and that no cock crow to him. That he may sow but may not reap... that neither land nor sea bring forth fruits for him... that he and all that belongs to him perish. Ruler Demeter, I pray to you since I have suffered injustice. Listen and grant, goddess,

---

[123] For example Iuvenalis 10, 56, *propter quae fas est genua incerare deorum;* Apul. *Apol.* 54 *votum in alicuius statuae femore assignasti* (and see A. Abt, *Die Apologie des Apuleius von Madaura und die antike Zauberei* (RVV 1908) *ad loc.*); Philostr. *Her.* 3, 2 καὶ νὴ Δία ἀλείφοντες τε καὶ ἐπισφραγιζόμενοι τὰς εὐχάς. Cf. K. Latte, *RRG*, 328; P. Friedländer, *Sittengeschichte Roms* III⁹ (1920) 196 n. 9. Is this the origin of the habit of pinning political slogans on statues? See R. MacMullen, *Enemies of the Roman Order* (Cambridge Mass. 1966) 297 n. 9.

[124] See above note 79. On the *pittakion*: Steinleitner, 100 f.

[125] Homolle, *BCH* 25 (1901) 413 ff.; *IG* XII, 7; J. Zingerle, *Österr. Jahresh.* 23 (1926) 67 ff., who dates it in the 2nd century B.C., contrary to Homolle and Björck, *op. cit.* (above note 79) 129 ff., who think of the imperial period. Cf. also K. Latte, *Heiliges Recht* (Tübingen 1920) 81.

and pass a righteous judgement... Queen listen and hear us sufferers, punish those who see us with joy in this condition'.

Many of the surviving personal prayers on lead or papyrus contain similar requests to the god to do justice.[126] These petitions were placed where it was expected that they would best reach the god: in a grave if they were intended for the gods of the underworld, on the statue of the deity when they were directed to the gods of the heavens. (The modern Greek also gives the dying letters for his dead loved ones).[127] We have a splendid example from the very borders of Antiquity: Gregory Thaumaturgus graciously permits Apollo to continue his oracular activity (Euseb. II, 2, 955, 9 Schwarz-Mommsen): *At ille* (sc. Gregory) *nihil moratus scribit epistulam in haec verba: 'Gregorius Apollini. Permitto tibi redire ad locum tuum et agere quae consuesti'. Hanc epistulam sacerdos accipit et ad fanum defert, positaque ea iuxta simulacrum adfuit daemon ac dedit responsa poscenti.* Gregory of Nyssa[128] tells us that the text of the letter ran: Γρηγόριος τῷ Σαθάνᾳ, εἴσελθε. Whoever might find all this somewhat arrogant is right, but the colloquial tone which contributes to this feature is peculiar to the epistolary style and also appears in reverential prayers, sometimes with surprising effects. The author of an Egyptian oracle question[129] ends his letter to the god with ἔρρωσο, which means no more than *vale*, 'all the best', and indeed, the friendly greeting with which the husbandman salutes the image of his favourite god on his land also amounts to little more than 'hallo'.[130] It is curious how ancient and modern devotion meet on this point. Philostratos *Vit. Soph.* I, 25, 4 says that when Asclepius appeared to Polemon at Pergamon and told him to keep away from water as a cure, he answered: βέλτιστε, εἰ δὲ βοῦν ἐθεράπευες; 'and what if you had to cure an ox?',[131] while G. Lewis reports that students in Istanbul write to Allah: 'Allahim ne olur. Bu sene sinifimi geçirim (*sic*) olmaz mi?' 'It is all the same to You,

---

[126] Very good treatment by G. Björck, *op. cit.* (above note 79).

[127] R. and E. Blum, *The Dangerous Hour* (London 1970) 68. Cf. the specifically Egyptian letters to the dead: A. H. Gardiner-K. Sethe, *Egyptian Letters to the Dead* (London 1928); and letters to gods: K.-Th. Zaurich, *Die demotischen Dokumente,* in *Textes et languages de l'Égypte pharaonique* III (Kairo 1974) 94; D. Wildung, *Imhotep und Amenhotep. Gottwerdung im alten Ägypten* (München-Berlin 1977).

[128] Greg. Nyss., Migne XLVI, 913 D ff. Cf. A. D. Nock, *Essays* I, 45; 328 n. 107.

[129] W. Schubart, *ÄZ* 67 (1931) 110 ff. n° 5 = *P.Ox.* VIII, 1148.

[130] See W. Burkert, *Griechische Religion der archaischen und klassischen Epoche* (Stuttgart-Berlin 1978) 126.

[131] Mentioned by O. Weinreich, *Antike Heilungswunder* (RVV 1909) 113, who gives more examples.

God, isn't it? I'll pass up this year, O.K.?'[131a] There was, and still is, a
busy vertical correspondence. The repetition, so characteristic of normal
prayer, which signifies intensity, also appears in this sphere: in the chapel
of the Holy Child in Aracoeli I found two identical letters, which were obviously written at the same time, from a girl asking for the recovery of her
father and mother. One letter was dispatched a week after the other and I
was unable to make out whether this was due to a distrust of horizontal
rather than vertical communications, or whether it was simply in order to
increase the intensity by repetition. The gods, moreover, frequently wrote
to humans.[132]

If the prayer was heard the token of thanks was often attached to the
image too. A good example,[133] which corresponds to modern usage, can
be found in Lucian, *Philopseudes*, 18 ff. where a certain Eucrates has a
miraculous image in his house which he has partially gilded in thanks for
his recovery from a fever. Other recoverers laid coins before the image or
fastened them to its thighs.

Apart from presents gratitude—to which I shall be returning—is
expressed in recognition by way of a title of honour ἐπήκοος or ὑπήκοος.
O. Weinreich has written the fundamental study on these terms,[134] and
since then many new data have come to light and supplementary observations been published. We can see that ἐπήκοος,[135] which started as a func-

---

[131a] G. Lewis, 'The Saint and the Major-General', *Anatol. Stud.* 22 (1972) 249-253.

[132] A very telling instance in the *ktisis*-story of the Serapeum of Thessalonike: R.
Merkelbach, *ZPE* 10 (1973) 49 ff., espec. 53; Cf. W. Speyer, *Bücherfunde in der Glaubenswer-
tung in der Antike* (Göttingen 1970) 17 and 32-39; E. R. Dodds, *The Greeks and the Irrational*[6]
(1968) 106-108 and n. 19.

[133] More examples: Prudent. *Hamartig.* 403; *idem, c. Symm.* I, 204; *idem, Apophth.* 457. A
nice example of a votive pinax near the image of the god: Herond. *Mimiamb.* IV, 19-20, ἐκ
δεξιῆς τὸν πίνακα, Κοττάλη, στῆσον τῆς Ὑγιείης, with the comments by R. Wünsch, *ARW* 7
(1904) 107 ff. On these *pinakes* in general see D. Wachsmuth, Πόμπιμος ὁ δαίμων (Diss. Berlin
1967) 134 ff.; 141 n. 246, and J. Boardman, 'Painted Votive Plaques' *ABSA* 49 (1954)
183-201. And cf. F. T. van Straten, below p. 79 ff.

[134] O. Weinreich, *op. cit.* (above note 104); *Phil. Wochenschr.* (1930) 980; *Hermes* 51 (1926)
627; *Ausgewählte Schriften* I (1969) 175-186. Practically every new find breeds a new paper on
this subject, which does not always imply progress: L. Robert, *Rev. Phil.* (1974) 198 n. 103
and 104. Modern ἐπήκοοι: Weinreich, 44 ff.; P. Kretschmer, *Glotta* 21 (1933) 171 on the
epithets of the Panagia Ἀπακοή, τῆς Ὑπακοῆς. Cf. P. Lambrechts et L. Vanden Berghe, 'La
divinité-oreille dans les religions antiques', *Bull. de l'inst. hist. belge de Rome* 29 (1955)
177-197.

[135] Next to this also εὐάντητος, particularly in the case of the Mater deorum: Weinreich,
o.c. (preceding note) 41 n. 1; M. J. Vermaseren, in *Festoen, opgedragen aan A. N. Zadoks-
Josephus Jitta* (Groningen-Bussum 1975) 589. Cf. P. Herrmann, *Denkschr. Oest. Ak. Wiss.*

tional and predicative epithet like *audiens* or *audientissimus*,[136] turned into the standard cult epithet of a certain type of god. A good example of the original predicative usage is to be found in Aristoph. *Thesmoph.* 1154 ff.

μόλετον, ἔλθετον, ἀντόμεθ', ὦ Θεσμοφόρω πολυποτνία, εἰ καὶ πρότερόν ποτ' ἐπηκόω ἤλθετε, νῦν ἀφίκεσθ' ἱκετεύομεν, ἐνθαδ' ἡμῖν.

It emerges from the epigraphical material that the term was applied in Greece above all to gods of healing of the Asclepius type and was then associated, in Asia Minor and elsewhere, primarily with Oriental gods. We can seek an explanation of this phenomenon in the fact that, ever since the fourth century B.C., the feeling of personal dependency on the god obtained increasing emphasis amongst the faithful, the call for help and salvation became ever more frequent and the gods appeared to be more imposing and majestic, a process which is discussed by H. W. Pleket in this book. The god who hears was great or the greatest, and vice versa: one could expect to be heard by a great god. Hence the multiple combinations μέγας ἐπήκοος, μέγιστος ἐπήκοος, ὕψιστος ἐπήκοος. Hence the fact that hearing was equated with rescuing and ἐπήκοος was virtually the same as σωτήρ,[137] until we end up with cumulations like Διὶ Ἡλίῳ μεγάλῳ Σαράπιδι σωτῆρι πλουτοδότῃ ἐπηκόῳ εὐεργέτῃ ἀνεικήτῳ Μίθρᾳ χαριστήριον.[138]

One of the paradoxes of this religious mentality[139] is that the exalted and omnipotent god owed much of his inaccessible majesty to the fact that he lent an ear to lowly mortals. An example with an almost Old Testamentary patina is the plea of the knight Lenaios[140] whose horse has had a stroke and gone blind. Blindness was often interpreted as a divine punishment, and, as though he were pleading 'for a brother or a son', Lenaios shows the great god Serapis that horses cannot sin—an argument which convinces the god. The horse recovers. A particularly concrete manner of expressing the hearing quality of the god was the dedication of representa-

---

Phil-Hist. Kl. 77 (1959) 15 f. (reference by Pleket). Cf. for other variants Van Straten, below p. 71, n. 28.

[136] Dessau *ILS* 2996 ff.

[137] See on the identification of terms as κύριος, ἐπήκοος and σωτήρ: I. Chirassi Colombo, in *Les syncrétismes dans les religions de l'antiquité* (ed. F. Dunand et P. Lévêque, Leiden 1975) 104-105, and Y. Grandjean, *Une nouvelle arétalogie d'Isis à Maronée* (Leiden 1975) 30-31, where the editor reads [ἐπήκ]ουσας (cf. below notes 147, 148). This conjecture is not beyond all doubt, however: L. Vidman, *Gnomon* (1978) 214.

[138] L. Vidman, *SIRIS*, n° 389.

[139] I have illustrated one of these paradoxical aspects in my inaugural address *De tyrannie verdrijven?* (Rede Leiden 1978).

[140] Aelian. *Hist. Anim.* 11, 34.

tions of ears, of which we have many examples, especially from the cult of Oriental θεοὶ ἐπήκοοι. A final consequence then, was that the believer did not pray to the god but to the ears of the god. Dedications and prayers *auribus* or ἀκοαῖς,[141] still obstinately misinterpreted here and there, are the plastic attestations of these scenes, of which I shall give a single example: Καρποκράτη, ἀκοαῖς τῆς ῎Ισιδος, ᾽Οσείριδι ἐπηκόῳ, ῾Εστίᾳ κουροτρόφῳ.[142] It is again in Egypt that we encounter the greatest excess.[143] There we come across gods with 'many eyes and numerous ears'—a magical papyrus attributes 77 eyes and 77 ears to the god Chnoem, and besides gods 'who listen' we get an entirely new, independent, god called 'Mestasut-mis', 'the listening ear'.

The emperor resembled the great god in various respects: for one thing, petitions to the emperor, especially in Egypt but also elsewhere in the East, were laid at the foot of his statue.[144] For, as Artemidorus III, 13 remarks: 'rulers, like gods, also have the power to treat people well or badly'. So we should not be surprised to find the term ἐπήκοος also attributed to the emperor, although we only have one sure example in an inscription from Aegina, ὁ ἀφ' ῾Ηλίου νέος Διόνυσος Θεὸς μέγας ἐπήκοος, Heliogabalus or Caracalla.[145] Emperors could be divine ἐπήκοοι; so could the dead, as we

---

[141] Massive information in O. Weinreich, *op. cit.* (above note 104) 55. On the ambiguity: ear of the god or healed ear of a human being see Chr. Habicht, *op. cit.* (above note 24) n° 91 with rich literature. On misunderstandings L. Robert, *op. cit.* (above note 134). Cf. also F. T. van Straten, below p. 83.

[142] R. Harder, *Abh. Preuss. Ak.* 1943, no. 14; L. Vidman, *SIRIS*, n° 88.

[143] See J. Quaegebeur, 'Egyptische goden die luisteren', *Alumni* 49 (1978) 9-19, with interesting material and the relevant literature. I owe the reference to this paper to Dr. G. Schepens.

[144] For example in *P. Oxy.* XVII, 2130, where a plaintiff has first put his case before a college of gymnasiarchs, line 17 ff., καὶ μὴ προσεθέντων τούτων ἀνεθέμην ἐν τῷ αὐτ[ό]θι Σεβαστείῳ πρὸς τοῖς θείοις ἴχνεσι τοῦ κυρίου ἡμῶν Αὐτοκράτορος Γαλλιηνοῦ Σεβάστου διαπεμφθησόμενα ὑπὸ τοῦ στατίζοντος τῷ λαμπροτάτῳ ἡγεμόνι. Another case in *Corp. Pap. Raineri*, ed. C. Wessely I (Vienna 1895) n° XX, also about 250 A.D. See on this Hunt in his commentary *ad loc.*, who remarks (p. 232) that the reasons for this type of action have not been clearly explained. For statues of emperors as place of supplication and as asylum: Preisigke, *Wörterbuch* s.v. ἴχνος, and P. J. Alexander, *The Oracle of Baalbek* (Washington 1967) 31 ff. On the basis of these data F. Millar, in *Le culte des souverains dans l'empire romain* (Entretiens Hardt 1973) 148 is right in maintaining the manuscr. version in the Acta of Dasius ἴχνεσι. In the discussion around the emperor cult these passages have not received sufficient attention.

[145] A. D. Nock, *Aegyptus* 33 (1953) 295 (Caracalla); *idem, JRS* 47 (1957) 121 = *Essays* II, 843, and Nilsson, *GGR* II² (518) (Heliogabalus). In *Inschr. Milet* I, 7, p. 349 n° 7, βασιλεῖ ἐπηκόῳ εὐχήν is not directed at a human prince according to Rehm. It may be relevant to note that there are more types of human ἐπήκοοι. An inscription from Kyme mentions an

see from a dedication by parents to their dead child: θεῷ ἰδίῳ ἐπηκόῳ.[146] In such cases we may indeed wonder what ἐπήκοος still means. That a process of linguistic debasement is at play is certain. Words lose their original meaning and need to be reinforced. Ἐπήκοος actually means 'whose nature it is to hear', but unfortunately this property is not always realised in practice. We consequently get sporadic inscriptions like Ἀρτεμίδωρος Μενελάου Μητρὶ Θεοῦ καὶ Διὶ Σελευκέῳ ἐπακούσασι [εὐχ]ήν, about which L. Robert observed:[147] 'Il ne semble pas qu'on ait encore d'exemple dans un dédicace de ce participe aoriste au lieu de l'épithète de nature ἐπήκοος'. But in 1973 the same scholar mentioned an inscription from Iasos with the amazing text Ἀφροδίτης ἐπακουούσης καὶ ἐπηκόου,[148] from which I can only deduce the satisfied ascertainment that the goddess has really put her quality into practice.

Gods who 'hear' and gods who 'grant', epithets which imply hope and acknowledgement. But gods did *not* always listen. How did ancient man react when his prayer was not heard, when the god, in the unique words of Callimachus *Delian hymn* 116, was ἀνήκοος?

VI. *Deaf gods and angry men*

In a papyrus in which the writer invokes someone's help we read that, if this person is not prepared to help him, ὥσπερ [ὁ]ι θεοὶ οὐκ ἐφίσαντό μ[ο]υ, οὕτως κἀγὼ θεῶ[ν] οὐ φί[σ]ομαι 'just as the gods paid no heed to me, I shall pay no heed to them'.[149] We have already seen on repeated occasions that the believer of Antiquity approached his god, in word and deed, as though

---

ἐπάκοος, interpreted by H. Engelmann, *Die Inschriften von Kyme*, n° 11, p. 18, as a kind of judge. Cf. Hesych. δ 4542. The divine ἐπήκοοι functioned in the juridical sphere as well.

[146] H. W. Pleket, *Epigraphica* II (Leiden 1969) n° 55, and *idem*, *HThR* 58 (1965) 334 n. 14. Cf. H. D. Klitsch, *Eine inschriftliche Krankengeschichte des 3e Jh. n. Chr. Das Grabgedicht für den fünfjährigen Lucius Minicius Anthimianus* (Diss. Erlangen-Nürnberg 1976) 38-40.

[147] L. Robert, *Hellenica* VI, 24 n. 2 (Manisa Mus. n° 103), but cf. above note 137.

[148] After G. Pugliese Carratelli, *Annuar. Sc. Arch. At.* 47-8 (1969-70) 371-403, n° 19, who translates the text 'Veneris quae preces audit et exaudit'. This cannot be right. The difference between the two terms does not lie in the meaning of the stem ἐπακούειν = *exaudire* in both cases, but in the actualization or lack of actualization of the quality of the goddess. The praesens remains puzzling. Is there some similarity with expressions as πολλὰς εὐεργεσίας καὶ τετελεκότα καὶ τελοῦντα (P. Herrmann, 'Ergebnisse einer Reise nach Nordost Lydien', *Öst. Ak. Wiss. Phil. Hist. Kl.* 80 (1962) n° 25)? Anyhow it is clear that the writer wished to brush up the worn epithet, just as in a dedication κἀλῷ καλοχαίρῳ, where 'the beautiful season' has already become 'summer' and needs an additional καλός, since not every summer is really a beautiful season.: L. Robert, *Hellenica* IX, 51-66.

[149] Mitteis-Wilcken, *Chrestomathie* I, 2, n° 120.

he was a great and powerful human being. Indeed, he had few other alternatives, either psychological or linguistic. The negative reactions, too, are
often strikingly human and, especially in their expression of disappointment, tragi-comical.

Everyone is familiar with outbursts of emotion and fury directed, even
today, particularly in somewhat warmer climates, at disappointing saints
and their images.[150] In Portugal, Italy and Spain it is customary to
threaten the local saint with hanging on the occasion of epidemics, too
little rain or too much rain; images are placed in the blazing sun so that
they themselves can feel it; they are tied up, spat upon, whipped and hung
upside down in a well. St. Anthony of Castel Branco was punished by his
worshippers when he allowed the village to be plundered by the Spaniards:
all his images were broken and his most venerated statue was beheaded
and given the head of St. Francis whose name it bore ever after.[151] This
was a typical *damnatio memoriae*, comparable to that of the Roman emperors
whose statues also received the head of a worthier successor. Indeed, there
are still more pronounced parallels: Augustus had the image of Neptune
removed from the *pompa deorum* as punishment for a storm caused by the
deity (Suet. *Aug.* 16), and, with a very different attitude Caligula ordered
ut simulacra numinum religione et arte praeclara, inter quae Olympii Iovis, apportarentur e Graecia, quibus capite dempto suum imponeret (Suet. *Cal.* 22).

Whoever thinks that Catholics only treat their saints (and their images)
in so 'classical' a manner in order not to come to grips with God Himself is
wrong. On a farm in Southern Germany we can read: 'Dieses Haus stand
in Gottes Hand und ist dreimal abgebrannt; das vierte Mal ist's wieder
aufgebaut und jetzt dem Hlg. Florian anvertraut',[152] and Heiler[153] tells
of a German Protestant farmer who clenched his fist at heaven after a
long drought and shouted: 'Du verfluchter Lieber Gott'. Saints (even
God himself) must do what people want them to do, no less and—
preferably—no more: a French king had the following text placed in a
churchyard where too many miracles were taking place: 'De par le roi

---

[150] Material in J. G. Frazer, *The Golden Bough* I. *The Magic Art and the Evolution of Kings* I
(London 1911) 296 ff.; A. S. F. Gow, *ad* Theocr. VII, 108 Binding of St. Antony to the
mast: L. Radermacher, *ARW* 7 (1904) 451 f.; L. Friedländer, *Sittengeschichte Roms* III⁹ (1920)
196-7.

[151] R. Gallop, *Portugal. A Book of Folk-Ways*² (Cambridge 1961) 134.

[152] Quoted by O. Weinreich, *op. cit.* (above note 70) where one also reads 'Dieses Haus
steht in St. Florians Hand; verbrennt es, ist's ihm eine Schand'. (p. 30).

[153] *Op. cit.* (above p. 3) 84.

défense à Dieu de faire miracles à ce lieu'.[154] In short, if gods and saints refuse to do what men want them to do, men get angry and odd things happen. This goes for Antiquity too.[155]

The best example of a god being punished is Xerxes' decision to have the Hellespont flogged and shackled and thenceforth to declare the god no longer entitled to sacrifices.[156] The Greeks thought it absurd, obviously failing to realise that there were plenty of rites in their own country which were not so very different from this spontaneous reaction. When, in Arcadia (admittedly a backward area), the flocks ceased to prosper and there ensued a lack of meat, boys scourged the image of the god Pan, as a punishment and so that he should do better.[157] Since they flogged him with onions this has been regarded as a fertility rite[158]—unnecessarily in my opinion. We also come across other examples of the flagrant chastisement of divine images in Antiquity. Babrius 119 describes the scene of a poor craftsman who sacrifices to Hermes regularly every day without ever getting anything in return. He ends up by flinging the statue on the ground in fury and breaking it into tiny pieces—with an unexpected result. Statues were regularly thrown about. The most impressive example I know is described by Suetonius *Cal.* 5, where by the people, deeply shaken by the death of Germanicus, *lapidata sunt templa, subversae deum arae, Lares a quibusdam familiares in publicum abiecti, partus coniugum expositi.*[159] A double punishment was reserved for the image of the dead athlete Theagenes of Thasos which was flogged every night by a jealous rival but which fell and killed the culprit one evening and was cast into the sea as a punishment.[160]

---

[154] I read this in a review of E. and M.-L. Keller, *Miracles in Dispute*, in *TLS* 25-6-1970, p. 692.

[155] See besides Friedländer (above note 150), L. Schmidt, *Die Ethik der alten Griechen* II (Berlin 1882) 43 ff. and 64. H. Braune, Περὶ εὐχῆς. *Veterum de precibus sententiae* (Diss. Marburg 1935) 20 n. 8, has collected some prayers where gods are being abused, and in apparent embarrassment adds: 'Hae sane preces nominandae non sunt, quarum formulas usitatas homines magna animi perturbatione commoti perrumpunt.'!

[156] Herod. 7, 34 f., on which N. Tergazhi, 'Die Geiselung des Hellespontos', *ARW* 11 (1908) 145-150, with an unacceptable interpretation; cf. R. M. Meyer, *ibid.*, 324.

[157] Theocr. VII, 106 ff.

[158] See A. S. F. Gow, *ad loc.*

[159] I have discussed this remarkable type of reaction in 'Destruction, Devotio and Despair in a Situation of Anomy: The Mourning for Germanicus in Triple Perspective', in G. Piccaluga (ed). *Perennitas. In onore di A. Brelich* (Roma 1980) 541-618.

[160] Pausan. 6, 11, 5 ff. (and Frazer *ad loc.*) = Parke-Wormell, *The Delphic Oracle*, n° 389-391; cf. *ibid.* n° 520 = Pausan. 5, 27, 10. Parallels in O. Weinreich, *op. cit.* (above note 131) 143 n. 1. There are points of contact with the punishment of animals or objects:

Images of heroes were frequently punished by burial: Artemidorus IV, 78
refers to statues of heroes 'mishandled by certain people or buried in the
ground' and in II, 33 he talks of the 'destruction of divine images, throwing them out of doors, raising a temple to the ground'. It can hardly be ob-
jected that this author was describing dreams and that dreams are illusory:
these are clearly scenes from daily life. Rage and disappointment were expressed thus; Epictetus (*Diss.* III, 4, 7) says it himself: καὶ τί θαυμαστόν; οἱ
γεωργοὶ τὸν Δία οὐ λοιδοροῦσιν, ὅταν ἐμποδίζωνται ὑπ' αὐτοῦ; οἱ ναῦται οὐ
λοιδοροῦσι;[161] In later Antiquity gods were even customarily insulted and
threatened in an attempt to spur them into action.[162] It must, of course, be
admitted that anthropomorphic representations of gods facilitated such
deeds. In this connection and with reference to Homeric scenes, E.
Vermeule observed: 'It amused the Greeks to "kill" their gods in such
fables'.[163]

Such behaviour was naturally not always exempt from punishment. Admittedly it was said of the Rhodians: *etiam deos aliqui verbis ferocioribus incre-
pant, neve ideo quemquam fulmine ictum audimus* (Liv. XLV, 23, 19), but the
tyrant Philanthropos (!), who set fire to the sanctuary of Olympia in his
fury at a prayer not being granted, was nevertheless killed by lightning
(Anon. in Westermann, *Paradox. Gr.* 221, 14). The human reaction could
also have a more drastic variant: frustrated by the fact that a perjuror was
not punished by the gods Diagoras of Melos concluded that no gods existed
and thus became the first true atheist in Greece.[164] Comparable, although

M. Mühl, 'Relikte der Tier- und Sachstrafe bei Homer', *REG* 84 (1971) 1-16. In Nonnos,
Dionys. 48, 690 ff. Aura, who has been violated by Dionysos, scourges an image of Aphrodite
and flings it into the river.

[161] Cf. Aelian. fr. 36 (H) from Suid. ὁ δὲ ἐξέπλευσεν τῶν φρενῶν, καὶ πολλὰ ἐς τὸ ἄγαλμα
παρῴνησεν.

[162] Examples in F. Cumont, *L'Egypte des astrologues* (Bruxelles 1937) 136. These are mostly
cases of the well-known λοιδορία, which had the purpose of spurring gods into action, a
custom which originated in Egypt. S. Eitrem, Διαβολή, *SO* 2 (1924) 47-48. It is a variant of
the βιαστικαὶ ἀπειλαί (Wünsch, Praef. *Defixiones Atticae*, XXVI; A. Abt, *op. cit.* (above note
123) 48 f.; L. Fahz, *De poetarum Romanorum doctrina magica* (RVV 1904) 52 f.; A. D. Nock,
Essays I, 185; A. Wiedemann, *Magie und Zauberei im alten Ägypten* (Der alte Orient 1905) 13 ff.;
Th. Hopfner, *Griechisch-Ägyptische Offenbarungszauber* I (1921) 204 ff) Herodotus 4, 184
already knows that the Libyan Atarantes scold the sun when the heath is unbearable καὶ πάντα τὰ αἰσχρὰ λοιδορέονται. Cf. Strabo 17, 822. In Philostr. *Vita Apoll.* 11, 4 the Saint abuses a
vampire ἐλοιδορεῖτο τῇ Ἐμπούσῃ. I leave out the somewhat deviating custom of binding images of gods, although there are similarities. See R. Merkelbach, 'Gefesselte Götter', *Antaios*
12 (1971) 549-565, and his contributions to K. Meuli, *Gesammelte Schriften* II, 1035 ff.

[163] E. Vermeule, *Aspects of Death in Early Art and Poetry* (Berkeley-Los Angeles 1979) 125.

[164] Sext. *Math* 9, 53; Schol. Aristoph. *Nub.* 830. See the contribution of P. A. Meijer.

less general, conclusions, were often drawn individually. A god who did not lend an ear had to beware: people easily decided that the god was not worth much or perhaps did not even exist. A large number of Roman gods died owing to their loss of function, although this was usually determined socially and through no fault of their own. In Plautus' *Casina* 347-9, however, someone already says: *nam omnes mortales dis sunt freti, sed tamen vidi ego dis fretos saepe multos decipi.*[165] But I have found no more moving an expression of disenchantment than in the inscription of a gladiator—a dead gladiator—*CIL* V, 3466 = *ILS* 5121, concerning the great goddess of the gladiators Nemesis: *In Nemese ne fidem habeatis. Sic sum deceptus...* That is diametrically opposed to a formula of praise like σὺ εἶ ἡ ἐλπὶς τῶν ἀπηλπισμένων from a Christian-magical text.[166]

Hope and disappointment are the two poles between which religious life, and therefore the life of the deity, oscillated. The two reactions to disenchantment, rage and disbelief, do not, however, always lie in the same domain. On the contrary: when the Neapolitans abuse their St Januarius as a 'vecchio ladrone', 'birbone', 'scelerato',[167] this, like Job's clenched fist, is a sign of faith. Fury is vented on someone who *exists*, as relationship therapeutists still have to teach us. Yet this does not detract from the fact that there are indeed some substantial stages of transition from emotional protest to defeatist denial. In papyrus Bremen n° 10[168] the alarmed mother Eudaimonis says ἴσθι δὲ ὅτι οὐ μέλλω θεῷ σχολάζειν (pay attention to) εἰ μὴ πρότερον ἀπαρτίσω τὸν υἱόν μου, and the same lady, 'eine sehr temperamentvolle und sanguinische alte Dame', wrote elsewhere[169] οὔτ[ε ἐ]λουσάμην [οὔ]τε προσεκύνησα θεοὺς φοβουμένη σου τὸ μετέωρον whereat Hunt[170] rightly observed: 'These ... passages illustrate the tendency in

---

[165] See J. A. Hanson, 'Plautus as a Source Book for Roman Religion', *TAPA* 90 (1959) 48-101, espec. 99.

[166] Quoted by Björck, *op. cit.* (above note 79) 58. *Elpis* is a central religious concept in the Hellenistic period. See on *euergetai* who give *elpis* to the people, L. Robert, *BE* 1973, 427.

[167] I read this in G. F. Schoemann, *Griechische Alterthümer* II (Berlin 1859) 167. Only at the 4th of May 1976 I came to understand why the Saint sometimes refuses his assistance: the cause may be the legalization of abortion and the derision by a communist mayor (*Nieuwe Rotterdamse Courant* 4-5-1976).

[168] = n° 63 in U. Wilcken, 'Die Bremer Papyri', *Abh. Preuss. Ak. Berlin* (1936) who exclaims on p. 141: 'ja was heisst ἀπαρτίσω?' Cf. his discussion on p. 144. In my opinion it is likely to understand 'unless I have my son back in good health'.

[169] Mitteis-Wilcken, *Chrestomathie* I, 1, p. 125. μετέωρον implies an unfinished and therefore threatening affair.

[170] *P. Oxy.* VII, n° 1065.

popular religion to regard the relationship between gods and men as one of
strict reciprocity. If the gods neglected their duty and afflicted their
devotees, the sufferers retaliated by turning their backs on the gods'.[171]
The relationship between fury and (acquiescent) neglect would be the subject of an interesting study. All we can say is that gods who were hard of
hearing had to beware: they were in danger of becoming smaller,
sometimes a whole head smaller. Gods who heard, on the other hand,
grew larger, and this was not kept secret as we shall see in the following
section.

VII. *Prayers of gratitude*

In my room there hangs a stone tile with the initials of the Virgin Mary
and the text 'Dank om een bekomen gunst'. ('Thanks for a favour
received'). This looks like Dutch, but is *not* Dutch, and the explanation for
this curious jargon lies in the fact that I borrowed[172] the object from a
place of pilgrimage called 'Klein Lourdes' near Ghent in Belgium: an im-
itation cave where, judging from the crutches and professions of gratitude
displayed, considerable miracles are performed. We here see the grateful
reaction of the faithful to the granting of prayers which I mentioned at the
beginning of this survey, and, in the collections to which I referred, we
find numerous formulas of thanks such as 'Merci à notre Dame pour les
grâces accordées', 'Herzlichen Dank für die Gebetserhörung',[173] etc.
Antiquity offers thousands of attestations of gratitude, often in the shape of
votive gifts, sometimes, but not always, with the reason for the gift added
in the inscription. These are the subject of F. T. van Straten's paper.
What interests us here is the question of whether Antiquity was acquainted
with the prayer of gratitude as well as with the prayer of supplication, and,
if so, what its characteristics were. The answer to this question is less
obvious than we might at first think.

---

[171] Cf. S. Bonnet, *op. cit.* (above note 1) 33: 'guérison rapide source d'une réelle dévotion
mariale ou rien'; 37: 'St. Joseph, faites que cette année je forme une famille.... je sens que je
perds la foi'. 33: 'Oh, St. Joseph ayez pitié de moi..... (a number of requests). Je m'adressai
plutot à la Sainte Vierge c'est la première fois que je vous demande une grace, tachez de
faire un petit effort...'
[172] My colleague J. Strubbe warns me that the person who abstracts such a votive tablet is
punished with the sickness from which the giver has been cured. Therefore I wish to stress
that I only borrowed it and it was an old and damaged piece.
[173] Bonnet, *op. cit.* (above note 1) *passim*; W. Heim, *op. cit.* (above note 3) 48.
[174] P. Stengel, *Die griechischen Kultusaltertümer*[2] (München 1898) 72.

In his *Die griechischen Kultusaltertümer* P. Stengel[174] already observed that in Homer, as well as later, prayers of gratitude are scarce and that even when they do appear there is no question of effusiveness. Sudhaus,[175] who quotes these lines, only knows of a single example—albeit a very fine one—of a passionate prayer of thanks from the Hellenistic period: Terence, *Heautontim.* 879 ff. (= Menander), where a man, irritated by the obviously somewhat exaggerated prayers of thanks pronounced by his wife on the return of her daughter, says:

> *Ohe, iam desine deos, uxor, gratulando obtundere*
> *tuam esse inventam gnatam, nisi illos ex tuo ingenio iudicas*
> *ut nil credas intellegere nisi idem dictumst centiens.*

We must of course be cautious where such topics are concerned: nobody has read the *whole* of ancient literature, and there is always more than a couple of scholars, however learned they might be, can tell us. There is no place for absolute statements in a subject like this. We have, for example, a scene of great purity where Cyrus brings sacrifices of gratitude (χαριστήρια) to the gods at the end of his life because they have always pointed out the right path to him through oracles and portents and, in a prayer, he gives thanks (χάρις) for their concern (Xen. *Cyropaed.* 8, 7, 3). This might well have been a Persian custom, but, in his brief but learned study on prayer in Antiquity, H. Braune[176] gives further examples of what we would call prayers of gratitude, and quotes Cicero (*N.D.* 3, 87) who writes: *At vero aut honoribus aucti aut re familiari, aut si aliud quippiam nacti sumus fortuiti boni aut depulimus mali, tum diis gratias agimus.* Although Braune has to admit that there is no prayer of gratitude in Virgil's *Aeneid*, it is nevertheless true that short expressions of thanks to the gods are far from lacking, especially in Roman comedy. Take Plautus, *Poen.* 1274, *Dei deae- que omnes, vobis habeo merito magnas gratias*; Plautus, *Capt.* 622, *Iovi disque ago gratias merito magnas*, with, in both cases, an extensive explanation of the profession of gratitude.[177] Nor should we underestimate the fervour of the

---

[175] *Op. cit.* (above note 96) 195-201 and espec. 189 n. 1.

[176] *Op. cit.* (above note 155) 20 ff. with reference to H. Lehr, *Religion und Kult in Vergils Aeneis* (Diss. Giessen 1934) 22.

[177] On the *gratulatio*, particularly as the opening of a monologue in Plautus, see E. Fraenkel, *Plautinisches im Plautus* (Berlin 1922) 236 ff. They are for the greater part parodies on the triumphal formulas: H. Kleinknecht, *Gebetsparodie*, 161 ff. and L. Halkin, 'La parodie d'une demande de triomphe dans l'Amphitryon de Plaute', *L'AC* (1948) 297 ff.

gratulationes[178] which the masses gave the gods on appointed days, as in Livy 27, 51, 9: *eam supplicationem C. Hostilius praetor edixit. Celebrata a viris feminisque est; omnia templa per totum triduum aequalem turbam habuere, cum matronae amplissima veste cum liberis, perinde ac si debellatum foret, omni solutae metu deis immortalibus grates agerent.* And whoever is tempted to question the spontaneous nature of the phenomenon because of the *edixit*, or the Roman contribution, in view of the possible Greek origin of the *supplicatio*,[179] may be convinced by the reactions of the Roman people to the rumour of Germanicus' recovery: Suet. *Cal.* 6, *passim cum luminibus et victimis in Capitolium concursum est ac paene revolsae templi fores, ne quid gestientis vota reddere moraretur, expergefactus e somno Tiberius gratulantium vocibus.*

In such cases it is difficult to decide whether to attribute the formula to a derivation from the Greek idiom or to a spontaneous parallelism, as for example, in similar situations in the following comparable formulas of Cyrus (via Xenophon) and Scipio (via Livy): Xen. *Cyrop.* IV, 1, 2, πρῶτον μὲν τοὺς θεοὺς ἐγὼ ἐπαινῶ ὅσον δύναμαι (....) νίκης τε γὰρ τετυχήκαμεν καὶ σωτηρίας.[180] Liv. 26, 48, 3... *primum dis immortalibus laudes gratesque egit...*, formulas to which I shall again be returning.

However this may be, the brief formulas of thanks, *gratias habeo / ago, gratulor, grates laudesque fero*,[181] are referred in Latin literature just as frequently to divine as to human benefactors. But how frequently *is* that, what was their exact meaning and what was the position of the formula of thanks in Greece? Stengel was not the only scholar to point out the rarity of prayers of gratitude. Carolus Ausfeld[182] had already lamented: 'mirum videtur quam paucae inveniantur gratulationes', and in more recent times Rudhardt wrote:[183] 'Il faut avouer toutefois que la prière de pure action de grâce parait relativement rare'. How should we account for this? Rudhardt gives the following answer: 'pour exprimer sa gratitude ou,

---

[178] A complete survey of all the *supplicationes* and *gratulationes* in L. Halkin, *La supplication d'action de grâces chez les romains* (Paris 1953).

[179] See on the Roman character and particularly the element of gratitude in the *gratulatio* G. Freyburger, 'La supplication d'action de grâces dans la religion romaine archaïque', *Latom.* 36 (1977) 283-315.

[180] Cf. also Philostr. *Vit. Apoll.* 4, 38.

[181] Material in Appel, *op. cit.* (above note 56) 182-183; Brissonius, *De formulis et sollemnibus populi Romani verbis* (Paris 1583) I, 80 ff.

[182] *Op. cit.* (above note 29) 509, who in the mean time does give a few examples. In the *RAC* article 'Gebet' the prayer of gratitude is not mentioned at all.

[183] J. Rudhardt, *Notions fondamentales de la pensée religieuse et actes constitutifs du culte dans la Grèce classique* (Genève 1958) 187-212. The quotation on p. 199.

après un succès, le sentiment de son accord avec les dieux, le Grec ne se contente pas de parler; il chante. Sa prière prend la proportion d'un hymne'. This is a standard example of an unjustified extrapolation leading to dubious conclusions. Rudhardt, moreover, bases himself almost exclusively on literary material. Are we really to believe that a peasant who finds his pick-axe thanks to a hint by the deity, that the woman who does not die in childbirth or that the man who escapes from a mad dog will burst spontaneously into 'a perfect hymn? I do not deny that there is an element of truth in what Rudhardt says, but we should, I think, approach the matter from an entirely different angle.

The modern Greek word for 'thank you', εὐχαριστῶ, εὐχαριστοῦμεν, can be found with the same meaning in many votive inscriptions from Antiquity.[184] It is a typical term with which gods and men are thanked, but, surprisingly enough, this short formula only appears in inscriptions of the imperial period and even then primarily in Asia Minor.[185] So how did people express themselves on stone in the earlier periods? Well, they made do with well-known formulas like εὐξάμενος εὐχὴν ἀνέθηκεν, or simply εὐχή(ν),[186] and sometimes, though not always, with the reason for the dedication. True words of thanks are seldom or never to be met with in these inscriptions, just as the Roman also contented himself with formulas such as v(otum) s(olvit) l(aetus) l(ibens) m(erito) etc. In the great collection of votive inscriptions assembled by M. L. Lazzarini[187] for the Greek archaic period we do not have a single example of an *unequivocal* word of thanks. But by using terms such as 'true words of thanks' or 'unequivocal words of thanks' we are of course introducing a subjective element into the discussion which deserves closer investigation. What follows is no more than a superficial survey of the terrain. Moreover, in this case, even more than in the preceding sections, there is the danger of neglecting possible

---

[184] See Th. Schermann, 'Eucharistia und eucharistein in ihrem Bedeutungswandel bis 200 n. Chr.', *Philol.* 69 (1910) 375-410.

[185] L. Robert has treated these terms several times: *Hellenica* X, 55-62; XI-XII, 27; *BE* 1965, 256; *Studii Clasice* 16 (1974) 80 n. 8 and 60 ff. The term does occur in the Hellenistic period with the meaning 'cherish a feeling of gratitude' (Schermann, 376 ff.), but not, as far as I see, in inscriptions.

[186] Nearly always in the accusative. Only sporadically the nominative is found: L. Robert, *Hellenica* VI, 106 and n. 7; 111; 117 n. 3; *BE* 1969, 393; 1973, 297; Th. Drew-Bear, *GRBS* 17 (1976) 253. Cf. also A. Corlu, *Recherches sur les mots relatifs à l'idée de prière d'Homère aux tragiques* (Paris 1966) 207 ff.

[187] Maria L. Lazzarini, *Le formule delle dediche votive nella Grecia arcaica* (Acc. Lincei ser. VII, vol XIX, 1976).

developments and evolutions. Most of the material dates from the
Hellenistic or the Imperial age. Yet I believe that earlier periods provide
sufficient data to justify a more general approach. It is, however, perfectly
possible that—as Pleket shows for different elements of religious
behaviour—a development from incidental towards structural phenomena
has taken place. All this implies that the subject 'thanks, thankfulness,
prayers of gratitude' requires a monographic study, which cannot be
provided here.

In his great work on prayer Heiler[188] reminds us that languages exist
which have no such thing as a term with which to express the concept 'to
thank', something which obviously has direct consequences where prayers
of gratitude are concerned. Whoever takes the troubie to investigate the
etymological origin of words of thanks in modern languages will see that a
significant evolution has usually taken place. The term 'thanks' in the
Germanic languages has developed from a concept of 'to think', 'to commemorate', (denken, gedenken), whereby the concept of gratitude is obviously expressed by thinking about and commemorating a favour. Something
similar is expressed by the Dutch word 'erkentelijkheid': the 'erkenning'
or acknowledgement of a favour is a sign of gratitude. The Romance
languages derive their word of thanks from the Latin merces in the sense of
'mercy', and this is apparently not so very far removed from what we
know about the Greek and Latin terms, χάρις and gratia. But we would be
well advised to exercise a certain caution when it comes to a simple identification of modern 'thanks' with these ancient terms.

Theophrastus gives three reasons why sacrifices should be made: τριῶν
ἕνεκα θυτέον τοῖς θεοῖς, ἢ γὰρ διὰ τιμὴν ἢ διὰ χάριν ἢ διὰ χρείαν τῶν ἀγαθῶν 'in
order to honour the gods, or to thank them or to ask them for something
good'.[189] This brings us to the fourth century B.C. and there can be no
doubt that χάρις here is more or less completely covered by the translation
'thanks', especially if we keep in mind that, according to the research of
Hewitt,[190] ever since the days of Xenophon 'the neuter plural of the words
σωτήριον and χαριστήριον has taken on a technical significance and denotes
thank-offering'. Hewitt continues: 'from Xenophon to about the time of
the Christian era the two words are rare; they become common only when

---

[188] Op. cit. (above p. 3) 44.
[189] Cf. also F. T. van Straten, below p. 66 and the references given there.
[190] J. W. Hewitt, 'On the Development of the Thankoffering among the Greeks', TAPA
43 (1912) 95-111. The quotations on p. 105.

we find the thank-offering itself fully developed'. This corresponds to the fact that in honorary inscriptions, for example, next to expressions like μνήμης, ἀρετῆς, εὐνοίας, τιμῆς χάριν or ἔνεκα we also frequently find εὐχαριστίας ἔνεκα, but only in later Hellenism and above all in the imperial period.[191]

On the other hand the question of what a term like χάρις meant in an earlier religious or secular context is easier to ask than to answer. In a votive inscription quoted by Van Straten (below p. 72) from c. 450 B.C. we find the recurrent formula σοι χάριν ἀντ[ιδιδός]. There can obviously be no objection to rendering it as 'giving thanks to you' if it *must* be translated, but I do not believe I am alone in preferring, did I have the choice, to leave this expression untranslated. Words of the root χαρ- appear frequently in early votive inscriptions and in the rest of literature, as we see for instance in the ensuing epigram quoted by Van Straten (p. 73), one of the earliest surviving Greek votive inscriptions τὸ δὲ .... δίδοι χαρίϝ ετταν ἀμοι ϝ[άν], which has a close parallel in *Od.* 3, 58 δίδου χαρίεσσαν ἀμοιβήν. Here it is almost certain that something is being expressed like 'a return service producing gaiety and joy'. Besides we meet formulas of the type χάριν γὰρ τροφεῦσιν ἀμείβων (Aeschyl. *Agam.* 728 f.), which W. Peek used to complete a sixth-century votive inscription from Olympia as follows:

[..... ἀνέθε]χε Εὐρυστρατίδας τάδε τὰ hόπλα
τ[ὸ Λακεδ]αιμονίο· τὺ δὲ τôι χάριν αἰὲς ἄ[μειβε].

and he translated the last phrase as 'du aber statte ihm stets huldvollen Dank ab'.[192] I do not wish to maintain that gods could not be grateful to humans, but I would point out that there is no compelling reason to read the element of 'thanks' into the term χάρις in texts such as these. For the return service, the reaction to the favour, can already be found in the terms ἀντιδιδόναι,[193] ἀμείβειν, just as it also lies in the substantive ἀμοιβή,

---

[191] See E. Nachmanson, 'Zu den Motivformeln der griechischen Ehreninschriften', *Eranos* 11 (1911) 190-196, espec. 181.

[192] W. Peek, *Philol.* 94 (1941) 330 ff., now discussed by L. Semmlinger, *Weih-, Sieger-, und Ehreninschriften aus Olympia und seiner Umgebung* (Diss. Erlangen 1974) n° 13.

[193] Expressions with the simplex διδόναι occur, but rarely. A. E. Raubitschek, *Dedications from the Athenian Akropolis* (1949) n° 295 proposes the following text: hερμεί[αι τόδε] ἄγαλμα [διδὸς] χάριν ἐν[θάδε ἔ]θεκεν / Οἰν[όβιο]ς χέρυχς μ[νεμ]οσύνες hέ[νεκα]. We find διδόναι instead of ἀντιδιδόναι in Soph. *Oedip. Col.* 1489 f.; Peek, *Griechische Versinschriften*, 1264. See R. Kassel, *ZPE* 12 (1973) 16; B. Kramer, *ZPE* 20 (1976) 18.

which leaves the possibility open that, in such texts, in which it is also repeatedly wished that the god χαρίζεται (shows his favour, obliges, gratifies, etc.), the term χάρις itself can be understood as 'favour' or something close to it. This hesitation about the 'correct' rendering of χάρις can be observed again and again, precisely because there is no single correct translation. It is instructive, for example, to see how W. Burkert sets about it in his great work on Greek religion.[194] On p. 291 he writes: 'Und doch bedürfen die Menschen der Götter ganz anders als die Götter der Menschen; sie leben von der Hoffnung auf gegenseitige Freundlichkeit, *cháris*'; on p. 409, in a passage on the attitude of men to gods, we read: 'Man versucht, den "Gefallen" der Götter zu finden, (…) am schönsten ist lächelndes Gewähren, *cháris*, wie man den Gott gleich einem Bekannten mit *chaire* grüsst, "freue dich"; die Uebersetzung "Gnade" gibt nur die eine Seite der *cháris* wieder'. Only on the penultimate page of his book (494), about the human reaction to the gods in Plato, do we read: 'aber für die aus ihrer Güte fliessenden Gaben können sie auf traditionelle Weise Dank und freundliche Verbundenheit zum Ausdruck bringen, *cháris*'—an unintentional demonstration of how polyvalent terms like *charis* are. Some aspects of this issue were recently discussed by Maria Rocchi in a study on the Charites,[195] in which she tries to explain the —to us—very different meanings of *charis*, 'favore' and 'ringraziamento', on the basis of Mauss' theories about the gift and the duty of returning the gift. I believe, however, that the crux of the matter has been expressed so succinctly in two pages by G. B. Philipp[196] that I take pleasure in reproducing a few of his remarks to the letter. We must start, as O. Loew[197] demonstrated eighty years ago, with the meaning of χάρις as 'res laetificans', 'das Erfreuende'. The connection between χάρις and χαίρω in this sense can be found in an utterance of Hippocrates *Aer*. 22, 9 (Diller p. 74, line 17 ff.) εἰ τιμώμενοι δὴ χαίρουσι οἱ θεοὶ καὶ θαυμαζόμενοι ὑπ' ἀνθρώπων καὶ ἀντὶ τούτων χάριτας ἀποδιδόασιν. Philipp quite rightly comments at this point: 'Der Plural χάριτας bezeichnet nichts anderes als facta laetificantia, "Dinge, die erfreuen"… Wir übersetzen zwar gewöhnlich mit "Dank", müssen uns aber bewusst bleiben dass dieser Begriff nicht in χάριτας enthalten ist,

---

[194] *Op. cit.* (above note 130).

[195] M. Rocchi, 'Contributi allo studio delle Charites', *Studii Clasice* 18 (1979) 5-16, espec. 5-7.

[196] G. B. Philipp. 'Kritzeleien eines erleichterten Lehrers auf einem hölzernen Buchdeckel', *Gymnasium* 85 (1978) 157-159.

[197] O. Loew, *ΧΑΡΙΣ* (Diss. Marburg 1908).

sondern das Motiv der Erwiderung durch die Präposition ἀπό (...), an anderen Stellen etwa durch ὀφείλειν oder τίνειν suggeriert wird'. We saw above that we can also think of ἀμείβειν in this connection. This has consequences for such expressions as χάριν οἶδα, which means 'ich bin mir der erwiesenen Gefälligkeit bewusst', χάριν ἔχω (sc. μνήμῃ) 'ich behalte das mir erwiesene Erfreuliche im Sinn'. I point out in passing the parallelism which this displays with the above-mentioned evolution 'think/thank' and 'acknowledgement' and will return to the μνήμη suggested by Philipp and to the important text of Hippocrates later.

If what has hitherto been said puts into doubt the *automatic* rendering of χάρις by 'thanks', at least as far as the archaic and early classical periods are concerned, similar doubts may rise concerning the meaning of Latin *gratia* in expressions like *gratias/grates agere/ferre* etc. Here too I must limit myself to a few brief observations. We are naturally accustomed to render these expressions by 'giving thanks', but there is a problem. The basic etymological meaning of the root $*g^{u}er$ is unequivocally, as Walde-Hofmann[198] have it: 'loben, preisen' and also 'singen, ankündigen', and we therefore have to ask ourselves how long this basic meaning lasted in Latin or at least how long it continued to play a part as a connotation. It is no mere chance that the combination *grates laudesque fero* should be so frequent. When Theophrastus distinguishes between τιμή and χάρις we may well wonder whether the Latin formula expressed two *different* concepts or rather a single concept *in two manners*. M. Leumann[199] and Cl. Moussy,[200] who has devoted a monograph to the word family of *gratia*, both regard *laudes gratesque* in this formula as an expressive doublet in which the central part is played not by the concept of 'thanks' but by that of 'praise'. Let us keep this problem in mind and, before we tie up the loose ends, look at a third and different sort of difficulty.

Anyone who studies Greek texts is inevitably struck by the fact that those terms which we virtuously learnt in our youth, χάριν εἰδέναι, ἔχειν, φέρειν, actually appear very seldom in Greek conversation—let us say in Plato's dialogues or in conversations in tragedy and comedy. Just as J. H.

---

[198] Walde-Hofmann, *LEW*, s.v. *gratus.*

[199] *Gnomon* 13 (1937) 34 f.

[200] Cl. Moussy, *Gratia et sa famille*, Public. de la Fac. des Lettres et Sciences humaines de l'université de Clermont Ferrand 25 (Paris 1966) 35-50. As we shall observe, the praise of the god is a means to make him great. This is a trait characteristic of I. E. languages: G. Dumézil, *Servius et la fortune. Essai sur la fonction sociale de la louange et du blâme et sur les éléments indo-européens du cens romain* (Paris 1943) 63 ff.

Quincey,[201] who wrote an article on the Greek way of expressing thanks, says: 'as readers of Greek literature will have become aware, if only sub-consciously, these combinations are not to be found used responsively in the prose or verse of the classical period'. The terms appear to be descriptive, not affirmative. This complicates the entire business: not only do terms which we are accustomed to translate as 'to thank' not necessarily possess this notion, but some of the most important expressions which we have thus 'misused' almost seem to be lacking altogether in active linguistic usage and only serve a descriptive purpose. And again we are confronted with the question: how did the Greek—if we limit ourselves to this linguistic area—express his gratitude to god and man in general? When I provided an answer to this question in the Dutch version of this paper I did not have most of the studies I have just mentioned at my disposal. Nevertheless they confirm strikingly the conclusions which I reached basing myself on Quincey and others.

The term with which the Greek of the classical period expressed his gratitude is not so much a word of the family of χάρις, as, both in religious and secular texts, above all (ἔπ)αινος, ἐπαινεῖν. I wish to emphasize the word 'express' in this last sentence, and I am far from suggesting that ἐπαινεῖν is a verb which must (always) be translated as 'to thank' and therefore primarily be given this meaning in dictionaries. The point is that the Greek who wished to *express* the feelings which *we* call gratitude pre-ferred to use terms which are translated in our modern languages as 'to commend', or 'to praise'. There are numerous honorary decrees in which government and people decide to ἐπαινέσαι a benefactor or a friendly city, and this is always—I do not say: wrongly—translated as 'to praise', 'to honour', etc.[202] Πρῶτον μὲν τοὺς θεοὺς ἐγὼ ἐπαίνω said Xenophon and Livy said it after him. The Delian Serapis hymn has ἐπαινοῦμεν τοὺς θεοὺς ἀξίαν χάριν ἀποδίδοντες,[203] and many parallels show that these were the standard turns of phrase used in a situation of gratitude to the gods[204] in as far as

---

[201] J. H. Quincey, 'Greek Expressions of Thanks', *JHS* 86 (1966) 133-158, who in-vestigates the prophane context of these expressions. I owe this reference to J. M. Bremer.

[202] I. Calabi Limentani, 'La formula di lode nei decreti ateniesi per stranieri', *Iura* 24 (1973) 1-27.

[203] Ed. H. Engelmann, *op. cit.* (above note 117) line 27-8. en cf. τιμῶσα χάριν σήν, quoted by Van Straten, below p. 74.

[204] ἔπαινος as expression of gratitude to gods: Aristoph. *Plut.* 745; Xen. *Symp.* 4, 49. Cf. also Thesaurus. *Gratias et laudes fero* for example in Liv. 7, 36, 7; 27, 13, 2. In Tac. *Ann.* 1, 69 directed to a human being. Further examples in Brissonius, *op. cit.* (above note 181) 80 ff.;

anyone felt it necessary to use a special term[205]—for I do not wish to maintain that these terms are that numerous in inscriptions of thanksgiving. But in this case it can be proved that they were frequently replaced on stones by an extensive substitute. Before this proof is provided, however, it should be pointed out that what we have found so far points to a fundamental aspect of the attitude of ancient man towards his benefactor.

Admittedly in our own language 'praise God' is close to 'thank God', in the true *laus Deo* tradition; admittedly we too can, *on the whole*, define 'to thank' as an acknowledgement, usually pronounced out loud, of a favour conferred by someone else—an acknowledgement which implies the superiority of the benefactor, although neither modern nor ancient man is likely to go to the extremes of Thessalos of Tralles who entreated, and then thanked, a priest as follows:[206] κλαίων τῶν ποδῶν εἰχόμην τοῦ ἀρχιερέως and ἠσπασάμην αὐτοῦ τὴν δεξίαν καὶ ηὐχαρίστουν κρουνηδόν μοι τῶν δακρύων φερομένων. But none of this detracts from the fact that, in professions of praise and honour as a token of gratitude, we have discovered a form of expression specifically characteristic of Antiquity. The benefactor of Antiquity was impelled primarily by φιλοτιμία: if anything emerges clearly from P. Veyne's book on euergetism, this is it.[207] His greatest delight was to surpass a rival; he found the greatest token of appreciation in the numerous honours conferred on him by grateful fellow-townsmen. This applied both to men and gods. When, in Aristoph. *Pax*, 413 ff., Trygaeus promises Hermes that henceforth all Athenian festivals will be celebrated exclusively in his honour this also contains the charm of the *agon* for the deity. Variations on the praise of a deity in gratitude for a favour developed in numerous manners, particularly in post-classical times.

The most direct method was to proclaim the great deeds of the god in public, as happened literally in the sanctuary of Asclepius on the Insula Tiberina: καὶ ἐσώθη καὶ ἐλθὼν δημοσίᾳ ηὐχαρίστησεν ἔμπροσθεν τοῦ δήμου.[208]

Kleinknecht, *op. cit.*, (above note 177) 161 ff. Cf. ἐπαινεῖτε οἱ παριόντες, quoted by Van Straten below p. 74.

[205] Generally terms like (προσ)εύχεσθαι are being used; cf. Aesch. *Ag.* 317; Eur. *El.* 764 and see Corlu *op. cit.* (above note 186) 235 f.

[206] H.-V. Friedrich, *Thessalos von Tralles* (Meisenheim 1968) col. 51, 6 and 16 = Prooem. 16 and 19. One of the rare places where tears occur in a situation of gratitude, but Thessalos says himself φυσικῶς γὰρ χαρὰ πλείονα λύπης ἐκκαλεῖται δάκρυα. It is noteworthy that the Medieval latin translation of ηὐχαρίστουν is *dando gloriam*!

[207] P. Veyne, *Le pain et le cirque* (Paris 1976), who on p. 330 n. 25 refers to H. W. Pleket, *Lampas* (1971) 372.

[208] *Sylloge* 1173; O. Weinreich, *op. cit.* (above note 131) 108-9 gives more material.

In some cases the short formula εὐχαριστῶ is replaced in the thanks-giving inscriptions from Asia Minor by another one: (ἀπὸ νῦν) εὐλογῶ '(henceforth) I praise your name',[209] in which Jewish influence has—perhaps wrongly—been detected. The promise to propagate the name and miracle of the god is also to be found in literature: Prop. IV, 17, 19 f. *quod superest vitae per te et tua cornua vivam virtutis tuae, Bacche, poeta ferar* (which is in an old aretalogical tradition)[210] and in inscriptions (which are not, of course, necessarily unliterary), like this close of an epigram discovered in the Asclepius sanctuary of Pergamon:

[ἀνθ' ὧν σὸν τιμ]ῶ τε καὶ ἄζομαι οὔν[ομα, Σῶτερ]
[κληίζων χω]ρῆς πε[ίρ]ατ' [ἐς ἡμεδαπῆς].[211]

I have deliberately selected this heavily mutilated specimen because it is by Aelius Aristides, the second-century Sophist, who has also left us the redemption of this or a related vow: his hymn to Serapis[212] (Aristides was prepared to bulk various gods together if he stood to gain by it) is explicitly called a ὕμνος χαριστήριος. It is only in this light that we can accept Rudhardt's remark quoted above, and we must keep in mind that there were many more ways to 'praise god' than by singing a hymn. This, at all events, shows how, at a certain moment, poems and prayers could be regarded as a sacrifice to the gods. The explanation must be sought in the essential τιμή-character which these three categories have in common. Sacrifice was among other things always a 'token of honour' to the deity. Not only do we find this in Theophrastus: it emerges clearly from countless texts in which offerings are regarded as, and dubbed τιμή and γέρας, 'gift of honour'.[213] What is indicative, for example, is the fact that

---

[209] See for instance Steinleitner, *op. cit.* (above note 79) 112; R. Reitzenstein, *Die hellenistischen Mysterienreligionen* (reprint Darmstadt 1966) 160. Εὐλογέω in this sense occurs already in Eurip. *Ion* 136. See now the ample treatment of the term by H. W. Pleket, below p. 183 ff., whose tentative reconstruction of the development of the term I fully endorse.

[210] R. J. Littlewood, 'Two elegiac Hymns', *Latomus* 34 (1975) 667 f.

[211] Habicht, *op. cit.* (above note 24) n° 145; the inscription has been fully discussed by R. Herzog, 'Ein Asklepios-Hymnus des Aristides von Smyrna', *S.B. Berlin* (1934) 753-769.

[212] Ael. Arist. *Or.* 45, 34 on which A. Höfler, *Der Sarapishymnus des Aelios Aristides* (Tübingen 1935) 113.

[213] On sacrifice as τιμή see W. Poetscher, *Theophrastos, Περὶ Εὐσεβείας* (Leiden 1964) *ad loc.*; *idem*, 'Moira, Themis und τιμή im homerischen Denken', *WS* 73 (1960) 5. The aristocratic valuesystem that is in the background is discussed by A. W. H. Adkins in numerous works. On τιμή as the 'province' of each god: G. Arrighetti, 'Uomini e dei in Esiodo', *Graz. Beitr.* 7 (1978) 15-35.

many oracle questions with the elements τίνι θεῶν εὐχόμενος καὶ θύων often received the answer: you must *honour* (τιμᾶν) such and such a god.[214] So on the one hand one could βωμοὺς ἑορταῖς γεραίρειν (Pindar *Ol.* 3, 2) 'honour the gods with sacrifices', but at the same time men ἐπινικίοις γεραίρειν and γένος θεῶν γεραίρειν φωνῇ (Aristoph. *Thesm.* 961) 'honour the race of the gods with the voice'. This could imply singing a hymn in which the great deeds of the gods were glorified, for—as we shall see later—the god was as great as his deeds,[215] as Aelius Aristides says elsewhere (II, p. 357 Keil) about Serapis: οὐ γὰρ ἀλλοῖός ἐστιν ἢ οἷος ἐκ τῶν ἔργων ἐπιφαίνεται καὶ δείκνυται. Only thus can we understand the strange Latin expressions of the type *Iunoni fer rite preces* (Virgil *Aen.* 8, 60) which, it was noticed even in Antiquity,[216] runs parallel to the expression *sacra ferre*. We find them combined, for example, in Val. Flacc. 2, 336: *date vina precesque*.

Sacrifice and prayer (of gratitude) were both τιμαί, just like a hymn or a poem to the deity, and could thus be offered to the gods.[217] The primary concern of the gods was obviously honour and admiration, as emerges clearly from the passage of Hippocrates quoted above. W. Burkert was right to say: 'Religion kann man auf griechisch kaum anders ausdrücken als "Ehren der Götter", θεῶν τιμαί'. (*op. cit.* 406). The various manners in which verbal praise of the god(s) could be expressed, deserve further attention.

A much quoted inscription, brief and to the point, albeit not entirely unequivocal, Ἀφιὰς Θεοδότου εὐχαριστῶ Μητρὶ Λητωῖ ὅτι ἐξ ἀδυνάτων δυνατὰ πυεῖ (= ποιεῖ)[218] propagates the acknowledgement and divulgence of

---

[214] Parke-Wormell, *passim*, e.g. n°'s 238 ff.

[215] 'Miracle proved deity', says Nock, *Conversion* 91, referring to Terent. *Ad.* 535 f.

[216] Serv. Dan. *ad loc.*

[217] See on poems as a sacrifice S. Østerud, 'Sacrifice and Bookburning in Catullus' Poem 36', *Hermes* 106 (1978) 138-155, espec. 151 ff.

[218] Steinleitner, *op. cit.* (above note 79) does not give any interpretation. J. Zingerle, *op. cit.* (above note 85) 11, regards it as an 'Allmachtsformel', comparable with Luk. 18, 27 and Matth. 19, 26. Cf. also Origen. Περὶ εὐχῆς I, 1, δυνατὸν ἐξ ἀδυνάτου γίνεται διὰ τοῦ Κυρίου ἡμῶν Ἰησοῦ Χριστοῦ. It is often quoted as such in modern literature. Yet W. H. Buckler's translation (*ABSA* 21 (1914-5) 172f., 'because from things without strength she maketh things that are strong' is not impossible either. (This interpretation is followed by H. W. Pleket, below p. 178 n. 124). Anyhow, a total reversal in the circumstances is used frequently to indicate omnipotence: *PGM* XXIX δὸς τὰ [ἄβ]ατα εὔβατα, *PGM* I, 125, ὁπόταν τε θέλῃς [τὰ θερ]μὰ ψυχρὰ ποιῆσαι καὶ τὰ ψυχρὰ θερμά, λύχνους ἀνά[ψει κ]αὶ κατασβέσει πάλιν and very circumstantially in *PGM* IV, 1511. These examples are mentioned by A. Cameron, *op. cit.* (above note 5), who points out that similar expressions already occur in Sappho. Hesiod, *Erga* 1-10, is, however, a better testimony. Line 6 ῥεῖα δ'ἀρίζηλον μινύθει καὶ ἄδηλον ἀέξει has

the goddess' miracle. We find numerous similar examples in the so-called 'confession-inscriptions' of the second and third century A.D. in which ἀρετή has assumed the meaning of 'miracle'[219] and the aretalogy as a description of this miracle—frequently on the instructions of the god—turns into a testimony (see below). The most extensive specimens are the great Isis hymns, which were also sometimes published in thanks for a miracle.[220] But in substance the numerous attestations of miraculous cures by Asclepius mainly from the 4th century B.C., are aretalogies *avant la lettre*: praise and thanks in one. Is the report of a one-eyed man who retrieves his eye, of a bald man who retrieves his hair overnight,[221] not just as much an aretalogy as the many *pinakes* with paintings of shipwrecks and rescue, the votive offerings consisting of the clothes and hair of the survivors in the temples?[222] And are they not implicitly what the ὕμνος χαριστήριος or the εὐχαριστῶ are explicitly? Diogen. Laert. V, 76 tells us that Demetrius of Phaleron, in thanks for an eye cure performed by Serapis, τοὺς παιᾶνας ποιῆσαι τοὺς μέχρι νῦν ᾀδομένους.[223] We read that a contemporary of Euripides, the tragedian Aristarchus,[224] wrote the tragedy 'Asclepius' as χαριστήριον after a cure performed by Asclepius, at the god's request—and indeed the gods frequently demanded that their

some similarity with Isis hymn Kyme 50, ἐγὼ τὰ πλωτὰ ἄπλωτα ποι[ῶ, ὅ]ταν ἐμοὶ δόξῃ. Although R. M. Grant, *Miracle and Natural Law in Graeco-Roman and Early Christian Thought* (Amsterdam 1952) 127, says about our inscription 'that it need not be anything but Greek', it is of course true that this type of 'Allmachtsformel' is typical of Near-Eastern religious language.

[219] The best short survey with recent literature in Y. Grandjean, *Une nouvelle arétalogie d'Isis à Maronée* (Leiden 1975) 1-15. The typical evolution of the term ἀρετή and the genre of the aretalogy must be attributed to the Hellenistic era, but an inscription of the mid-fourth century B.C. (*Sylloge* 1131) has already Ἀθηνάαι Μένεια ἀνέθηκεν ὄψιν ἰδοῦσα ἀρετὴν τῆς θεοῦ, whose importance has been valued by A. Kiefer, *Aretalogische Studien* (Diss. Freiburg 1929) 21 f. Cf. also F. T. van Straten, below p. 77, and H. W. Pleket, below p. 157.

[220] So explicitly in the hymn of Maronea: Grandjean, *op. cit.* (above note 219).

[221] R. Herzog, *Die Wunderheilungen von Epidauros* (Philol. Suppl. XXII, 1931) n°'s IV and IX; n° XX.

[222] D. Wachsmuth, *op. cit.* (above note 21) 120 ff. and 141 n. 243 (hair and clothes); 134 ff.; 141 n. 246.

[223] Demetrius fr. 68 (Wehrli). A number of these 'aretalogies' are collected in Weinreich, *op. cit.* (above note 131) 4 ff.; R. Merkelbach, *Roman und Mysterium in der Antike* (München-Berlin 1962) 113 n. 2; Wachsmuth, *op. cit.*, 142 n. 247. Cf. also Engelmann, *op. cit.* (above note 117) 37.

[224] Suda s.v. *Aristarchos*. The latter cases show that this type of 'advertisement' already occurred before the Hellenistic period, which fact does not detract from Pleket's correct distinction between incidental and structural manifestations of this kind.

miracles be recorded as a reward: ἐκέλευσεν δὲ καὶ ἀναγράψαι ταῦτα.[225] And this even led to the use of a characteristic verb in the confession-inscriptions: στηλογραφεῖν. In a papyrus[226] we come across the title of a book Διὸς Ἡλίου μεγάλου Σαράπιδος ἀρετὴ ἡ περὶ Συρίωνα τὸν κυβερνήτην: the description of a journey as a psalm of praise, in the same way as Hanno dedicated his log-book.[227]

One of the reasons for the development of this type of token of gratitude was undoubtedly that, while a mere peasant or craftsman dedicated part of his products to the deity, the artist, scholar or musician could do as much with the fruits of his own work. He too dedicated the *primitiae* of his art to the god: ἀπάρχονται or ἀπαρχὰν ποιοῦσιν ἀπὸ τοῦ μαθήματος, τῆς τέχνης and so on.[228] We find an exceptional example of an *epideixis* of the talents of a juggler as a sign of his veneration of the god in Seneca (*apud* Augustine, *C.D.* 6, 10), who describes how an aged leader of a troupe of actors gave a daily performance on the Capitol 'as though the gods were to derive pleasure from an actor in whom the public was no longer interested'.[229]

If the illiterate poor could get by with a small gift or a simple, stereotyped formula, the rich man was sometimes instructed to use professional specialists. In addition to his oracular texts Apollo often gave orders that a hymn of thanksgiving should be composed by the *hymnologoi* next-door (see the result below p. 202), a by no means unique form of cooperation between various clerical specialities,[230] which, incidentally, do indeed

---

[225] Inscription from Epidaurus, *IG* IV, 955; Asklepieion of Lebena (*Sylloge* 1172), ἰδοῦσαν] δὲ με πλείονας ἀρετὰ[ς τοῦ θεοῦ καθ᾿ ὕπν]ον [ἀν]αγράφειν ὁ θεὸ[ς ἐκέλευσε τὰς ὄψ]εις, with the commentary *ad loc.* Delian hymn of Serapis, line 2: ἀνέγραψεν κατὰ πρόσταγμα τοῦ θεοῦ.

[226] *P. Oxy* 1382.

[227] Lit. D. Wachsmuth, *op. cit.* (above note 21) 143 n. 247. Artemidorus II, 44, knows several books on the miracles of Serapis.

[228] See Ad. Wilhelm, *Anz. Ak. Wien* (1922) 14 f.; L. Robert, *Études épigraphiques et philologiques* (Paris 1138) 38-45. On the *aparchai* of craftsmen and the like see F. T. van Straten, below p. 92 ff.

[229] This anecdote is compared by Veyne, *op. cit.* (above note 207) 449 n. 58, with the story about a pious mime in 211 B.C. On the phenomenon of the *epideixis* as an honour of the gods see L. Robert, *op. cit.* (preceding note) 38-45.

[230] Cf. Firm. Maternus, *Math.* III, 103, where there is a distinction between two categories (apart from others) in the cult of the Mater Magna: *qui deorum monitu futura praenoscant*, and *hymnologi*. The latter are the specialists *qui laudes deorum..... decantent* (*ibid.* III, 5, 33). See on a new inscription with *hymnologi*: Patrizia Sabbatini Tumolesi Longo, 'Due iscrizioni inedite di Roma', *Epigrafica* 38 (1976) 37 ff. On an inscription with a *melopoios* and a choir of boys ὑμνήσοντες τὸν θεόν see L. Robert, 'Des Carpathes à la Propontide', *Studii Clasice* 16 (1974) 74-80. The 'hymn-writer for life' mentioned by J. M. Bremer (below p. 202) belongs in this context.

also appear in combination, as is proved by an ὀνειροκρίτης καὶ ἀρεταλόγος.[231] Specialists in honouring the gods with aretalogies sometimes combined their activities with writing, composing poems and pronouncing eulogies of human beings, particularly of rulers. There thus developed the genre of encomiography which flourished in the imperial period and was even practised in contests.[232] This again draws our attention to the fact, which I have already mentioned several times, that even in the manner in which they were honoured by grateful mortals the gods were really regarded as 'great, immortal men', and a few words should now be said about this highly relevant correlation.

We have observed that thanks to gods and men was primarily given in the form of praise and honour. Even a superficial glance at a few of the commonest formulas in both categories automatically brings us *in medias res*: the essential purpose served by the numerous honorary and thanksgiving inscriptions. First of all, however, it will be useful to ascertain that in Antiquity nothing was given free: neither gods nor men turned up their noses at favours returned, as Hesiod[233] well knew: Δῶρα θεοὺς πείθει, δῶρ' αἰδοίους βασιλῆας. The element of exchange was fundamental to dealings with the deities: J. Festugière gave a study on this subject the title of one of the most characteristic formulas in votive prayers: Ἀνθ' ὧν.[234] Man gave and the god had to answer with another gift and *vice versa*. The commercial nature of the transaction was often prosaically expressed by calling the favour returned a 'debt' which had to be 'paid'. We find a splendid example in an epigram attributed to Callimachus and quoted by Van Straten (p. 71). It even contains a sort of receipt or proof of payment: no wonder, if we think that Apollo in his turn demanded *misthos* for his oracles, just as Asclepius did for his cures.[235] Consequently gift and return-gift should stand in a rational relationship to each other. We repeatedly come across texts[236] in which a man offers a simple present to the god, but adds (for

---

[231] From the Isis cult: P. Roussel, *Les cultes égyptiens à Délos* (1916) n° 119; cf. n° 120.

[232] L. Robert, *op. cit.* (above note 228) 21 ff. Cf. J. M. Bremer, below p. 202.

[233] Hesiod, fr. 361 (Merkelbach-West), of which the immortal part became proverbial: Suda δ 1451; cf. Plato, *Res Publ.* III, 390 E.

[234] A. J. Festugière, "Ἀνθ' ὧν. La formule 'en échange de quoi' dans la prière grecque hellénistique', *Rev. Sc. Phil. Théol.* 60 (1976) 389-418.

[235] Cf. Lucian, *Charon* 11. The latin *vota solvere* has the very same connotation. Already in the hymn to Demeter (l. 369) we find the expression ἐναίσιμα δῶρα τελοῦντες, for which see W. Burkert, *Gnomon* 49 (1977) 445 n. 14 with further references.

[236] For instance *Anthol. Graec.* VI, 238; 299; 415 ff. and more in Festugière, *op. cit.* (above note 234).

example in *Anthol. Graeca* VI, 152): ..... ἔργων ἐξ ὀλίγων ὀλίγην δόσιν. ἢν δέ τι μεῖζον δωρήσῃ, τίσει τῶνδε πολυπλάσια, 'if you (god) give something larger the recipient will also offer you many times more gifts than he is giving today'. This is expressed with curious directness in the wishful dream of Hippolytus who laments that it must be possible to obtain children without the irksome intervention of women[237]

ἀλλ' ἀντιθέντας σοῖσιν ἐν ναοῖς βροτοὺς
ἢ χρυσὸν ἢ σίδηρον ἢ χαλκοῦ βάρος
παίδων πρίασθαι σπέρμα, τοῦ τιμήματος
τῆς ἀξίας ἕκαστον.......

'But in your shrines mortal men could have offered up
either gold or iron or heavy weight of bronze
to purchase their breed of offspring, each paid in sons or daughters
according to his own gift's worth...'.

Of course, this *commercium* character is regarded as characteristic of the Roman religious attitude in practically every textbook on the subject. We can conclude this short excursus with the observation that the rapidity with which the god responded tended to determine the gratitude with which the mortal reacted (a Panagia of modern Greece is called 'Gorgoepekoos', 'the fast hearer', a word which can also be found in Antiquity).[238]

Returning to my central issue, the basic ideology behind the expressions of gratitude, I shall now devote some attention to the human benefactors and their rewards. No doubt there were obvious differences between mortals and immortals when it came to the material form in which the gratitude was expressed. Here, Prometheus may be held responsible: bones, fat and smoke of the roasted sacrificial meat suited gods, not men. The slightly insane physician Menecrates, who claimed to be divine, was *not* amused and less than satiated when, at the court of the witty Philip II, he was treated to a typical γέρας of the gods. The terminology of the story is very relevant to my subject:[239] Εἱστία ποτὲ μεγαλοπρεπῶς ὁ Φίλιππος, καὶ δὴ καὶ τοῦτον ἐπὶ θοίνην ἐκάλεσε, καὶ ἰδίᾳ κλίνην αὐτῷ ἐκέλευσε παρεσκευάσθαι, καὶ κατακλινέντι θυμιατήριον παρέθηκε, καὶ ἐθυμιᾶτο αὐτῷ· οἱ δὲ λοιποὶ

---

[237] Eur. *Hipp.* 620 ff.
[238] See R. E. Witt, *Isis in the Graeco-Roman World* (London 1971) 136. The term is to be found in Ael. Arist. 49, 49. It should be noted that adhortations of the type τάχυ are certainly not restricted to magical texts. See A. Cameron, *op. cit.* (above note 5) 9.
[239] Aelian. *Var. Hist.* 12, 51.

εἱστιῶντο, καὶ ἦν μεγαλοπρεπὲς τὸ δεῖπνον. ὁ τοίνυν Μενεκράτης τὰ μὲν πρῶτα
ἐνεκαρτέρει, καὶ ἔχαιρε τῇ τιμῇ· ἐπεὶ δὲ κατὰ μικρὸν ὁ λιμὸς περιῆλθεν αὐτόν, καὶ
ἠλέγχετο ὅτι ἦν ἄνθρωπος, καὶ ταῦτα εὐήθης, ἐξαναστὰς ἀπιὼν ᾤχετο, καὶ
ἔλεγεν ὑβρίσθαι, ἐμμελῶς πάνυ τοῦ Φιλίππου τὴν ἄνοιαν αὐτοῦ ἐκκαλύψαντος.
Although rulers were indeed venerated in the long run with honours both
material and divine, like temples, altars and sacrifices, it was more
obvious to give human benefactors other tokens of thanks. Cyrus, as
Xenophon tells us, treated his friends as follows (Xen. *Cyrop.* 8, 1, 39):
τούτους καὶ δώροις καὶ ἀρχαῖς καὶ ἕδραις καὶ πάσαις τιμαῖς ἐγέγαιρεν. It is,
however, not the external form of the gifts, but the ideology as expressed
in the honorary phrases that will show us the close correspondence between the acts of gratitude towards benefactors, divine and human.

Let us start with an honorary inscription which is truly exemplary from
all points of view.[240] It comes from the town of Teos, was made for Antiochus the Great, and contains an unequivocal expression of the element
of service and return service. On the one hand it is said of the king (I, 16):
θέλων χαρίζεσθαι τῶι τε δήμωι καὶ τῶι κοινῶι τῶν περὶ τὸν Διόνυσον
τεχνιτῶν,[241] whereupon the people of Teos react with the words (I, 40 ff.):
ἵνα οὖν καὶ ἡμῖς ἐμ [πα]ντὶ κα[ιρῶ]ι φαινώμεθα χάριτας ἀξίας ἀποδιδόντες τῶι τε
βασι[λε]ῖ καὶ τῇ [βα]σιλίσσῃ καὶ ὑπερτιθέμενοι ἡαυτοὺς ἐν ταῖς τ[ιμ]αῖς ταῖς πρὸς
[τ]ούτους κα[τὰ] τὰς εὐεργεσίας καὶ φανερὸς ᾖ πᾶσιν ὁ δῆ[μος] εὐπορίστως
διακίμε[ν]ος πρὸς χάριτος ἀπόδοσιν· τύχῃ ἀγαθῇ. Here we see quite clearly
that the king has 'done favours' (χαρίζεσθαι) to Teos. The town now wishes
to react with due χάριτας (I am still reluctant to translate this, although we
are in c. 200 B.C.), and this is later expressed as χάριτος ἀπόδοσιν. The
means of this reaction is equally explicit: the people want to surpass
themselves in tokens of honour ἐν ταῖς τ[ιμ]αῖς. An exceptional feature is
that one of the many tokens of honour mentioned is the dedication of a
spring to the sister of king Antiochus, Laodice. The argumentation is so
important that I shall quote it in its entirety (II 64 ff.): ἵνα δὲ καὶ τῇ ἀδελφῇ
τοῦ βασιλέως βασιλίσσῃ Λαοδίκῃ πρὸς [ταῖς] ἄλλαις ταῖς δεδομέναις τιμαῖς
ὑπάρχωσιν ἄλλαι μὴ μόνον χ[άριν] ἔχουσαι τὴμ παραυτίκα ἀλλὰ καὶ μνήμην
ποιοῦσαι τὴν εἰς τὸ[ν ἄ]παντα χρόνον καὶ τοῖς εἰς τὴμ πόλιν ἀφικνουμένοις τῶν
ξένων [παρά]δειγμα πᾶσιν ὑπάρχον ἐμ μέσωι φαίνηται τῆς εὐχαριστίας το[ῦ

---

[240] P. Herrmann, 'Antiochus der Grosse und Teos', *Anadolu* (*Anatolia*) 9 (1965) (1967)
29-160.

[241] On the words βουλόμενος χαρίζεσθαι on another decree from Teos see *BCH* 58 (1934)
309b, 13 and commentary p. 313.

δή]μου καὶ προσηκούσας ἑκάστοις φαινώμεθα τὰς τιμὰς ψηφιζόμ[ενοι,] κατασκευάσαι τὴγ κρήνην τὴν ἐν τῇ ἀγορᾶι.

The object is clearly not only to provide an *ephemeral* token of thanks but to provide one that will remain visible as a *durable* memento or 'acknowledgement' so that others (foreigners, for example) will be aware of it both as a 'display of gratitude' and as proof that 'suitable tokens of honour' have been given. It is not by chance in this context that an annual sacrifice is made (II 34) τῶι τε βασιλεῖ καὶ Χάρισιν καὶ Μνήμη and, as the commentator P. Herrmann remarked, it is even less fortuitous that in one of the few other inscriptions in which the goddess Mneme appears, she is also coupled with the Charites.[242] Χάρις, τιμή and μνήμη—it is with this completion of the original couple that we have come to the essence of the matter.

In the article I mentioned previously Philipp suggests that we should seek the genuine Greek word for '(to) thank' in μνήμη/μιμνήσκεσθαι.[243] He only gives one reference in literature for this. I myself am reluctant to go so far as to decide on a simple *identity* of μνήμη = 'thanks', just as I am reluctant to conclude that ἔπαινος is to be *identified* with the notion 'thanks'. But our text shows that in this whole complex of gratitude these terms do indeed play a very central rôle. The inscription I quoted from the Athenian Acropolis ends with μνεμοσύνες ἡένεκα. Still more indicative is the fact that the verb μνησιδωρεῖν, which appears in oracular answers, does indeed always mean 'offer public thanksgiving' (LSJ) and is exactly the same as the Roman *gratulationes*. It is also worth noting that in Arrian *Anab.* 5, 29, 1 the soldiers of Alexander who had at last reached the Indian borders gave: χαριστήρια τοῖς θεοῖς ἐς τοσόνδε ἀγαγοῦσιν αὐτὸν νικῶντα καὶ μνημεῖα τῶν αὑτοῦ πόνων.

Let us once more return to the argumentation in the Antiochus inscription: the object is that his favours (and those of his family) be recorded so that they be, and remain, visible to a larger circle than the contemporary inhabitants of Teos. This motive returns word for word in an inscription in honour of an athlete from Aphrodisias:[244] μὴ μέχρις μόνης τῆς γνώσεως

---

[242] In the famous *lex sacra* of a private sanctuary at Philadelphia in Lydia: O. Weinreich, *SB Heidelberg* (1919) n° 16, p. 34 ff. On Mnème see L. Robert, *Hellenica* IX, 54 ff.

[243] There is a very full bibliography on the idea expressed by μνήμη in J. Jeremias, *Die Abendmahlsworte Jesu*⁴ (Göttingen 1967) 230-232 and 246; cf. also *TWNT* s.v. And cf. the remarks by F. T. van Straten, below p. 76.

[244] L. Robert, *OMS* I, 614 ff.

τῶν παρόντων μηδὲ τῶν ἀπαντησάντων κατὰ καιρὸν τῷ σταδίῳ στῆναι τὴν περὶ τούτων μαρτυρίαν, ἀλλὰ γὰρ καὶ παρακατάθεσθ[αι] δι[ὰ] τούτου τοῦ ψηφίσματος ἔτι μᾶ[λ]λον αὐτὸν τῇ πατρίδι. Here we have an 'attestation' which is not only intended to reach those who happen to be present at, or visiting the stadium, but also to obtain greater celebrity throughout the country. And the term μαρτυρία contained in the motivation catches the essential purpose of numerous honorary inscriptions.[245] There are numerous decrees in which benefactors are honoured because they have performed deeds ὡς τετειμῆσθαι, ὡς μεμαρτυρῆσθαι, ὡς θαυμάζεσθαι. Following Ad. Wilhelm, L. Robert[246] gives plenty of examples of combinations such as ἐπαίνων καὶ τειμῶν καὶ μαρτυριῶν τετευχέναι and there were official genres of ψηφίσματα μαρτυρητικὰ καὶ τειμητικά.[247] As in the case of the μιμνῄσκεσθαι these decrees are 'testimonies', the proclamation in a large circle of the favours of the euergetes. The point was the advertisement[248] which these testimonies provided and which presented the euergetes, whether he was human or divine, as superior, unique and excellent. Men and gods liked to be thanked, but they preferred to be honoured[249] and to be admired. Hippocrates, as we saw, mentions θαυμάζειν as a typical action towards the gods. A single expression of admiration of a favour, however, satisfies neither god nor man. The Delian Serapis hymn includes the phrase: ἅπας δ'ἄρα λαὸς ἐκείνωι σὴν ἀρετὴν θάμβησεν ἐν ἤματι and Engelmann gives examples in which the importance of the observation of the miracle by many is

[245] On μαρτυρία inscriptions and their meaning see P. Veyne, op. cit. (above note 207) 268 and notes 226 and 227. Cf. above all L. Robert, Hellenica III, 21 f.; H. Engelmann, Die Inschriften von Kyme (Bonn 1976) n° 19 line 22 ἐπαίνων τε καὶ τειμίων .... μαρτυρίαν and commentary. In the Delian Serapis hymn verse 90 f. we read ἅπας δ'ἄρα λαὸς ἐκείνωι σὴν ἀρετὴν θάμβησεν ἐν ἤματι, where Engelmann gives further examples illustrating the importance of the miracle being observed by many onlookers. Cf. on μαρτυρία in agonistic situations: R. Merkelbach, ZPE 18 (1975) 129 ff. Cf. also H. Häusle, Das Denkmal als Garant des Nachruhms. Eine Studie zu einem Motiv in lateinischen Inschriften (Zetemata 1980).

[246] Ad. Wilhelm, Anatolian Studies Ramsay, 423; L. Robert, Hellenica III, 22 f.

[247] L. Robert, Hellenica XIII, 207 n. 5.

[248] Björck, op. cit. (above note 79) 125, calls the Epidaurean miracle-inscriptions 'Reklame', and compares them rightly with the confession-stelai. On advertising pinakes see P. Veyne, Ann. Coll. France 76 (1976) 579 f. Much information on this matter in A. D. Nock, Conversion (Oxford 1961), 90 ff. On 'advertisement' in general see H. W. Pleket, below p. 183 ff. It is on the supposed similarity of the Epidaurean and the later 'eulogies' (as defended by Björck, Nock, Kudlien—cf. Pleket, notes 135 and 137a—) that Pleket and I do not totally agree.

[249] Perfect, in this connection, is Eur. Hippol. 7 f.
ἔνεστι γὰρ δὴ κἀν θεῶν γένει τόδε,
τιμώμενοι χαίρουσιν ἀνθρώπων ὕπο.

emphasized.[250] But ἐκείνωι ἐν ἤματι means literally, 'ephemeral', and that is too little. The *aretè* must be publicised so that lasting μνημή and μαρτυρία be ensured for still more people. How else, according to an established formula of Hellenism and the imperial period, could admired athletes, benefactors and princes be πρῶτος καὶ μόνος εἰς αἰῶνα?[251]

This is exemplarily expressed on a human level in an inscription from Kourion,[252] Cyprus (one of many). The decision has been taken to ἐπαινέσαι a benefactor and τὰ δεδογμένα [ταῦτα ἀναγρ]άψαντες εἰς στήλην ἀνθεῖναι [πρὸς τῶι ἀνδ]ριάντι ὅπως ἡ τ'ἀνδ(ρ)ὸς ἀρετὴ [φανερὰ ἄπασ]ιν καθεστήκηι. The implicit ὅπως εἰδῶσι πάντες is a strictly conventional request for publication,[253] but the charming part of it is that here it is the ἀρετή (excellence) of a man which is being proclaimed, while elsewhere the aim is that all should know the ἀρετή (miracle) and δύναμις of the god. And this is the point: the glorious name and the deed must be propagated. This could also be intended as a cautionary example, as we sometimes see in confession-inscriptions: παραγγέλλω πᾶσιν μηδένα καταφρονεῖν τοῦ θεοῦ, ἐπεὶ ἕξει τὴν στήλην ἐξενπλάριον,[254] the Latin 'example'—*exemplum*—of which recurs in a magical text: *ut omnes cog(n)os(cant) exempl(um e)or(um)*.[255] Apuleius *Metam.* 11, expresses it as follows: *videant irreligiosi, videant et errorem suum recognoscant*. Even Asclepius made obvious examples in cases of mockery and disbelief. Mockers were punished with the name Ἄπιστος or had to dedicate a silver pig ὑπόμναμα (!) τῆς ἀμαθίας,[256] actually a token of remembrance (ὅπως εἰδῶσι πάντες!), since the description of the miraculous punishment was publicised. But what was positively desired was, above all, renown, as—to enter another (though in fact exactly the same) sphere—the Biblical γνωρίω αὐτοῖς τὴν δύναμίν μου, καὶ γνώσονται ὅτι ὄνομα μου Κύριος (Jeremiah 16, 21) and its many variants show. Augustine[257] tells of miracles performed by a martyr in the name of God: *de quibus libelli*

---

[250] See above note 245.

[251] On this and similar formulas L. Robert, *op. cit.* (above note 228) 108-111; *Hellenica* X, 61; XIII, 216. The expression in a latinized form on a mosaic: *Isaona*. See J. W. Salomonson, *BABesch.* 35 (1960) 34 f.

[252] T. B. Mitford, *The Inscriptions of Kourion* (Philadelphia 1971) n° 76.

[253] Cf. Engelmann, *op. cit.* (above note 245) n° 2 and commentary.

[254] Steinleitner, *op. cit.* (above note 79) 113, a recurrent formula.

[255] R. Wünsch, *Sethianische Verfluchungstafeln aus Rom* (Leipzig 1898) n° 3 = Audollent, *Defixionum Tabellae*, n° 142.

[256] R. Herzog, *op. cit.* (above note 221) n° III and IV.

[257] *De civ. Dei* 22, 8.

dati sunt, qui recitarentur in populis, and the epigram by Aelius Aristides quoted previously is a pagan version of the same idea.

The log-book with the accounts of marvellous journeys of *P. Oxy.* 1382 ends as follows: καὶ καταχωρίζεται ἡ ἀρετὴ ἐν ταῖς Μερκουρίου (Thot) βιβλιοθήκαις. Οἱ παρόντες εἴπατε· 'εἷς Ζεὺς Σάραπις'. Indeed, the miraculous narrative itself could be stored away[258]—although there are examples showing that people sang the παιᾶν μέχρι νῦν[259] or that someone πᾶν δὲ κατ' ἦμαρ σὰς ἀρετὰς ἤειδεν[260], or, to remain 'classical': αὐτὰρ ἐγὼ καὶ σεῖο καὶ ἄλλης μνήσομ' ἀοιδῆς. But the reaction, the 'amen says my soul to this', was no longer drowned by the whole of Antiquity. 'Great', 'unique', 'our one and only god', chanted the fervid believers, sometimes hour after hour,[261] and that was the highest form of praise as well as the highest form of thanks, for although these acclamations did not necessarily imply monotheism, they definitely implied an exaltation of one god over the others. Stammering with reverence, the worshippers created new, double or treble superlatives: ὁ μεγιστότατος Ἥλιος we read in a magical text beside the familiar τρισμέγιστος. Nor, of course, did the human ruler lag behind: he ended up in the Byzantine period as *protopansebastohupertatos*.[262]

This, then, was the inevitable hypertrophy of gratitude in a world 'in der wohl das Bitten eine durchaus wesentliche und beachtliche Rolle spielt, wo aber der Gegenpol des Bittens nicht primär das Danken, sondern das Loben ist. Und dieses Loben ist ein so stärker, lebendiger und weiter Begriff, dass er unser ''Danken'' in sich fasst; das Danken ist hier noch ganz drinnen im Loben'.[263]

---

[258] Aelius Aristides, *Serapis hymn* 29 (II, 360 Keil), mentions ἱεραὶ θῆκαι βίβλων ἱερῶν, where numerous miracles are stored up.

[259] Above note 223. Cf. for similar phenomena J. M. Bremer, below p. 200.

[260] Delian Serapis hymn, ed. Engelmann, line 48 f.

[261] The most famous instance being the demonstration by the people of Ephesus against Paul and Barnabas, where the masses continued shouting μεγάλη ἡ Ἄρτεμις Ἐφεσίων for two hours. Even in this connection the divine and human worlds meet: senators used to spend an afternoon now and then with spontaneous cheers to the emperor and among their exclamations we find examples of the following type ὁ καλὸς Καῖσαρ, ὁ Ἀπόλλων, ὁ Αὔγουστος, εἷς ὡς Πύθιος, μά σε Καῖσαρ, οὐδείς σε νικᾷ (Cass. Dio 61, 20, 5). Cf. the examples given in my article quoted next note, 397 n. 138, and above all A. Alföldi, *Die monarchische Repräsentation im römischen Kaiserreiche* (Darmstadt 1970) 79 ff.

[262] I have collected some material in 'A Parody on Hymns in Martial V, 24 and some Trinitarian Problems', *Mnem.* 27 (1974) 365-405.

[263] Cl. Westermann, *Lob und Klage in den Psalmen* (Göttingen 1977) (= 5e erweiterte Auflage von *Das Loben Gottes in den Psalmen*) 20. On page 20-25 he gives an elucidation of the fact that terms of 'thanks' are lacking in Hebrew and he discusses the consequences for the

VIII. *The end of a circle*

Thus the circle closes which we followed from prayer of supplication to prayer of gratitude. It *is* a circle, for, when ancient man 'thanked' his human or divine benefactor in word or deed he was most reluctant to do so without also ensuring his future. The honorary decrees, to which I have already referred, regularly ended with a so-called adhortative formula in which we find the following elements: 'the city thus honours her *euergetes* to prove that she is grateful, that she knows how to honour good citizens, so that these good citizens will have many imitators, to spur each man on to follow their example and to stimulate a still greater devotion to the city'.[264] The women in Herodas' 4th mimiambus may be naive, but they are also exemplary when, after having sacrificed a cock in gratitude for a cure, they promise to return with still larger sacrifices together with their husbands and children (cf. above: 'Demain je reviendrai avec mes petits'!) *provided they remain in good health* (v. 86-88) χύγίη πολλῆ ἔλθοιμεν αὖτις μέζον' ἴρ' ἀγινεῦσαι σὺν ἀνδράσιν καὶ παῖσι, and this would appear to be a topos which already appears in votive epigrams in the archaic period:

Φαρθένε ἐν ἀκροπόλει Τελεσῖνος ἄγαλμ' ἀνέθεκεν
Κέτιος hõι χαίροσα διδοίες ἄλο ἀναθẽναι

'Athena Parthenos on the Acropolis. Telesinos has dedicated this show-piece to you. Be content with it and grant that he may be able to dedicate another'.[265] The habit of pronouncing new wishes at the same time as gratefully redeeming an old vow[266] flourished, above all in Rome, in the

ways in which gratitude is shown to God. There are significant similarities with the conclusions of Quincey (above note 201), who notes on p. 157: 'The Greeks' habit in accepting an offer, service etc. was to confer praise and not thanks. The difference between their usage and ours is not just a verbal one but reflects a fundamental difference of outlook. The Englishman with his "Thank you" is content to express his feelings, the Greeks, although no less sensible of the force of χάρις, saw an obligation created by a favour received and sought, in their practical, direct way, to discharge it' (very illustrative: Plato *Resp.* 338b). It is noteworthy that the Greek Jew Philo connects Greek and Jewish concepts also in this regard. In *De special. legg.* I (*de vict.* 9), n. 224 (Cohn V, 55, 8) he analyses the O.T. concept of θυσία αἰνέσεως (Lev. 7:12, 13, 15; 22:29) as follows: ὕμνοι, εὐδαιμονισμοί, εὐχαί, θυσίαι καὶ αἱ ἄλλαι εὐχαριστίαι.

[264] See on the adhortative formula L. Robert, *Ann. de l'école des hautes études* (1968-9) 165; P. Veyne, *op. cit.* (above note 207) 269.

[265] A. E. Raubitschek, *Dedications from the Athenian Acropolis* (Princeton 1949) n° 40. A collection of similar inscriptions is to be found in Lazzarini, *op. cit.* (above note 187) n° 786 ff. Cf. Van Straten, below p. 72 f.

[266] On this phenomenon see D. Wachsmuth, 'Weihungen', *Der Kleine Pauly*, col. 1356; W. Burkert, *op. cit.* (above note 130) 155. How difficult this combination appears to be for

supplicationes,[267] the New Year *vota*, the *vota quinquennalia*, etc. Life was a concatenation of threats and dangers; hardly had a man survived the old year than he started to fear some disaster in the new one. The gods of Antiquity did not have a moment's rest; they were called upon day in day out. 'One must not leave the gods alone, one must tire them', later theurgy informs us. I cannot help feeling that the ancient gods died of weariness.

the modern reader is shown by J. W. Hewitt, *op. cit.* (above note 190) who refuses to recognize obvious thank offerings as such, for the sole reason that at the same time new wishes for the future are being pronounced. The same misunderstanding concerning the προχαριστήρια, *ibid.* p. 106. Cf. also Herzog, *op. cit.* (above note 221) 134 f.

[267] *RE*, 'Supplicatio', 946, various examples of 'Doppel-Supplicationes von denen ein Tag dem Danke, der andere der Bitte gilt'. The same idea is hidden in such simple formulas as *Lari patrio Ladronius Avitis filius votum soluit, propitius sis rogo.* A greedy variant of about 150 B.C. (*CIL* I², 1531; X, 5708; Degrassi, *ILLRP* 136): *Semol te orant se [v]oti crebro condemnes.* The same principle in modern prayer: Bonnet, 20 'Merci pour cette Merveilleuse année que nous venons de passer tous les deux ma femme et moi donne nous encore beaucoup d'autres Merci'; 27: 'Voici deux semaines que je viens apporter des remerciements j'espère que la semaine prochaine j'en aurai d'autres', 23: 'Merci pour mon bonheur, celui des autres-Faites qu'il dure'. Dutch laconic in the name of a farm: 'Dank en hoop' (Thanks and hope).

F. T. VAN STRATEN

GIFTS FOR THE GODS*

οὐ μέγεθος πίνακος θαυμαστέον ἀλλὰ τὸ θεῖον

I. *Introduction*

In order to enter into and sustain a good personal relationship with his gods the ancient Greek resorted primarily to three means: prayer, sacrifice and the votive offering.[1] These three are normally closely connected. Whoever decides to study one of them will usually find that he must deal with the other two as well. The subject of the present paper is the votive offering in so far as it sheds light on the personal religiosity of the Greeks. I shall also be devoting some attention to sacrifices, albeit far less than such an important aspect of the Greek cult would require in order to be properly understood. For a thorough treatment of prayer the reader should turn to the article by H. S. Versnel.

What follows will be mainly confined to the archaic and classical periods of the Greek world (6th-4th century B.C.). I shall not, however, be restricting myself too narrowly to these chronological limits. Whenever it might be illuminating material will also be taken from other periods and areas. Whoever goes into this subject soon finds that, over the years,

* Abbreviations, in addition to those in general use:

BE = J. & L. Robert, *Bulletin Épigraphique*.

Lazzarini = M. L. Lazzarini, *Le formule delle dediche votive nella Grecia arcaica* (*MAL* Ser. VIII, XIX 2, 1976).

Nilsson I-II = M. P. Nilsson, *Geschichte der griechischen Religion* I² (1955), II² (1961).

Raubitschek = A. E. Raubitschek, *Dedications from the Athenian Akropolis* (1949).

Rouse = W. H. D. Rouse, *Greek votive offerings* (1902).

SEG = Supplementum Epigraphicum Graecum.

Sokolowski, *LS* = F. Sokolowski, *Lois sacrées des cités grecques* (1969).

Sokolowski, *LSS* = Idem, *Idem, Supplément* (1962).

Sokolowski, *LSA* = Idem, *Lois sacrées de l'Asie Mineure* (1955).

Svoronos = J. N. Svoronos, *Das Athener Nationalmuseum* (1908-1937).

For various helpful suggestions and informations I am indebted to H. S. Versnel, Irina Diakonoff, L. B. van der Meer, T. H. Tjia and R. A. Tybout.

[1] Prayer, sacrifice and votive offering mentioned together in the inscription *BE* 1960, 223 (Bulgaria): εὐξάμενος θυσίαις εὐχὴν ἀνέθηκα τὸ δῶρον.

votive religion displays a considerable number of constant components, some of which survived in Roman Catholic and Greek Orthodox circles and persist until modern times.[2]

It comes as no surprise to find sacrifices and votive offerings often mentioned in the same breath in ancient sources.[3] At a superficial glance they have an obvious feature in common: in both cases something is offered to the gods.[4] On the other hand, as long as we limit ourselves to fairly broad lines, the difference between the two is not difficult to determine. We talk of sacrifices when the object offered is intended for consumption (human or divine), while votive offerings are basically durable—a general definition which does indeed serve our purpose, although it does not do justice to the complex of phenomena contained in the term 'sacrifice'.

What are the motives and considerations which could play a rôle in the presentation of a sacrifice or a votive offering? Let us begin with the *sacrifice*.[5] Why was a sacrifice made? Theophrastus gives a clear answer: τριῶν ἕνεκα θυτέον τοῖς θεοῖς· ἢ γὰρ διὰ τιμὴν ἢ διὰ χάριν ἢ διὰ χρείαν τῶν ἀγαθῶν.[6]

We must sacrifice to the gods in order to honour them or to thank them or to ask them for something (good). But Theophrastus' clear and rational division is far from reflecting the current Greek concepts of sacrifice in anything like an exhaustive manner, as we shall see from the following examples.

[2] A thorough treatment of modern ex votos, and general questions concerning votive offerings, is to be found in the beautifully illustrated book by L. Kriss-Rettenbeck, *Ex Voto—Zeichen, Bild und Abbild im christlichen Votivbrauchtum* (1972); for a slightly different approach see R. Kriss, Zum Problem der religiösen Magie und ihre Rolle im volkstümlichen Opferbrauchtum und Sakramentalien-Wesen, in L. Petzoldt (ed.), *Magie und Religion* (1978) 385-403. Further references in Appendix, C4.

[3] Plato, *Leg.* 909-910; Herondas IV 11-19; for presenting a votive offering, elsewhere ἀνατίθημι, in Arcadian ἀναθύω or ὑνθύω are used: *IG* V 2, 554 and 555; *SEG* 11, 1162; *Hesperia* 28 (1959) 153; Lazzarini p. 72.

[4] The votive offering is often called δῶρον: Lazzarini 750 ff.; *SEG* 1, 248; above nt. 1. Cf. Eurip., *Med.* 964 πείθειν δῶρα καὶ θεούς, λόγος.

[5] For the essential data concerning Greek sacrificial rites see: P. Stengel, *Opferbräuche der Griechen* (1910); Idem, *Die griech. Kultusaltertümer* ³(1920); L. Ziehen, *RE* s.v. 'Opfer', 'Nephalia', 'Sphagia'; K. Hanell, *RE* s.v. 'Trankopfer'. On terminology: J. Rudhardt, *Notions fondamentales de la pensée religieuse et actes constitutifs du culte dans la Grèce classique* (1958). Of many other valuable and fascinating, occasionally perhaps a little speculative, works, I only mention S. Eitrem, *Opferritus und Voropfer der Griech. u. Röm.* (1915); K. Meuli, *Griech. Opferbräuche*, in *Phyllobolia P. von der Mühll* (1946); W. Burkert, *Homo Necans* (*RgVV* 1972); M. Detienne & J.-P. Vernant, *La cuisine du sacrifice en pays grec* (1979) with useful bibliography at p. 309-323.

[6] Theophr., *Peri euseb.* fr. 12 Pötscher, 42-44.

In certain sacrifices the rule was that only a part of the sacrificial beast was to be burnt for the gods and that the rest of it was to be eaten by the author of the sacrifice. No sensible explanation of this custom is to be found in Theophrastus' scheme—but then he was against the habit, and was opposed to animal sacrifices in general.[7] Most Greeks, on the other hand, would have regarded the eating of sacrificial flesh as a very concrete participation in the divine sphere, a μεταλαγχάνειν δαιμονίου καὶ θείας ἱερουργίας.[8] In other cases the sacrificial animal was completely destroyed (burnt, buried or cast into the sea), without the sacrificer eating any part of it. Such *sphágia* or *thysíai ágeustoi* were given above all in moments of crisis.[9] A good example is to be found in the Homeric hymn to the Dioscuri. A ship is endangered by a storm. The passengers have assembled in the stern and invoke the assistance of the Dioscuri, at the same time sacrificing white lambs:

εὐχόμενοι καλέουσι Διὸς κούρους μεγάλοιο
ἄρνεσσιν λευκοῖσιν ...[10]

It is clear from the formulation that sacrifice and prayer are regarded as an indivisible act the object of which is to achieve the redemptive epiphany of the Dioscuri. But Theophrastus' scheme does not do justice to this sort of sacrifice either.

Finally, sacrificial rites display a variety of peculiarities which can only be appreciated if we are prepared to acknowledge that there are more sides to sacrifice than Theophrastus would have us suppose. This can be illustrated by an example taken from an archeological source: on an Attic black-figured cup of 575-550 B.C. (*Fig. 1a*)[11] we see a sacrifice and a choral dance in combination with a man sowing and a man ploughing—in other words a sacrificial celebration on the occasion of sowing. But the woman at the altar bringing the sacrifice (detail *Fig. 1b*) carries a *liknon* or winnow, a tool used at the time of threshing, that is after a successful harvest. In order to understand the use of the *liknon* at a sowing sacrifice

---

[7] *Ibid.* fr. 6 and 7. On philosophical criticism of animal sacrifice see Burkert, *Homo Necans* 15.

[8] Polyaenus, *Strat.* 8, 43.

[9] Ziehen, *RE* s.v. 'Sphagia'; A. D. Nock, 'The cult of heroes', *Essays* II (1972) 575 ff.

[10] Hom. hym. 33 (Diosc.), 9-10.

[11] London, B.M. 1906. 12-15.1: Beazley, *ABV* 90/7; B. Ashmole, *JHS* 66 (1946) 8 ff., pl. II-III.

we should probably attribute to it a sort of inductive, more or less magical function.[12]

It is not only the question why and to what purpose he must sacrifice that preoccupied the believer, but also the questions what and how much. And the 'how much' is connected with an ethical problem. What do the gods prefer—a rich sacrifice or little given in the right spirit? Theophrastus opts for the latter. 'The gods like what is cheap', he writes, 'and the deity attaches more importance to the disposition (*êthos*) of the sacrificers than to the quantity (*plêthos*) of what is sacrificed... Those who introduced extravagance in sacrifice do not realise that they have thereby introduced a mass of evil...'[13] A similar idea can be found at an earlier period, in Xenophon, who says: 'How can we sacrifice to the gods in a pleasing manner if we also commit evil deeds?'[14] But Xenophon and Theophrastus are simply two Greeks, and this is different from 'the Greeks'. Theirs can consequently be regarded as *a* Greek attitude, and not as *the* Greek attitude, towards this matter, and we do not have to look very far to find other points of view.

The women in Herondas' fourth mimiambus ask Asklepios to accept their simple animal sacrifice, a cock, as a side-dish, since they are by no means well-off. Otherwise they would have offered an ox or a fatted pig.[15] The theme of the poor sacrificer who apologises for the exiguity of his gift by referring to his reduced circumstances also occurs in the votive epigrams in the Anthologia Palatina,[16] where it is assumed that, if one can afford it, a large and expensive sacrifice is preferable—and such was undoubtedly also the opinion of the man who composed the following inscription in duplicate in Cyrene in the fourth or third century B.C.[17]:

[12] *Liknon*: C. Bérard, *AK* 19 (1976) 101 ff.; M.-A. Zagdoun, *Fouilles de Delphes* IV 6 (1977) 34-35.

[13] Theophr., *Peri euseb*. fr. 7, 52-54 and fr. 8, 8-10 Pötscher.

[14] Xen. *Anab*. V 7, 32.

[15] Herondas IV 11-18.

[16] *Anth. Pal*. VI 98 and 191. The author of a votive inscription from Phthiotic Melitaia went one better: he assures the goddess Ino that although he lives in a humble hut—δημότις χαλιή—, he gives lavishly ὥς τις ἀπὸ κτεάνων πολλῶν, W. Peek, *Philologus* 117 (1973) 66-69. The same text is printed with a translation in J. Roux, *Euripide: Les Bacchantes II, Commentaire* (1972) 634; Roux reads Καλίη instead of χαλιή, taking it as the name of the dedicator's daughter, who would then only make an appearance in this text to have herself called δημότις.

[17] *ASAA* 39-40 (1961-62) 312-313 Nos. 161-162. Other remarkable numbers of sacrificial animals mentioned in inscriptions: A. Wilhelm, *SBWien* 180, 2 (1917) 49 and *ICret* I, XXII, 9.

μνᾶμα τόδ' Ἑρμήσανδρος ὑπὲρ κράνας ὁ Φίλωνος
θῆκε θεᾶι θύσας 'Αρτέμιτος τελετᾶι
βοῦς ἑκατὸν κατάγων καὶ ἴκατι· τῶι τάδε κεῖται
κόσμος καὶ μνᾶμα καὶ κλέος εὐδόκιμον,

'Hermesandros, the son of Philon, placed this in remembrance over the spring when he brought 120 oxen as a sacrifice to the goddess Artemis on her feast-day; this stands here as an ornament, a memento and an honour for him'.

It would have been too bad had the display of wealth of the man who paid for 120 oxen sunk into oblivion,—and, after the last slice of sacrificial meat had been consumed, no tangible memento of sacrifices remained. Such an idea was unacceptable, particularly to the man, so brilliantly characterised by Theophrastus, who is afflicted with petty ambition (*mikrophilotimía*): admittedly he only sacrifices a single ox, but he nails its skull directly opposite the entrance to his house, entwined by huge ribbons, so that whoever comes in can see that he has sacrificed an ox.[18]

The desire to retain a tangible memento of a sacrifice brings us automatically to the *votive offerings* which remained in the sanctuary, perceptible and tangible, after their presentation. We shall now investigate those motives and considerations which played a rôle in the presentation of the votive offering, just as we have done in the case of the sacrifice. Where the sacrifice was concerned, however, it was necessary to rely chiefly on literary sources, and here our task was complicated by the fact that the most outspoken views to be found are in Theophrastus who was hardly an average Greek. With regard to votive offerings, on the other hand, we have a store of epigraphical information: the votive inscriptions which bring us far more closely into contact with the 'average' Greek.[19]

---

[18] Theophr., *Char.* 21, 7. Vase paintings with sacrificial scenes often feature skulls of animals previously sacrificed, see e.g. E. von Mercklin, *AA* 1935, 78-79; βουκέφαλα and προμετωπίδια originating from important sacrifices were kept in the sanctuary of Athena Lindia at Lindos: *Lindos* II, No. 2, lines C 103, 110, 114. See also Ch. Börker, Bukranion und Bukephalion, *AA* 1975, 244-250, and Burkert, *Homo Necans* 13-14.

[19] The only comprehensive study of Greek votive offerings is by W. H. D. Rouse (1902), occasionally inaccurate, and now rather out of date, but still useful. A good concise article with helpful references: D. Wachsmuth, 'Weihungen', *Kleine Pauly* V (1975) 1355-1359. On votive inscriptions: G. Naumann, *Griech. Weihinschriften* (1933), meagre; M. L. Lazzarini, *Le formule delle dediche votive nella Grecia arcaica* (*MAL* Ser. VIII, XIX 2, 1976) has a convenient collection of 1000 votive inscriptions.

We see from the inscriptions that votive offerings, just like sacrifices,[20] were often presented to redeem a *vow* previously made in a prayer. This could be expressed by the participle εὐξάμενος connected with the subject of ἀνέθηκε or by εὐχήν, εὐχωλήν in apposition to the object. Both formulations can be found in the (late-) archaic votive inscriptions of the Athenian Akropolis:

Πείχον εὐχσά|μενος χερα|μεὺς δεχάτεν | ἀνέθεχεν | τἀθεναίαι,
'Peikon the potter dedicated this as a tithe to Athena by a vow'.[21]

'Αλ|χίμαχος μ' ἀνέ{σ}θεχε Διὸς χόρει τόδ' ἄγαλμα ε|ὐ|χολέν (---),
'Alkimachos dedicated me, a magnificent votive offering, to Zeus' daughter as a (redemption of his) vow'.[22]

A later inscription from Tomis (Rumania) gives us the Latin formulation beside the Greek one:[23]

C. HERENNIUS CHARITO VOTVM SOLVIT
Γ. ΕΡΕΝΝΙΟΣ ΧΑΡΙΤΩΝ ΕΥΞΑΜΕΝΟΣ.

The same idea can be expressed by κατ' εὐχήν.[24] The Latin version, *ex voto*, appears so frequently that it came to be used as a noun meaning 'votive offering'. Yet the offerer of the votive offering was not always the same man as he who promised it. There were occasions on which children redeemed the vow of their parents, expressed in inscriptions by τῶ πατρὸς εὐχσαμένο[25] or μετρὸς ἐπευχσαμένες.[26]

The *euché* referred to in the inscriptions mentioned should usually be regarded as a prayer of supplication combined with a vow whose redemption is conditionally connected with the answering of the prayer. Sometimes the votive inscriptions furnish us with further details in this domain. On occasion the emphasis is laid on the participation of the deity in this transaction, the answering of the prayer (Thespiai):[27]

---

[20] Cf. Plato, *Leg.* 909-910.
[21] Raubitschek 44.
[22] Raubitschek 6.
[23] *BE* 1966, 267.
[24] *IG* VII 225; *IG* XII 3, 263; *BE* 1953, 218.
[25] Raubitschek 221; Lazzarini 737. Cf. κατ' εὐχὴν τοῦ πατρὸς αὐτοῦ *BE* 1959, 454; κατὰ τὴν πατρῴαν (ὑπόσχεσιν vel.sim.) *IGBulg* I² 267.
[26] Raubitschek 236; Lazzarini 736.
[27] *IG* VII 1794. Cf. ἀντ' ἀγαθῶν ἔργων --- δῶρα *IG* IV² 1, 237.

εὐχὰν ἐκτελέσαντι Διονύσοι | Νεομέδες
ἔργον ἀντ' ἀγαθὸν | μνᾶμ' ἀνέθεκε τόδε,
'To Dionysos who has answered his prayer Neomedes dedicates this in remembrance, in exchange for favours'.

The deity is called *epékoos*, *euántetos;*[28] the dedicator has obtained what he asked for (Bulgaria):[29]

'Απολλώνιος 'Ροιμη|τάλκου εὐξάμενος | καὶ ἐπιτυχὼν 'Απόλ|λωνι Αὐλαρχην(ῷ) | εὐχαριστήριον,
'Apollonios, son of Rhoimetalkes, having prayed and having received, to Apollo Aularchenos, as a token of gratitude'.

On another occasion the due of the believer, the redemption of the vow, is mentioned explicitly (Melos, sixth century B.C.):[30]

Παῖ Διὸς Εκφhαντοι δέκσαι τόδ' ἀμ[ε]νπhὲς ἄγαλμα
σοὶ γὰρ ἐπευχhόμενος τοῦτ' ἐτέλεσσε Γρόφhον,
'Child of Zeus, receive on behalf of (?) Ekphantos this perfect show-piece, for Grophon has completed it for you according to his vow'.

The god might otherwise forget that the human had already satisfied his obligations, as is suggested in an epigram of Callimachus:[31]

τὸ χρέος ὡς ἀπέχεις, 'Ασκληπιέ, τὸ πρὸ γυναικὸς
Δημοδίκης 'Ακέσων ὤφελεν εὐξάμενος,
γινώσκειν· ἢν δ' ἄρα λάθῃ καὶ ⟨ δίς ⟩ μιν ἀπαιτῇς,
φησὶ παρέξεσθαι μαρτυρίην ὁ πίναξ,
'Know that you have received the debt, Asklepios, which Akeson owed you because of his prayer for his wife Demodike; were you to forget it and claim it a second time, the votive tablet will serve as evidence'.

---

[28] εὐάντητος: *IG* II² 4714, 4759, 4760; *BE* 1960, 356. εὐκτέος: Haspels, *Highlands of Phrygia* 297 No. 7. εὐήκοος: S. Charitonides, *Epigr. Lesb. Sympl.* (1968) 31, 32; ἐπήκοος: Weinreich, *MDAI(A)* 37 (1912) 1 ff., see Appendix, B 3. Cf. H. S. Versnel, above p. 34 ff.

[29] *Berytus* 16 (1966) 22. Cf. τυχὼν ὑγείας *IG* II² 4743; τυχὼν ἀπάντων *IG* II² 4924; εὐξάμενος καὶ ἐπιτυχὼν *JÖAI* 23 (1926) Bbl. 121 No. 10 (cf. Appendix, A 19); ἔτυχα παρὰ τοῦ 'Ερμοῦ καὶ τῆς 'Εκάτης καὶ τῆς 'Αθηνᾶς τὰ αὐτοὶ ἠθέλησαν *ASAA* 30-32 (1952-54) 264 No. 12.

[30] *IG* XII 3, 1075. The interpretation presents difficulties: M. Guarducci, *Epigrafia greca* I (1967) 323; L. H. Jeffery, *The local scripts of archaic Greece* (1961) 320 No. 23; Lazzarini 826; cf. L. Semmlinger, *Weih-, Sieger-, und Ehreninschriften Olympia* (1974) p. 71 ff.

[31] *Anth. Pal.* VI 147.

Callimachus' poem may not have been intended as a serious votive epigram for real use, although this cannot be altogether excluded. It is perfectly possible to imagine the offerer worrying about this sort of thing since the failure to redeem a vow made could entail a terrible punishment.[32]

We have seen that it is possible to regard the votive offering as a part of a more or less commercial transaction between man and god. But we can also formulate it in a different manner and regard the votive offering as a tangible proof of *gratitude* towards the deity for answering a prayer or for help and assistance in general. Such gratitude is occasionally mentioned in the inscriptions. Our first example again comes from the Athenian Akropolis (c. 500 B.C.):[33] hΕρμεί[αι: τόδε] | ἄγαλμα [: διδὸς] | χάριν: ἐν[θάδε: ἔ]θεχεν: Οἰν[όβιο]|ς: χῆρυχς: μ[νεμ]|οσύνες: hέ[νεχα], 'The herald Oinobios has gratefully placed this beautiful votive offering here to Hermes, in remembrance'.

In later votive inscriptions, especially from the imperial period, we often find the concept of gratitude expressed by the addition of εὐχαριστῶν to the subject, or εὐχαριστήριον to the object of the dedication.[34] We also come across votive inscriptions of the type Διὶ 'Ορνέῳ εὐχαριστοῦμεν ναῦται 'Ηρακλεῶται ('To Zeus Orneos we bring thanks, the sailors of Herakleia').[35]

Even if a prayer was answered and a votive offering was presented in redemption of the vow contained in that prayer, the matter was still not generally regarded as settled. Needless to say the believer also hoped for the help and protection of his deity in the future, and he was not ashamed to *ask* for it at the very moment when the god was thought to be particularly well disposed towards him through his delight at having received the votive offering. This is clearly stated in a votive inscription from the Athenian Akropolis (c. 450 B.C.):[36]

Πότνι' ἀπαρχὲν τένδε Μένανδρο[ς -- ἀνέθεχεν]
εὐχολὲν τελέσας σοὶ χάριν ἀντ[ιδιδὸς]

---

[32] See R. Herzog, *Die Wunderheilungen von Epidauros* (*Philologus Sup.* 22, 3, 1931) No. 47.
[33] Raubitschek 295.
[34] L. Robert, *Hellenica* X (1955) 55 ff. Cf. the discussion by Versnel above p. 45 ff.
[35] *BE* 1976, 559.
[36] Raubitschek 218. Cf. σὺ δὲ τõι χάριν αἰὲς ἄ[μειβε] Semmlinger, *Weih- etc. Olympia* No. 13; ἀντὶ δὲ δώρων πένπε ὑγίειαν ἄμωμον *IG* V 1, 1119; τὺ δὲ δὸ[ς χα]ρίεσαν ἀμοι Ϝάν on a pinax from Penteskouphia: Furtwängler, *Beschr. Vasen Berlin* No. 834.

Αἰγιλιεὺς huιὸς Δεμετρίο hõι [σὺ τὸν ὄλβον]
σõιζε Διὸς θύγατερ τόνδε χαρ[ισαμένε],

'Mistress, Menandros, son of Demetrios, from the *demos* Aigilia, has dedicated this ... as a first fruit, redeeming his vow and giving you thanks; stand by him and protect his wealth'.

But we already come across this *do-ut-des* concept connected with a votive offering in a far earlier period, for instance in the inscription scratched on the thighs of a bronze statuette of Apollo from Thebes (*Fig. 2*, shortly after 700 B.C., one of the oldest Greek votive inscriptions in existence):[37]

Μάντιχλος μ' ἀνέθεχε Ϝεχαβόλοι ἀργυροτόχσοι
τᾶς δεχάτας, τὺ δέ, Φοῖβε, δίδοι χαρίϝετταν ἀμοιϝ[άν],

'Mantiklos has dedicated me to Him Who Strikes From Afar with the Silver Bow (as a part) of his tithe, grant in exchange, Phoibos, an agreeable reward'.

Or, slightly less materialistic (Athenian Akropolis, c. 500 B.C.):[38]

[---]νες καὶ παῖδες 'Α[θ]εν[α]ίαι τόδ' ἄγ[αλμα]
[ἄνθεσα]ν he δ' αὐτ[οῖ]ς π[ρό]φρονα θυμὸ[ν ἔχοι],

'...nes and his sons have presented this beautiful votive offering to Athena; may she be well-disposed towards them'.

The series prayer/vow—gratification—votive offering/new prayer can easily be extended into a continuous interaction between man and god. A votive epigram by Callimachus can serve as an example:[39]

καὶ πάλιν, Εἰλήθυια, Λυκαινίδος ἐλθὲ καλεύσης
εὔλοχος ὠδίνων ὧδε σὺν εὐτοχίη·
ὡς τόδε νῦν μέν, ἄνασσα, κόρης ὕπερ, ἀντὶ δὲ παιδὸς
ὕστερον εὐώδης ἄλλο τι νηὸς ἔχοι,

'Come again, Eilethyia, answering the call of Lykainis, thus alleviating the birth pangs and producing a fortunate delivery. Just as you have now received this, mistress, as thanks for a daughter, so will your fragrant temple receive something else in thanks for a son'.

---

[37] Boston M. F. A. 03.997: M. Comstock & C. Vermeule, *Gr. Etr. Rom. Br. M. F. A. Boston* (1971) No. 15; Jeffery, *Local scripts* 46, 90, 94; Guarducci, *Epigrafia greca* I 145; Lazzarini 795.
[38] Raubitschek 64.
[39] *Anth. Pal.* VI 146.

Prayers pronounced at the presentation of a votive offering and ultimately included in the votive inscription had the obvious advantage of not sinking so soon into oblivion. Through their connection with the durable votive offering they obtained, as it were, a permanent effectiveness. The votive offering, a tangible proof of the relationship which had come into being between man and god, remained visibly effective as long as it hung in the sanctuary. Nevertheless the Greeks also felt the need to 'recharge' their votive offerings at certain times, as though they were to lose some of their power in the long run. To that end they were sometimes equipped with a special device, as we see in a votive relief to Artemis or Hekate (*Fig. 3*, from Thera?):[40] in the lower righthand corner it has a small conchiform basin which may have been used to hold a burning lamp or to receive a small offering or a couple of coins. The latter habit was by no means rare. In inscriptions with inventories of sanctuaries we read repeatedly of coins contained in or on votive offerings,[41] or which have fallen out of them (τὸ νόμισμα τὸ ἐκπεπτωκός).[42]

The attentive reader will have noticed by now that the votive inscriptions contain two recurrent motives—thanks for favours received and a prayer for new favours in the future—which tally with two of the three reasons for which, according to Theophrastus, sacrifices must be made.[6] Can we also find parallels in the votive inscriptions to his third reason, *honouring* the gods? Well, we do indeed find certain examples, although they are far from numerous in classical Greece.[43] An Athenian votive offering from the fourth century B.C. is dedicated by the offerer to Athena τιμῶσα χάριν σήν: 'honouring your mercy'.[44] A fourth-century votive relief representing the female genitals, from the sanctuary of Aphrodite on the Sacred Way between Athens and Eleusis, invites the passers-by to praise the goddess: ἐπαινεῖτε οἱ παριόντες (*Fig. 63*).[45] A eulogy (*eulogia*) is a more or less regular component of the inscriptions on the so-called confession

---

[40] Athens, N.M. 1416: Svoronos 361, pl. 66; *BCH* 90 (1966) 454; cf. *Lindos* II No. 138, 175-177, 224; *JDAI* 16 (1901) 163.

[41] *IG* II² 1533, 20 ff. Cf. Lucian, *Philopseudes* 20: πολλοὶ --- ἔκειντ' ὀβολοὶ πρὸς τοῖν ποδοῖν αὐτοῦ (the cult statue) καὶ ἄλλα νομίσματα, ἔνια ἀργυρᾶ, πρὸς τὸν μηρὸν κηρῷ κεκολλημένα καὶ πέταλα ἐξ ἀργύρου, εὐχαί τινος ἢ μισθὸς ἐπὶ τῇ ἰάσει.

[42] *IG* VII 303, see Appendix, A 16.3.

[43] Cf. the oracle *Milet* I 7 (1924) 302 No. 205 b. Cf. on the theme of honouring the Gods H. S. Versnel above p. 50-62.

[44] *IG* II² 4334.

[45] Appendix, A 11.4.

stelai, large quantities of which were erected in the imperial period in parts
of Lydia and Phrygia.[46]

The properties by which the votive offering differs from the fleeting
prayer and the swiftly consumed sacrifice, its relative durability and its
permanent presence in the temple, are expressed in various manners in
the votive inscriptions. The votive offering is frequently called a show-
piece, something beautiful which will delight the deity: ἄγαλμα,[47] καλ Ϝὸν
ἄγαλμα,[48] ἀμεμφὲς ἄγαλμα,[49] σεμνὸν ἄγαλμα.[50] It is an ornament for the
place of worship (Athens, c. 450 B.C.):[51]

> [ἀ]ρρήτο τελετῆς πρόπολος σῆς, πότνια Δηοῖ,
> καὶ θυγατρὸς προθύρο κόσμον ἄγαλμα τόδε
> ἔστησεν Στεφάνω Λυσιστράτη, οὐδὲ παρόντων
> φείδεται ἀλλὰ θεοῖς ἄφθονος ἐς δύναμιν,
>
> 'The servant of your holy rites, oh mistress Deo, and of those of your
> daughter, Stephanos' daughter[52] Lysistrata, has presented this show
> piece as an ornament of your portal, and she does not spare her prop-
> erty but makes abundant gifts to the gods according to her wealth'.

In this last case ágalma undoubtedly means an image, but that was not
always so. The term can also refer to a tiny bronze vase.[53] Not only did
the agálmata give pleasure to the gods, but they were also admired by the
people who visited the sanctuary. When the visitors of the Asklepieion in
Herondas' fourth mimiambus, which we encountered earlier, have set
down their own modest offering, they look around. They then gape with
amazement: μᾶ καλῶν, φίλη Κυννοῖ, ἀγαλμάτων, what splendid works of
art![54]

---

[46] F. Steinleitner, *Die Beicht im Zusammenhange mit der sakralen Rechtspflege in der Antike*
(1913); references to later finds: L. Robert, *Nouvelles inscriptions de Sardes* I (1964) 23 ff.; E.
Lane, *Corpus Monumentorum Religionis Dei Menis* III (1976) 17 ff.; I. Diakonoff, 'Artemidi
Anaeiti anestesen', *BABesch* 54 (1979) 140 ff. See for a discussion of *eulogia* H. W. Pleket
below p. 183-189.

[47] Lazzarini p. 95-98. There is a discussion of μνήμη in inscriptions in the contribution by
H. S. Versnel above p. 58 ff.

[48] Lazzarini 796; cf. *IG* II² 4828.

[49] *IG* XII 3, 1075; Lazzarini 826.

[50] *ICret* I, XVI, 7.

[51] *SEG* 10, 321.

[52] Thus Lazzarini 715 and p. 64. P. Maas, *Hesperia* 15 (1946) 72 takes στεφανώ to be the
title of a priestess of Demeter.

[53] Paris, Louvre MNC 614: *IG* V 1, 231; Lazzarini 720.

[54] Herondas IV 20-21.

It also followed from the durable nature of the votive offering that it could serve as *a memento, a remembrance*: μνῆμα. In the votive inscription of Oinobios mentioned above we read that the *ágalma* is dedicated out of gratitude and μνημοσύνης ἕνεκα: in remembrance.[33] But in remembrance of what? Here the offerers express very different views. Some of them were primarily concerned with perpetuating the remembrance of their own excellence, their wealth, generosity and piety. We have already come across this motive on more than one occasion—in Theophrastus' *mikrophilótimos*,[18] in Hermesandros of Cyrene (the man of the 120 oxen),[17] and also in the Athenian priestess of Demeter Lysistrata.[51] Here are two further examples; a dedication from the Athenian Akropolis (500-490 B.C.):[55]

[ἔργο]ν θαλόντον πολιέοχε πότνι' 'Αθάνα
Σμίκρο καὶ παῖδον μνῆμ' ἔχοι ἥδε πόλις,
'Protectress of the city, mistress Athena, may this city keep (this in) remembrance of the prosperity of the trade of Smikros and sons'.

And, still more extensive, an inscription from Erythrai (4th-3rd century B.C.):[56]

[Σ]ιμὼ τήν[δ' ἔστη]σ[α] γυνὴ Ζωΐλου Διονύσωι
[ἱε]ρέα πρὸ πόλεως Παγκρατίδεω θυγάτηρ,
[εἰ]κ[ό]να μὲ[μ] μορφῆς ἀρετῆς δ' ἐπίδειγμα καὶ ὄλβου,
[ἀθ]άνατον μνήμην παισί τε καὶ προγόνοις,
'I, Simo, wife of Zoilos, priestess of Dionysos before the city, daughter of Pankratides, have presented this image as a proof both of my beauty and my virtue and wealth, as an eternal memento for the children and the children's children'.[57]

Texts such as these may well give rise to considerations about the fact that modesty was hardly a characteristic of the Greeks, since, even before the gods, they were primarily concerned with their own fame and honour. Such considerations, however, run the risk of giving a one-sided and distorted picture of the situation. For the inscriptions quoted are indeed written by Greeks, but are not necessarily representative of *the* Greeks.

---

[55] Raubitschek 53.

[56] Engelmann & Merkelbach, *Inschr. Erythrai und Klazomenai* (1973) 210 a; cf. *IG* IV² 1, 228.

[57] For this unusual meaning of πρόγονοι cf. *BE* 1943, 28.

There are others, like the one written by the Athenian Myron on his votive offering (4th century B.C.):[58]

[σ]ῆς ἀρετῆς αλλ[.] παρά[δειγμ]α πᾶσιν ἰδέσθαι
σωθεὶς ἐ[χ ---] ἀνέ[θ]ηχε Μύρω[ν],

'As proof of your miraculous power, for all to see, Myron, rescued from ..., has dedicated this'.

Here too the main concern is to preserve the memory of an *areté*; not, however, the *areté* of the offerer but that of the god.[59] *Areté* in the sense of miraculous power, of concrete miracles performed by the gods, also appears in another fourth-century Athenian votive inscription:[60]

'Αθηνάαι Μένεια ἀνέθηκεν | ὄψιν ἰδοῦσα ἀρετὴν τῆς θεοῦ,

'Meneia has dedicated this to Athena, having seen the *areté* of the goddess in a vision'.

Whoever had experienced divine *areté* personally, in his own flesh, was thoroughly permeated by the awareness of how small were his own merits. This is what happened to Kleo, a woman who visited the Asklepieion of Epidauros in order to ask the god for help after a particularly long and difficult pregnancy. With the help of Asklepios she finally gave birth to a well-made son. On the votive tablet which she hung up out of gratitude in the Asklepieion Kleo wrote (4th century B.C.):[61]

οὐ μέγε | [θο]ς πίναχος θαυμαστέον, ἀλλὰ τὸ θεῖον,
πένθ' ἔτη ὡς ἐχύησε ἐγ γασ | τρὶ Κλεὼ βάρος,
ἔστε ἐγχατεχοιμάθη χαί μιν ἔθηχε ὑγιῆ,

'No one should wonder at the size of the tablet but at the divine action (the miracle): Kleo was pregnant with the burden in her belly for five years until she slept in the sanctuary and He made her healthy'.

The data assembled in this section is far from exhausting the information to be derived from the votive inscriptions. Yet I hope that what I have said has provided some insight into the essentials, and that it will assist the reader in following my investigation of the votive offerings themselves—a study in which I will be making repeated and grateful use of further epigraphical data.

[58] *IG* II² 4908. Cf. ἱστορίας μνᾶμ' *IG* IV² 1, 236.
[59] *BABesch* 51 (1976) 16.
[60] *IG* II² 4326.
[61] Herzog, *Wunderheilungen von Epidauros* No. 1.

II. *Votive offerings*

When Diagoras of Melos, nicknamed *Atheos*, was at Samothrace, he visited the sanctuary of the Great Gods who were chiefly honoured as the rescuers of sailors in distress.[62] On this occasion a friend asked him: 'You who believe that the gods do not care about human affairs, do you not see from the vast quantity of painted votive tablets how many men have been delivered from the violence of the storm through their prayers and vows and have reached the harbour safely?' 'That', replied Diagoras, 'is because the men who were shipwrecked and died at sea are not painted anywhere'. This anecdote handed down to us by Cicero,[63] contains a piece of information which is of particular interest for our subject: the sanctuary of Samothrace was full of votive offerings. And from this point of view it was no exception; other famous sanctuaries of great assisting gods, like the Asklepieia of Epidauros, Kos, etc., were cluttered with votive gifts as we know from Pausanias, Strabo and other ancient authors.[64]

Whoever visits a Greek temple nowadays and can experience some sense of archaeological or aesthetic pleasure from the more or less decrepit ruins, should, if he wishes to appreciate these temples as places of divine worship, remember that the *live* sanctuaries were *full*. They were sometimes so full that the cult-image could hardly even be seen.[65] All the walls were decked with votive tablets, festoons, wreaths, and it was only with the greatest difficulty that the believer made his way past the votive offerings standing all over the place. In certain cases it was necessary to lay down special rules, as we see in an inscription from the Asklepieion of Rhodes (3rd century B.C.):[66]

(--) μὴ ἐξέστω μηθενὶ αἰτήσασ |[θαι ἀνά]θεσιν ἀνδριάντος μηδὲ ἄλλου
[ἀναθ]ήματος μηδενὸς ἐς τὸ κάτω μέρος | [τοῦ τ]εμένευς (---)
ἢ ἐς ἄλλον τινὰ τόπον ἐν ᾧ στα|θέντα τὰ ἀναθήματα κωλύσει τοὺς
περιπάτους (---),

'No one is permitted to request that an image be raised or some other votive offering set up in the lower part of the sanctuary (...) or in any other spot where votive offerings prevent people walking past'.

---

[62] B. Hemberg, *Die Kabiren* (1950); Nilsson I 670 and II 102.

[63] Cicero, *De natura deorum* III 89.

[64] Strabo VIII 374; Pausanias II 11, 6; III 26, 1; Diod. Sic. V 63; cf. Herondas IV and Plato, *Leg.* 909-910. Such well-stocked sanctuaries were likely to attract thieves: Aelian, *De nat. anim.* VII 13.

[65] Pausanias II 11, 6 and III 26, 1.

[66] Sokolowski, *LSS* 107; cf. *ibid.* 123.

It was not only the great and famous sanctuaries to which the faithful came from far and wide that were full of votive offerings, but also the modest shrines of deities with a more limited, local significance, such as heroes and Nymphs. Even if it was true that the latter had a more limited sphere of activity, this mattered little to the simple Greek whose entire life took place within the confines of his own village. Indeed, because of the closeness and familiarity of the local deities, he would have felt more at his ease with them. He could submit all his daily worries to them and, out of gratitude for their help and protection, their shrines too were crowded with gifts which may have been of less value, but were presented with no less piety than the ones in larger sanctuaries. Thus, for example, two cave sanctuaries of the Nymphs and Pan in Attika, at Vari[67] and at Phyle,[68] have yielded countless remnants of votive offerings. From a grotto also belonging to the Nymphs and Pan as well as to other divinities at Pharsalos, we have an interesting inscription (4th century B.C.)[69] in which a certain Pantalkes, who regarded himself as an overseer, caretaker and gardener of the shrine personally appointed by the Nymphs, cordially invites the passers-by to enter the santuary:

ἱαρώτατ᾽ ἐν αὐτῶι
ἔμφυτα καὶ πίνακες καὶ ἀγάλματα δῶρά τε πολλ[ά],
'within there are very holy plants and tablets and fine dedications, offerings in great quantities'.

Of the numberless gifts which the Greeks brought to their gods many have been lost. This is partly owing to the material with which they were made, which, although relatively durable, was no match for century after century of Greek climate. Of the many painted wooden panels (*pinakes*), which were popular as votive offerings not only in Samothrace but also elsewhere, only a couple have been retrieved which are reasonably intact (cf. *Fig. 13*).[70]

Another part of the votive offerings has been lost because they were too valuable. This applies, for example, to the small gold and silver plates with

[67] *BABesch* 51 (1976) 19 nt. 264.
[68] *Ibid.* nt. 269. The scene of Menander's *Dyskolos* is laid here.
[69] *SEG* 1, 248.
[70] Orlandos, *Enc. dell'Arte Ant.* VI s.v. 'Pitsa'; F. Muthmann, *Mutter und Quelle* (1975) 95 ff. Sometimes bronze inscribed labels attached to perishable votive offerings have survived: G. Dunst, *MDAI(A)* 87 (1972) 106 ff.; W.-D. Albert, *Perg. Forsch.* 1 (1972) 1-42.

a depiction in repoussé relief (they are called τύποι ἔγμακτοι or κατάμακτοι,[71] and correspond to the *támata* which one finds in many Greek churches).[72] Suchlike *týpoi* have been found in a Demeter sanctuary excavated in 1973 in the Thracian Mesembria (*Fig. 7, 59-60*).[73] On the whole, however, they have not survived: these and other gold and silver votive offerings were usually melted down from time to time, in order to make new ritual vessels for the temple, for example. On such an occasion, however, a list was made of the votive offerings which were melted, with a brief description of each object, its weight, and the name of the offerer, 'so that the memory of the votive offerings should remain for the offerer' (ἵνα τοῖς ἀναθεῖσιν ὑπομνήματα ἦι τῶν ἀναθημάτων).[74]

Many more votive offerings have survived in other materials (terracotta, stone, bronze). Altogether they form a rich, although not always an easily accessible, source of information about various aspects of personal religiosity in ancient Greece.

At a first encounter many readers will be surprised by the enormous variety of Greek votive offerings. It looks as though anything could be dedicated: not only votive gifts which were made as such, but also objects which originally had a completely different purpose, such as utensils, tools, etc. In what follows I shall endeavour to introduce some order into this chaos by a *classification of the motifs* (iconographical motifs in a somewhat loose sense of the term) displayed by the votive offerings in their form, and in the representations which they sometimes bear. In order to avoid misunderstanding, I should point out that I am concerned with a classification not of the votive offerings themselves but of the motifs, one or more of which appear on each individual votive gift. My underlying principle will be the *relationship* which can be perceived between the *form and the representation* of the votive offering on the one hand, and on the other its *function*, as we learned to know it in the introductory section.

If we regard the votive offering as a means, used in close connection with prayer and sacrifice, to bring about and sustain a relationship between man and god, and if we also realise that the presentation of a votive gift was often brought about by something that had happened in the (recent) past and that a certain effect was also intended for the future, we

---

[71] *IG* II² 1534 *passim.*
[72] For references see Appendix, C 4.
[73] A. K. Vavritsa, *PAAH* 1973, 70-82; *Ergon* 1973, 54.
[74] *IG* VII 303, cf. Appendix, A 16.3.

can draw up as a working hypothesis the following classification scheme of motifs to be expected:

1. participants and concomitants; a) God, b) Man, c) Prayer, d) Sacrifice;
2. occasion; a) Initiation, b) The course of life, c) Contests, d) Work, e) Disasters and dangers, f) Illness;
3. desired effect.

Let us proceed to check this scheme against the material available.

1. *Participants and concomitants*

a) *God*

A relatively large quantity of votive offerings consist in a representation of the deity to whom they were offered. To this category belong the bronze statuette of Apollo (*Fig. 2*)[37] and the relief with Artemis/Hekate (*Fig. 3*).[40] *Fig. 4* is an example from the Athenian Akropolis, a bronze statuette of Athena of c. 480 B.C.[75] with the votive inscription on its pedestal: Μελεσὸ ἀνέθεκεν δεκάτεν τἀθεναίαι, 'Meleso has dedicated it as a tithe to Athena'.

In this same group I should like to include the votive offerings which represent a symbol or attribute of the deity, for example a *kylix* or a *thyrsos* for Dionysos,[76] and the shield that Phrygia the bread seller dedicated to Athena (*Fig. 5* from the Athenian Akropolis: Φρυγία : ἀνέθεχέ μ[ε τ]ἀθ[ε]ναίαι hε ἀρτόπολ[ις]).[77]

b) *Man*

Votive gifts representing the offerer or offerers themselves are also easy to find. In a votive inscription to Apollo Ptoios in Boeotia (4th-3rd century B.C.), the offerer mentions an image of himself as the object of the offering: εἰκόνα ἑαυτοῦ.[78] A large votive gift from the Heraion of Samos, signed by the sculptor Geneleos (*Fig. 6*, 560-550 B.C.),[79] shows us a family con-

---

[75] Athens, N.M. 6447: A. de Ridder, *Cat. des bronzes trouvés sur l'Acropole d'Athènes* (1896) 796; W. Lamb, *Gr. and R. Bronzes* (1929) 144; *IG* I² 426.

[76] Kylix: *BCH* 88 (1964) 828 fig. 11; thyrsos: *BE* 1967, 511; a small terracotta disc with a suspension hole, decorated with a relief of Apollo's lyre, from the sanctuary of Apollo Maleatas at Epidauros: *Ergon* 1978, 42 fig. 46.

[77] Athens, N.M. 6837: De Ridder, *Cat. br. Acrop.* 264; *IG* I² 444.

[78] *BE* 1943, 28; P. Guillon, *Les trépieds du Ptoion* (1943) 109-114; 143-146; cf. note 56.

[79] E. Buschor, *Altsamische Standbilder* II (1934) 26 ff. with faulty reading of the inscription; G. M. A. Richter, *Korai* (1968) 49 ff.; Lazzarini 166.

sisting of a (seated) mother Phileia, a boy and a girl whose names have been lost, Philippe, Ornithe, and, on the far right in reclining posture, the father with the inscription: [--]νάρχης ἡμέας ἀνέθηκε τῆι Ἥρηι, '...narches has dedicated us to Hera'.

As examples of categories 1a and 1b I have chosen votive offerings representing only the god and the offerer respectively. We shall now see—and this will come as no surprise—that god and offerer frequently appear on votive offerings in association with other themes.

c) *Prayer*

Prayer, which is in itself invisible, can be visualised in various manners. The most obvious is a reproduction of the offerer in an attitude of prayer, as we see in various metal votive tablets from the Demeter sanctuary of Mesembria (*Fig. 7*).[80] This representation can obviously be extended to include a representation of the god to whom the prayer is directed. On the votive relief of *Fig. 8*, originating from Piraeus (4th century B.C.),[81] we see Zeus Meilichios in the shape of a bearded man with scepter and phiale, sitting at his altar. The god, as was customary, is larger than the men.[82] In another fourth-century votive relief from Piraeus, probably from the same sanctuary (*Fig. 10*),[83] we see Zeus Meilichios on the right, again larger than the worshippers approaching from the left, but in this case he has assumed the form of a snake. It is interesting to observe that the same god in the same place and at the same time was worshipped both anthropomorphically and theriomorphically.

Figs. 7, 8, 10 show us the worshippers in the attitude of prayer which is most frequent in Greek iconographical material: standing and with the right hand (sometimes both hands) raised. In a third votive relief to Zeus Meilichios, also from Piraeus and dating from the fourth century (*Fig.*

[80] To describe the metal repoussés from Mesembria illustrated in *PAAH* 1973, pl. 92 ff., one might borrow the words of some entries in the inventories from the Athenian Asklepieion: e.g. *IG* II² 1534, 63: τύπος κατάμακτος πρὸς πινακίωι, ἔνι προσευχόμενος; *ibid.* 87: τύπος μέγας κατάμακτος, ἔνεισι προσευχόμενοι Καλλιστώ, Ἀφόβητος. Cf. *ibid.* 62: τύπος κατάμακτος, ἐν ᾧ ἔνι θεὸς καὶ προσευχόμενος.

[81] Athens, N.M. 1431: Svoronos 436, pl. 70; *BABesch* 49 (1974) 164; *IG* II² 4618.

[82] U. Hausmann, *Griech. Weihreliefs* (1960) 57; L. Deubner, *De incubatione* (1899) 12; F. Pfister, *RE* s.v. 'Epiphanie', 314; H. Rauscher, *Anisokephalie* (1971).

[83] Berlin, St. M. K 91; C. Blümel, *Die klass. griech. Sk. St. M. Berlin* (1966) 75 No. 88; *BABesch* 49 (1974) 179-180; E. Mitropoulou, *Deities and heroes in the form of snakes* (1977) 129 No. 22.

9),[84] we see the foremost female worshipper kneeling before the deity, however. If we examine all the material available we find a number of other kneeling worshippers in this same period. It would appear that Greeks, and, more frequently still, Greek women, did indeed throw themselves on their knees before the deities from whom they expected assistance and salvation, in particular circumstances and in fervent prayers of supplication.[85]

In certain votive reliefs the offerer, depicted standing with his right hand raised in worship, has his left hand clenched with the thumb closed inwards. Ludwig Deubner has recognised this as the gesture described in magical texts as κρατεῖν τὸν ἀντίχειρα, *premere pollicem*.[86] The purpose was probably to give the prayer a magical, coercive power.

Hitherto we have seen how the prayer was made visible in the shape of the praying offerer. But the matter can also be approached from another angle and the prayer visualised by a reference to the listening deity. We see an example of this in *Fig. 11*:[87] two bronze ears from Delos with the inscription on a *tabula ansata* below: Διογένης | Διογένου Ἀντιο|χεὺς Ἴσιδι ἐπη|κόωι εὐχήν, 'Diogenes, son of Diogenes, from Antioch, to Isis the listening one, as (redemption of his) vow'. The ears are those of the deity, whose listening character they emphasise,[88] as is strikingly illustrated in a relief (*Fig. 12*)[89] showing two enormous ears depicted on either side of a bust of Sarapis, as an enlarged projection of the god's most fervently desired quality.

d) *Sacrifice*

Like the prayer the sacrifice is a frequent theme in votive offerings. To start with we have a wooden votive *pinax* from the cave of the Nymphs at

---

[84] Athens, N.M. 1408: Svoronos 357, pl. 65; *BABesch* 49 (1974) 163.

[85] F. T. van Straten, 'Did the Greeks kneel before their gods?', *BABesch* 49 (1974) 159-189.

[86] L. Deubner, *JDAI* 58 (1943) 88 ff.; U. Hausmann, *Kunst und Heiltum* (1948) 97; see also the terracotta arms and hands from Paros: O. Rubensohn, *Das Delion von Paros* (1962) 167 Nos. 96-97, pl. 33.

[87] Delos A 1858: Ph. Bruneau, *Recherches sur les cultes de Délos* (1970) 167-168, pl. VII 5; *ID* 2173.

[88] See Appendix, B 3.

[89] London, Wellcome Inst. Hist. Med. R 6665/1936: L. Curtius, *Fests. J. Loeb* (1930) 62 fig. 12; W. Hornbostel, *Sarapis* (*EPRO* 32, 1973) 192 ff., fig. 137. Cf. also H. S. Versnel above p. 36.

Pitsà near Sikyon, dating from 540-520 B.C. (*Fig. 13*).[90] Before the altar smeared with blood[91] represented on the right stands a small procession of sacrificers consisting in a woman with a jug and, on her head, a tray with sacrificial instruments; a boy leading the sacrificial animal, a sheep; two boys providing the musical accompaniment of the solemnity with a flute and a stringed instrument since Pan, the constant companion of the Nymphs, does not like silent sacrifices;[92] and finally the offerers with sprays and ribbons in their hands. Their names are given in the damaged inscription which also contains the dedication to the Nymphs and the signature of the painter of the *pinax* who came from Corinth.

The deities who receive the sacrifice are not here depicted in person. They often are in votive reliefs with representations of sacrifices. In a fourth-century votive relief from the Amphiareion of Oropos (*Fig. 14*),[93] however, the god Amphiaraos, who was undoubtedly represented on the right hand side of the relief, is broken off. All that remains are the offerers, a married couple with a child, and, on the far left, a servant with, on her head, a cylindrical basket covered with a cloth: this is the *kíste* in which the sacrificial cakes (*pópana*) and other requisites were conveyed.[94] Diagonally in front of her walks a boy leading the sacrificial animals, a sheep and a pig,[95] and carrying in his right hand a *kanoûn* barely recognisable owing to the damage. The *kanoûn* is a flat sacrificial hamper with three raised 'ears' containing grains of barley (*olaí*), ribbons (*stémmata*), and the sacrificial knife (*máchaira*).[96] A similar *kanoûn* is in a better state of preservation in a relief from Eleusis (*Fig. 15*, fourth century B.C.),[97] with the sacrifice of a pig to the goddesses depicted on the right, Demeter with a libation cup and (lost) scepter, and Kore with two torches and ears of corn.

In a votive relief for Asklepios and Hygieia (*Fig. 16*, c. 300 B.C.)[98] we see the beginning of the actual sacrificial ceremony. The bearded sacrificer

---

[90] Athens, N.M. (the photograph is of a painted copy made immediately after the discovery): Orlandos, *Enc. dell' Arte Ant.* VI s.v. 'Pitsa'; Muthmann, *Mutter und Quelle* 95 ff.

[91] Ziehen, *RE* s.v. 'Opfer', 613.

[92] Menander, *Dysk.* 432-434.

[93] Athens, N.M. 1395; Svoronos 346, pl. 59; Hausmann, *Kunst und Heiltum* 181 No. 180; Petrakou, *Ὠρωπός* (1968) 123 No. 20.

[94] Aristoph. *Thesm.* 284-285.

[95] Cf. Pausanias I 34, 5.

[96] Aristoph., *Pax* 939; J. Schelp, *Das Kanoun: der griech. Opferkorb* (1975).

[97] Paris, Louvre 752: J. Charbonneaux, *Sc. gr. et rom. Louvre* (1964) 120; A. Peschlow-Bindokat, *JDAI* 87 (1972) 156 R67.

[98] Paris, Louvre 755: Hausmann, *Kunst und Heiltum* 178 No. 146.

to the right of the altar has taken something (presumably grains of barley) from the *kanoûn* held out to him by the boy standing next to him and is placing it on the altar. Another boy is holding down the sacrificial bull.

The killing of the sacrificial animal is seldom represented in material from archaic and classical Greece, though we do indeed see it in a later relief from the vicinity of Kyzikos (*Fig. 17*, 1st century B.C. or A.D.)[99] with the legend:

Εὐοδίων ἱερεὺς θεοῦ Διὸς ᾿Ολβίου
ὑπὲρ τῶν ἰδίων πάντων καθὼς ἐκέλευσεν ἀνέθηκα εὐχαριστήριον,
'I Euodion, priest of the god Zeus Olbios, have dedicated this for the sake of all that is mine / my own family, as he has ordered, in token of gratitude'.

Zeus Olbios himself stands in the upper part of the votive relief. On the lower level we see a man raising an axe in order to slay the sacrificial bull tied to a ring on the altar.

We can assume that sacrificial representations on votive offerings which stood in the sanctuary where the sacrifice depicted had been performed were usually executed according to the regulations and customs which prevailed in that particular sanctuary. They therefore constitute an important source for our knowledge of the sacrificial rites in the Greek shrines and they provide a welcome supplement to the information which can be derived from inscriptions with sacrificial instructions and from literary texts.

A votive relief from the Athenian Akropolis (*Fig. 18*, 500-480 B.C.)[100] thus shows a pregnant sow being brought as a sacrifice to Athena (far left) by a man, a woman, two boys and a girl. The theme of the pregnant sacrificial animal is one which we also find elsewhere,[101] but that pregnant animals were offered on occasion to Athena on the Akropolis is something we only know from this relief.

In addition to animal sacrifices the votive reliefs also depict the offering of bloodless gifts. In a relief from the Athenian Asklepieion (*Fig. 19*, 4th

[99] Istanbul: Mendel, *Cat. sc.* No. 836; *BABesch* 51 (1976) 11.
[100] Athens, Akr. M. 581: M. S. Brouskari, *The Acrop. Mus.* (1974) 52-53; E. Mitropoulou, *Corpus* I (1977) No. 21; Ziehen, *RE* s.v. 'Opfer' 595.
[101] Nilsson I 151-152; see also the indices on Sokolowski, *LS*, *LSS*, and *LSA*.

century B.C.)[102] a sacrificial table (*hierà trápeza*) laden with cakes, and possibly also with fruit, is set before Asklepios and Hygieia. The inquisitive reader may wonder what actually became of these sacrificial cakes, etc. The answer is simple: after they had lain for a certain amount of time on the *hierà trápeza* they were usually all collected by the priest. He did not take unlawful possession of them, as Aristophanes suggests,[103] but they were his by law.[104] There was nothing mysterious about this; the priest's right could be read by anyone in the public regulations of the sanctuary.[105] The fascinating part of the custom is that, although the believers knew this perfectly well, they had no difficulty in imagining that the gods themselves partook of these gifts. In terracotta reliefs from Taranto (*Fig. 20*, fourth century B.C.)[106] we see the Dioscuri galloping through the air to the copious provisions covering their table in their sanctuary.

A relief from Tegea (*Fig. 21*, c. 400 B.C.),[107] representative of a widespread type, shows how a god or hero, whose name in this case is unknown to us, is reclining together with his snake, at the table full of sacrificial cakes and fruit.

Another form of bloodless sacrifice, a libation offering, is depicted in a votive relief from a Nymph sanctuary on Pentelikon in Attika (*Fig. 22*, late 4th century B.C., inscription: Ἀγαθήμερος | Νύμφαις | ἀνέθηκε, 'Agathemeros has dedicated it to the Nymphs').[108] In the sanctuary depicted as a cave we see, on the left, the three Nymphs, Hermes and Pan with panpipes. On the right, above an altar of rough boulders, Agathemeros and an assistant bring the libation offering. For this purpose he uses a so-called *kantharos*, a form of cup which shows beyond a doubt that the offering is one of wine. In the light of a statement by Polemon that the Athenians only give wineless sacrifices (νηφάλια ἱερά) to the Nymphs, this is an interesting feature.[109]

[102] Athens, N.M. 1335: Svoronos 254, pl. 36; Hausmann, *Kunst und Heiltum* 178 No. 145; *IG* II² 4402.

[103] Aristoph., *Plut.* 676 ff.

[104] D. Gill, *HThR* 67 (1974) 117-137, esp. 127-132.

[105] E.g. Sokolowski, *LSA* 13.

[106] E. Petersen, *MDAI(R)* 15 (1900) 24; Nilsson I 408; L. Pirzio Biroli Stefanelli, Tabelle fittili tarantine relative al culto dei Dioscuri, *ArchClass* 29 (1977) 310-398, esp. 356 ff.

[107] Tegea 132: R. Thönges-Stringaris, *MDAI(A)* 80 (1965) 70 No. 6.

[108] Athens, N.M. 4466: Hausmann, *Griech. Weihreliefs* 61; W. Fuchs, *MDAI(A)* 77 (1962) 248; P. Zoridis, *AE* 1977 (published 1979), Chron. 4-11.

[109] Schol. Soph., *O.C.* 100; Stengel, *Opferbräuche* 181.

Besides votive offerings with a representation of the sacrificial rite we also have votive gifts which consist solely in a representation of the offering. This is an extremely numerous group from which I shall mention only a few examples. Terracotta cockerels from the Asklepieia of Corinth and Athens.[110] A bronze sheep from the Athenian Akropolis (*Fig. 24*)[111] with the inscription on its belly: Πέσιδος ἱχεσία, '(This is) the supplication of Peisis' (we should observe how here too sacrifice and prayer are regarded as a single unit). In the Thasian Thesmophorion several terracotta piglets were found with slit bellies, exposing the entrails.[112] The sanctuary of Demeter and Kore on Acrocorinth, moreover, has yielded a number of miniature terracotta models of *likna* filled with sacrificial cakes and fruit (*Fig. 25*).[113]

In the light of what has just been said we might tend to interpret these votive gifts as replicas and mementos of sacrifices which were actually made. But the following monument may lead us to modify this idea somewhat. It is a stele from Ayazviran (Lydia), dated 235/6 A.D.: we are thus on the very edge of the Greek world, both chronologically and geographically (*Fig. 26*).[114] On the left of the relief the god Men is depicted between lions, and on the right we have a bull. The inscription beneath runs:

Μηνὶ ᾿Αξιοττηνῷ Τατιανὴ Ερ|που εὐξαμένη ταῦρον ὑ|πὲρ ἀδελφῶν καὶ ἀκουσ|θεῖσα, μὴ δυνασθεῖσα δὲ | ἀποδοῦναι ταῦρον, ἠρώτη|σε τὸν θεὸν καὶ συνεχώρησε | ἀπολαβεῖν στήλλην. ἔτους τχ᾿, | μη(νὸς) Πανήμου ι᾿,

'To Men Axiottenos. Tatiane, daughter of Erpos, having promised a bull in a prayer for the sake of her brothers and having been gratified, but not in a position to give the bull due, asked the god—and he agreed—to satisfy himself with this stele (bearing the depiction of a bull). In the year 320 (Sullan era), the tenth of the month Panemos'.

We should therefore reckon with the possibility that in some cases the bronze, stone and terracotta replicas of sacrifices were not offered as

[110] Corinth: C. Roebuck, *Corinth* XIV (1951) 143 No. 50; cf. M. Lang, *Cure and cult in ancient Corinth* (1977) title page. Athens: E. Holländer, *Plastik und Medizin* (1912) 100 fig. 41. Cf. Plato, *Phaedo* 118.
[111] Athens, N.M. 6695: De Ridder, *Cat. br. Acrop.* 529; *IG* I² 434.
[112] Thesmophorion Thasos: C. Rolley, *BCH* 89 (1965) 441-483, esp. 470 fig. 30-31.
[113] R. Stroud, *Hesperia* 34 (1965) 23, pl. 11. On terracotta cakes and cake moulds found in sanctuaries: P. Zancani-Montuoro, *ASMG* 6-7 (1965-66) 83.
[114] Ayazviran: Lane, *CMRDM* I No. 50.

mementos, but in the place, of true sacrifices. There are various indications that such substitutes, particularly sacrificial animals made of paste
instead of real ones, were not wholly alien to the Greeks.[115]

2. *Occasion*

The number of conceivable causes for the offering of a votive gift is virtually unlimited. Here I shall only illustrate some of the most recurrent
and interesting ones. In connection with what has just been said, I shall
start with occasions of a religious nature.

a) *Initiation*

Initiation into mysteries entailed, for the believers, a religious experience which created an uncommonly close bond between them and the
deities. It filled them with good expectations for the future, both in this life
and the next. That they wanted to commemorate this experience with
votive offerings is perfectly understandable. Let us examine an example
which is connected with what are perhaps the best known mysteries, the
Eleusinian ones. This is the painted terracotta *pínax* which would appear
from the inscription to be dedicated by Niinnion to the two goddesses
Demeter and Kore: Νιίννιον τοῖν θεο[ῖ]ν ἀ[νέθηκε] (*Fig. 27*, first half of the
4th century B.C.).[116] Certain points of the interpretation are disputed, but
what follows seems to me to be plausible. In the main field we see, one on
top of the other, two separate events which are not simultaneous. Below
we have the procession of *mystai* making its way from Athens to Eleusis.
The participants carry pouches on sticks over their shoulders. Iakchos, in
a beautifully decorated garment and with two torches, walks before them
to Demeter, who awaits them seated on the right. On the upper level we
see the same (?) initiates in the sanctuary before Demeter, seated, and
Kore, standing with two torches. The triangular pediment bears a
representation of the night-festival (*pannychís*) which followed the arrival in
Eleusis. It would seem obvious to identify the woman in white in the mid-

---

[115] *Fab. Aesop.* 28 (Hausrath-Hunger); *Anth. Pal.* VI 40. Also compare the sacrifice at the
Diasia: L. Deubner, *Attische Feste* (1932) 155 ff., H. W. Parke, *Festivals of the Athenians* (1977)
120 ff.; the *boûs hébdomos*: Stengel, *Opferbräuche* 222 ff.; see also Sokolowski, *LS* 52, 25 and G.
Capdeville, 'Substitution de victimes ...', *MEFR* 83 (1971) 283.

[116] Athens, N.M. 11036: Peschlow-Bindokat, *JDAI* 87 (1972) 105 ff. with references to
older literature; Nilsson I 474. Other votive offerings referring to initiations: e.g. votive
relief Athens, N.M. 3942: O. Walter, *JÖAI* 31 (1939) 59 ff.; Cabiric skyphos: P. Wolters &
G. Bruns, *Das Kabirenheiligtum bei Theben* I (1940) 106 ff. M4.

dle of the pediment, the third woman from the left on the upper level and the second from the left on the lower level, with the *kérnos*[117] on her head, with Niinnion herself. It is clear, moreover, that although the essence of the mysteries could not be represented, the various events taking place contain a sufficient amount of themes eligible for representation on a votive offering.

b) *The course of life*

Transition from one phase of life to the next was normally accompanied by religious actions. At the time of the Apatouria festival in Athens the newborn children were officially received in the *phratry* of their father (*eisagogé*), whereby a small sacrifice, the so-called *meíon*, was made to Zeus Phratrios and Athena Phratria. On the threshold of adulthood the *mellépheboi* were inscribed once and for all in the *phratries*, also during the Apatouria. The sacrifice offered on this occasion was called *koúreion*, which is undoubtedly connected with χείρειν ('clip, shear'), since, on this occasion, their hair, which had hitherto grown long, was cut.[118] At about the same time as the *koúreion* the young men were introduced to Herakles in one of his sanctuaries (so numerous in Attika) at a festive gathering at which wine was libated and drunk (*oinistéria*).[119] It is with this last event that the votive relief of *Fig. 28* is connected (Athens, 400-375 B.C.):[120] a father introduces his son, standing before him, to Herakles, depicted on the left with club and lionskin. This relief is part of a series of closely linked monuments all displaying the strange building consisting of four columns on a rectangular surface, connected above by four architraves. By comparing it with a vase painting Otto Walter has been able to demonstrate that this construction served as a permanent frame which could, on occasion, be decked with branches and foliage and turned into an attractive summer-house where a feast was prepared for Herakles.[121]

---

[117] *Kernoi*: H. G. Pringsheim, *Archäologische Beiträge zur Gesch. des Eleus. Kults* (1905) 69 ff.; C. Rolley, *BCH* 89 (1965) 471 ff.: Thasos; J. J. Pollitt, Kernoi from the Athenian Agora, *Hesperia* 48 (1979) 205-233.

[118] E. Samter, *Familienfeste der Gr. und R.* (1901) 71 ff., Deubner, *Att. Feste* 232 ff.; Parke, *Fest. Ath.* 88 ff.; Nilsson I 137.

[119] S. Woodford, *Stud. Hanfmann* (1971) 211 ff.; F. T. van Straten, 'The lebes of Herakles', *BABesch* 54 (1979) 189 ff.

[120] Athens, N.M. 2723: Svoronos 379, pl. 101, 121; J. Travlos, *Bildlexikon zur Topographie des antiken Athen* (1971) 274 ff.

[121] O. Walter, *MDAI(A)* 62 (1937) 41 ff.

In addition to the above-mentioned official celebrations it was quite customary for parents to commend their children to the protection of certain deities with whom they had a special relationship, and later to give thanks to these deities for the assistance provided. On the support of a large votive relief of c. 400 B.C. found in Phaleron (*Fig. 23*)[122] we read:

Ξενοκράτεια Κηφισō ἱερ| ὸν ἱδρύσατο καὶ ἀνέθηκεν |
ξυνβώμοις τε θεοῖς διδασκαλ|ίας τόδε δῶρον,
Ξενιάδο θυγάτ|ηρ καὶ μήτηρ ἐκ Χολλειδῶν,

'Xenokrateia has founded the sanctuary of Kephisos, and has dedicated this gift to him and the gods who share his altar for the upbringing (of her son), (Xenokrateia:) daughter and mother of a Xeniades, from Cholleidai'.

On the relief Xenokrateia is represented with her little son Xeniades before her, stretching out his hand to the river-god Kephisos. They are standing in the midst of a dozen other gods and goddesses, the *xýnbomoi theoí*. Nymphs and river-gods were regarded as the protectors of youth *par excellence*. The hair cut from the head of boys when they reached adulthood was often dedicated to them, and Pausanias mentions a votive offering in the form of a boy who is cutting off his hair for Kephisos.[123]

The solemn dedication of locks of hair could also be celebrated by the presentation of a votive offering. In a votive relief from Phthiotic Thebes (*Fig. 29*)[124] we see two plaits presented to Poseidon by Philombrotos and Aphthonetos, the sons of Deinomachos: Φιλόμβροτος ᾿Αφθόνητος Δεινομάχου Ποσειδῶνι.[125]

On reaching a marriageable age, or on the occasion of their marriage, it was customary for girls to dedicate their dolls and other toys, as well as musical instruments they used to play with.[126] They also gave their

---

[122] Athens, N.M. 2756: Svoronos 493, pl. 181; Walter, *AE* 1937 I, 97 ff.; A. Linfert, *MDAI(A)* 82 (1967) 149 ff. with comprehensive bibliography; Mitropoulou, *Corpus* I No. 65; M. Guarducci, *Phoros-B. D. Meritt* (1974) 57 ff. suggests a somewhat far fetched interpretation for διδασκαλίας τόδε δῶρον.

[123] Pausanias I 37, 3; cf. Theophr. *Char.* 21, 3; *IG* XII 5, 173.

[124] London, B.M. 798: Smith, *Cat. sc.* I 798; *Br. Mus. Inscr.* No. 163.

[125] It is not altogether inconceivable that a shipwreck occasioned these hair offerings, see nt. 159.

[126] E.g. *Anth. Pal.* VI 280, cf. G. Daux, *ZPE* 12 (1973) 225-234; *CRAI* 1973, 389-393. Two tympana, one with a dedication to (Artemis) Limnatis, coming from Laconia or Messenia, the other with an Arcadian votive inscription to Kora (here probably also Artemis), would seem to have been offered on a similar occasion: *IG* V 1, 1497 and V 2, 554

children's clothes, and in particular their girdle, to Artemis Lysizonos.[127] This ceremony would seem to be the subject represented on an Athenian red-figured lekythos of about the middle of the 5th century B.C.: a woman is untying her girdle before Artemis who holds a torch, bow and arrows (*Fig. 30*).[128]

c) *Contests*

The winners of contests which usually took place in a religious context thanked the gods for their triumph with votive offerings. Both the prizes won as well as the instruments used for a particular sport (such as the *halteres* of a long jumper or the discus of a discus-thrower) were potential objects of dedication.[129] It was also possible to have a votive relief executed for the occasion, like the one reproduced (*Fig. 31*, 4th century B.C.),[130] dedicated after a victory in the *lampadedromía* (a sort of relay race with torches) in honour of the Thracian goddess Bendis in Piraeus. What we see represented is the winning team with its two captains or trainers, the foremost of whom holds the *lampás* in his right hand. The goddess is standing on the right. The Athenians had various torch races, such as the ones at the Panathenaia, and at the festivals in honour of Hephaistos, Prometheus and Pan.[131] The *lampadedromía* for Bendis was exceptional in that it was run on horseback.[132]

(Lazzarini 87 and 111 calls them phialai, but there can be no doubt that they are tympana, see the illustrations in M. Fränkel, *AZ* 1876, 28 ff.).

[127] G. van Hoorn, *De vita atque cultu puerorum monumentis antiquis explanato* (1909) 98. There is some confusion in the ancient sources on whether the girdle was dedicated to Artemis Lysizonos on reaching a marriageable age, or at the birth of the first child.

[128] Syracuse 21186: Beazley, *ARV²* 993/80 (Achilles Painter); D. C. Kurtz, *Athenian white lekythoi* (1975) pl. 32, 2.

[129] Rouse 149 ff.; Lazzarini 827-868.

[130] London. B.M. 2155: Smith, *Cat. sc.* III 2155; Nilsson, *Op. Sel.* III (1960) 55 ff.

[131] Jüthner, *RE* s.v. 'Lampadedromia'; Deubner, *Att. Feste* 211 ff.; G. Q. Giglioli, *ArchClass* 3 (1951) 147 ff.; H. Metzger, *Les représentations dans la céramique attique du IVe siècle* (1951) 351 ff. Some other votive reliefs dedicated for victories—torch races: Athens, Akr. M. 3012 + London, B.M. 813, Walter, *Beschr.* No. 213-213a; Athens, N.M. 2332 + Rhamnous 1960 BK 1452, Petrakou, *PAAH* 1976, 53, pl. 20γ; London, B.M. 1953. 5-30.1 + Athens, N.M. 2331, B. Ashmole, *AJA* 66 (1962) 233 ff., pl. 59; Athens, N.M. 4467, A. K. Orlandos, Τὰ ὑλικὰ δομῆς II (1958) 124 f., παρενθ.πιν. A, with erroneous interpretation.—Chariot races: London, B.M. 814 + Athens, Br. School S. 24, G. B. Waywell, *ABSA* 62 (1967) 19 ff., pl. 3; Palermo, *EV* 563, Waywell, *ibid.* 21.—Apobates race: list of reliefs in J. Borchhardt, *MDAI(I)* 19-20 (1969-70) 198 ff.

[132] Plato, *Rep.* beginning.

d) *Work*

Despite the depreciatory remarks which recur in Greek literature about many, if not all, forms of work,[133] for most Greeks it was the only possible means of providing for their subsistence. In daily work the need for divine support and protection was felt virtually every day. As thanks for their assistance the gods received a proportionate share of the earnings, usually called *aparché* (first fruit) or *dekáte* (tithe) in the inscriptions. Here are a few examples. Athens, fourth century B.C.:[134]

χερσί τε καὶ τέχ[ν]αις ἔργων | τόλμαις τε δικαίαις |
θρεφαμένη τέκνων γεν[εὰ]ν | ἀνέθηκε Μέλιννα |
σοὶ τήνδε μνήμην, θεὰ Ἐργάνη, | ὧν ἐπόνησεν |
μοῖραν ἀπαρξαμένη κτεάνων | τιμῶσα χάριν σήν,

'Having brought up her children with her hands, and with skill in her work, and with a decent spirit of enterprise, Melinna has dedicated this memento to you, goddess (Athena) Ergane: of the possessions which she has assembled through hard work she offers a part as a first fruit to you, honouring your mercy'.

Athens, c. 500 B.C.:[135]

Παλάδι Ἀθαναίαι Λύσον ἀνέθεκεν ἀπαρχὲν
hὸν αὐτῶ κτ[εά]νον τεῖ δὲ θεῶι χαρίεν.
Θεβάδες ἐπ[οίεσεν ho Κ]ύ[ρ]νο παῖς τόδ' ἄγαλμα,

'Lyson has dedicated this to Pallas Athena as *aparché* of his own possessions, acceptable to the goddess. Thebades, son of Kyrnos, has made this splendid votive gift'.

Athens c. 480 B.C.:[136]

[τέ]νδε κόρεν ἀνέθεκεν ἀπαρχὲν | [Ἰσό]λοχος ἄγρας:
ἔν οἱ ποντομέδ|[ον χρυ]σοτρία[ι]ν' ἔπορεν,

'Isolochos has dedicated this *kore* as *aparché* of the catch which the Ruler of the Sea with the Golden Trident has provided for him'.

---

[133] E.g. Xen., *Oecon.* IV 1-4; Aristot., *Pol.* VII 1328 B 37-1329 A 2. M. M. Austin & P. Vidal-Naquet, *Economic and social history of ancient Greece* (1977) 11 ff., 168 ff.
[134] *IG* II² 4334. See also H. Beer, *Aparché und verwandte Ausdrücke in griech. Weihinschriften* (1914).
[135] Raubitschek 290.
[136] Raubitschek 229.

Epidauros:[137]

Τιμαίνετος ἀνέθηκε 'Ανάκοιν δεκάταν αἰγῶν,
'Timainetos has dedicated this to both Anakes as *dekáte* of (the produce of) the goats'.

Kalymnos, 3rd century B.C.:[138]

Νικίας με ἀνέθηκεν 'Α | πόλλωνι υἱὸς Θρασυμήδεος |
ἔργων ὧν ὁ πατὴρ ἠργά | σατο τὴν δεκάτην σοι,
'Nikias the son of Thrasymedes has dedicated me to Apollo, as the *dekáte* due to you of the work performed by his father'.

Athena, who was the protectress of crafts in her quality as Ergane, received numerous votive offerings from craftsmen in her sanctuary on the Athenian Akropolis. How near the goddess was to these men (at least in the archaic and early classical period) is evident in a votive relief with a unique theme (*Fig. 32*, 475-450 B.C.).[139] On the right a craftsman is sitting behind a bench (exactly what his trade is, we do not know). At the same time he is handing his *aparché* to Athena, who is physically present in his workshop.

Craftsmen could of course present a product of their own workshop as a votive offering. This was not a rule: a potter sometimes gave a valuable stone image.[140] Yet there is always something touching about men dedicating their own work and proudly reporting the fact in the inscription. Take, for instance, the one on a bronze *strigilis* from Olympia (5th century B.C.):[141]

[τέν]δε Δίκον Διὶ δῶρον ἀπ' [ἐργαρί]ας | ἀνέθεκεν
αὐτὸς ποιέ[σ]ας [καὶ γὰρ] | ἔ[χ]ει σοφίαν,
'Dikon has dedicated this to Zeus as a present from his business; he made it himself since he possesses great skill'.

---

[137] *BE* 1976, 261.

[138] *ASAA* 22-23 (1944-45) 146 No. 100.

[139] Athens, Akr. M. 577: Dickins, *Cat.* I 1912; P. Perdrizet, *Mél. Perrot* (1902) 261; Mitropoulou, *Corpus* I 29.

[140] E.g. Raubitschek 197. But a terracotta shrine model from the Potters' Quarter in Corinth shows three miniature terracotta figures of a common type lying on the altar-tables: *Corinth* XV 2, 208 No. XXXIII 1, pl. 45.

[141] Lazzarini 819; E. Kunze, *AD* 19 (1964) B' 2, 170. See also Lazzarini 812-826; M. K. Langdon, *The sanctuary of Zeus on Mount Hymettos (Hesperia Sup.* 16, 1976) Nos. 27, 29, 30; Haspels, *Highlands of Phrygia* 300 No. 14.

The negative attitudes towards crafts (*banausikaì téchnai*) which we find in Greek literature were probably seldom shared by the craftsmen themselves.[142]

When a personal product was dedicated it was often specially executed for the occasion. A smith in Kamiros dedicated a cartwheel (*Fig. 33*, 550-525 B.C.).[143] On the rim he wrote:

Ὀνησός ⋮ με ἀνήθεκη ⋮ τὸπόλονι ⋮ ὁ χαλχοτύπος ⋮ τρο Ϙ ὸν ἄρματος,
'Onesos the smith has dedicated me to Apollo: a cartwheel'.

The only thing is that it is not a genuine cartwheel, but a bronze miniature barely 7.5 cms. across.

If a potter dedicated a vase he frequently made sure that it had a suitable decoration. On a fragment of a crater, presented as a votive offering to Athena on the Athenian Akropolis (*Fig. 34*, 475-450 B.C.),[144] we see on the upper level a scene from the potter's shop: on the right a pot is being shaped on a potter's wheel, while on the left a pot is being painted. Below, a part of a sacrificial scene has been preserved. A sacrifice to Athena had been paid for with the *aparché* or *dekate* of the income from the potter's shop, and at the same time this vase was presented in remembrance, as a votive offering.

In the sanctuary of Poseidon in Penteskouphia near Corinth a large quantity of painted terracotta votive tablets from the sixth century have come to light. Some of them bear representations of the work of the potters who dedicated (and executed) them.[145] On the example reproduced here (*Fig. 35*) we see the potter climbing up his oven in order to close the air-hole with a hook: a highly critical moment in the baking process of Corinthian (and Attic) pottery.[146]

At first sight even the relief of the mason who immortalised himself in the rock wall of the Nymph grotto at Vari (*Fig. 36*)[147] would seem to

---

[142] See nt. 133.

[143] Rhodos 14464: I. D. Kontis, *ASAA* 27-29 (1949-51) 347; Lazzarini 779. A list of votive wheels in G. Dunst, *MDAI(A)* 87 (1972) 139; some new ones from the sanctuary of Apollo Maleatas at Epidauros: *PAAH* 1975, 174, pl. 152 d and *Ergon* 1978, 41 fig. 46.

[144] Athens, N.M. Akr 739: Graef-Langlotz 69 No. 739; Beazley, *ARV²* 1092/76.

[145] *Fig. 35* shows the reverse of Berlin P280 (obv.: Poseidon): Furtwängler, *Beschr.* No. 802; *Antike Denkmäler* I (1886) pl. 7-8; II (1901) pl. 23-24, 29-30, 39-40; J. V. Noble, *The techniques of painted Attic pottery* (1965) fig. 75, 231-238.

[146] Noble, *Techniques* p. 72-73, 77.

[147] *BABesch* 51 (1976) 19 nt. 264.

belong to the series of votive offerings representing craftsmen at work. Nevertheless, it is an exception in this particular group. The man in question is Archedemos of Thera, a congenial spirit to Pantalkes from Pharsalos,[69] who was only a mason by taste. Towards the end of the fifth century Archedemos had come from Thera to Attika where he led a secluded existence at the cave of Vari, wholly devoted to the Nymphs. In one of the inscriptions which he left he named himself νυμφόληπτος: 'seized by the Nymphs'. On the Nymphs' instructions he decorated their grotto, laid a garden and made a dancing floor.[148]

A further category of votive offerings, which contain clear references to the work of the offerer, consists of tools. One example is the bronze axe from Calabria. (*Fig. 37*, 525-500 B.C.)[149] with the inscription:

τᾶς ἡέρας hιαρός | ἐμι τᾶς ἐν πεδί|οι ϙυνίσϙο|ς με ἀνέθε|κε ὄρταμο|ς Ϝέργον | δεκάταν,

'I am the dedicated property of Hera in the plain. Kyniskos the butcher dedicated me as a tithe of his work'.

Sometimes the votive offerings simply consisted in representations of the tool.[150] But the man who retired from work in his old age often hung up the genuine tool with which he had earned his bread until that day, as a votive gift in a temple.[151]

A merchant who had found a ready market overseas for his freight of pottery dedicated a terracotta *pínax* with a representation of his merchant ship and a number of pots (*Fig. 38*, from the sanctuary of Poseidon in Penteskouphia, 6th century B.C.).[152] Votive offerings from men who sail the sea, however, usually belong to category 2e on account of the attendant risks.

Political and religious functions, which are here classified under 'work' for the sake of convenience, could give rise to the presentation of votive offerings if certain duties were performed satisfactorily. We can take an example from the religious sphere. In the sanctuary of Artemis Orthia in

---

[148] *IG* I² 784, 785, 788.

[149] London, B.M. 252: Walters, *Cat. br.* 252; Lazzarini 701.

[150] E.g. New York: *Metr. Mus. Bul.* 21 (1926) 260 fig. 6; Athens, N.M. 1378: Svoronos 324, pl. 47.

[151] Rouse 70 ff. with references to *Anth. Pal.* VI; see also *IG* II² 47.

[152] Berlin P303 reverse (obv.: Poseidon): Furtwängler, *Beschr.* No. 831; *Ant. Denkm.* I pl. 8, 3 a; L. Casson, *Ships and seamanship in the ancient world* (1971) fig. 98.

Messene a number of votive statues of girls have come to light. One of them holds an old-fashioned looking image of the goddess. An inscription found on the same spot and belonging to a similar statue (which has been lost) casts more light on the significance:[153]

[Δαμόνικος --]ς, Τιμαρχὶς Δαμαρχίδα ἱερατεύσαντες
[Μεγὼ] τὰν θυγατέρα.
τᾷ Παρθένῳ τὰν παῖδα σοί με, πότνια
'Ορθεία, Δαμόνικος ἡ δ' ὁμευνέτις
Τιμαρχίς, ἐσθλοῦ πατρός, ἄνθεσαν Μεγὼ
τεὸν χερὶ κρατεύσασαν, "Αρτεμι, βρέτας
ἄν τε πρὸ βωμῶν σῶν ἔτεινα λαμπάδα.
εἴη δὲ κἀμὲ τὰν ἐπιπρεπέα χάριν
τεῖσαι γονεῦσιν | ἔνδικον γὰρ ἔπλετο
καὶ παισὶν τιμᾶν ἐμ μέρει φυτοσπόρους,

'Damonikos, son of..., Timarchis, daughter of Damarchidas (have dedicated an image of) their daughter Mego at the time of their priestship. To you, the Maid, mistress Orthia, Damonikos and his wife Timarchis, of noble parentage, have dedicated me, their child Mego, who have carried Your image, oh Artemis, in my hand and (they have dedicated) the torch which I have held up before your altar. May I also be permitted to give the thanks due to my parents, because it is meet that children should honour their begetters in their turn'.

e) *Disasters and dangers*

Need teaches us to pray. And a Greek prayer led in many cases to a votive offering.[154] The disasters and dangers about which the votive inscriptions tell us range from a mad dog,[155] via falling rocks,[156] to an earthquake.[157] A large group within this category of inscriptions comes from seafarers who ran into danger at sea.[158] When they had survived a shipwreck or the threat of a shipwreck, they dedicated their clothes or their

[153] *Ergon* 1962, 128 ff., fig. 155; *BE* 1964, 193; Daux, *BCH* 99 (1975) 156 ff.
[154] Plato, *Leg.* 909-910.
[155] Mihailov, *IGBulg* 1385.
[156] *IG* II² 3456, L. Beschi, *ASAA* 47-48 (1969-70) 86.
[157] *IG* XII 1, 23. On earthquakes in inscriptions see L. Robert, *BCH* 102 (1978) 395-408.
[158] On all religious matters concerning the sea and sailing see D. Wachsmuth, *Pompimos ho Daimon* (1967).

hair to the gods of the sea.[159] Their apparel, or a not too indispensable part of their body, was given in exchange for their physical safety.

A number of terracotta *pínakes* and stone votive reliefs offered by rescued sailors have also survived. Our first example is a relief from Piraeus (*Fig. 39*, 4th-3rd century B.C.).[160] On the right we have the front view of a boat in which a small figure of the skipper is standing. His right hand is raised in worship before his *sotêres*, the two Dioscuri. They have gallopped through the air to his assistance, and now, in the calm after the storm, one of the Dioscuri has dismounted in order to receive the thanks of their protégé.

A later relief (*Fig. 40*, 1st century A.D.)[161] comes from Tomis on the Black Sea with the inscription:

εὐχὴν Ἥωι Μανιμαζωι | Διοσκουρίδης | ᾿Αρίστωνος | ἀνέθηκεν,
'This has been dedicated by Dioskourides, the son of Ariston, in redemption of his vow to Heros Manimazos'.

In the upper part of the relief we see the hero on horseback by an altar on which a sacrifice is being offered to him. Below, a ship is depicted in shallow relief with the skipper and his boy in the centre imploring the help of the hero with raised hands.

What is striking is the fact that the votive offerings given by sailors which have survived from Antiquity never provide a realistic reproduction of the dangers from which they have been saved. Nevertheless we can conclude from a series of literary allusions that at least in the Roman period the (lost) wooden votive *pínakes* from the survivors of shipwrecks were decorated with highly realistic and dramatic depictions of their misfortunes.[162]

f) *Illness*

Strictly speaking illnesses should be classified under the preceding, more general category. When he is ill, just as when he is wrecked at sea, man acquires a heightened awareness of his own mortality. Thus invalids,

[159] *Anth. Pal.* VI 164, 245.
[160] Athens, N.M. 1409: Svoronos 358, pl. 33; Wachsmuth, *Pomp. Daim.* 156.
[161] Bucarest L 595: G. Bordenache, *Scult. Bucarest* I (1969) No. 203; Wachsmuth, *Pomp. Daim.* 157 ff.; for Manimazos: Mihailov, *IGBulg* 77-78.
[162] Juvenal 12, 22-28 with schol.; Idem 14, 301-302; Horace, *Sat.* 2, 1, 32-34 with schol.; Horace, *Ep.* 2, 3, 19-21 with schol.; Wachsmuth, *Pomp. Daim.* 141 ff.

too, dedicated their hair or articles of clothing to the gods.[163] Since votive gifts from invalids have survived in a large quantity, however, and since they display a number of specific characteristics, it is more practical to place them in a separate group.

The sick who sought their cure in the sanctuaries of Asklepios or similar gods of healing spent one or more nights in the *enkoimetérion*. The god appeared to them in their sleep and performed an operation, administered a medicine or produced some other form of cure. Inscriptions reporting miraculous cures (the richest collection, from the 4th century B.C., has been preserved in Epidauros) provide us with detailed information about the course of events.[164] The healing appearance of the god in the *enkoimetérion* is also the subject of a series of votive reliefs. A well-preserved example comes from the Asklepieion in Piraeus (*Fig. 41*, c. 400 B.C.).[165] In the centre lies the patient on a bench covered with the skin of a sacrificial animal.[166] On the right stands Asklepios, treating the shoulder of the invalid, together with Hygieia. On the left we see the grateful relatives venerating the miracle.

A similar occurrence some six centuries later is depicted in a similar way (*Fig. 42*):[167] the emaciated patient reclining on a couch tries to sit up, welcoming the apparition of the divine healer who is represented in the left-hand part of the relief. By the Cerberus at his side the god can be recognised as Sarapis, who in the Hellenistic-Roman period rose to the status of a healer god equal to Asklepios.[168]

In view of the great risks which accompanied pregnancy and confinement in Antiquity—and long after—it comes as no surprise when we

---

[163] Pausanias II 11, 16; Roebuck, *Corinth* XIV No. 116: terracotta plait of hair.

[164] Herzog, *Wunderheilungen von Epidauros*; E. J. & L. Edelstein, *Asclepius* I (1945) 194 ff.; Nilsson I 538 ff., 806 ff.

[165] Piraeus 405: Hausmann, *Kunst und Heiltum* 166 No. 1; Mitropoulou, *Corpus* I 126. On this and other votive offerings dedicated on the strength of a dream vision see F. T. van Straten, 'Daikrates' Dream—A votive relief from Kos and some other *kat 'onar* dedications', *BABesch* 51 (1976) 1 ff.

[166] Cf. Pausanias I 34, 5.

[167] The left-hand part of the relief is now in Budapest: A. Hekler, *Samml. Ant. Sk. Budapest* (1929) 142 ff., No. 136; the right-hand part is in the Vatican: G. Kaschnitz-Weinberg, *Scult. magazz. Mus. Vatic.* (1936-37) No. 405, pl. 75. Some drawings of the relief exist, made in Rome in the 16th century when it was still complete: G. Dehn, *JDAI* 28 (1913) 399-403, fig. 3-7. Cf. Hausmann, *Kunst und Heiltum* 50, nt. 219.

[168] Asklepios and Sarapis practising in a similar manner: Cicero, *Div.* II 123: '*an Aesculapius, an Serapis potest nobis praescribere per somnum curationem valetudinis, ...*'; Tac., *Hist.* IV 84, 5; A. Henrichs, *ZPE* 3 (1968) 66 ff.; Bruneau, *Cultes de Délos* 375.

encounter numerous pregnant women among the patients in the
Asklepieia.[169] At the same time expectant mothers invoked the assistance
of more specialised goddesses, like Eileithyia and Artemis. In Attika it was
above all Artemis Brauronia who was the protectress of women in labour,
and it was a common custom to dedicate clothes to her which had been
worn at the time of pregnancy.[170] Needless to say none of these votive gifts
have survived, but we do have a number of inscriptions with inventories
of the articles of clothing offered in the sanctuary of Artemis Brauronia.
The brief excerpt from one which follows (347/6 B.C.) can serve as an
example:[171]

χιτωνίσκος ἀλουργὸς περιποίκι ἐμ πλαισίωι, Θυαίνη καὶ
Μαλθάκη ἀνέθηκαν· Φίλη ζῶμα· Φείδυλλα ἱμάτιον
λευκὸν γυναικεῖον ἐμ πλαι: Μνησὼ βατραχίδα·
Ναυσὶς ἱμάτιον γυναικεῖον πλατυαλουργὲς περχυμάτιον,

'An underdress dyed purple with decor. all round in an oblong box,
Thyaine and Malthake have dedicated it; Phile a belt; Pheidylla a
woman's cloak, white, in obl. box; Mneso a green gown; Nausis a
woman's cloak with broad purple hem and a wave motif all round'.

It must all have looked something like a large women's clothes store at an
end-of-season clearance sale.

Other pertinent votive offerings are figures of pregnant women,[172]
replicas of the womb,[173] or representations of child-birth (e.g. *Fig. 44*, one
of several similar terracotta groups from Cyprus, 6th century B.C.):[174] A

---

[169] Herzog, *Wunderheilungen von Epidauros* p. 71 ff.

[170] Eurip., *I.T.* 1462 ff.; Nilsson I 485; L. Kahil, *AK* 8 (1965) 20 ff.; 20 (1977) 86 ff.

[171] *IG* II² 1514 ff.; the quotation is from *IG* II² 1515, 6 ff. Cf. T. Linders, *Studies in the treasure records of Artemis Brauronia found in Athens* (1972).

[172] Pregnant women, terracotta figures: Tsoutsouros (Inatos, Crete), sanctuary of Eileithyia: P. Faure, *Fonctions des cavernes Crétoises* (1965) 90f.; Th. Hadzisteliou Price, *Kourotrophos* (1978) fig. 2c.—Pitsà, cave of the Nymphs: *Enc. dell'Arte Ant.* VI 206 fig. 229.—Kos, Asklepieion (?): Appendix, A 30.7.—fragments of a votive relief from Delos, sanctuary of Artemis Lochia: A. Plassart, *EAD* XI 293-308, fig. 248; Bruneau, *Cultes de Délos* 191.

[173] Uteri: Appendix, A 15.118?, 25 *e*, 30.10.

[174] Child-birth: Cyprus: P. Dikaios, *Guide Cypr. Mus.* [3](1961) pl. 31, 3 (here *Fig. 44*); L. Heuzey, *Fig. ant. t.c. Louvre* (1883) pl. 9, 7; J. L. Myres, *Hbk Cesnola coll.* (1914) 188f., No. 1226; Athens, N.M. 12205 and 12206, exhibited in the exposition on Children in Antiquity (1979).—Lato (Crete): *BCH* 93 (1969) 819 ff., fig. 31-33.—Sparta: Tod & Wace, *Cat. Sparta Mus.* 171f., No. 364.—Paestum, Foce del Sele: M. W. Stoop, *Floral figurines from South Italy* (1960) 24-41, pl. I. Terracotta figures of women in labour, in a private collection:

distinctly magical connotation is present in the custom to offer keys to a goddess in order to facilitate parturition.[175]

A votive relief presented in gratitude for a successful confinement is illustrated in *Fig. 43* (425-400 B.C.).[176] The woman in child-bed is seated on a chair, leaning back in exhaustion. On the right stands the midwife supporting her with one hand and carrying the child in her other arm. On the left a goddess and the hand of a second deity can be seen, perhaps Hygieia and Asklepios.

Equally typical of the cult of gods of healing is a group of votive offerings usually referred to with the term 'Gliederweihungen' or 'anatomical ex votos'. They are representations of limbs or parts of the body which have been cured and which are presented in gratitude to the deity (see Appendix).

A relief from the sanctuary of the Athenian hero of healing Amynos (*Fig. 52* c. 340 B.C.)[177] shows the grateful Lysimachides dedicating a gigantic fake leg with a varicose vein to the hero. There are already two votive offerings in the shape of feet.

A splendid collection of terracotta anatomical votive offerings was found in the Asklepieion of Corinth (*Fig. 51*),[178] while some silver votive tablets with parts of the body in repoussé relief come from the sanctuary of Demeter in Mesembria (*Fig. 59-60*:[179] the distribution of functions and specialisations in the Greek pantheon was not applied quite as rigorously as is often supposed). Various sanctuaries in Athens, and the Amphiareion of Oropos, were also full of similar metal *týpoi*. None have come to light there, but they are reported in the inventories which I have already

K. Schefold, *AA* 1954, 217-224. A curious relief depicting child-birth is illustrated in H. E. Sigerist, *Anfänge der Medizin* (1963) II and E. D. Phillips, *Greek medicine* (1973) fig. 3.

[175] Keys: Festus, *De verb. sign.* 39, 56 L: *clavim mulieribus consuetudo erat donare ob significandam partus facilitatem*; cf. Aristoph., *Thesm.* 973-976. The numerous keys found in the sanctuary at Foce del Sele are thus interpreted by P. Zancani-Montuoro, *ASMG* 6-7 (1965-66) 152 ff., pl. 44. To this day keys and *támata* depicting keys are hung on the miraculous icon of Ayía Iríni Chrysovalándou at Lykovrísi (Attika). For other modern parallels see L. Kriss-Rettenbeck, *Ex Voto* 120 and 292. The flexibility of votive types in a society where votive religion is still very much alive was brought home to me, when on my inquiry after the meaning of *támata* with keys, the owner of a shop in Athens where they were sold answered that they might be dedicated when a person had lost his key, or wanted to buy a house.

[176] New York, M. M. A. 24.97.92: G. M. A. Richter, *Cat. Gr. sc.* (1954) No. 67; Mitropoulou, *Corpus* I 66.

[177] Appendix, A 2.1.

[178] Appendix, A 15.1-118.

[179] Appendix, A 22.1-12.

had occasion to mention. The following can serve as a small illustration (Amphiareion, c. 200 B.C.):[180]

Μέλανος προσώπιον ὁλκὴ ΔΔΠΗΗΗ, Βοίσκου
πρόσωπον ὁλκὴ ΠΗΗΗ, Φιλίας τιτθὸς ὁλκὴ ΠΗΗΗ,
'Αρσίνου αἰδοῖον ὁλκὴ ΠΗ, Καλλιμάχης ὀφίδ[ιο]ν ὁλκὴ Π,
["Ι]ππωνος αἰδοῖον ὁλκὴ ΗΗΗ, Εὐφροσύνης τ[ιτθ]ὸς ὁλκὴ Π |,
Φαττίου χεὶρ ὁλκὴ ΗΗΗ,

'From Melas a face, weight 29 drachmas (c. 125 grammes), from Boiskos a face, weight 9 dr., from Philia a breast, weight 9 dr., from Arsinos a genital organ, weight 6 dr., from Kallimache a small snake, weight 5 dr., from Hippon a genital organ, weight 4 dr., from Euphrosyne a breast, weight 6 dr., from Phattios a hand, weight 4 dr.'.

Anatomical votive offerings were spread over a large area both in time and in space. In Antiquity they appeared not only in the Greek world but also in Italy, and they can be found in numerous other places in more recent times.[181] The repertoire of the parts of the body thus dedicated varies according to the cultural sphere. Among the ancient Greek specimens, for example, we only exceptionally find internal organs while in Italy a great many have come to light and some are found in modern Greece. In modern Greece, on the other hand, we hardly ever come across the genitals, which are so frequent amongst the ancient votive offerings.[182]

In connection with category 2f, and anatomical votives in particular, I propose to make a few observations concerning particular representations on confession stelai from Lydia and Phrygia.[46] At their most complete the inscriptions on these stelai display the following pattern. Someone was stricken by illness or by an accident. This was regarded as divine punishment for an offence committed, and, after establishing, sometimes with considerable difficulty, what his offence was, the culprit confessed his guilt, gave satisfaction and, if he was lucky, recovered. He raised a stele with his history and praised the deity and his miraculous power (areté, dýnamis).

---

[180] Appendix, A 16.3.

[181] Appendix, C.

[182] See Appendix. Some exceptional modern votive genitals: R. Kriss & H. Kriss-Heinrich, *Rheinisches Jahrbuch für Volkskunde* 12 (1961) 152 Nos. 78-79, Abb. 20, Cyprus; R. Kriss, *Zeitschrift für Volkskunde* N.F. 2 (1930) 262 f., Italy.

In a number of cases these stelai are provided with reliefs which, by way of the parts of the body depicted, refer to the illness with which the culprit is punished. The Lydian stele of *Fig. 45* is an example.[183] What has happened is briefly summarised in the inscription:

Διεὶ Σαβαζίῳ καὶ Μη-
τρεὶ Εἵπτᾳ Διοκλῆς
Τροφίμου· ἐπεὶ ἐπεί-
ασα περιστερὰς τῶν
θεῶν ἐκολάσθην ἰς
τοὺς ὀφθαλμοὺς καὶ
ἐνέγραψα τὴν ἀρετήν,

'To Zeus Sabazios and Meter Hipta, Diokles the son of Trophimos; since I caught doves of the gods I was punished in my eyes and I have recorded the *arete*'.

In the relief we see Diokles' stricken eyes, but at the same time, in a manner typical of certain confession stelai, the misdemeanour committed is referred to by the representation of the doves. A similar representation, of what, for the sake of convenience, I shall call the *corpus delicti*, is to be found on a confessional stele from Köleköy in N.-E. Lydia (*Fig. 46* 164/5 A.D.).[184] In the upper relief field there stands the god Men to whom the stele is dedicated. Left, on a lower level, we probably have the punished sinner who had stolen a cloak (χλαπέντος οὖν εἱματίου in line 4 of the inscription). And, left of Men, above the thief, we see the stolen cloak.

3. *Desired effect*

We have seen that the form and representation of the votive offerings often contain very precise references to the cause of the dedication. Since we frequently find a prayer for the future in the votive inscriptions it is worth investigating whether what was desired for the future was sometimes also expressed in the form or the representation. At first sight there are no references to the desired effect which are as specifically and directly recognisable as certain references to the causes. Yet we can indeed find some if we call a couple of texts to our assistance.

---

[183] Appendix, A 44.5.

[184] Herrmann, *Denkschr. Wien* 80 (1962) 30 ff., No. 21; Lane, *CMRDM* I 69. Two other representations of the corpus delicti: from Divlit/Sandal, Diakonoff, *BABesch* 54 (1979) 148 No. 20: trees, -- ἐπειδὴ κατὰ ἄγνοιαν ἐκ τοῦ ἄλσου(ς) ἔκοψα δένδρα θεῶν --; from the Kula region, Keil, *Anz. Wien* 1960, 3-7: the pot with stolen money (?), --χλαπέντος ἀργυρίου --.

In the last section we assumed that the votive gifts in the shape of parts of the body were dedicated in gratitude for cures received. In so far as the epigraphical data are explicit they do indeed point in this direction. In Aelius Aristides, however, who can certainly be regarded as an expert in this domain, we read that these votive offerings were presented in order to ask for the part of the body depicted to be cured.[185] Of course the one need not necessarily exclude the other. Let us suppose that the anatomical dedications not only could serve as thanks, but also as a prayer, for a cure. In the latter case the representation would refer to the desired effect: it would have been used to commend the infected part of the body to the attention of the healing deity. In the extension of this process we can equally well assume that, even when the votive offering was intended as thanks for a cure received, the placing of a representation of the part of the body cured in the temple also entrusted it to the lasting care and protection of the deity in the future.

We can even go a step further and suppose that in the many cases in which the dedicator himself was represented on the votive offering this was done with the intention of commending himself to the permanent attention of the god in times to come. This assumption would seem to find confirmation in an inscription which belonged to a votive image of a priestess of Aphrodite in Argos (3rd century B.C.):[186]

[K]ύπρι μάκαιρα, μέλου Τιμανθίδος, ἇς ὑπερ εὐχᾶι
εἰκόνα Τιμάνθης τάνδε καθιδρύεται,
ὥς τις καὶ μετέπειτα, θεά, τέμενος τόδε πρῶνος
νισόμενος μνάμαν τᾶσδ' ἔχηι ἀμφιπόλου,
'Blessed Kypris, look after Timanthis; with / on account of a prayer for her sake Timanthes sets up this image so that later too, oh goddess, when this sanctuary on the promontory is visited, a thought be given to this servant of yours'.

The image was to serve to perpetuate the memory of Timanthis amongst men—a familiar motive—but it also invoked the lasting protection of the goddess.

The offerers were not always solely concerned with themselves. Parents often asked for protection for their children. A badly damaged relief from

---

[185] Aelius Aristides VI 66-67 Dind., XLII 7 Keil, see text at the end of the Appendix. Cf. *IGBulg* III 1, 984: εἰς δέησιν.

[186] F. Croissant, *BCH* 96 (1972) 138 ff.; *BE* 1973, 181.

Athens representing a woman bringing a sacrifice to Herakles together with her children, bears the inscription (4th century B.C.):[187] Λυσιστράτη | ὑπὲρ τῶν παιδ[ίων] | Ἡρακλεῖ ἀνέθηκε. This can be taken to mean that the votive offering is supposed to redeem a vow made in a prayer for the children. At the same time, however, the relief and the inscription ensure that the children will continue to remain under the protection of Herakles.

In the magnificent votive relief of Aristonike, found in Brauron (*Fig. 47*, 2nd half of the 4th century B.C.),[188] we see four couples sacrificing an ox to Artemis Brauronia. On this solemn occasion the children are allowed to accompany their parents to the temple, and they will remain for ever in the sanctuary and under the observation and protection of the goddess immortalised in the marble of the relief.

The devout farmer also required divine protection for his cattle. We therefore come across various dedications ὑπὲρ τῶν κτήνων, ὑπὲρ τῶν τετραπόδων, ὑπὲρ τῶν βοῶν, etc.,[189] especially from Asia Minor. A round stele probably from the neighbourhood of Dorylaion (*Fig. 48*, imperial period: Διονύσιος | Γλαύκου | ὑπὲρ τῶν ὑπαρ|χόντων Δὶ ’Αν|πελίτη εὐχήν)[190] was dedicated by a certain Dionysios for the sake of his property. The relief demonstrates the purport of his prayer: he places his entire herd, eight full-grown oxen and two calves, under the protection of Zeus Ampelites (depicted as a bust), just as a Greek farmer of our own time assures himself of the protective presence of St Modestos amongst his own livestock (*Fig. 49*).[191] The believer wishfully depicts the god as he likes to imagine him, as the personal protector of himself and his belongings. One Nikephoros, who in the 2nd century B.C. dedicated a statuette of the Pergamenian Mother of the Gods, gave verbal expression to the same idea: in the inscription on the base he called her τὴν ἰδίαν προστάτιν—'his own guardian'.[192]

---

[187] Athens, Epigr. M. 8793: Svoronos pl. 218; Hausmann, *Kunst und Heiltum* 180 No. 164; *IG* II² 4613.

[188] Brauron 5: *Ergon* 1958, 35 fig. 37; Kontis, *AD* 22 (1967) 195, pl. 104 a.

[189] Robert, *Hellenica* X 34-36.

[190] *100 Jahre deutsche Ausgrabungen in Olympia, Ausstellung München* (1972) 144. For the shape of the relief compare F. Cumont, *Cat. Bruxelles* (1913) No. 53, G. Rodenwaldt, *JDAI* 34 (1919) 77 ff.; Robert, *Hellenica* X 94 ff., pl. XI 3. On Zeus Ampelites: Robert, *BE* 1974, 557 and *OpMin* IV 261-262. ὑπὲρ τῶν ὑπαρχόντων: Robert, *OpMin* II 1355-1356.

[191] Bought in Athens, September 1977.

[192] Vienna I 1113, h. 50 cm: R. Fleischer, *Artemis von Ephesos* (*EPRO* 33, 1973) 84f., pl. 58; R. Noll, *Gr. und lat. Inschr. Wiener Antikensamml.* (1962) No. 79.—Some other inscriptions expressing an intimate personal relationship with the gods: Πᾶσι φίλοις *IG* II² 4828; φίλε μοι

APPENDIX

Votive offerings representing parts of the human body (the Greek world)

Excavations have yielded a considerable number of ancient Greek votive replicas of human members, dedicated in gratitude for a cure (or, in other cases, to pray for a cure). Of many others which were destroyed, epigraphical records have survived. Unfortunately the material is not always easily accessible. Part of the finds were never published, and what dispersed publications there are, are often regrettably incomplete or inaccurate.

Among the votive offerings, which in general have not received overmuch attention from archaeologists (presumably on account of their often slight aesthetic merit), the particular class of anatomical ex votos has repeatedly been subjected to downright contempt. 'This custom (of dedicating models of the diseased part) shows how low the artistic taste of the Greeks had already fallen, but it is not without its moral interest', judged W. H. D. Rouse (*Greek votive offerings*, 1902, 210-211), whose verdict, by virtue of his special interest in the subject, may be considered to have been exceptionally lenient. Before trying to pass this off as a survival of a 19th century attitude, one should realize that half a century later 'alcune figurazioni della maternità, ottenute riproducendo la metà inferiore di un corpo femminile in stato di gravidanza' (from the Italic Temple in Paestum), provoked the exclamation: 'Ma quale differenza dalla delicata rappresentazione dell'Eileithyia (from Foce del Sele), pudica pur nella sua nudità, e idealizzata nella perfezione delle sue forme' (P. C. Sestieri, *Il nuovo museo di Paestum*, [2]1955, 18). That beauty was not the primary concern of the dedicators and manufacturers of these objects, seems to have been little understood.

Some of the published ex votos inscribed with a dedication lead a double life, so to speak: one in the archaeological literature, the other in the epigraphical publications, without cross references between the two.

Inasmuch as this class of votive offerings is not entirely without interest, it seemed useful to assemble the published material and collate the various publications in the following catalogue. I have left out no evidence that I know of. Yet I fear that the list is less exhaustive than one might wish. References have been selected on the principle that they should easily lead those interested to further literature.

A. *Catalogue*

Attika:

1. Athens, Asklepieion on the South slope of the Akropolis.
    J. Travlos, *Bildlexikon zur Topographie des antiken Athen* (1971) 127-137; R. Martin & H. Metzger, *La religion grecque* (1976) 81-84.

Πᾶν *IG* II² 4831; 'Αρτέμιδος Σωτείρας ἡμετέρας *ASAA* 41-42 (1963-64) 324 No. 24; τῇ ἐμαυτοῦ σωτείρῃ on a statuette of Hygieia *IG* IV² 1, 570; σεβασμομένη μου Μῆτερ (?) *ASAA* 6-7 (1923-24) 420 f., No. 120.

In addition to a number of marble reliefs (1.1-1.24), we have evidence of many gold and silver ex votos which have not survived, in the inscriptions 1.25-1.31.

1.1 (*Fig. 50*) Woman kneeling before Herakles (Menytes?); behind the woman, probably suspended against a wall, are:
a) head and upper part of a body, with arm stumps, female;
b) abdomen and both thighs, female;
c) two arms, about mid upper arm to hand;
d) two lower legs, knee to foot.
a-d might be put together to form one complete female body.
4th century B.C.
Athens, Akr.M. 7232: O. Walter, *Beschreibung der Reliefs im kleinen Akropolis-museum in Athen* (1923) No. 108; on the kneeling woman see *BABesch* 49 (1974) 168 No. 11.

1.2 Upper left corner of a votive relief. Of a seated Asklepios with Hygieia standing beside him, only the head, resp. head and upper part of the body, are preserved. In the background immediately to the right of the head of Hygieia and partly covered by it, is a large eye, probably intended as being fastened to the wall of Asklepios' temple.
Inscription on the epistyle: Λάκαινα ᾽Α[σκληπιῶι ---].
4th century B.C.
Athens, Epigr.M. 2777: Svoronos pl. 225, p. 670; W. Peek, *MDAI(A)* 67 (1942) 69.

1.3 Lower left corner of a votive relief, with part of one female worshipper (and traces of a second?) facing right; below a large eye is carved in very shallow relief.
Athens, N.M. 2544B: Svoronos pl. 158, p. 647.

1.4 Semicircular painted marble relief representing the upper half of a face: forehead, eyes and part of the nose. This relief was fitted into a cavity in a limestone pillar. Several other cavities in the pillar were found empty, but once also must have contained small votive reliefs.
Inscription on the pillar: ὑπὲρ τῆς γυναικὸς | εὐξάμενος | Πραξίας ᾽Ασκληπιῶι.
4th century B.C.
S. A. Koumanoudis, *᾽Αθήναιον* 5 (1876) 411-415, sketch of the pillar on p. 413; *IG* II² 4372.

1.5 Pair of ears (presumably, but not necessarily, from the Asklepieion).
4th century B.C. (?)
Cassel: M. Bieber, *MDAI(A)* 35 (1910) 1ff., 5ff., pl. I, 1; M. Bieber, *Die antiken Skulpturen und Bronzen ... in Cassel* (1915) 37 No. 76, pl. 33.

1.6 Dorsal view of male body (broken off above and below; preserved from little above the waist to the left knee).
Inscription: Λύκος | [᾽Α]σκλη|[πι]ῶ εὐ|[χὴν ἀ]νέ|[θηκεν].
2nd century A.D.
Athens, Epigr.M.: Svoronos pl. 232, III, 132p, p. 672; *IG* II² 4518.

1.7   Dorsal view of male body.
Inscription: Εὐτυχίδ[ης 'Ασκληπιῷ] | καὶ Ὑγείᾳ : εὐ[χήν].
1st-2nd century A.D.
IG II² 4503.

1.8   Pair of female breasts.
Inscription: Φίλη 'Ασκληπιῶ[ι].
4th century B.C.
Athens, Epigr.M.: Svoronos pl. 232, II, 1482, p. 673; *IG* II² 4407.

1.9   Female breast.
Inscription: Ἡρὼ Ἀ[σ]|κληπ[ιῷ] | εὐχή[ν].
1st-2nd century A.D.
Athens, Epigr.M. 8418: Svoronos pl. 232, III, 132k, p. 673; *IG* II² 4504; *AD* 27 (1972) B', 11, pl. 15 a.

1.10   Female breast.
Inscription written from right to left on the breast itself: Ἑκάλης | ἀνάθεμα.
Probably 2nd century A.D.
Athens, Epigr.M. 3513: Svoronos pl. 232, p. 673; *IG* II² 4522.
The direction of writing is curious, considering the late date of the inscription. Koumanoudis, 'Ἀθήναιον 6 (1877) 281 No. 13, suggested that it might be due to an archaistic tendency, which may point to a Hadrianic date.

1.11   Frontal view of male abdomen, from below the navel to mid thigh.
Athens, Akr.M. 3687: Walter, *Beschreibung* No. 239.

1.12   Frontal view of male abdomen and right leg (broken off above the knee).
Athens, Akr.M. 3689: Walter, *Beschreibung* No. 240: 'Rechts und oben ist der Reliefgrund ganz roh bearbeitet, während er sonst wie das Relief schön geglättet ist; vielleicht hat man aus einem Relief mit einer nackten Jünglingsfigur eine derartige Votivgabe mit Darstellung erkrankter Gliedmassen angefertigt'.

1.13   Lateral view of male abdomen and right leg (broken off at mid thigh), facing right.
Athens, Akr.M. 3688: Walter, *Beschreibung* No. 241.

1.14   Vulva.
Athens, Akr.M. 3690: Walter, *Beschreibung* No. 243.

1.15   Frontal view of a pair of legs, thigh to foot, with the lower border of a short chiton above.
Athens, Akr. M. 4748: Walter, *Beschreibung* No. 242.
The exact provenance of 1.11-1.15 is not known. They must have been found on or near the Akropolis, and the Asklepieion would seem to be the most likely place in view of their nature. 1.11-1.14, however, may come from the sanctuary of Eros and Aphrodite on the North slope of the Akropolis, see below 4.1-6.

1.16   Frontal view of a pair of female thighs (top broken off).
Inscription: Ἀσκληπιῷ καὶ Ὑγείᾳ | Ζωσίμη εὐχήν.
2nd century A.D.
Athens, Epigr.M. 8414: Svoronos pl. 233, III, 132g, p. 673; *IG* II² 4517.

1.17   Lateral view of a leg, facing right (top broken off above knee).
Inscription: Με|νέσ|τρατ|ος εὐ|χὴν ἀ|ν[έθη]|χ[εν] | Δ[--].
Athens, Epigr.M. 8768: Svoronos pl. 232, II, 1503, p. 673;
IG II² 4706: 1st century B.C.; Kirchner, *Prosographia Attica* No. 9995 b: 3rd century B.C. (?)
The restoration Δ[ιί] in line 8 of the inscription, printed in *IG* II², seems rather arbitrary.

1.18   Lateral view of a leg, facing left (foot broken off above ankle).
Inscription: Σωσίβιος | Ἀσκληπιῷ καὶ | Ὑγείᾳ εὐχήν.
Athens, N.M. 2571: Svoronos pl. 164, p. 649; *IG* II² 4500.

1.19   Lateral view of a leg, facing right, from above knee downwards (broken off above ankle).
Inscription: [Ἀσκληπ]ιῷ Σωτῆρι καὶ Ὑγείᾳ | ε[ὐ]χὴν Τερτιανὸς ὑπὲρ τοῦ | υἱοῦ Κορνούτου.
Roman period.
Athens, Epigr.M. 8413: Svoronos pl. 233, III, 132h, p. 673; *IG* II² 4501.

1.20   Male leg.
Inscription: Εὐκαρπᾶς | εὐχήν.
1st-2nd century A.D.
IG II² 4506.

1.21   Lateral view of a leg, facing right (top broken off below the knee).
Athens, N.M. 2442: Svoronos pl. 157, p. 647.

1.22   Right foot.
Inscription: ......μος | Ἀσκληπιῶι | [ὑπ]ὲρ τοῦ παιδ|[ίο]υ εὐξάμεν|[ος] ἀν[έθηκεν].
4th-3rd century B.C.
Apparently lost: *IG* II² 4429.

1.23   Lateral view of a left foot with the lower part of the leg, facing right.
Inscription: [Τι]β. Ἀφροδεί|[σιο]ς Ἀσκληπι|[ῷ] καὶ Ὑγείᾳ|[εὐ]χὴν ἀνέ|[θ]ηκε.
1st-2nd century A.D.
Athens, Epigr.M. 8415: Svoronos pl. 232, III, 132, p. 673; *IG* II² 4502.

1.24   Pair of feet on a base.
Inscription: Φλ. Ἐπίκτητος | Ἀσκληπιῶι | καὶ Ὑγείᾳ | εὐχήν.
1st century A.D.
Athens, Epigr.M. 8419: Svoronos pl. 233, III, 132i, p. 673; *IG* II² 4488.

1.25-1.31   The inscriptions *IG* II² 1532-1537 and 1539 contain lists of votive offerings, mainly of gold and silver, which were dedicated in the Athenian

Asklepieion from shortly after the middle of the 4th century B.C. till the end of the 3rd century B.C. Among these, *týpoi* representing parts of the human body abound. I will first give the frequency of occurrence of each part. Since large portions of the inscriptions are missing, these numbers have no absolute value, but they may give an indication of the relative frequency of the various types of dedication. The count was based on the texts as they are printed in *IG* II². So some of the pairs of eyes (ὀφθαλμοί), where the ending of the word is restored, may in fact have been single eyes (ὀφθαλμός), but for the general picture that is of no consequence. On some of the problems raised by the entries here relevant a few brief notes will be added. They will in no way detract from the desirability of a comprehensive and penetrating study on these interesting texts.

a) body, σῶμα, σωμάτιον — 65 (19 male, 29 female, 17 not specified)
half body, σώματος ἥμυσυ — 1
dorsal view (or hinder part?) of body [σωμάτ]ιον ὀπίσθ[ιον], σῶμα ὀπ[ίσθιον] — 2
b) head, κεφαλή, κεφάλιον — 4
c) face, πρόσωπον — 17
face without ears, πρόσωπον ἄωτον — 1
lower part of face, προσώπου τὸ κάτω — 1
half face, προσώπο ἥμυσυ — 1
d) eye(s), ὀφθαλμός (-οί) — 154 (13 single, 141 pairs)
e) nose, ῥίς — 1
f) jaw, σιαγών — 2
g) mouth, στόμα — 8
h) teeth, ὀδόντες — 1
i) ear(s), οὖς (ὦτα), ὠτάριον (-α) — 25 (13 single, 11 pairs, 1 set of four?)
part of ear?, μήκων — 1
j) neck, τράχηλος — 1
k) chest, στῆθος — 2 (1 female, 1 uncertain)
l) female breast(s), τίτθη, τιτθός (-οί), τιτθίον (-α) — 13 (10 single, 3 pairs)
m) abdomen, ἦτρον — 1
n) pubic region, ἥβη — 3 (1 male, 2 female)
o) genitals, αἰδοῖον — 15 (10 male, 5 not specified)
p) heart, καρδία — 5
q) bladder, [κ]ύστις — 1
r) arm(s)/hand(s), χείρ (χεῖρες), χειρίδιον (-α) — 23 (18 single, 5 pairs)
[? ἀπ]ὸ τοῦ ὤμου — 1
s) finger(s), or possibly toe(s), δάκτυλος (-οι) — 3 (2 single, 1 set)
t) leg(s), σκέλος (-η) — 41 (34 single, 7 pairs)
u) hips, ἰσχία — 2 pairs
v) knee, γόνυ — 3
w) lower leg, κνήμη — 1
x) feet, πόδες — 2 pairs

a. In what way differed *týpoi* depicting a male or female σῶμα from others which are said to represent a man or a woman (ἄνδρα, γυναῖκα) or a worshipper (προσευχόμενον, προσευχομένην)? I suppose that the use of the word σῶμα indicates that the figure was represented nude, but one may also consider the possibility that in the present context σῶμα may perhaps stand for the human trunk without the extremities (cf. Corinth 15.19).

a and *c.* The half body and half face (σώματος ἥμυσυ 1534, 278; προσώπο ἥμυσυ 1534, 250) probably were lateral halves, since for the upper or lower half one would expect τὸ ἄνω or τὸ κάτω (προσώπου τὸ κάτω 1534, 239). The half body then may have looked somewhat like Corinth 15.18, or like Early and Middle Minoan votive terracotta figures from Crete (e.g. from Petsofá: *ABSA* 9, 1902-03, pl. XII 35). The half face recalls the terracotta half heads found in considerable quantities in ancient Italic sanctuaries (cf. references in this Appendix sub C). The half head illustrated in E. Holländer, *Plastik und Medizin* (1912) 182 fig. 96, and said to come from the Tegea region, when looked at does not seem to be beyond suspicion.

e. A nose is mentioned only once, combined with eyes (ὀφθαλμοὶ καὶ ῥίς 1534, 120). Presumably they were represented together on one *týpos*, as in 13.1 and 22.1-5. Separate votive noses do not seem to have been found. 'Da krankheiten der Nase doch so häufig sind, so ist es mir auffallend, das ich gar keine einzelne Nase gesehen habe; es wäre doch wünschenswerth, wenn man in den Museen sich nach Nasen umschauen wollte' (L. Stieda, *MDAI(R)* 14, 1899, 236). For modern Greek *támata* of noses see R. Kriss & H. Kriss-Heinrich, *Peregrinatio Neohellenika* (1954) 171 fig. 116: Istanbul, and the same authors in *Rheinisches Jahrbuch für Volkskunde* 12 (1961) 152 No. 77, Abb. 20, 10: Cyprus. A wax nose and mouth mounted on a plaque were recently acquired in Euboea by H. S. Versnel.

f. For the jaw or jaw-bone (σιαγών 1534, 53 and 70) again no actual parallels seem to have survived from ancient Greece. In the archaeological Museum of Madrid there is a terracotta lower jaw from Cales, Campania (J. M. Blazquez, *Archivo Esp. de Arqu.* 36, 1963, 38 No. XX, fig. 24). A unique ex voto which looks like its complement, a head modelled without the lower jaw, was found at Carsòli, N.E. of Rome (A. Cederna, *NSA* 1951, 218 No. 20, fig. 21).

g-h. Of ancient Greek votive offerings of a mouth (στόμα, eight examples in 1534) or a set of teeth (ὀδόντες 1534, 55) no surviving examples are known. Representations of the labial region do occur among ancient Italic ex votos, see L. Sambon, *British Medical Journal* 1895 II, 148, and L. Stieda, *Anatomische Hefte*, 1. Abteilung, Bd. 16, Hft. 50 (1901) 23. There is a single votive molar from Carnuntum (R. Töply, *JÖAI* 15, 1912, Bbl. 155 fig. 125), and there are modern Greek *támata* representing a mouth with parted lips, showing a lot of teeth in a rigid grin (Kriss & Kriss-Heinrich, *Peregrinatio Neohellenika* 170 fig. 115: Istanbul), and a set of teeth not unlike a denture (Kriss & Kriss-Heinrich, *Rheinisches Jahrbuch für Volkskunde* 12, 1961, 152 No. 75, Abb. 20,8: Cyprus).

i. The μήκων (1534, 234) might be just a poppy, but the word was also used as an anatomical term indicating the part of the ear at the root under the lobe (Pollux 2, 86), and that may well be intended in the present context.

j. For the neck (τράχηλος 1534, 92) no ancient parallels are known. A modern Italian wax ex voto in the form of a neck is illustrated by R. Kriss, *Zeitschrift für Volkskunde* 40 (1930, published 1931) 262, fig. 2. In Naples metal repoussé reliefs of a neck, including mouth and chin, are still on sale (*Fig. 57*).

m-n. In what way exactly the representations of ἦτρον (1534, 51) and ἥβη (1534, 225, 235 and 295) differed is difficult to establish. Perhaps ἦτρον is the entire abdomen, from navel to thighs (cf. Hippokrates, *Aph.* 2, 35; Timaeus, *Lexic. Plat.* s.v.) as in 1.1b, 8.13 and 30.8 (*Fig. 61*), and ἥβη only the area close to the genitals (cf. Hippokrates, *Epid.* 3, 4; Aristoph., *Nub.* 975-6), as in 1.11.

p-q. Heart (καρδία 1533, 16; 1534, 82, 230, 248 and 263) and bladder ([x]ύστις 1533, 84) are the only internal organs mentioned in the inscriptions from the Athenian Asklepieion. Ancient Greek votive offerings depicting internal organs are extremely rare, and as far as I know heart and bladder do not occur among the surviving examples. For ancient Italic terracotta votive hearts, see L. Sambon, *British Medical Journal* 1895 II, 148 fig. 6; F. Regnault, *Bul. Soc. Fr. Hist. Med.* 20 (1926) 142f., fig. 5; E. Greco, *Minerva Medica* vol. 51, No. 102 (1960) fig. 8.

In Italic ex votos showing the thoracic and abdominal viscera more or less in situ, either as if seen through an opening in the front of a human trunk, or mounted on a plaque, heart and bladder are often indicated (F. Regnault, *ibid.* 135-150 with references to older literature; illustrations in M. Tabanelli, *Gli ex-voto poliviscerali Etruschi e Romani*, 1962). A surprisingly accurate description of the heart, roughly contemporary with the dedications in the Athenian Asklepieion, which shows close observation, is to be found in the Hippocratic treatise Περὶ καρδίης (text: F. C. Unger, *Mnemosyne* 52, 1923, 50-57; translation by I. M. Lonie in G. E. R. Lloyd ed., *Hippocratic writings*, Pelican Books, 1978, 347-351). The votive bladder may have to do with the same sort of complaint as the catheters mentioned among the dedications to Asklepios (1534, 40 and 171, unless καθετήρ here means 'necklace' as Köhler argued in his edition of this inscription in *IG* II 835).

So far only the various parts of the body by themselves have been considered. Although generally the entries in the inscriptions are of the utmost brevity, occasionally some additional information may be gathered from the context. Sometimes the writers have expanded a little on the execution of the votive replicas and on the way they were displayed in the temple. Thus a small face was set in a miniature shrine or naiskos (πρόσωπον μικρὸν ἐν χαλιάδι 1533, 4-5, cf. 1533, 75). The gold and silver repoussé reliefs were often fastened to a small wooden (?) panel or tablet (τύπος ἔγμαχτος or κατάμαχτος πρὸς πινακίωι or ἐμ πινακίωι, e.g. 1534, 63, 64, 65, 67, etc.); in some of the surviving *týpoi*, from Mesembria (*PAAH* 1973, pl. 96a) and Kos 30.6, the nail-holes are still visible. Twice a *týpos* was set in a rectangular wooden box or frame (τύπος ἐμ πλαισίωι 1534, 75 and 76; on *plaision* see T. Linders, *Studies in the treasure records of Artemis Brauronia found in Athens*, 1972, 10).

Very frequently a single entry of a dedication by one person comprises more than one part of the body, though never such a complete series as in the marble relief 1.1. In general we are not explicitly informed whether these parts were co-ordinated in an organic unity, as may be supposed when they are contiguous (e.g. ὀφθαλμοὶ καὶ ῥίς 1534, 120), or represented separately, as is anyhow obvious in most cases (some examples from 1534: ὦτα δύο καὶ ὀδόντες 55; σκέλη δύο καὶ χείρ 60; ὦτα χρυσᾶ καὶ τράχηλον ἀ[ργυροῦν] 92; ὀφθαλμοὶ καὶ ἀ[ιδοῖ]ον 108; ὀφθαλμοὶ ἀργυροῖ δύο καὶ ὦτα ἐκ τοῦ αὐτοῦ 117; σκέλη δύο· στόμα 195; ὀφθαλμοί· σκέλος 217; οὖς καὶ σκέλος 310; etc.). Quite often also a replica of the diseased part is dedicated together with a complete representation of the dedicator (again some examples from 1534: τύποι: Δ: ἀνδρὸς καὶ γυναικὸς καὶ ὀφθαλμοὶ ἕτεροι χρυσοῖ 74; τύπος ἀνδρὸς καὶ γυναικὸς καὶ πρόσωπον 77; τύπος γυναικὸς καὶ ὀφ[θαλμοί or -ός] 77; τύπος, ἔνι προσευχόμενος καὶ στόμα 79; σῶμα γυναικὸς ἐν τύπωι καὶ ἰσχία 81; σῶμα καὶ τιτθός 262). A striking modern parallel to this practice of dedicating the part together with the whole was observed by R. Kriss in the church of the Madonna di Rimedio near Oristano, Sardinia (Österreichische Zeitschrift für Volkskunde 60, 1957, 101, Abb. 4). On a votive photograph glued onto a piece of cardboard a soldier is portrayed in his Sunday best, standing before a back-drop which shows Saint Peter in Rome. A life-size wooden model of an ear is fastened with a ribbon to a corner of the photograph. When man, either ancient or modern, thanks his god for a cure by offering a replica of the part which had been afflicted, he may be overcome by an acute awareness of the vulnerability of his mortal body, perhaps even heightened at the sight of numerous similar dedications in the sanctuary. It would not seem such a bad idea, then, to commend ones entire body to the benevolent attention of the god.

Somewhat intriguing are certain entries in the Asklepieion inscriptions which mention the dedication of more than one replica of the same part of the body by one person. Here the conciseness of the texts is at times frustrating. Various possible explanations may be contemplated. The four ears dedicated by Boidas (ὦτα: | | | | : ἃ ἀνέθηκε Βοΐδας 1534, 108), are they four separate ears, two pairs, or four ears represented together on one *týpos*, like the five pairs of eyes from Mesembria, below No. 22.11? And were they offered by Boidas on behalf of himself and another member of his family, or are they successive dedications for one person's ears? The latter possibility has a certain attraction in two cases where a gold and a silver *týpos*, each with two eyes, were offered by the same dedicator (τύποι δύο, ἔνι ὀφθαλμοί, χρυσοῦς καὶ ἀργυροῦς, καὶ ὀφίδιον χρυσοῦν : ἃ ἀνέθη : Ἡδύτιον 1534, 83; Ἀριστονίκη ὀφθαλμοὺς χρυσοῦς καὶ ἀργυροῦς 1534, 91). Did they offer the silver ones as a prayer for the eyes to be cured, and, when there was no improvement, resort to a stronger prayer with a gold *týpos*? Or—a more pleasant alternative—did they dedicate the silver ones as a prayer, and at the same time promise to offer gold ones when their prayer would be granted and the cure effected?

And what to think about the *týpos* with three bodies, of a certain Thallos (τύπος τρία σώματα ἔχων Θάλλο 1534, 244), or Mammia's body and two hearts (σῶμα καὶ καρδίαι δύο, Μαμμία 1534, 248)? Perhaps they are best understood as having been offered for the sake of (ὑπέρ) another person or persons as well. In some slightly more detailed entries this fact is explicitly mentioned, e.g. ὑπὲρ αὑτῆς καὶ τῶν παιδίων (1535, 70). Dedications ὑπέρ someone, especially a child, are not uncommon (e.g. αἰδοῖον, ἡ μήτηρ ὑπὲρ Φιλονίκου 1534, 286; χεὶρ χρυσῆ καὶ ἀργυρ[ᾶ] καὶ χ[αλκῆ] καὶ λιθίνη, ἣν ἀνέθηκε Φιλίππη ὑ[πὲρ ---] 1534, 71). We catch a glimpse of a serious case where both the mother and the grandmother added their votive *týpoi* to the child's one (τύπος Ἀρχεστράτο ⊦⊦, ἕτερον τυπίον ἡ τήθη ⊦⊦⊦, ἕτερον ἡ μήτηρ ||||: 1534, 229).

1.32 *IG* II² 4511 is a fragment of a list of dedications to Asklepios.

Among the dedicators is C. Iulius Antiochos Epiphanes Philopappos, who is known to have died c. 114-116 A.D. Thereby the date of the inscription is approximately fixed.

The following parts of the body are mentioned:

a) eyes, ὀφθαλμοί 2 pairs
b) ears, ὦτα 1 pair
c) breast, μασθός 2 single
d) genitals, αἰδοῖον 1
e) legs, σκέλη 1 pair
f) thigh, μηρός 1

2. Athens, sanctuary of Amynos West of the Akropolis.

A. Körte, 'Bezirk eines Heilgottes', *MDAI(A)* 18 (1893) 231-256; idem, *MDAI(A)* 21 (1896) 287-332; Travlos, *Bildlexikon* 76-78.

2.1-2.5 Marble reliefs.

2.1 (*Fig. 52*) A bearded man, facing left, is holding in both hands a colossal left leg with a thick varicose vein rendered in relief; the man is evidently placing his votive offering in the shrine. On the left, in a recessed panel, a pair of votive feet are represented, intended either as a general indication of the surroundings, or as an earlier dedication by the same man (cf. above, the comments on 1.25-1.31, at the end).

Inscription above the relief: [--- | --]οιων τευξα[-- | --]ων σεμνοτάτην [-- | Λυσιμαχί]δης Λυσιμάχου Ἀχαρνε[ύς].

Second half of 4th century B.C.

Athens, N.M. 3526: Svoronos pl. 237, p. 673 (not correct); Körte, *MDAI(A)* 18 (1893) 231, pl. XI; H. K. Süsserott, *Griechische Plastik des 4. Jhs v. Chr.* (1938) 28 nt. 5, 209; U. Hausmann, *Kunst und Heiltum* (1948) 45, 181 No. 171; Travlos, *Bildlexikon* 78 fig. 100; *IG* II² 4387. On the dedicator, who may be the eponymous archon of 339/8 B.C., see J. K. Davies, *Athenian propertied families 600-300 B.C.* (1971) 357 No. 9480.

2.2 Pair of ears.

Athens, N.M.: Svoronos pl. 238, 3; Körte, *MDAI(A)* 18 (1893) 242 No. 8, fig. 5; Travlos, *Bildlexikon* 78 fig. 101.

2.3 Female breast. Under the breast, in the plaque on which it is mounted, a nail-hole with the nail still in it.

Inscription: ῾Ηδεία ᾽Ασ|κληπι|ῶι.
4th century B.C.
Athens, N.M.: Körte, *MDAI(A)* 18 (1893) 241 No. 6, fig. 3; Travlos, *Bildlexikon* 78 fig. 101; *IG* II² 4422.

2.4   Male genitals on a plaque. Nail hole under the scrotum.
Athens, N.M.: Körte, *MDAI(A)* 18 (1893) 242 No. 7, fig. 4; Travlos, *Bildlexikon* 78 fig. 101.

2.5   Lateral view of a left leg and lower part of female body from the waist down, facing left.
Inscription: [Κλε?]ωνὶς Α[--- | ᾽Αμύ]νωι.
4th-3rd century B.C.
Athens, N.M.: Svoronos pl. 238, 1, p. 681 (incorrectly described as male); Körte, *MDAI(A)* 21 (1896) 291 No. 6; N. Yalouris, *AD* 29 (1973-74) B' 2 No. 8b, pl. 7a; *IG* II² 4435.

2.6-2.7   Two fingers.
Körte, *MDAI(A)* 18 (1893) 242-3 Nos. 11-12.

3.   Athens, sanctuary of the Heros Iatros.
Travlos, *Bildlexikon* 573; R. E. Wycherley, *Literary and epigraphical testimonia (The Ath. Agora* III, 1957) Nos. 340, 347, 498; H. A. Thompson & R. E. Wycherley, *The Agora of Athens (The Ath. Agora* XIV, 1972) 121 nt. 20, 125.
The site of this shrine, which apparently was close to the elusive Theseion, remains uncertain. Two substantial inscriptions with regulations concerning the melting down of dedications to the Heros Iatros were found on ᾽Αθηνᾶς street, at the intersection with Βύσσης and Βορέου. Remains of a building discovered there in 1937 may belong to his shrine. The votive eye 3.1 was found in the Athenian Agora excavations, but considering its small size it is not inconceivable that it has travelled some distance.

3.1   Left part of a marble relief depicting a right eye (the corresponding left eye was probably represented in the lost part).
Inscription: [ἥ]ρωι ᾽Ια[τρῶι ---].
3rd-2nd century B.C.
Athens Agora M. I 5968: B. D. Meritt, *Hesperia* 17 (1948) 39 No. 26, pl. 12.

3.2   One of the inscriptions referred to above (*IG* II² 839), with the text of a decree, dated at 221/0 B.C., regulating the melting down of silver and gold votives. Among the *týpoi*, a list of which is appended to the decree, the following parts of the body occur:

a) eyes, ὀφθαλμοί   3 pairs
b) chest, στῆθος   1 (male)
c) hand/arm, χείρ   1
d) thighs, μηροί   2 pairs

4.   Athens, sanctuary (sanctuaries?) of Aphrodite on the North (and South?) slope of the Akropolis.

Nos. 4.2-4.4, and probably 4.1, come from the sanctuary of Eros and Aphrodite on the North slope of the Akropolis: O. Broneer, *Hesperia* 1 (1932) 31-55; 2 (1933) 329-349; 4 (1935) 123-132; Travlos, *Bildlexikon* 228-232. It may seem tempting to ascribe No. 4.5, though it was reportedly found on the South slope, to the same sanctuary. On the other hand, there is some evidence that Aphrodite was worshipped on the South slope as well, cf. L. Beschi, *ASAA* 45-46 (1967-68) 418 and 420.

4.1 [A face, πρόσωπον]. The object itself is not preserved, but the votive inscription belonging to it survives. This inscription was discovered in the Athenian Agora, but there is a fair chance that it originates from the sanctuary on the North slope of the Akropolis.

['A]θηναγόρα | 'Αφροδίτει | τὸ πρόσωπ ⟨ο⟩ ν | [ἀ]νέθηκεν.
4th century B.C.
Athens, Agora M. I 2526: Meritt, *Hesperia* 10 (1941) 60 No. 24.

4.2 Vulva. Marble relief (only the lower left corner remains).
Athens, Agora M.: Broneer, *Hesperia* 4 (1935) 140f. No. 14, fig. 31.

4.3 Male genitals, on a plaque. Marble.
Athens, Agora M.: Broneer, *Hesperia* 4 (1935) 140 No. 13, fig. 30.

4.4 Male genitals, erect penis. Marble.
Athens, Agora M.: Broneer, *Hesperia* 2 (1933) 346.

Normally in votive offerings depicting the male genitals the penis is flacid, whereas erect phalloi regularly occur in apotropaic representations (e.g. Ph. Bruneau, *Recherches sur les cultes de Délos*, 1970, 642f.; J. Marcadé in *Études Déliennes*, *BCH Sup.* I, 1973, 329-334). However, a votive phallos does not seem to be out of place in a sanctuary of Eros and Aphrodite.

Broneer, *Hesperia* 4 (1935) 141 nt. 2, suggests that a large marble phallos in the annex of the Akropolis Museum may come from this sanctuary too.

See also above 1.11-1.14.

4.5 Pair of female breasts. Marble relief (the left half of the relief, with the right breast, is broken off).
Inscription: [---]N | ['Αφρο]δίτῃ | [.......]ΝΠΩΚΟΙΣ.
1st century A.D.
Athens, Epigr.M. 8420: Svoronos pl. 232, III, 130a, p. 673; *IG* II² 4729.

In line 3 of the inscription Svoronos (Philadelpheus) reads [---]νι τόκοις, implying a connection with child-birth which would be quite appropriate in this votive offering. Unfortunately the photograph favours the unintelligible reading of *IG* II² given above.

(4.6) A fragment of the comic poet Platon quoted by Athenaeus (X 441 e-f; cf. Broneer, *Hesperia* 4, 1935, 128), appears to allude to a practice of offering to Aphrodite cakes that were similar in shape to the marble votives: '(Aphrodite speaking) πρῶτα μὲν ἐμοὶ γὰρ κουροτρόφῳ προθύεται πλακοῦς ἐνόρχης (a cake with testicles in), ἄμυλος ἐγκύμων (a cake of fine flour pregnant)'. It is not clear whether Platon had any particular sanctuary in mind.

116   F. T. VAN STRATEN

5.   Athens, sanctuary of (Artemis) Kalliste and Ariste, on the road from the Dipylon to the Academy.
    A. Philadelpheus, 'Le sanctuaire d'Artémis Kallistè', *BCH* 51 (1927) 155-163; P. Roussel, *ibid.* 164-169; Travlos, *Bildlexikon* 301-302, 322.

5.1   Pair of female breasts. Marble relief.
    Inscription: ['Ιπ]ποστράτη | [Κα]λλίστει.
    3rd century B.C.
    Athens, N.M.: Philadelpheus, *BCH* 51 (1927) 159 No. 3, fig. 3; *IG* II² 4667; Travlos, *Bildlexikon* 322 fig. 424.

5.2-5.3   Vulvae. Marble reliefs.
    Athens, N.M.: Philadelpheus, *BCH* 51 (1927) 160 Nos. 5-6, fig. 4; Travlos, *Bildlexikon* 322 fig. 424.

6.   Athens, sanctuary of Artemis Kolainis.
    Apart from her well known sanctuary in the Attic deme of Myrrhinous (Pausanias I, 31, 4; Schol. Aristoph. *Av.* 873; *IG* II² 4746 and 4817), Artemis Kolainis must have had a shrine in Athens itself, where some dedications to her were found (votive altar Athens, Epigr.M. 138: Svoronos pl. 229, 1; *IG* II² 4731; also *IG* II² 4791). The location of the Athenian shrine is not known.

6.1   Female breast. Marble relief.
    Inscription: Καλλιστράτη | 'Αρτέμιδι Κολε|νίδι ἐπηκόῳ | εὐχήν.
    Roman imperial age.
    Athens, 'in domo privata': *IG* II² 4860.

7.   Athens, sanctuary of (Herakles) Pankrates and Palaimon on the Ilissos.
    I. Miliadis, *PAAH* 1953, 47-60; 1954, 41-49; Travlos, *Bildlexikon* 278-280. Cf. *BABesch* 49 (1974) 170-172.

7.1   Left leg, thigh to foot, facing right. Marble relief.
    Inscription: Πανκράτε[ι] | εὐχὴν Κλήσι[π]|πος (?).
    Roman period.
    Athens, 1st Ephoria: Travlos, *Bildlexikon* 279 fig. 357; *SEG* 16, 183; Robert, *BE* 1959, 124.

7.2   Arm. Marble relief.
    Athens, 1st Ephoria: Miliadis, *PAAH* 1953, 54.

8.   Athens, sanctuary of Zeus Hypsistos on the Pnyx.
    K. Kourouniotes & H. A. Thompson, The sanctuary of Zeus Hypsistos, *Hesperia* 1 (1932) 193-200; Travlos, *Bildlexikon* 569-572.
    The most conspicuous feature of the sanctuary are some 58 rectangular niches in the face of the scarp East of the *bema*, intended for votive offerings. The reliefs in London (8.1-3, 8.5-7, 8.14, 8.16-17, 8.19) were all found directly in front of these. Nos. 8.10-8.12 also have come to light on the Pnyx. The other ones were found elsewhere in Athens, but may be confidently assumed to have come from the same sanctuary.

All marble votive tablets (8.1-8.20) are of Roman imperial date, but the sanctuary itself must have been older (Travlos). The word θεραπευθεῖσα in the votive inscription *Hesperia* 5 (1936) 156 fig. 6, and the nature of the votive reliefs, make it clear that Zeus Hypsistos was here worshipped, mainly—if not exclusively—by women, as a healing god.

8.1 Face, from the eyebrows downwards.
Inscription: Τερτία Ὑψίστῳ | εὐχήν.
2nd-3rd century A.D.
London, B. M. 805: A. H. Smith, *A catalogue of sculpture ... British Museum* I (1892) No. 805; *Mus. Marbles* IX pl. 41, fig. 7; *Br. Mus. Inscr.* I, 131 No. 63; *IG* II² 4801; Travlos, *Bildlexikon* 571 fig. 716 f.

8.2 Pair of eyes.
Inscription: Φιληματιν | [ε]ὐχὴν ἀνέ||[θ]ηκεν.
2nd-3rd century A.D.
London, B. M. 801: Smith, *Cat.sc.* I No. 801; *Mus. Marbles.* IX pl. 41, fig. 5; *Br. Mus. Inscr.* I, 132 No. 68; *IG* II² 4805; Travlos, *Bildlexikon* 571 fig. 716 c. 'In the left eye is a horizontal incision as if to indicate that a surgical operation had been performed' (*Br. Mus. Inscr.*). Or is it accidental damage?

8.3 Pair of eyes (only the left eye remains).
Inscription: [--- Ὑψ]ίστῳ [εὐχήν].
2nd-3rd century A.D.
London, B.M. 802: Smith, *Cat.sc.* I No. 802; *Br. Mus. Inscr.* I, 133 No. 69; *IG* II² 4799: probably the same inscription as *IG* III 149 Εὔοδος Ὑψίστῳ εὐχήν.

8.4 Pair of eyes with the bridge of the nose.
Inscription: Εἰσιδότη Διὶ Ὑ|ψίστῳ.
2nd-3rd century A.D.
Berlin, St. M.: *Beschreibung der antiken Skulpturen ... Berlin* (1891) No. 720; *IG* II² 4808; E. Holländer, *Plastik und Medizin* (1912) 217 fig. 128.

8.5 Female breast.
Inscription: Ὀνησίμη εὐχὴν|Διὶ Ὑψίστῳ.
2nd-3rd century A.D.
London, B.M. 807: Smith, *Cat.sc.* I No. 807; *Mus. Marbles* IX pl. 41, fig. 1; *Br. Mus. Inscr.* I, 131 No. 65; *IG* II² 4802; Travlos, *Bildlexikon* 571 fig. 716 b.

8.6 Female breast.
Inscription: Εἰσιὰς Ὑψ[ίστῳ] | εὐχ[ήν].
2nd-3rd century A.D.
London, B.M. 800: Smith, *Cat.sc.* I No. 800; *Mus. Marbles* IX pl. 41, fig. 2; *Br. Mus. Inscr.* I, 132 No. 67; *IG* II² 4804; Travlos, *Bildlexikon* 571 fig. 716 e.

8.7 Female breast.
Inscription: Εὐτυχὶς Ὑψίστῳ εὐ|χή⟨ν⟩.
2nd-3rd century A.D.
London, B.M. 799: Smith, *Cat.sc.* I No. 799; *Mus. Marbles* IX pl. 41, fig. 3; *Br. Mus. Inscr.* I, 132 No. 66; *IG* II² 4803; Travlos, Bildlexikon 571 fig. 716 h.

8.8   Female breast.
Inscription: Εὐτυχία | Ὑφείστῳ | εὐχήν.
2nd-3rd century A.D.
Berlin, St. M.: *Beschreibung* No. 718; *IG* II² 4809; Holländer, *Plastik und Medizin*
217 fig. 127.

8.9   Female breast.
Inscription: Εὔπραξις | εὐχήν.
2nd-3rd century A.D.
Berlin, St. M.: *Beschreibung* No. 719; *IG* II² 4810.

8.10   Pair of female breasts.
Inscription: Διονυσία Ὑφίστῳ | εὐχήν.
2nd century A.D.
Athens, Agora M.: Kourouniotes & Thompson, *Hesperia* 1 (1932) 196 fig. 59;
IG II² 4783; Travlos, *Bildlexikon* 572 fig. 717.

8.11   Female breast.
Inscription: Ὑφίστῳ Γαμιχὴ | εὐχήν.
Athens, Agora M.: Thompson, *Hesperia* 5 (1936) 154f., fig. 4 a.

8.12   Female breast (fragment, with traces of inscription).
Athens, Agora M.: Thompson, *Hesperia* 5 (1936) 154f., fig. 4 b.

8.13   Female abdomen and thighs, from a little above the navel to the knees.
At the upper end the abdomen is finished off with a flat elliptic surface, sug-
gesting a foreshortened view of a transverse section of the trunk.
Berlin, St. M.: *Beschreibung* No. 721; Holländer, *Plastik und Medizin* 217 fig. 126.

8.14   Vulva.
Inscription: Ὀλυμπιὰς Ὑφίστῳ | εὐχήν.
London, B.M. 804: Smith, *Cat.sc.* I No. 804; *Br. Mus. Inscr.* I, 131 No. 62;
IG II² 4800.

8.15   Vulva.
Inscription: [Δι]ὶ Ὑφίστῳ Δάφνις | [εὐ]χὴν ἀνέθηκε.
Roman imperial age.
Boston, M. F. A. 08.34 b: M. B. Comstock & C. C. Vermeule, *Sculpture in stone
... Boston* (1976) 146 No. 235.

8.16   Part of a shoulder or a thigh (?)
Inscription: ---α θεῷ Ὑφί||στῳ ε]ὐχήν.
1st-2nd century A.D.
London, B.M. 808: Smith, *Cat.sc.* I No. 808; *Br. Mus. Inscr.* I, 133 No. 70;
IG II² 4807.

8.17   Pair of arms (the hands are missing).
Inscription: Κλαυδία Πρέπουσα | εὐχαριστῶ Ὑφίστῳ.
2nd-3rd century A.D.
London, B.M. 806: Smith, *Cat.sc.* I No. 806; *Mus. Marbles* IX pl. 41, fig. 6;
Br. Mus. Inscr. I, 131 No. 64; *IG* II² 4806; Travlos, *Bildlexikon* 571 fig. 716 d.

8.18   Pair of thighs (?) (top broken off).
Inscription: Χρυσάριν Ὑψίσ|τῳ εὐχήν.
2nd-3rd century A.D.
Athens, Agora M. I 4294: Meritt, *Hesperia* 29 (1960) 63 No. 107, pl. 20.

8.19   Right foot, facing right (only the toes and the forepart of the foot remain).
London, B.M. 803: Smith, *Cat. sc.* I No. 803; *Mus. Marbles* IX pl. 41, fig. 4;
Travlos, *Bildlexikon* 571 fig. 716 a. M. Bieber, *MDAI(A)* 35 (1910) 6: 'verkrüp-
pelter Fuss', seems to be over-interpreting.

8.20   Relief of a pair of footprints.
Inscription: Εὐτυχία εὐχὴν θεῷ | Ὑψίστῳ ἀνέθηκα.
1st-2nd century A.D.
Athens, Roman Agora: Kourouniotes & Thompson, *Hesperia* 1 (1932) 198 fig.
60; *IG* II² 4784; M. Guarducci, *RPAA* 19 (1942-43) 337; Travlos, *Bildlexikon* 572
fig. 718.
   This pair of footprints, belonging to the Athenian series of votives to Zeus Hypsistos, presumably refers to a cure. Usually, however, the meaning of this type of
representation is different, see under B4.

9.   Some presumably Athenian votive offerings of which the exact provenance
could not be determined.

9.1   Marble votive relief of the so called 'sepulchral banquet' type. The right-
hand part, with the reclining hero, is broken off. On the right of the remaining part
the heroine is represented, sitting on the kline, facing right. From the left a boy
leads a pig to an altar which stands before the kline, followed by a family of worshippers (man, woman, child, very small child on all fours). On the extreme left,
hanging from the upper left corner, a colossal leg, thigh to foot, facing right.
4th century B.C.
Athens, Kanellopoulos Mus.: M.-A. Zagdoun, *BCH* 102 (1978) 304 No. 14, fig.
18. On this type of relief, principally if not exclusively used as a votive relief
throughout the classical period, see R. N. Thönges-Stringaris, *MDAI(A)* 80 (1965)
1-99; *BABesch* 49 (1974) 173 nt. 107. To which healing god or hero this particular
relief was dedicated, cannot be ascertained.'

9.2   Marble tablet with a pair of eyes in relief.
Athens, N.M. 2277.

9.3   Female breast on a plaque. Marble.
Traces of inscription.
Athens, Epigr. M. 2524: Svoronos pl. 232, 11, p. 673.

9.4   Dorsal view of a male body, waist to mid thigh, on a base. Marble.
Traces of inscription on the base.
Athens, Epigr. M. 3221: Svoronos pl. 233, 4, p. 673.

9.5   Dorsal view of a male body, from the waist downwards (lower part broken off
at mid thigh). Marble relief.
Athens, Epigr. M. 2528: Svoronos pl. 232, 1, p. 672.

9.6   Left arm, shoulder to a little below elbow, facing left. Marble relief.
Inscription (faintly legible on photograph): ANN-- | XHN--- | ---PIΣT---.
Athens, Epigr. M. 2527: Svoronos pl. 232, 3, p. 672.

9.7   Pair of hands, palms foreward. Marble relief.
Athens, N.M. 2701: Svoronos pl. 164, p. 649.

9.8   Right hand, palm foreward. Marble relief.
Inscription (according to Svoronos): [Εὐ]νομίᾳ | ΔIITYXOΣ (?)
Athens, N.M. 2680: Svoronos pl. 164, p. 649; W. Peek, *MDAI(A)* 67 (1942) 53,
doubts whether anything is written after ΔII, but traces of --XOΣ or something like
it are visible on the photograph.

9.9   Left leg. Terracotta. A pierced lug for suspension is attached to the flat surface with which the thigh is finished off.
Athens, N.M.: displayed in the Temporary Exhibition of Ancient Medicine,
1979.

9.10   Left foot with sandal. Marble.
Roman period.
Berlin, St. M.: *Beschreibung* No. 661.

10.   Piraeus, Asklepieion.
W. Judeich, *Topographie von Athen* ²(1931) 441.

10.1   Lower part of male body, genitals, thighs. Marble relief.
Inscription: Ἀθηνόδωρος | Ἀσκληπιῷ ἐπη|κόῳ εὐχὴν ἀ|νέθηκε.
2nd-3rd century A.D.
Athens, 'in domo privata': *IG* II² 4527; *AD* 1888, 134 No. 20.

10.2   Marble votive relief with on the right Agathe Theos holding a cornucopia
and a phiale; on the left a worshipping couple. A leg is hanging from the upper left
corner, knee to foot, facing right.
Inscription: Ἀγαθῆι Θεῶι Πυθό|νικος εὐξάμενος |ἀνέθηκεν.
Late 4th—early 3rd century B.C.
Piraeus Mus.: A. Greifenhagen, *MDAI(R)* 52 (1937) 238 ff., pl. 50, 2; *IG* II²
4589; Hausmann, *Kunst und Heiltum* 180 No. 166; K. Latte, *Römische Religions-
geschichte* (1960) 228 nt. 2, fig. 20.
On the provenance of this relief Greifenhagen 239 nt. 2.
Cf. the 4th century relief of Agathe Tyche from the Athenian Asklepieion,
Athens, N.M. 1343: Svoronos pl. 34; *IG* II² 4644; Hausmann, *Kunst und Heiltum*
180 No. 165; Holländer, *Plastik und Medizin* 156 fig. 83.

(10.3)   Female breasts.
'Im Museum des Piraeus zwei Blöcke mit weiblichen Brüsten': M. Bieber,
MDAI(A) 35 (1910) 5 nt. 2.

11.   Daphni, sanctuary of Aphrodite on the Sacred Way from Athens to Eleusis.
S. Wide, Τὸ ἐν Δαφνίῳ ἱερὸν τῆς Ἀφροδίτης, *AE* 1910, 35-52; J. Travlos, *PAAH*
1937, 25-41; J. Travlos & K. Kourouniotis, *PAAH* 1938, 28-34; 1939, 39-41;

A. Delivorrias, 'Die Kultstatue der Aphrodite von Daphni', *Ant. Plastik* VIII (1968) 19-31.

Foundations of a small temple remain, and several niches in the face of the rock, some with inscriptions below them. Typical votive offerings are marble pigeons, two of which, picked up by Fauvel, have come to roost in the Rijksmuseum van Oudheden at Leiden (F. L. Bastet, *Het maansteenrif*, 1979, 60-81), and reliefs depicting the pudenda muliebria.

11.1 Vulva (?) attached to a marble pigeon.
Inscription: Φαλακρίων Ἀφροδίτει [ἀνέθηκεν.
4th century B.C.
Athens, N.M. 1592: Svoronos pl. 164, p. 648; *IG* II² 4577.

11.2 Vulva.
Inscription: Παμφίλη Ἀφροδί[τει].
4th century B.C.
Athens, N.M. 1594: Svoronos pl. 164, p. 648; *IG* II² 4576.

11.3 Vulva.
Inscription: Ἀφροδίτει.
Athens, N.M. 1595: Svoronos pl. 164, p. 648; Peek, *MDAI(A)* 67 (1942) 51.

11.4 (*Fig. 63*) Vulva.
Inscription: Φιλουμένη Ἀφρο[δ]ίτε[ι χ]αριζομέ|νη· ἐπαινεῖτε οἱ παριόντες.
4th century B.C.
Athens, N.M. 1821: Svoronos pl. 164, p. 648; *IG* II² 4575.

11.5 Vulva.
Inscription: Δωριὰς |Ἀφροδίτει ἀνέ[θηκεν].
4th century B.C.
Athens, N.M. 2730: Svoronos pl. 164, p. 649; *IG* II² 4635 and Peek, *MDAI(A)* 67 (1942) 51.

11.6 Vulva.
Athens, N.M. 1596: Svoronos pl. 164, p. 648.

11.7-8 Vulvae (fragments).
Travlos, *PAAH* 1937, 31 fig. 8.

12. Eleusis, Asklepieion.

12.1 Female breast. Marble relief.
Inscription: Ἰσιὰς | Ἀσκλη|πιῷ εὐχήν.
1st-2nd century A.D.
Lost?: *IG* II² 4505; Skias, *PAAH* 1898, 88 No. 3.

13. Eleusis, sanctuary of Demeter and Kore.
G. E. Mylonas, *Eleusis and the Eleusinian mysteries* (1961).
Found inside the sanctuary, close to the middle round tower of the southern peribolos:

13.1 (*Fig. 56*) Marble plaque in the shape of an antefix, decorated in relief and painting. In the upper part a female face and neck are depicted, with rays emanating from it (or from an invisible source behind it) on both sides. Above, a hole for suspension. The rectangular lower part shows a pair of eyes and a nose, and underneath the inscription: Δήμητρι Εὐκράτης.

4th century B.C.

Athens, N.M. A 11386: O. Kern, Δημήτηρ-Σελήνη, *AE* 1892, 113-118, pl. 5; *IG* II² 4639; O. Rubensohn, 'Demeter als Heilgottheit', *MDAI(A)* 20 (1895) 360-367; idem, 'Das Weihehaus von Eleusis und sein Allerheiligstes', *JDAI* 70 (1955) 40-42, fig. 1; Holländer, *Plastik und Medizin* 218 fig. 131.

'Inschrift und bildliche Darstellung sollen deutlich machen, das durch die Epiphanie der πυρφόρος θεά (Eurip., Hiketid. 261), der Herrin des mystischen Feuers, inmitten der Strahlen diese die Kraft erhalten, die erloschene Sehkraft wieder zu erwecken' (Rubensohn). Although we know that elsewhere Demeter was worshipped as a healing goddess (cf. e.g. Mesembria 22.1-12, Pergamon 36; Mihailov, *IGBulg* III 1, 1961, No. 932 from Philippopolis; Artemidoros, *Oneir.* II 39), we have no such evidence from Eleusis apart from this relief.

I would suggest the alternative interpretation, that it was not dedicated in gratitude for the recovery of the power of sight (ὅρασις, as in the votive relief from Philippopolis *IGBulg* III 932), but to commemorate Eukrates' attaining to the ἐποπτεία, the highest grade of initiation at the Eleusinian mysteries. For this—as the word *epopteía* indicates—primarily visual experience, eyes would be appropriate.

The Argolid and Corinth:

14. Epidauros, Asklepieion.

Bibliography in *Enc. dell'Arte Ant.* III (1960) 367; G. Roux, *L'architecture de l'Argolide aux IVe et IIIe siècles av. J.-C.* (1961); A. Burford, *The Greek temple builders at Epidauros* (1969).

This very important sanctuary has surprisingly little to contribute to our catalogue.

14.1 [Ear, ὠτίον ?] The object itself is not preserved, but mentioned (if the restoration is correct) in the votive inscription which belonged to it: [Σω]τῆρι Ἀσκ[ληπιῷ | Κρα?]των τὸ ὠ[τίον σὺν | τῶι] βωμῷ.

2nd-3rd century A.D.

Epidauros: *IG* IV² 1, 474.

14.2 Pair of ears on tabula ansata. Marble relief with traces of gilding.

Inscription: *Cutius has auris Gallus tibi voverat olim*
           Phoebigena, et posuit sanus ab auriculis.

Athens, N.M. 1428: Svoronos, pl. 70, p. 430; *IG* IV² 1, 440; *CIL* III, Sup. 1, 1311 No. 7266; Dessau, *ILS* II, 1, 3853; Weinreich, *MDAI(A)* 37 (1912) 63f.; R. Herzog, *Wunderheilungen von Epidauros* (*Philologus Sup.* 22, 3, 1931) 43 W78, 135.

Weinreich, following Svoronos, holds that this is obviously 'ein von der berechnenden Priesterschaft zu Reclamezwecken hergestelltes Weihgeschenk, das auf Namen des reichen Gallierkönigs Cutius gefälscht ist'. Herzog rejects this idea as too fanciful and thinks it extremely improbable that our Cutius can be identified with the Gallic praefectus of royal blood Cottius. It is indeed not likely that the Epidaurian priests, if this were a sample of their propagandistic creativeness, should have passed over in silence Cutius' or Cottius' high status.

15.   Corinth, Asklepieion.

C. Roebuck, *The Asklepieion and Lerna* (*Corinth* XIV, 1951); M. Lang, *Cure and cult in ancient Corinth—A guide to the Asklepieion* (1977).

The exceptionally rich finds of terracotta replicas of human members from the Corinthian Asklepieion have been favoured with an uncommonly thorough publication (*Fig. 51*).

With few exceptions the terracotta members were made in moulds, often with retouches added before firing, and painted after it (generally white for feminine and red for masculine parts; two, the eye 15.15 and the genitals 15.42, were gilded). Many are pierced by holes near the top for suspension. Fortunately the deposits from which the votives come are securely dated, ranging from the last quarter of the 5th to the last quarter of the 4th century B.C. (Roebuck p. 128-138). Otherwise well meaning archaeologists might have wanted to create some more distance between them and the Parthenon sculptures.[193] The distance may be there, but it is not to be measured in years or kilometres.

In the following list I have restricted myself to a bare enumeration of broad categories, keeping the numbering of Roebuck's publication, to which the reader is referred for all further information. It should be noted, that his catalogue only lists the better preserved examples of each type.

15.1-7   Heads.

15.7   Upper part of a face, originally representing the eyes, part of the nose between them, brow and hair, mounted on a plaque.

15.8-12   Ears.

15.13-15   Eyes.

15.16   Tongue? Compare the ancient Italic votive tongue described by L. Sambon, *British Medical Journal* 1895 II, 148. Also Cederna, *NSA* 1951, 202 (Carsoli); M. Moretti e.a., *Nuove scoperte e acquisizioni nell' Etruria meridionale* (1975) 125 No. 43 (Lucus Feroniae); M. Fenelli, *Arch Class* 27 (1975) 216 pl. XL 3 (Lavinium).

15.17-19   Male chests.

15.20-30   Female breasts.

15.31-48   Male genitals.

---

[193] In fact, Q. F. Maule & H. R. W. Smith, *Votive religion at Caere: Prolegomena* (1959) 90 note 16, obviously unaware of the final publication by Roebuck, believed that 'it may be that the anatomical terracottas which F. J. de Waele was so justly surprised (*AJA* 1933, 444) to find at Corinth should be redated in its Roman period'.

15.49-62   Arms and part arms.

15.63-73   Hands. 15.63 has a growth on the back.

15.74-76   Fingers. 15.76, found in Roman filling, is the only marble votive in the group.

15.77-97   Legs and part legs.

15.98-114   Feet.

15.115-118   Miscellaneous:

15.115   Terracotta base, of male genitals (?)

15.116   Plait of hair.

15.117   A small thigh bone.

15.118   Seems to represent an internal organ of doubtful identification. Roebuck suggests a stomach, but perhaps there is a somewhat closer resemblance to the *uterus* as it is represented, together with other viscera, in some ancient Italic ex votos (P. Decouflé, *La notion d'ex-voto anatomique chez les Étrusco-Romains*, 1964, pl. XI-XII, fig. 14-15: Berlin; M. Tabanelli, *Gli ex-voto poliviscerali Etruschi e Romani*, 1962, fig. 15: Caere; 25: Vatican; 27: Vatican; 28: Louvre. That the organ, situated excentrically in the lower left part of the abdomen,[194] is in fact intended as a uterus, is demonstrated by the specimen Vatican, Mus. Etr. 13962, Tabanelli fig. 27, where part of the head of the foetus is visible through an opening. See also L. Stieda, *Anatomische Hefte*, 1. Abteilung, Bd. 16, Hft. 50, 1901, pl. III/IV, 24, and P. Rouquette, *Bul. Soc. Fr. Hist. Med.* 10, 1911, 517f., fig. 7; *ibid.* 11, 1912, 371 fig. 2). Alternatively the Corinthian votive could represent a bladder. Bladder and uterus were supposed to be not dissimilar in shape, both resembling a bleeding-cup (σικύη, see Hippokrates, *V.M.* 22).

Boeotia:

16.   Oropos, the Amphiareion.
     B. Ch. Petrakou, Ὁ Ὠρωπὸς καὶ τὸ ἱερὸν τοῦ Ἀμφιαράου (1968).

16.1   Votive relief dedicated to Amphiaraos by Archinos. The relief shows what Archinos experienced when he slept in the *enkoimeterion*. On the left, as he himself saw it in his dream, Archinos' right shoulder is being treated by Amphiaraos; on the right, as the same event was witnessed by outsiders, a snake is licking his shoulder while he is asleep on a couch. There is a votive pinax on a pillar in the background, and on the extreme right a worshipper, probably Archinos again,

---

[194] That the uterus is placed excentrically in these specimens may not be as disconcerting as it seems. The ancients held the view that the uterus could freely move about inside the abdomen, as though it were an animal with a life of its own. See for instance Aretaeus Cappad. II, 11 (Hude): --- καὶ τὸ ξύμπαν ἐν τῇ ἀνθρώπῳ ἐστὶ ἡ ὑστέρη ὁκοῖόν τι ζῶον ἐν ζώῳ, and VI, 10 ἴη δ' ἄν κοτε καὶ ἔνθα καὶ ἔνθα, ποτὶ σπλῆνα καὶ ἧπαρ.

rendering thanks for his cure. The relief is framed, as often, by antae on either side and an epistyle with geison and row of tile ends above. On top, exactly in the middle, a pair of eyes is represented.

Inscription: Ἀρχῖνος Ἀμφιαράωι ἀνέθηκεν.

First half 4th century B.C.

Athens, N.M. 3369: V. Leonardos, *AE* 1916, 120; Herzog, *Wunderheil. v. Epidaur.* 88 ff.; Hausmann, *Kunst und Heiltum* 55 ff., 169 No. 31, pl. 2; Idem, *Griechische Weihreliefs* (1960) 19; Petrakou, Ὠρωπός 122, 133f.; pl. 40a; S. Karouzou, *Cat. Nat. Arch. Mus., Collection of sculpture* (1968) 149f.; *BABesch* 51 (1976) 4; E. Mitropoulou, *Five contributions to the problems of Greek reliefs* (1976) 35 ff.; G. Neumann, *Probleme des griechischen Weihreliefs* (1979) 51.

The two eyes, in this case, almost certainly do not refer to a cure. Archinos' illness evidently affected his shoulder. Should the eyes have been intended as a memento of a hypothetical earlier cure, they would rather have been represented in the relief field, as if hanging in the sanctuary (cf. 1.1, 1.2, 2.1, 9.1, 10.2). Most authors have interpreted the eyes on Archinos' relief as apotropaic (Herzog, Hausmann, Karouzou). However, apotropaic eyes, unparalleled in Greek votive reliefs, have no obvious relevance here. Mitropoulou rather unnecessarily proposes to regard the eyes at the top of the votive relief as derived from Egyptian prototypes; she expresses no opinion on their significance.

More or less analogous to what was suggested above regarding No. 13.1 one might perhaps consider the possibility that Archinos had the eyes added to his relief, not in gratitude for the recovery of the power of sight (ὅρασις), but to render thanks for the *vision* (ὅραμα, see *BABesch* 51, 1976, 13) he saw in his dream, which is the main subject of the relief.

16.2   Small hand and arm. Bronze.

Petrakou, Ὠρωπός 134, pl. 51a.

16.3   The inscription *IG* VII 303 (Petrakou, Ὠρωπός 188 ff.; Sokolowski, *LS* 70) consists of a decree, dated at 202/199 B.C., regulating the melting down of gold and silver votive offerings, a list of which is appended.

The following parts of the body are mentioned:

a) Face, πρόσωπον, προσώπιον	2	
b) Female breast, τιτθός	2 single	
c) Genitals, αἰδοῖον	2 male	
d) Hand/arm, χείρ	1	

17.   Boeotia, exact provenance not known.

17.1   The inscription *IG* VII 2424, of the 2nd or 1st century B.C., contains a list of votive offerings. Among many *phialai* and *skaphia*, there is one *typos* without further specifications, and a woman's votive offering consisting of two πρόσωπα.

17.2   Boeotian red-figure bell krater.

A: A bearded god or hero, wearing a wreath, reclines at a banquet, facing left. A table with cakes stands by his couch. On the left an enormous coiled snake is about to drink from the kantharos in his outstretched right hand.

B: A goddess or heroine holding a sceptre is seated on the right. From the left approaches a woman worshipper or priestess bringing an oinochoe and a tray with cakes, sprigs, and a lighted candle. Two legs and an arm/hand are suspended above.

Late 5th century B.C.

Athens, N.M. 1393: O. Kern, *AE* 1890, 131 ff., pl. 7; J. Harrison, *Prolegomena to the study of Greek religion* ³(1922) 347f.; fig. 101; L. Deubner, *Attische Feste* (1932) 205, pl. 23,2 (= B); R. Lullies, 'Zur boiotisch rotfigurigen Vasenmalerei', *MDAI(A)* 65 (1940) 21f., pl. 26; for the candle cf. J. de la Genière, *RA* 1972, 291 ff.

The iconographical type of the so called 'sepulchral banquet' reliefs (cf. above No. 9.1) is here spread out over two sides of a vase. Since we do not know which sanctuary the vase painter had in mind, the couple of healing deities here depicted cannot be named (Amphiaraos?, Trophonios?).

Phocis:

18.　Delphi, Asklepieion.

18.1　Marble stele. In the upper part, in a field framed by a lower ledge, two antae, and an epistyle, are two symmetrically placed holes for the attachement of two bronze ears, which are now lost. Underneath, the inscription: Ἀναξίλα Ἀσκλαπιῶι.

Delphi, Mus. 1598: P. Perdrizet, *Fouilles de Delphes* V (1908) 209; Weinreich, *MDAI(A)* 37 (1912) 64 fig. 12.

(The large marble eye *Fouilles de Delphes* V 209 No. 708, fig. 911, may be either votive or apotropaic).

Thessaly:

19.　Stele with a relief of a right hand, back forward. Above it the inscription: Αὐλὶς Ἀρίστου ΑΕΙ | Α(?) εὐξαμένα καὶ | κατατυχοῦσα.

2nd-1st century B.C.

Volos, Mus. E 185.

Macedonia:

20.　Philippi.

Among the numerous reliefs carved in the rock of the Akropolis, there are two pairs of votive eyes, one above the other, with a crescent between them.

Below the lower pair of eyes the inscription: *Galgest/ia Primil/la pro / filia De̜[a]ne / v.s.1.m.*

P. Collart & P. Ducrey, *Philippes I, Les reliefs rupestres* (= *BCH Sup.* II, 1975) No. 149.

21.　Herakleia Lynkestis (near Bitola, Yugoslavia), Asklepieion.

21.1　Stone relief depicting a pair of ears on either side of a pine cone.

Inscription: [ε]ὐχὴν Ἀσσκλη | [πι]ῷ Ἀσσκληπι | άδ[η]ς.

Herakleia, Mus.: G. Cvetković Tomašević & T. Janakievski, *Heraklea Lyncestis* (1973) 68 ff., fig. 28; S. Düll, *Die Götterkulte Nordmakedoniens in röm. Zeit* (1977) 428 No. 183 A, fig. 72. On Asklepios and pine cones cf. *BABesch* 51 (1976) 7-8.

Thrace:

22. Mesembria on the North coast of the Thracian Sea, sanctuary of Demeter. A. K. Vavritsa, *PAAH* 1973, 77-81.

In the sanctuary a hoard of votive repoussé reliefs (*týpoi*) was found together with sherds of a red-figure pelike, in which they had perhaps been buried. They are of bronze, silver and gold, some silvered or gilded. After their discovery they were taken to the Komotini museum for cleaning and restoration; now they are (all?) exhibited in the museum of Alexandroupolis. The *týpoi* represent the goddess (according to the type usually associated with Kybele), worshippers, or both together, and some parts of the human body. They are probably not later than the 4th century B.C.

22.1-5 (*Fig. 59*) Pair of eyes and nose.
PAAH 1973, pl. 93 b, Nos. 1, 2, 3, 5; *AAA* 11 (1978) 52 fig. 4, No. 5.

22.6-10 Pair of eyes.
PAAH 1973, pl. 93 b, No. 4; *AAA* 11 (1978) 52 fig. 4, Nos. 1-4.

22.11 A series of five pairs of eyes on one strip.
PAAH 1973, pl. 95 a.

22.12 (*Fig. 60*) Right arm, upper arm to hand.
PAAH 1973, pl. 95 b.

Islands of the Aegean:

23. Delos, Asklepieion.
F. Robert, *EAD* 20 (1952) 51-108; Ph. Bruneau, *Recherches sur les cultes de Délos* (1970) 355-377.

23.1 Male genitals on a plaque. Marble.
Delos A4203: Robert, *EAD* 20, 107 No. 1; Bruneau, *Cultes* 371 No. 1, pl. IV a.

23.2 Right hand.
Delos A4205: Robert, *EAD* 20, 107 No. 2; Bruneau, *Cultes* 371 No. 2.

24. Delos, Thesmophorion (sanctuary of Demeter and Kore).
Bruneau, *Cultes* 269-293.
The inventories mention several votive offerings representing eyes, and one leg:

a) Eyes, ὀφθαλμοὶ ἐπὶ σανιδίου   *ID* 1444 (141/0 B.C.), Ba, 2, 10, 11, 16, 17.

ὀφθαλμὸς χρυσοῦς   *ID* 1444, Ba, 11.
ὀφθαλμῶν τύπια   *ID* 1444, Ba, 18.
(the same eyes were also mentioned   in *ID* 1442 and 1443).
b) Leg, σκέλος ἐπὶ σανιδίου   *ID* 1444, Ba, 9.
(also mentioned *ID* 1425 and 1443).

25. Delos, sanctuaries of the Egyptian gods.

P. Roussel, *Les cultes égyptiens à Délos* (1915-16); Bruneau, *Cultes* 457-466; L. Vidman, *Sylloge inscriptionum religionis Isiacae et Sarapiacae* (*RgVV* 28, 1969) at p. 80-87 has a convenient 'index donariorum' on the Delian inscriptions. Several offerings recur in the inventories of consecutive years; these, of course, are counted only once.

a) Face, πρόσωπον, προσώπιον: 3 (?), some of these may depict the face of a god, like the Ἡλίου πρόσωπον in *ID* 1417, B I, 10.

b) Eyes, ὀφθαλμός (-οί): 20 (2 single, 18 pairs), some of the votive eyes may have had no connection with a cure, see below sub B.

c) Ears, ὠτίον, ὠτάριον: 3 single; the bronze votive ears found in Delos are not listed in this catalogue, see below sub B.

d) Genitals, αἰδοῖον: 1 (probably male), in the temple of Isis.

e) Uteri, ὑστέρας ἀργυρᾶς δύο, ἀνάθημα Ἀρτεμοῦς, in the Isideion: *ID* 1442, A, 55 (145/4 B.C.). These are the only votive uteri from Greece that are entirely above suspicion; cf. Corinth 15.118 and Kos 30.10.

f) Arm, βραχιόνιον: 1

26. Rhodos: Lindos, sanctuary of Athena Lindia.
Lindos I-III (1931-1960); H. Kähler, *Lindos* (1971).

26.1 Pair of feet. Terracotta.
Istanbul Mus.: G. Mendel, *Catalogue des figurines grecques de terre cuite* (Istanbul, 1908) No. 39; *Lindos* I, 469 No. 1896, pl. 84.

27. Rhodos, exact provenance not known.

27.1 Male genitals. Marble.
Berlin, St. M.: *Beschreibung* No. 728.

28. Lesbos: Mytilene.

28.1 (Pair of) eye(s), on a plaque (only the left half of the plaque with a right eye remains).
Inscription: Ἀθηνᾶι .[---] | Βηρύλλα [---] | τὸ[ν ὀφθαλμόν] or το[ὺς ὀφθαλμούς]?
2nd century A.D.
IG XII 2, 121.
Line 1 of the inscription might also be read as Ἀθηνᾷ Ἰσ[---] or Ἰο[---], or Ἀθηναιο[---].

29. Melos, Asklepieion.

29.1 Left leg from above the knee, facing left. Marble relief.
Inscription: Ἀσκλη|πιῷ | καὶ | Ὑγείᾳ | Τύχη | εὐχαρισ|τήριον.
Roman period.
London, B.M. 809: Smith, *Cat.sc.* I No. 809; *Br. Mus. Inscr.* II, 141 No. 365; *IG* XII 3, 1086.

29.2 (*Fig. 53*) Foot with lower part of leg, facing left, and left ear. Marble relief (top probably broken off).

Inscription: [-- 'A]σ|[κλη]πι|[ῷ κ]αὶ 'Υ|[γ]είᾳ | [ε]ὐχήν.
Hellenistic or Roman period.
Athens, Epigr. M. 3224: Svoronos pl. 232, p. 673; *IG* XII 3, 1087; Weinreich, *MDAI(A)* 37 (1912) 62 fig. 10.
Svoronos and Weinreich were unaware of the Melian origin of this relief and its identity with *IG* XII 3, 1087.

30.   Kos, Asklepieion.
R. Herzog & P. Schazmann, *Kos* I, *Asklepieion* (1932); bibliography in *Enc. dell'Arte Ant.* II (1959) 800.
'Die Tätigkeit der Kalkbrenner zeigt sich auf dem ganzen Gebiet (---). Daraus erklärt sich auch, dass von ganzen Denkmälerklassen, wie figürlichen Weihreliefs nach Art der athenischen, und marmornen geweihten Gliedmassen, nur eben soviel erhalten ist, dass wir ihr Vorkommen im koischen Asklepieion nachweisen können' (Herzog, *AA* 1905, 10).
The marble replicas of parts of the human body found in Herzog's excavation, and briefly mentioned in his *Wunderheilungen von Epidauros* 148 nt. 15, are:

30.1   Ear.

30.2   Female breast.

30.3   Male genitals ('krankhaft' according to Herzog).

In 1910 a group of interesting ex votos (mainly terracottas), allegedly found on the site of the Asklepieion, was acquired in Kos, together with some ancient medical instruments, by Th. Meyer-Steineg, historian of medicine and former oculist from Jena.
Th. Meyer-Steineg, *Chirurgische Instrumente des Altertums* (= *Jenaer medizin-historische Beiträge* 1, 1912) and *Darstellungen normaler und krankhaft veränderter Körperteile an antiken Weihgaben* (= *Jenaer medizin-historische Beiträge* 2, 1912).
The circumstances under which these objects came into his possession are described as follows: 'Weit günstigere Erfolge hatte ich dagegen in Kleinasien und auf den der Westküste vorgelagerten Inseln. Diese verdankte ich hauptsächlich dem Umstande, dass ich, dem Rate eines Kenners der dortigen Verhältnisse folgend, mich reichlich mit Medikamenten und Instrumenten zur augenärztlichen Behandlung ausgerüstet hatte und meinen ehemaligen Beruf als Augenarzt, soweit dies im Umherziehen möglich war, unter der Bevölkerung ausübte, bei der neben allen möglichen anderen Augenleiden namentlich das Trachom mit allen seinen Folgezuständen ausserordentlich verbreitet ist.
Der Erfolg meiner Bemühungen bestand für mich darin, dass die 'dankbaren Patienten', deren manchem ich in der Tat einen guten Rat zu erteilen vermochte, mir auf meine Nachfragen zahlreiche antike Werkzeuge brachten, die sie—nur zum Teil mit Recht—für ärztliche hielten. (---) Einen zweiten umfangreicheren Fund chirurgischer Instrumente erhielt ich gleichzeitig mit einigen interessanten Exvotos auf der Insel Kos. Die Gegenstanden sollen angeblich aus dem Gebiete des von Herzog ausgegrabenen Asklepieions stammen. Näheres über die Stelle, wo und über die Umstände, unter denen sie gefunden wurden, vermochte ich

nicht festzustellen, als dass sie 'in der Ecke eines alten Mauerwerks unter einem grossen Stein' gelegen hätten' (*Jenaer Beitr.* 1, 5-6).

We should bear in mind that Herzog's discovery of the Asklepieion had occurred only a few years before Meyer-Steineg's visit. It had caused great excitement among the Coans, who felt very much involved:

'Die Bevölkerung von Kos, deren Traum das Asklepieion mit seinem Ruhm und seinen Schätzen war, hatte unser Beginnen mit mitleidigem Unglauben verfolgt. Denn sie war der festen Überzeugung, dass das Asklepieion an einem geheimnisvollen Ort in der Ebene liege, den nur ein alter Werkmeister kannte. (---) Die Koer aber verliessen ihn (when it turned out that Herzog was digging in the right place) und wandten sich dem aufsteigenden Gestirn zu, indem sie in Scharen heraufpilgerten, von Inschriften mit goldenen Buchstaben und anderen Schätzen, die wir gefunden haben sollten, zu erzählen wussten, und einerseits den Entdecker des Heiligtums als ihren grössten Wohltäter priesen, andererseits die unverschämtesten Entschädigungsforderungen für die Grabungen auf ihren Grundstücken von ihm zu erpressen suchten' (Herzog, *AA* 1903, 6).

When Meyer-Steineg came to the island, and showed an interest in antiquities connected with ancient medicine, it must have been absolutely unthinkable to the people of Kos to disappoint their guest, even benefactor, and to put 'their' Asklepieion to shame. They may have gone to great lengths to provide Meyer-Steineg with the things he wanted. Under the circumstances, the votives 'from the Asklepieion' are perhaps not entirely above suspicion. That is not to say that they are all forgeries. But in so far as they are genuine votive offerings, they are not necessarily ancient, and in so far as they are ancient, they are not necessarily from Kos. In any case it is not likely that they should all be lumped together, for there is a marked difference in clay between the two heads 30.4-5, the lungs 30.9, and the other terracottas (see Meyer-Steineg, *Jenaer Beitr.* 2, 14).

It is regrettable that we cannot rely on the authenticity of this group of ex votos, for they exhibit some types that are very unusual, even unparalleled among the surviving Greek votives. This in itself should not unduly increase our doubts. We have seen that several of the votives mentioned in the inscriptions from the Athenian Asklepieion have no Greek parallel either; evidently, what survives is not a representative sample. Nor should we discount the possibility, that there existed local variants, more or less restricted to one sanctuary.

So with all proper reserves I include the Meyer-Steineg votives in this catalogue.

30.4   Terracotta head of a boy. Neck finished off flat, with traces of a lug attached to the flat surface.

The right eye, bulging from its socket, is clearly affected by a fatal tumor. Meyer-Steineg, *Jenaer Beitr.* 2, 14f., pl. I 1-2.

(R. Zahn examined this head and suggested a possible Alexandrian origin, quoted *ibid.* 13 nt. 2)

30.5   Terracotta head of a man of advanced age. Neck as in 30.4.

The face is curiously lop-sided; the entire left part looks limp and drooping. Paralysis of the facial nerves of the left side may be diagnosed.

Meyer-Steineg, *Jenaer Beitr.* 2, 17, pl. I 4-5.

Votive heads occur elsewhere in Greece as well: Athens 1.25-1.31 *b*, Corinth 15.1-7. The realistic rendering of the disease, however, is remarkable.

30.6   Bronze repoussé relief with a pair of eyes. Traces of silvering remain. There is a small hole in each of the shorter sides for fastening the *týpos* to a piece of wood.

Meyer-Steineg, *Jenaer Beitr.* 2, 26f., pl. II 2.

Votive repoussé eyes are as common in modern Greece as they were in ancient Greece.

30.7   Small female trunk. Terracotta, made in a mould; the neck and the stumps of arms and legs are finished off flat. The swollen state of the abdomen indicates either pregnancy (Holländer) or dropsy (Meyer-Steineg).

Meyer-Steineg, *Jenaer Beitr.* 2, 17f., pl. I 3; Holländer, *Plastik und Medizin* 267 fig. 159.

For another votive trunk see Corinth 15.19 and perhaps Athens 1.25-1.31 a. A comparison with the terracotta figure of a pregnant woman from the cave of Pitsà (*Enc. dell'Arte Ant.* VI 206 fig. 229 b: a fragment of an entire figure, not a separate trunk) would seem to tell in favour of Holländer's diagnosis.

30.8   (*Fig. 61*) Terracotta plaque: in a recessed panel the relief of a female abdomen, from a little above the navel downwards, and including the upper part of the thighs. Below it an inscription: Ἀριστάρχ[η ---] | Ἀσκλη[πιῷ ---]. (The fragment containing the letters ΑΡΧ of the first line was accidentally not included in the photograph).

Meyer-Steineg, *Jenaer Beitr.* 2, 21f., pl. III 1.

Some other ancient Greek votives representing approximately the same part of the body are Athens 1.1 b and 8.13, Samos 33.1. The letter forms agree well with those current in the 2nd-3rd century A.D., suggesting rather more familiarity with the niceties of Greek epigraphy than is to be expected of a hypothetical Coan forger around 1910.

30.9   (*Fig. 62*) Terracotta plaque with the human organs of respiration depicted in relief: cricoid cartilage, trachea, bronchi, lungs.

Meyer-Steineg, *Jenaer Beitr.* 2, 19f., pl. II 1.

The relief betrayes a considerable anatomical knowledge. The cricoid cartilage and the cartilaginous rings of the windpipe are indicated, the difference in width and length between the left and right bronchus is observed, and even the fissures dividing the left lung into two and the right lung into three lobes are rendered by grooves (cf. Galen, *De anat. adm.*, Book VII, esp. ch. 11; the two and three lobes of the lungs are also visible in the famous opened up marble torso in the Vatican, Gal. Stat. 382: Helbig, *Führer* I⁴,1963, No. 195; Stieda, *Anatomische Hefte*, 1. Abteilung, Bd. 16, Hft 50, 1901, 44 ff., pl. II 7; Holländer, *Plastik und Medizin* 207 fig. 119; Rouquette, *Bul. Soc. Fr. Hist. Med.* 11, 1912, 271 ff. fig. 1; Regnault, *ibid.* 20, 1926, 140f.; Tabanelli, *Ex-voto poliviscerali* 31 No. 1, fig. 6). There is a fragmentary terracotta relief with a rough model of the larynx and trachea in Rome, Mus. Naz. Terme 56320 (Sambon, *British Medical Journal* 1895 II, 149 fig. 7; Tabanelli, *Ex-voto*

poliviscerali fig. 36; Stieda, *MDAI(R)* 14, 1899, 239f.: from the Insula Tiberina?),
but I have not found an ancient parallel, either Greek or Italic, to Meyer-Steineg's
votive lungs. Modern Greek *támata* with lungs, still on sale in Athens, are rather
similar.

30.10   (*Fig. 64*) Oval terracotta plaque with a relief representing a uterus with a
lateral appendage. Suspension hole at the top.
   Meyer-Steineg, *Jenaer Beitr.* 2, 22 ff., pl. IV 1.
   (Another terracotta relief in Meyer-Steineg's collection, representing an infant
wrapped in swaddling bands, is very similar in execution; it preserves traces of
silver plating).
   The identification of the curious object represented in this relief as a uterus is
based on its likeness to the votive uteri which are found in such enormous quantities in ancient Italic sanctuaries (for a circumstantial treatment of the latter see
Rouquette, *Bul. Soc. Fr. Hist. Med.* 11, 1912, 370-414; the identification of the
Italic uteri is put beyond doubt by a votive terracotta female abdomen in Florence,
Mus. Arch. 4775: G. Bartoloni, *SE* 38, 1970, 266 No. 17, pl. 22 a, where such an
organ of proportionally large dimensions, indicating pregnancy (?), is represented
in approximately the correct position on the abdomen). The Italic uteri with few
exceptions also have a lateral appendage, and it is nearly always on the left (for the
beholder), as in Meyer-Steineg's example. There is, however, a remarkable difference as well. The Italic separate votive uteri are all, with very few exceptions
indeed (and these are without lateral appendage), covered with transverse wrinkles
or folds, whereas the one from Kos has a smooth surface. Some smooth uteri do occur in Italic ex votos where they are represented surrounded by other abdominal
viscera (see references given above at No. 15.118).
   If the Coan terracotta should be taken as a forgery, it presupposes a thorough
familiarity with the Italic examples, and an intelligent combination and rearrange-
ment of the data they provide. It is questionable whether such knowledge was
available, even in Kos, in 1910. If it is genuine, the Coan and Italic uteri may be
satisfactorily explained as regional variants of the same basic conception, ultimately deriving from medical knowledge about the appearance of the womb as we find
it in Greco-Roman medical literature (e.g. Hippokrates, *V.M.* 22; Soranus, I 3).
Anyway, ancient Greek parallels for votive uteri are not entirely absent (see Delos
25 *e*; perhaps Corinth 15.118).
   The lateral appendage of the Coan and Italic uteri poses a problem. The
historians of medicine disagree on its interpretation. Some think that it is intended
as an ovary (Rouquette, *Bul. Soc. Fr. Hist. Med.* 11, 1912, 376-395, defends this
opinion with much learning; also Tabanelli, *Ex-voto poliviscerali* 74). There is,
however, never more than one. Others regard it as a representation of the bladder
(Stieda, *Anatomische Hefte*, 1. Abteilung, Bd. 16, Hft. 50, 1901, 70-72; Meyer-
Steineg, *Jenaer Beitr.* 2, 24). If the choice is strictly between these two possibilities,
the fact that uterus and appendage in the Coan example have separate openings
would at least there seem to plead in favour of a bladder.

31. Paros, Asklepieion.
O. Rubensohn, *MDAI(A)* 27 (1902) 224-230, 235-238; Idem, *RE* XVIII, 'Paros', col. 1852.

31.1 Pair of hands. Marble relief.
Inscription: --- | Ἰσμηνίου Ἀσ|κληπιῷ | καὶ Ὑγίᾳ.
Roman period.
IG XII 5, 158.

31.2 Hand. Marble relief (from the Asklepieion?).
Rubensohn, *MDAI(A)* 27 (1902) 224.

31.3 Foot. Marble relief.
Inscription: ---ικος Ἀριστο |[-- Ἀσ]κληπιῷ Ὑπα |[ταίῳ κ]αὶ Ὑγείᾳ εὐχα |
[ριστήρ]ιον.
Roman period.
IG XII 5, 156.

31.4 Foot. Marble relief.
Inscription: Αὐωνία Ζωσίμη | Ἀσκληπιῷ | εὐχήν.
IG XII 5, 157.

32. Paros, sanctuary of Eileithyia.
Rubensohn, *RE* XVIII, 'Paros', col. 1847-8.

32.1 (*Fig. 58*) Pair of female breasts on a plaque. Marble, two holes in top corners.
Inscription: Ὥρα Διφάνου | Εἰλιθυίᾳ εὐχήν.
Roman period.
Paros, Mus.: *IG* XII 5, 198 with photograph; Holländer, *Plastik und Medizin* 217 fig. 129.

33. Samos, exact provenance not known.

33.1 Female abdomen with upper part of the thighs. Marble relief.
Inscription: Ζμαράγδιν εὐχήν Ἀφροδίτῃ.
Roman period.
Samos, Vathy Mus.: Th. Wiegand, *MDAI(A)* 25 (1900) 174 No. 53.

33.2 Foot with sandal. Marble relief.
Samos, Vathy Mus.: Wiegand, *MDAI(A)* 25 (1900) 174 No. 54.

34. Crete, Eleutherna (Prinès).

34.1 Female breast on a plaque. Limestone.
Inscription: Σετηρία | Ἀρτέμιδι δυνατηρᾷ εὐχήν.
1st-2nd century A.D.
Rhethymnon Mus. 139: *ICret.* II, XII 24. On the epithet δυνατηρά see H. W. Pleket, p. 182.

Asia Minor:

35.   Pergamon, Asklepieion.
Bibliography *Enc. dell'Arte Ant.* VI (1965) 50-51, other volumes of *Altertümer von Pergamon* have appeared since; W. Radt, *Pergamon-Führer* (1973).

35.1   Pair of eyes. Bronze.
Inscription: Ταπαρι 'Ασ|κληπιῷ εὐχή ⟨ν⟩.
Bergama Mus. M 59/3: Chr. Habicht, *AvPerg.* VIII 3 (1969) No. 111 b, pl. 30; G. de Luca, *AvPerg.* XI 1 (1968) 172 B, pl. 62; W.-D. Albert, Tabulae ansatae aus Pergamon, *Perg. Forschungen* 1 (1972) 41 No. 21, fig. 44-45 at p. 12.

35.2   Ear. Bronze plaque, only the ear itself, executed in repoussé relief, is gilded. Nail holes at top and bottom.
Inscription: 'Ασκληπιῷ Σω|τῆρι Φαβία Σεκοῦν|δα κατ' ὄνειρον.
Bergama Mus. M 59/127: Habicht, *AvPerg.* VIII 3, No. 91, pl. 30; De Luca, *AvPerg.* XI 1, 171 A, pl. 62; Albert, *Perg. Forsch.* 1, 41 No. 20, fig. 42-43 at p. 11.

35.3   Pair of ears. Bronze.
Inscription: 'Απόλλωνι | Πρόκλος | εὐχήν.
Roman imperial age.
Bergama Mus. VT M 64/34: Habicht, *AvPerg.* VIII 3, No. 115 b, pl. 30; De Luca, *AvPerg.* XI 1, 171; Albert, *Perg. Forsch.* 1, 41 No. 19, fig. 40-41 at p. 9.

35.4   Pair of ears. Bronze.
Inscription: 'Αγαθῇ Τύχῃ |'Ασκληπιῷ | Σωτῆρι 'Αττικὶ | εὐχὴν ἀνέθη|κα.
Roman imperial age.
Bergama Mus.: Th. Wiegand, *Abh. D. A. W. Berlin* 1932, 34f. B 9; Habicht, *AvPerg.* VIII 3, No. 89.

35.5.   Ear. Bronze.
Bergama Mus. M 61/167: De Luca, *AvPerg.* XI 1, 172.

35.6   Pair of ears. Bronze, gilded.
Inscription: Καλιας τῷ | 'Ασσκληπιῷ | εὐχήν.
2nd century A.D.
Berlin, St. M. 31393: K. Vierneisel (ed.), *Römisches im Antikenmuseum* (Berlin 1978) 36 fig. 24.

36.   Pergamon, sanctuary of Demeter.
In this sanctuary many terracotta eyes were found (one in 1909, a large group with 15 different types in 1938, and again some in 1968). They are probably datable to the 3rd century B.C.
E. Töpperwein, *Terrakotten von Pergamon* (1976) 140, 241 Nos. 588-590, pl. 85; C. H. Bohtz & W.-D. Albert, *AA* 1970, 402 fig. 21-24.

37.   Pergamon, exact provenance not known.

37.1   Ear. Stone relief.
Berlin: F. Winter, *AvPerg.* VII 2 (1908) 266 No. 337.

37.2 Pair of female breasts on a plaque. Stone.
Bergama: Winter, *AvPerg.* VII 2, 267.

38. Ephesos, Artemision.
D. G. Hogarth, *Excavations at Ephesus* (1908). Hogarth found several tiny replicas of human members, executed in thin gold and electrum foil, and some of ivory, datable to the early phase of the sanctuary, i.e. end of 8th-first half of 7th century B.C.

38.1-6 Pairs of eyes. Gold and electrum.
Hogarth, *Ephesus* 108, pl. VII 35, 36, 42, 44; F. H. Marshall, *Catalogue of jewellery Br. Mus.* (1911) No. 922, pl. IX.

38.7-23 Single eyes. Gold and electrum.
Hogarth, *Ephesus* 108, pl. VII 39, 40, 41, 47; Marshall, *Cat. jew.* Nos. 917, 919, 920, pl. IX.

38.24-26 Ears. Gold.
Hogarth, *Ephesus* 108, pl. VII 48; Marshall, *Cat. jew.* No. 923, pl. IX.

38.27 Vulva?? Gold.
Marshall, *Cat. jew.* No. 924, pl. IX.

38.28-29 Hand and forearm. Electrum.
Hogarth, *Ephesus* 107, pl. VII 22; Marshall, *Cat. jew.* No. 916, pl. IX.

38.30-31 Leg and foot. Electrum.
Hogarth, *Ephesus* 107, pl. VII 21, 23; Marshall, *Cat. jew.* No. 915, pl. IX.

38.32 Arm. Ivory.
Hogarth, *Ephesus* 198, pl. XLII 5.

38.33 Left foot. Ivory.
Hogarth, *Ephesus* 196, pl. XLII 10-11.

39. Ephesos, exact provenance not known.

39.1 Ear. Terracotta.
Istanbul Mus.: Mendel, *Cat. t.c.* No. 1937.

39.2 Foot, shod. Terracotta.
Istanbul Mus.: Mendel, *Cat. t.c.* No. 1936.

Lydia and Phrygia:

Among the numerous marble (and some limestone) votive stelai found in Lydia and Phrygia, several bear reliefs depicting parts of the human body. Most of these are just votive offerings dedicated in gratitude for a cure, but some belong to the class of the 'confession stelai' (viz. 40.2, 42.1?, 44.2, 44.3?, 44.4, 44.5, 46.1, 47.3, 48.2; cf. p. 101).

40. Sardes.

40.1   Pair of eyes (fragment).
Inscription: [θεᾷ] ἀγνῇ Ἰα[σοῖ? | ἔτου]ς σνζ᾽ Ἀπφι |[ον Ἀπολ]λωνίου | [ἔστησεν] εὐχήν.
172/3 A.D.
W. H. Buckler & D. M. Robinson, *Sardis* VII 1 (1932) 99 No. 97, fig. 86.

40.2   Pair of eyes (fragment).
Inscription: Ἀρτέμιδι Ἀναείτ[ι] | Ἀμμιὰς Ματρίδος Ε[.] | ΚΤΙΣΣΕΩΣ χολασθ[---].
2nd century A.D.?
Buckler & Robinson, *Sardis* VII 1, 97f. No. 95, fig. 83; I. Diakonoff, 'Artemidi Anaeiti anestesen'. *BABesch* 54 (1979) 154 No. 48.

41.   Alaşehir (Philadelpheia).

41.1   Lateral view of lower part of male body, with genitals, and leg.
Inscription: Μητρὶ Φιλεῖ ἐπη|κόῳ Ἀλεξᾶς ἐπὶ | τοῦ ἰδίου σώματο |ς τὴν εὐχὴν ἀπέ | δωκεν.
3rd century A.D.
J. Keil & A. von Premerstein, 'Zweite Reise in Lydien', *Denkschr. Wien* 54, 2 (1911) 25 No. 34.

42.   Aivatlar (Katakekaumene), sanctuary of Artemis Anaeitis.

42.1   Pair of female breasts; lateral view of a right leg, from mid thigh downwards, facing right; pair of eyes.
Inscription: θεᾷ Ἀναείτι καὶ Μηνὶ Τιάμου etc.
236/7 A.D.
Leiden, Rijksmuseum van Oudheden S.Ns. 309: E. N. Lane, *Corpus Monumentorum Religionis Dei Menis* I (*EPRO* 19, 1971) 23 No. 35; Diakonoff, *BABesch* 54 (1979) 144 No. 6, fig. 10.

42.2   Pair of eyes, to the right of a recessed panel in which a female worshipper is represented.
Inscription: Ἀρτέμιδι Ἀναείτι Στρα |τονείκη Μελτίνης ὑπὲρ | ὑγείας τῶν ὀφθαλμῶν | εὐχὴν ἀνέστησεν.
Ca. 210-240 A.D. (Diakonoff).
Leiden, Rijksmuseum van Oudheden S.Ns 312: Diakonoff, *BABesch* 54 (1979) 144 No. 5, fig. 8.

43.   Gölde (Katakekaumene), various sanctuaries.

43.1   Leg.
Inscription: Μηνὶ Ἀξιεττηνῷ ἐξ Ἐπι |κράτου Ἑρμογένης ἐπὶ χά |ριτος εὐχήν.
Once Smyrna, now lost?: Lane, *CMRDM* I No. 31.

43.2   Pair of eyes.
Inscription: Μηνὶ Οὐρανίῳ | Μηνὶ Ἀξιοττηνῷ | ...λία Ποπλίου.
Once Smyrna, now lost?: Lane, *CMRDM* I No. 32.

43.3 (*Fig. 54*) Lateral view of a left leg, mid thigh to foot, facing left, in a recessed panel.

Inscription: Θειῷ Ὁσίῳ καὶ Δικαίῳ etc.

172/3 A.D.

Once Smyrna, now lost?: Fontrier, *Μουσεῖον* 3 (1878-80) 169 No. τμγ'; for further references see P. Herrmann & K. Z. Polatkan, *SBWien* 265, 1 (1969) 49; photograph in Holländer, *Plastik und Medizin* 296 fig. 185.

43.4 Five worshippers in a recessed panel, the third and fourth from the left taller than the others; two pairs of eyes, above the second and third figure from the left (presumably Meltine and her daughter).

Inscription: θεᾷ Τασηνῇ Μελτίνη ὑπ[ὲρ ἑαυ]|τῆς καὶ τῆς θυγατρός [--].

Ph. Le Bas & W. M. Waddington, *Voyage archéologique* III 218 No. 688; Ph. Le Bas & S. Reinach, *Monuments figurés* pl. 137, 1; L. Robert, *Nouvelles inscriptions de Sardes* (1964) 27 nt. 2.

43.5 Pair of female breasts.

Keil & von Premerstein, *Zweite Reise* 94 No. 6.

43.6 Right hand, palm forewards, in a recessed panel.

Keil & von Premerstein, *Zweite Reise* 93 No. 7.

44. Kula (Katakekaumene), various sanctuaries.

44.1 Pair of feet.

Inscription: Ἀρτέμιδι Ἀναείτι καὶ | [Μ]ηνὶ Τιάμου Μελτίνη | [ὑπ]ὲρ τῆς ὁλοκληρίας| [τῶν] ποδῶν εὐχὴν | [ἀνέ]στησεν.

Lane, *CMRDM* I No. 59; Diakonoff, *BABesch* 54 (1979) 150 No. 28. On ὁλοκληρία see Robert, *Hellenica* X (1955) 97-99.

44.2 Lateral view of lower part of female body and right leg, facing left (rather a pronounced buttock).

Inscription: Γλυκία Ἰουλί|ου τοῦ Ἀγρίου | κολασθεῖ|σα ὑπὸ τῆ|ς Ἀναείτιδος τῆς ἐγ Μητρῳ τ|ὸν γλουθρουν ἐ|πιζητήσασα ἀν[έθ]|ηκεν.

3rd century A.D.

H. W. Pleket, *Talanta* 10-11 (1978-79) 88 No. 13; Diakonoff, *BABesch* 54 (1979) 151 No. 31. γλουθρουν: cf. γλουτός, 'buttock'.

44.3 Men standing between two lions; under him a rider, and a man standing by the horse's head, on a ledge carrying the first line of the inscription; under it a right leg, from a little above the knee, facing right.

Inscription: Μηνὶ Ἀξιττηνῷ | Ὀνησίμη ἡ μήτηρ ὑπὲρ | τοῦ υἱοῦ Τυράννου, ἐπει|δὴ τὸν πόδα πονήσας εὐ|λογοῦσα ἀνέθηκα etc.

269/70 A.D.

P. Herrmann, *Denkschr. Wien* 80 (1962) 46 No. 39; Lane, *CMRDM* I No. 65.

44.4 Pair of female breasts.

Inscription: (date) ἐχολάσθη Ἀμμιὰς | οἰπὸ Μητρὸς Φιλεῖδος | ἰς τοὺς μαστούς etc.

125/6 A.D.

Fontrier, *Μουσεῖον* 3 (1878-80) 165 No. τλδ'; F. Steinleitner, *Die Beicht* (1913) 39 No. 12.

44.5   (*Fig. 45*) Pair of eyes above two pigeons, in a recessed panel.

Inscription: Διεὶ Σαβαζίῳ καὶ Μη|τρεὶ Εἴπτα Διοκλῆς | Τροφίμου· ἐπεὶ ἐπεί|ασα περιστερὰς τῶν | θεῶν ἐκολάσθην ἱς | τοὺς ὀφθαλμοὺς καὶ | ἐνέγραψα τὴν ἀρετήν.

W. H. Buckler, *ABSA* 21 (1914-16) 169 ff., pl. XV 1; Herrmann, *Denkschr. Wien* 80 (1962) 51; Robert, *JS* 1971, 95.

45.   Menye (Katakekaumene), sanctuary of Thea Bryzi.

45.1   Foot (leg?, only the lower part remains).

Inscription: θεᾷ Βρυζι Λοῦκις 'Ονησί|μου ὑπὲρ τοῦ ποδὸς εὐ|χὴν ἀνέστησεν.
Herrmann, *Denkschr. Wien* 80 (1962) 53 No. 47.

45.2   Leg; standing figure on either side.

Inscription: θεᾷ Βρυζι ἁγνῇ 'Αδυτη||[ν]ῇ Εὐτυχιανὴ Μελίτω|νος τῶν Φ / ΠΥΡΩΝ ὑπὲρ το[ῦ] | ποδὸς εὐχαριστοῦσ[α | ε]ὐχὴν ἀνέστησεν.
Herrmann, *Denkschr. Wien* 80 (1962) 53.

46.   Sandal (Katakekaumene).

46.1   Arm, the hand broken off, in a recessed panel.

Inscription: (date) Μητρόδω|ρος Γλύκωνος παιδίον ὢν ἀκου|σίως κατεάξας στηλλάριον τῆς | θεοῦ ἐπεζήτησε ἀνασταθῆ|ναι ὑπὸ αὐτοῦ ἄλλο.
118/9 A.D.
Keil & von Premerstein, *Zweite Reise* 99 No. 197; Diakonoff, *BABesch* 54 (1979) 154 No. D1.

47.   Katakekaumene, exact provenance not known.

47.1   Pair of female breasts.

Inscription: 'Αρτέμιδι 'Αναε[ίτι] καὶ Μηνὶ Τιάμου 'Α[λε]|ξάνδρα ὑπὲρ τῶν | [μ]αστῶν εὐχὴν | ἀνέστησεν.
Ca. 210-240 A.D. (Diakonoff)
Manisa Mus.: Robert, *Hellenica* X (1955) 163, pl. 29, 1; Lane, *CMRDM* I No. 74; Diakonoff, *BABesch* 54 (1979) 152 No. 33, fig. 9.

47.2   (*Fig. 55*) Lateral view of a right leg, thigh to foot, facing left, in a recessed panel.

Inscription: (date) Λούκιος ὑπὲρ | Τροφίμου τοῦ θρε|π ⟨τ⟩ οῦ θεᾷ Οὐρανίᾳ | εὐχήν.
202/3 A.D.
Once Smyrna, now lost?: 'Αρμονία (Smyrna) May 31st, 1900, No. 7; photograph in Holländer, *Plastik und Medizin* 295 fig. 184.

47.3-6   Some unpublished stelai from the Katakekaumene in the museum of Uşak carry representations of parts of the human body.

47.3   Pair of eyes, θεοὶ οἱ ἐν Περεύδῳ, 194/5 A.D.

47.4   Pair of female breasts, and female worshipper, θεῷ 'Υφίστῳ ἐπηκόῳ, 206/7 A.D.

47.5   One female breast, Μηνὶ Λαβανᾷ καὶ Διί, 147/8 A.D.

47.6 Leg, and forearm with hand, θεᾷ.

48.   Dionysopolis (Phrygia).

48.1 Pair of legs, with feet pointing inwards.
Inscription: Μελιτίνη Μη|νογένους Διὶ | Τυλισσου ἀναδε|ξαμένη εὐξαμένη ἀνέθη[κα].
MAMA IV 266. The epithet of Zeus in line 3 possibly Τρωσσου?, see T. Drew-Bear, GRBS 17 (1976) 262.

48.2 A pair of legs, turned to the right, and male genitals, are carved below a confession inscription, which is written in Greek so faulty as to be largely unintelligible.
3rd century A.D.
MAMA IV 283.

49.   From the region of the Emir Dağ (Phrygia) come several votive stelai to Zeus Petarenos, Zeus Alsenos, and Zeus Orochoreites.
L. Tuğrul, Annual Archaeol. Mus. Istanbul 13-14 (1966) 175-185, pl. 8-13;
Robert, BE 1968, 526.
Some of these are carved with representations of human members:

49.1 Pair of eyes.
Inscription: Δημοσ|θένη Δὶ 'Α|λσηνῷ | εὐχήν.
Istanbul Mus. 5738: Tuğrul, Ann. Ist. 13-14 (1966) 180 No. 10, pl. X.

49.2 Right arm (only the forearm remains).
Inscription: [Διὶ Πε]|ταρηνῷ | 'Αφφία ὑπὲρ | ἰδίου σώμα|[το]ς εὐχήν.
Istanbul Mus. 5590: Tuğrul, Ann. Ist. 13-14 (1966) 183 No. 19, pl. XII.

49.3 Right arm.
Inscription: Πρωτάρχη Δεὶ 'Ο|ροχω|ρείτη ε|ὐχήν.
Istanbul Mus. 5592: Tuğrul, Ann. Ist. 13-14 (1966) 184 No. 21, pl. XII.

49.4 Leg, thigh to foot, facing right.
Inscription: 'Αρίστω|ν | Διὶ | 'Αλισην|ῷ | εὐχή|ν.
Istanbul Mus. 5591: Tuğrul, Ann. Ist. 13-14 (1966) 181 No. 12, pl. X.

49.5 Pair of legs, facing right.
Inscription: "Ηλιο[ς] | Διὶ 'Αλ|σην|ῷ | εὐχήν.
Istanbul Mus. 5720: Tuğrul, Ann. Ist. 13-14 (1966) 181 No. 11, pl. X.

49.6 Leg, facing right.
Inscription: 'Ερμογέ|νης | Διὶ ε|ὐχὴ|ν 'Ορο(χωρείτη?).
Istanbul Mus. 5593: Tuğrul, Ann. Ist. 13-14 (1966) 184 No. 22, pl. XIII.

49.7-8 Two stelai in a private collection, illustrated by D. Pinkwart in the catalogue of the Pergamon-Ausstellung (Ingelheim am Rhein, 1972) Nos. 37 b-c, probably come from the same region:

49.7   Pair of eyes.
Inscription: Πρείμα Διὶ Πετα|ρηνῷ | εὐχήν.
Pergamon-Ausstellung (1972) No. 37 b.

49.8   Lateral view of a right leg, thigh to foot, facing right.
Inscription: Σύντροφος ’Αριστο|μάχου Δεὶ Πε|ταρηνῷ εὐ|χήν.
Pergamon-Ausstellung (1972) No. 37 c.

Cyprus:

50.   Golgoi.
Several limestone plaques with representations of parts of the human body were collected by L. Palma di Cesnola. They now form part of the Cesnola collection in the New York Metropolitan Museum of Art.
L. Palma di Cesnola, *Cyprus, its ancient cities, tombs, and temples* (1877); J. L. Myres, *Handbook of the Cesnola collection* (1914).

50.1   Face.
Cesnola, *Cyprus* 158, 1.

50.2   Eye.
Cesnola, *Cyprus* 158, 3; Myres, *Hbk.* No. 1683.

50.3-5   Pairs of eyes.
Cesnola, *Cyprus* 158, 6; Myres, *Hbk.* Nos. 1685-1687.

50.6   Pair of eyes and mouth.
Cesnola, *Cyprus* 158, 5; Myres, *Hbk.* No. 1684.

50.7   Ear with earring.
Cesnola, *Cyprus* 158, 2; Myres, *Hbk.* No. 1682.

50.8-9   Ears, with syllabic inscriptions on the lobe (interpretation uncertain).
O. Masson, *Inscr. Chypr. Syllab.* (1961) 293f., Nos. 288-289; Myres, *Hbk.* Nos. 1881-1882.

50.10   Pair of ears.
Cesnola, *Cyprus* 158, 7.

50.11   Female breast.
Myres, *Hbk.* No. 1676.

50.12   Pair of female breasts; below them a grape-like growth (or some internal organ?)
Cesnola, *Cyprus* 158, 8; Myres, *Hbk.* No. 1227; Holländer, *Plastik und Medizin* 300 fig. 192.

50.13   Hand.
Myres, *Hbk.* No. 1679.

50.14-15   Fingers (or toes?)
Cesnola, *Cyprus* 158, 4; Myres, *Hbk.* Nos. 1680-1681.

50.16-17   Feet.
Myres, *Hbk.* Nos. 1677-1678.

51.   Cyprus, exact provenance not known.
Several limestone plaques in the Louvre, some of which were studied by P. Perdrizet when in the possession of an art dealer at Larnaka (*BCH* 20, 1896, 361-363), may with reasonable probability also be attributed to the Golgoi area.
A. Caubet & B. Helly, 'Ex-voto chypriotes au musée du Louvre', *Revue du Louvre* 21 (1971) 331-334.

51.1   Pair of eyes, painted (suspension hole in top centre).
Inscription: θεῷ Ὑψίστῳ εὐξάμενος | Χαρίτων ἀπέδωκεν.
3rd-4th century A.D.
Paris, Louvre AM 670: Perdrizet, *BCH* 20 (1896) 361f., No. 2; Caubet & Helly, *RevLouvre* 21 (1971) 331f., fig. 1; O. Masson, *BCH* 95 (1971) 331 No. 12, fig. 20.

51.2   Pair of eyes, painted (suspension hole in top centre).
Inscription: θεῷ Ὑψίστῳ ἀνέ|θηκεν εὐξάμενος | Μᾶρχος ---.
3rd-4th century A.D.
Paris, Louvre AM 565: Caubet & Helly, *RevLouvre* 21 (1971) 331f., fig. 2; Masson, *BCH* 95 (1971) 331 No. 12 bis, fig. 21.

51.3   Similar plaque with a hardly recognisable painted representation; Dain suggests a nose (?).
Inscription: θεῷ Ὑψ[ίστῳ] | Ἀφροδεί|σις | ἀνέθηκεν | εὐξάμε|νος.
Paris, Louvre AM 669: A. Dain, *Inscr. gr. Louvre* ... (1933) 83f. No. 71; Masson, *BCH* 95 (1971) 331 No. 13, fig. 22.

51.4   Three eyes, incised relief.
Paris, Louvre AM 3351: Caubet & Helly, *RevLouvre* 21 (1971) 333 note 8, fig. 3a.

51.5   Face of a youth, right profile; pair of eyes; forepart of a left foot with only the first three toes. Relief.
Paris, Louvre MNB 324: Caubet & Helly, *RevLouvre* 21 (1971) 333f., fig. 4.

51.6   Pair of female breasts, relief.
Inscription: θεῷ Ὑψίστῳ ἀνέθη|χεν Προχτυος εὐξαμέ|[ν]η.
Paris, Louvre AM 668: Perdrizet, *BCH* 20 (1896) 361 No. 1; Masson, *BCH* 95 (1971) 331 No. 11, fig. 19.

51.7   Frontal view of a male trunk, approximately from the lower part of the thorax to the upper part of the thighs, relief.
Paris, Louvre AM 3354: Caubet & Helly, *RevLouvre* 21 (1971) 333 note 8, fig. 3c.

51.8-9   Two feet, separately carved.
Paris, Louvre AM 3349 and 3350: Caubet & Helly, *RevLouvre* 21 (1971) 333 note 8, fig. 3b.

51.10-14   Male genitals, relief.
Perdrizet, *BCH* 20 (1896) 362 No. 3; cf. Caubet & Helly, *RevLouvre* 21 (1971) 333.

51.15 etc. Some other votive replicas in the Louvre (i.a. arms), and in the Cyprus Museum, Nicosia (face, ear, male genitals, arms, legs) are briefly mentioned by Caubet & Helly, *RevLouvre* 21 (1971) 333 and 334.

Sicily:

52. Gela.

52.1 Foot with sandal. Terracotta.
Ca. 300 B.C.
Gela Mus.: P. Orlandini, *ArchClass* 9 (1957) 160 pl. 61, 1.

Italy:

53. Policoro (Herakleia).

53.1 Pair of eyes with the bridge of the nose. Bronze.
Late 5th century B.C.
Policoro Mus.: W. Hermann, *AA* 1966, 297 fig. 51; B. Neutsch, *AA* 1968, 765 fig. 10 a.

54. Francavilla Marittima (Cal.), sanctuary of Athena.
M. W. Stoop, *BABesch* 54 (1979) 76-90.

54.1 Left leg, knee to foot. Bronze; pierced lug for suspension.
First half 5th century B.C.
M. W. Stoop, *BABesch* 55 (1980) fasc. 2, 164, fig. 3-5.

55. Rome, Tiberine Island, Asklepieion.
M. Besnier, *L'Isle Tibérine dans l'Antiquité* (1902); M. Guarducci, 'L'isola Tiberina e la sua tradizione ospitaliera', *RAL* Ser. VIII 26 (1971) 267-281; E. Nash, *Bildlexikon zur Topographie des antiken Rom* I (1961) 508. Probably from this Asklepieion:

55.1 [Silver spleen]. Only its inscribed marble base remains: Ἀσκληπιῷ θε[ῷ] | μεγίστῳ [σ]ωτῆ[ρι] | εὐερ[γ]έτῃ ὄνχο[ν] | σπληνὸς σωθεὶς | ἀπὸ σῶν χιρῶν | οὗ τόδε δῖγ-μα ἀρ|γύρεον εὐχαριστ[ή]|ριον θεῷ Νεοχάρ[ης | Σ]εβαστο[ῦ ἀπ]ελ[εύ|θ]ερος Ἰουλιαν[ός].
Second half of the 2nd century A.D.
Moretti, *IGUrbRom* No. 105.

To include second century Rome in the Greek world, to which this catalogue is restricted, stretches Horace's *Graecia capta* rather far. Although in this case god and dedicator both are of Greek extraction, and correspond in Greek, Neochares' silver spleen appears to be more at home among Italic votive offerings, where internal organs are infinitely more common than in Greece. Typical Italic terracotta anatomical ex votos have in fact been found in large numbers on and near the Insula Tiberina, cf. below under C.

56. Unknown provenance.

56.1   Marble relief: a pair of ears is represented in the middle; on either side a snake, twisting itself up, touches one of the ears with its mouth or tongue; on the extreme left and right two identical plants.

Inscription: [τ]οῦ ὠτί[ο]υ θεραπεί|[ας] Μαριδία Πώλλα | [ἱε]ρηὶς εὐχαρι|[σ]τήριον. Roman period.

Woburn Abbey: Conze, AZ 1864, 213 pl. A1; A. Michaelis, *Ancient marbles in Great Britain* (1882) 746 No. 193; Weinreich, *MDAI(A)* 37 (1912) 65f., fig. 14. On miraculous cures performed by licking snakes see Herzog, *Wunderheilungen von Epidauros* p. 87 ff. and above No. 16.1.

(56.2?)   *Anth. Pal.* VI 166 (Loukillios):

εἰκόνα τῆς κήλης Διονύσιος ὧδ' ἀνέθηκεν
σωθεὶς ἐκ ναυτῶν τεσσαράκοντα μόνος·
τοῖς μηροῖς αὐτὴν γὰρ ὑπερδήσας ἐκολύμβα.
ἔστω καὶ κήλης ἔν τισιν εὐτυχίη.

This bizarre text can hardly be taken as a serious votive epigram. It may have been inspired by some such Italic anatomical votive with a realistic representation of a hernia, as is illustrated by Rouquette, *Bul. Soc. Fr. Hist. Med.* 11 (1912) 284.

Addenda

15 bis. Messene.
Limestone plaque with relief of a left (?) hand (broken off at the wrist).
P. Themelis, *AD* 21 (1966) B 164, pl. 157b.

19 bis. Demetrias.
Vulva. Marble relief.
Volos, Mus. E 467: Arndt-Amelung, *Einzelaufnahmen* No. 3399 (text F. Stählin and G. Lippold).

B.   *Confusions and exclusions*

A number of votive offerings that at one time or another have been taken by other authors as replicas of diseased parts of the body dedicated out of gratitude for a cure, were deliberately excluded from the above catalogue. They may belong to one of the following categories.

1. *Fragments*.   In the case of arms, legs, etc. that are broken off, it is often impossible to determine whether they were once separate votive limbs, or parts of complete figures. When in doubt, I refrained from including them. Cf. for example some fragments from the Delian Asklepieion already eliminated by Bruneau (*Cultes de Délos* 371).

Bronze male genitals from the Athenian Asklepieion, which were included among the 'Gliederweihungen' by M. Bieber, *MDAI(A)* 35 (1910) 5 nt. 2, in fact belonged to a herm, as is apparent from the description in 'Ἀθήναιον 5 (1876) 163 No. 28: part of the shaft of the herm, to which the bronze genitals are attached with lead, remains. For a similar case from the Amphiareion see A. Greifenhagen, *AA* 1964, 630.

2. *Ambiguous words.* Some curious misunderstandings have been caused by the use of certain ambiguous words in inscriptions with lists of votive offerings. Thus Roebuck, *Corinth* XIV 114, follows Rouse, *Greek votive offerings* 212, in regarding Amphiaraos at Oropos as a specialist in lung complaints, on the strength of the frequency of votive μαστοί in *IG* VII 3498. That several dozens of these were dedicated by the same Sophainetos, might have sounded the alarm. Since all the other votive offerings in this list are silver vessels, the context compels us to understand μαστός (μαστίον) here as the cup which derives its name from the fact that it is shaped like a woman's breast (Athenaeus XI 487 b; Hesychius s.v.). The same applies to the μαστοί in Delos (Vidman, *Sylloge* p. 83; *ID* 442, B 44 and 93).

Rouse, *ibid.* interpreted the χρυσοῦς τύπος μητρικὸς πρὸς ξύλωι, *ID* 442, B 202, as a representation of the pudenda muliebria, apparently deriving the adjective from μήτρα, 'womb'. But the same object recurs in other Delian inscriptions, then sometimes called τύπος μητρωικός, τύπιον μητ[ρωικ]όν (*ID* 1409, Ba, I 100 and 1443, B, I 110; cf. Bruneau, *Cultes de Délos* 432), and therefore can only have borne a depiction of the Μήτηρ, the Mother of the Gods.

The silver καρκίνος, *IG* II² 1534, 237, from the Athenian Asklepieion, interpreted by Rouse, *ibid.* 214, as a model of an ulcer, may more plausibly be regarded as a forceps; either a personal toilet article of the woman who dedicated it, or a medical forceps like the καρκίνοι ἰατρικοί listed with other medical instruments in *IG* II² 47 from the Asklepieion in Piraeus (see also J. S. Milne, *Surgical instruments in Greek and Roman times*, 1907, 16). Medical instruments dedicated by a patient, in whose cure they had been instrumental, have a striking parallel in the 17th century votive offering to S. Domenico at Soriano, illustrated in E. Greco, *Minerva Medica* Vol. 51, No. 102 (1960) 4406-4415, fig. 20.

3. *Ears.* Votive ears may be either replicas of the dedicator's ears which were afflicted by a disease, or representations of the listening ears of the god (*theòs epékoos*, cf. p. 83). Only in the first case do they belong in our list. It is, however, often impossible to be sure. When no direct or circumstantial evidence was available to impose a choice for either possibility, I have drawn the line somewhat arbitrarily: all ears dedicated to deities that are in the first place healing gods are included; those from sanctuaries of the Egyptian gods have been excluded.

The classic study by O. Weinreich, Θεοὶ ἐπήκοοι, *MDAI(A)* 37 (1912) 1-68, has lost nothing of its value. See now also Bruneau, *Cultes de Délos* 167-168. Conclusive evidence that the word ἀκοή (ἀκοαί) was used to denote the votive representations of the ears of the listening god is provided by some dedications from Thessalonica, see L. Robert, *RPh* 48 (1974) 198.

Eyes. It is possible that votive eyes too in some instances are intended as the eyes of the god. At least for the Egyptian gods Clemens of Alexandria (*Strom.* V 7, 42) supports such a supposition. For the Greek world, however, the matter is much less clear than in the case of the ears. Therefore all eyes have been included. For two other suggestions see catalogue Nos. 13.1 and 16.1.

4. *Footprints.* It seemed reasonable to take the footprints No. 8.20, in agreement with the other votive plaques from the same sanctuary, as referring to a cure.

Usually footprints, carved in relief or simply outlined by an incised or painted contour, have another meaning: They serve as proof and memento that the owner of the feet was there. Often they are human footprints, left by pilgrims in a sanctuary (outlines of hands are found as well; both also occur in secular contexts). In other cases, however, they represent the imprint of divine feet. The footprints left by a deity as a visible token of his epiphany are sometimes referred to in the accompanying inscriptions as ἴχνος or βῆμα (βήματα).

Roussel, *Cultes ég. Délos* 115f.; M. Guarducci, Le impronte del Quo Vadis, *RPAA* 19 (1942-43) 305-344; G. Manganaro, *Siculorum Gymnasium* N.S. 16 (1961) 184-190; Idem, *ArchClass* 16 (1964) 291-293; P. Herrmann & K. Z. Polatkan, *SBWien* 265, 1 (1969) 54f.,; C. H. E. Haspels, *The Highlands of Phrygia* (1971) 300 No. 14; Bruneau, *Cultes de Délos* 464.

(There is an interesting modern parallel in Italy on Monte S. Angelo, Gargano: both the archangel Michael, who is worshipped there, and his worshippers, have left their footprints. See R. Kriss, *Zeitschrift für Volkskunde* N.F. 2, 1930, 254f.; R. Kriss & H. Kriss-Heinrich, *Peregrinatio Neohellenika*, 1955, 129 ff.)

5. *The foot of Sarapis.* A characteristic type of object connected with the cult of Sarapis consists of a large, usually marble, foot surmounted by a bust (sometimes a complete figure, or related symbols) of the god. Here again the divine foot is intended, probably with special reference to its healing power.

Weinreich, *MDAI(A)* 37 (1912) 37-39 gives a list of such feet, which has been enlarged by S. Dow & F. S. Upson, The foot of Sarapis, *Hesperia* 13 (1944) 58-77 and D. K. Hill, *Hesperia* 15 (1946) 69-72; M. Le Glay, in *Hommages M. J. Vermaseren* (1978) 573-589. On their meaning see also Weinreich, *Antike Heilungswunder* (*RgVV* VIII 1, 1909) 67-73 and A. Henrichs, Vespasian's visit to Alexandria, *ZPE* 3 (1968) 68 ff.

6. *The hand of Sabazios.* The numerous bronze hands of Sabazios are characterised by a typical position of the fingers: thumb, index, and middle finger are stretched, the other two fingers are closed inwards (as in the gesture of the 'benedictio latina'). Usually these hands are covered with a multitude of attributes and symbols. Representations of Sabazios show the god himself making the gesture described above, which apparently had some specific significance in his cult. The separate bronze hands may be taken as images of the god's benedictory and beneficent hand.

The basic study is Chr. Blinkenberg, *Archäologische Studien* (1904) 67-100. Furthermore: O. Elia, *RAAN* 35 (1960) 5-10; D. K. Hill, *Essays in the memory of K. Lehmann* (1964) 132 ff.; E. Lane, *Muse* 4 (1970) 43-48; Catalogue of the exposition *Pompeii A.D. 79* (Boston, 1978) II 182 No. 189; W. F. Jashemski, *The gardens of Pompeii* (1979) 135-137, fig. 215; Y. Hajjar, in *Hommages M. J. Vermaseren* (1978) 455-472. Similar hands borrowed by Jupiter Dolichenus: G. Tonczewa, *Archeologiya* (Sofia) 4 (1950) 51 and M. Tačeva-Hitova, *ibid.* 16, 2 (1974) 23-27; J. Wagner, in *Hommages M. J. Vermaseren* (1978) 1300-1308.

7. *'Fluchhände'.* Two raised hands, with part of the forearms, palms turned forewards, are frequently depicted on later Greek grave reliefs of the eastern part of

the Greek world. They also accompany some curse inscriptions, e.g. *ID* 2531 (found in the Delian sanctuary of the Syrian gods), where we read in lines 2-3: αἴρει τὰς χεῖρας τῷ Ἡλίῳ καὶ τῇ Ἁγνῇ θεᾷ. The hands are those of the injured author of the inscription, appealing to the Sun for vengeance. On grave reliefs the hands are either an appeal for vengeance of a suspected murder, or directed against potential robbers and desecrators of the tomb.

The fundamental treatment of these representations and their Syrian background is by F. Cumont, Il Sole vindice dei delitti ed il simbolo delle mane alzate, *MemPontAcc* Ser. III 1 (1923) 65-80; see also Idem, *Syria* 14 (1933) 392-395; Bruneau, *Cultes de Délos* 449, 486; E. Pfuhl & H. Möbius, *Die ostgriechischen Grabreliefs* II (1979) 537; D. R. Jordan, *BCH* 103 (1979) 521-525.

C. *Comparative material*

For items in our catalogue that had no parallel in the ancient Greek world itself, comparative material from other areas and periods was occasionally adduced. There is comfort even in foreign company. In this section some references are assembled for the convenience of those who want to look farther afield.

1. *Minoan Crete.* The Early and Middle Minoan peak sanctuaries have produced many terracottas representing human figures, half figures, separately modelled limbs, etc. We may infer that a healing deity was venerated in these sanctuaries, although M. P. Nilsson, *The Minoan-Mycenaean Religion* ²(1950) 74-75, expressed serious doubts, on the ground that some parts of the body are absent which are very prominent in later healing sanctuaries, whereas the Cretan half figures and arm with quarter trunk cannot, in his opinion, be explained in this way. Of Nilsson's 'unsurmountable difficulties' the latter is easily surmounted if one looks at the material mentioned in our catalogue at Nos. 1.25-1.31 *a* and *c*. Of the wanting types that bothered Nilsson, most have been provided subsequently by new finds and belated publications of earlier finds. Finally the argument is clinched by a figure from the peak sanctuary of Traostalos, near Zakro. It represents a seated woman (once a complete figure) with a hideously swollen left leg (illustrated in C. Davaras, *Guide to the Cretan antiquities*, 1976, fig. 138). The deities worshipped in the peak sanctuaries had healing power, though it may have been only one of their aspects.

J. L. Myres, The sanctuary-site of Petsofá, *ABSA* 9 (1902-03) 356-387; N. Platon, Τὸ ἱερὸν Μαζᾶ καὶ τὰ Μινωικὰ ἱερὰ κορυφῆς, *ΚρΧρον* 5 (1951) 96-160; B. Rutkowski, Minoan cults and history, *Historia* 20 (1971) 1-19; Idem, *Cult places in the Aegean world* (1972); S. Hiller, *Das minoische Kreta nach den Ausgrabungen des letzten Jahrzehnts* (1977) 168-173.

2. *Ancient Italy.* Anatomical ex votos, mainly of terracotta, are extremely numerous in ancient Italy. They are very incompletely published. Some of the more interesting local groups, and a selection of general and special studies, are listed here. For an extensive survey see M. Fenelli, *ArchClass* 27 (1975) 206-252.

Bolsena (Pozzarello): E. Gabrici, *MonAL* 16 (1906) 169-240.

Caere (Manganello): R. Mengarelli, *SE* 9 (1935) 83-94.

Cales: J. M. Blazquez, *Zephyrus* 12 (1961) 25-42; Idem, *Archivo Esp. de Arqu.* 36 (1963) 20-39.

Capua: M. Bonghi Jovino, *Capua Preromana, Terrecotte votive* I-II (1965-1971); M. Bedello, *idem* III (1974).

Carsòli: A. Cederna, *NSA* 1951, 169-224; Idem, *ArchClass* 5 (1953) 187-209.

Lavinium: B. M. Thomasson, *ORom* 3 (1961) 123-138; M. Fenelli, *ArchClass* 27 (1975) 206 ff.

Lucera: R. Bartoccini, *Iapigia* 11 (1940) 185-213; E. Greco, *Minerva Medica* Vol. 51, No. 102 (1960) 4406-4415; Idem, *Riv. Storia della Medicina* 5 (1961) 193 ff.

Lucus Feroniae: M. Moretti (ed.), *Nuove scoperte e acquisizioni nell' Etruria meridionale* (1975) 93 ff.

Nemi: L. Morpurgo, *MonAL* 13 (1903) 297-368, bibliography at col. 324.

Paestum (Italic Temple): P. C. Sestieri, *Il nuovo museo di Paestum* ²(1955) 18; B. Neutsch, *AA* 1956, 445.

Praeneste: S. J. de Laet & M. Desittere, *AntClass* 38 (1969) 16-27.

Rome (Esquiline, Minerva Medica): L. Gatti Lo Guzzo, *Il deposito votivo dall'Esquilino detto di Minerva Medica* (1978).

Rome (Insula Tiberina, Tiber): M. Besnier, *L'Isle Tibérine dans l'Antiquité* (1902); M. Guarducci, 'L'Isola Tiberina e la sua tradizione ospitaliera', *RAL* Ser. VIII 26 (1971) 267-281; P. Pensabene e.a., *Terracotte votive dal Tevere* (= *Studi Miscellanei* 25, 1980).

S. Giuliano: P. Villa d'Amelio, *NSA* 1963, 1-76, esp. 65-69.

Teano (Teanum Sidicinum): W. Johannowski, *BA* 48 (1963) 131-165.

Veii (Campetti): L. Vagnetti, *Il deposito votivo di Campetti a Veio ... scavi 1937-38* (1971); M. Torelli & J. Pohl, *NSA* 1973, 40-258, esp. 227-248; see also the studies of Stieda and Alexander mentioned below.

Vulci: S. Paglieri, *RIA* 9 (1960) 74-96.

General and special studies:

L. Sambon, 'Donaria of medical interest in the Oppenheimer collection', *British Medical Journal* 1895 II, 146-150, 216-219.

L. Stieda, 'Anatomisches über alt-italische Weihgeschenke', *Anatomische Hefte*, 1. Abteilung, Bd. 16, Hft. 50 (1901) 1-83.

G. Alexander, 'Zur Kenntnis der etruskischen Weihgeschenke', *ibid.* Bd. 30, Hft. 90 (1905) 155-198.

P. Rouquette, 'Les ex-voto médicaux d'organes internes dans l'antiquité romaine I-III', *Bul. Soc. Fr. Hist. Med.* 10 (1911) 504-519; 11 (1912) 270-287 and 370-414.

E. Holländer, *Plastik und Medizin* (1912).

F. Regnault, 'Les ex-voto polysplanchniques de l'antiquité', *Bul. Soc. Fr. Hist. Med.* 20 (1926) 135-150.

N. Breitenstein, *Catalogue of terracottas, Danish National Museum, Copenhagen* (1941) Nos. 769-832.

Q. F. Maule & H. R. W. Smith, *Votive religion at Caere: prolegomena* (1959).

M. Tabanelli, *Gli ex-voto poliviscerali Etruschi e Romani* (1962).

P. Decouflé, *La notion d'ex-voto anatomique chez les Étrusco-Romains* (1964).

G. Bartoloni, Alcune terrecotte votive delle collezioni Medicee ora al Museo Archeologico di Firenze, *SE* 38 (1970) 257-270.

M. Bonghi Jovino, *Depositi votivi d'Etruria* (1976).

3. *Gallia.* Anatomical votives have been found in some Gallo-Roman sanctuaries. The largest and most interesting group comes from the sanctuary of Dea Sequana at the sources of the Seine. Older finds included parts of the human body carved in limestone, or cut out of thin bronze foil, see R. Bernard & P. Vassal, Étude médicale des ex-voto des sources de la Seine, *RAE* 9 (1958) 328-359 (perhaps at times a little over-interpreting with regard to supposed indications of specific diseases).

In 1963 a surprising discovery was made in the same sanctuary of some two hundred wood sculptures, which had been relatively well preserved in the marshy soil: R. Martin, Sculptures en bois découvertes aux sources de la Seine, *RAE* 14 (1963) 7-35. More were found in 1966 and 1967. Among these wood sculptures, which are firmly dated in the early 1st century A.D., are a number of most unusual anatomical representations, some sculptured in the round, others in the form of carved plaques. The majority represent the thorax, or the thoracic and part of the abdominal viscera, in an extremely schematic fashion. An extensive and sensible preliminary publication of these unique objects has been produced with gratifying promptness by Simone Deyts.

S. Deyts, Note préliminaire sur les sculptures anatomiques en bois trouvées aux sources de la Seine, *RAE* 16 (1965) 245-258; Nouvelles figurations anatomiques en bois des sources de la Seine, *RAE* 20 (1969) 235-245. See also, by the same author, Les différents 'styles' de sculptures en bois des sources de la Seine, *RAE* 17 (1966) 198-211, esp. 202-206; À propos d'une statue en bois des sources de la Seine, *RAE* 21 (1970) 437-460; *Ex-voto de bois, de pierre et de bronze du sanctuaire des sources de la Seine* (Catal. of exhibition Paris, Musée Carnavalet, 1966); *Sanctuaires et cultes des divinités des sources à l'époque gallo-romaine en Bourgogne* (1967).

4. *Modern anatomical votives.* There exists an extensive literature on modern ex votos, including the anatomical ones. Only a few of the more pertinent studies are listed here. Full bibliographies may be found in the first two books mentioned.

L. Kriss-Rettenbeck, *Ex Voto, Zeichen, Bild und Abbild im christlichen Votivbrauchtum* (1972).

M. Brauneck, *Religiöse Volkskunst* (1978).

Modern Greece and Cyprus:

R. Kriss & H. Kriss-Heinrich, *Peregrinatio Neohellenika* (*Veröff. Österr. Mus. für Volksk.* VI, 1955).

R. Kriss & H. Kriss-Heinrich, 'Beiträge zum religiösen Volksleben auf der Insel Cypern mit besonderer Berücksichtigung des Wallfahrtswesens', *Rheinisches Jahrbuch für Volkskunde* 12 (1961) 135-210.

N. Papadakis, *Greek folk silver votive offerings* (1971).

Modern Italy and Sardinia:

R. Kriss, 'Votive und Weihegaben des italienischen Volkes', *Zeitschrift für Volkskunde* 40, N.F. 2 (1930, published 1931) 249-271.

E. Greco, 'Gli ex-voto anatomici', *Minerva Medica* Vol. 51, No. 102 (1960) 4406-4415 (some interesting illustrations of modern ex votos).

R. Kriss, 'Beitrag zur Wallfahrtsvolkskunde von Sardinien', *Österreichische Zeitschrift für Volkskunde* 60, N.S. 11 (1957) 97-128.

G. Eckert, 'Zum Votivwesen in Nordwest-Sardinien', *Zeitschrift für Ethnologie* 82 (1957) 261-266.

Southern France:

F. Benoit & S. Gagnière, 'Pour une histoire de l'ex-voto: ex-voto en métal découpé de la région de Saint-Rémy-de-Provence', *Arts et Traditions Populaires* 1954, 23-34.

D. *Summary*

After the Minoan anatomical votive offerings, datable to the end of the 3rd and the first half of the 2nd millennium B.C., the earliest to be found in the Greek world are the Ephesian ones (end 8th-first half 7th century B.C.). Then there is a gap again till the 5th century B.C., when we see some rare examples in South Italy (catalogue 54.1 and 53.1) and, towards the turn of the century, the beginning of the Corinthian terracotta votive limbs (15). From the 4th century onwards, Greek anatomical ex votos are much more numerous, though never as overwhelmingly abundant as in Italy.

The majority come from sanctuaries of typical healer gods, like Asklepios, Amphiaraos, Amynos, Heros Iatros. Asklepios, a general practitioner by vocation, probably received the widest variety of parts of the human body. Women, with the typical problems of their sex connected with fertility, pregnancy and child-birth, could also turn to Asklepios for help, but they might prefer one of the deities who specialized in gynaecology, such as Artemis or Aphrodite. Besides, many of the other gods practiced a little medicine as a side-line.

The Asklepieia received patients with all sorts of complaints. Yet it is conceivable that a certain degree of local differentiation may have developed, to the effect that different diseases were considered to be, not exclusively, but on the whole more successfully cured in different Asklepieia. Such a limited differentiation, which may also be observed among the healing saints of modern Greece, has in fact been suggested for the ancient Asklepieia of Athens and Corinth, and the Amphiareion at Oropos (Rouse, *Greek votive offerings* 212; Roebuck, *Corinth* XIV 114). Amphiaraos as a specialist in lung complaints had to be dismissed (above B 2), but a comparison of the Athenian and the Corinthian Asklepieia, with regard to the relative frequency of certain parts of the body among the votives, seems promising, since these are the two sanctuaries from which the greatest numbers of anatomical ex votos are known to us.

The Athenian Asklepios' claim as a successful oculist (Rouse, Roebuck) is well founded: eyes are by far the most frequent among the Athenian votives (1.2-4,

1.25-1.31 *d*), whereas Corinth has only three (15.13-15). In Corinth, Asklepios appears to have had a certain bias towards legs and feet (15.77-114).

However, we should bear in mind that these conclusions are only valid, if we assume that the known votive offerings from these sanctuaries form a representative selection. I doubt whether that is true. The striking predominance of eyes in Athens is incontestable, but their scarcety at Corinth is another matter. After all, out of the more than 150 Athenian dedications of eyes, only three (1.2-4) really remain. All the other ones were gold and silver votives that do not survive, but of which we happen to have an epigraphical record because the Athenians were rather given to inscribing all sorts of decrees and inventories on stone. For all we know, the Asklepieia of Corinth and Epidauros may have been just as rich in gold and silver *týpoi*, which, like the Athenian ones, have left no tangible trace, and, unlike the Athenian ones, no epigraphical record either. That gold and silver votives indeed occurred there may perhaps be inferred from the gilded marble relief found at Epidauros (14.2), and the gilded terracottas from Corinth (15.15 and 15.42).

The parts of the body dedicated by the patients give us only a general idea of the types of diseases from which they suffered. More specific information, in the form of a realistic or at least recognizable rendering of the symptoms of the disease, is found in very few instances only (2.1, 8.2?, 15.63, 30.3-30.6, 44.2?, 46.1, 48.1?, 50.12?). Most of the Corinthian terracottas were made in a mould. Presumably the manufacturer kept a stock of standard types, from which the dedicator could select one. But we should allow for the possibility that then some realistic details were painted on in the appropriate places, as Kriss observed in a Sicilian shop of wax votives: 'Kommt dann ein Käufer, so wird er gefragt, ob er an dem ausgewählten Objekte irgendeine bestimmte Krankheit oder Verwundung angedeutet haben wolle; ist dies der Fall, so wird das gekaufte Votiv von der Geschäftsinhaberin in ganz primitiver Weise an der vom Käufer bezeichneten Stelle mit roten Flecken bemalt' (*Zeitschr. für Volkskunde* N.F. 2, 1931, 263).

The amount of medical information that may be gathered from the ex votos is also limited by the fact, that their forms are to a certain extent governed by convention. It has repeatedly been observed that internal organs are very rare in Greece (1.25-1.31 *p* and *q*, 15.117: bone, 15.118, 25 *e*, 30.9, 30.10, 55.1: Rome), as compared with Italy. Surely no one will consider this a significant piece of information on the state of public health in both countries. In the case of an internal complaint the common practice in Greece obviously was to dedicate an exterior view of the corresponding part of the body.

Replicas of the diseased part of the body were dedicated to thank for a cure, and also, according to Aelius Aristides (quoted below), as a prayer for a cure. Meyer-Steineg shrewdly remarks that for the two heads from Kos (30.4 and 30.5) only the latter possibility is acceptable, since both show clear symptoms of an incurable disease, and therefore can never have been dedicated to thank for a cure. Perhaps the learned doctor from Jena for a moment forgot, that there is a difference between himself and Asklepios: Asklepios could perform miracles.

We may have caught a glimpse of a woman clinging to her faith in the miraculous power of Asklepios to cure her oncoming blindness, offering silver eyes, then insisting with gold ones (1.25-1.31 commentary). But generally speaking the possibilities of the anatomical ex votos as a means of religious expression are rather slight. That may have been the reason why sometimes the dedicators preferred to incorporate the replica of the diseased member in a more comprehensive scene of worship. The actual presentation of the votive offering is depicted on Lysimachides' relief (2.1), not without a certain amount of (*mikro?*)*philotimía* perhaps: it is a remarkably tall leg; but after all, Lysimachides was not just a nobody. In other cases prayer and sacrifice, which accompanied the votive offering, are represented (1.1., 1.2?, 1.3?, 10.2, 42.2, 43.4, 45.2?, 47.4; 9.1). And we have seen that the patients that were cured in the Athenian Asklepieion frequently offered a *týpos* of themselves worshipping the god, in addition to the replica of the diseased part (1.25-1.31 commentary). Thus they gave visual expression to their adoration, and at the same time asked Asklepios, not to limit his attention to the part of their body that happened to trouble them at that moment, but to encompass their whole physical well-being with his healing and guarding power, as he did for Aristides: ἀλλὰ καὶ μέλη τοῦ σώματος αἰτῶνταί τινες, καὶ ἄνδρες λέγω καὶ γυναῖκες, προνοίᾳ τοῦ θεοῦ γενέσθαι σφίσι, τῶν παρὰ τῆς φύσεως διαφθαρέντων. καὶ καταλέγουσιν ἄλλος ἄλλο τι, οἱ μὲν ἀπὸ στόματος οὑτωσὶ φράζοντες, οἱ δ' ἐν τοῖς ἀναθήμασιν ἐξηγούμενοι. ἡμῖν τοίνυν οὐχὶ μέρος τοῦ σώματος ἀλλ' ἅπαν τὸ σῶμα συνθείς τε καὶ συμπήξας αὐτὸς ἔδωκε δωρεάν (VI 66-67 Dind., XLII 7 Keil).

H. W. PLEKET

RELIGIOUS HISTORY AS THE HISTORY OF MENTALITY: THE 'BELIEVER' AS SERVANT OF THE DEITY IN THE GREEK WORLD

I. *Introduction*

One can argue as long and as violently as one likes about the exact object of religious history. F. Dunand seems to me to have given a good answer recently—an answer which at least calls for a great deal of concrete investigation. On the one hand, she says, we should study religion in any particular society as a sort of social binding agent, operating with an ideology which either confirms the structure of society or attacks it (and in the latter case only holds one particular social group together); on the other hand we can try to get an idea of the manner in which, in a (part of a) particular society, the 'believers' experience their relationship with the world of the gods. At this point, the French proceed to indulge in flowers of speech like 'le sacré-vécu'.[1]

Nowadays research into the world of religious experience usually ends as the study of a *collective mentality*. What is at stake is not the single votive or funerary inscription in which the single believer puts into words his relationship with the deity or his vision of death (and hence also his relationship with the god(s) of the afterlife); nor is it the individual author and his personal vision of the various problems—no, our endeavour should, indeed must, be to study a *series* of documents in order to get at the common characteristics of the world of religious experience in a given society or group. In the case of a literary source we must study the expressions of an author and use these, together with the serial data from this same author's environment, to press through to the common traits of the conceptual world of a particular society.[2]

Thus, basing himself on the study of a few *thousand* wills, M. Vovelle recently tried to reach some general conclusions about the (development

---

[1] F. Dunand, Pour ou contre une Science des Religions, *Dialogues d'Histoire Ancienne* II 1976 (Paris) 479-491.

[2] Cf. my remarks in 'Griekse epigrammen op steen en de "Histoire des Mentalités",' *Handelingen van het 29e Vlaams Filologen Congres* (1973) 145-159, esp. 145-150.

of) attitudes towards death and the afterlife in seventeenth- and eighteenth-century France; in the 1930s L. Febvre used the work of Rabelais as a starting-point for a study of the attitude of sixteenth-century man towards the phenomenon of '(dis)belief'. In 1978 D. Pikhaus published a serial study, based on hundreds of funerary inscriptions, of the views of death and the afterlife in the Roman imperial period.[3]

It is on this level, on the level of a collective mentality, that I propose to approach one particular problem: from the vague but extensive group of problems covered by the label 'relationship of the believers with the world of the gods' I shall isolate the question of to what extent the believers experienced the deity as a great god possessing and exercising power, before whom the worshipper appears as a subordinate. Certain limitations are necessary for so brief an exploratory investigation. My primary concern will be to provide a *terminological* study. Yet religious behaviour expresses itself not only in words but also in deeds, so it will be essential, for example, to know the extent to which the worshipper did—or did not—kneel before his god. Since this problem has recently been treated in depth by F. T. van Straten[4] I shall merely touch on it, but will otherwise leave out iconography. Within the context of *terminology* I shall confine myself largely to epigraphical sources. It is above all the votive inscriptions which tell us about the way in which the worshippers gave shape to their relationship with the deity. They do so, moreover, in a 'serial' manner, so that we run less of a risk of taking personal peculiarities as the characteristics of a collective mentality. I shall concentrate on the following key words, to be divided under the categories 'Deity' and 'Worshipper'.

Deity	Worshipper	
commands (e.g. προστάττειν, ἐπιταγή)	ὑπουργός ὑπηρέτης	'servant'
power (e.g. δύναμις, παντοκράτωρ)	λάτρις	
epithets like κύριος, δεσπότης, τύραννος	δοῦλος τοῦ θεοῦ θεραπευτής εὐλογέω/-ία	

I shall refer very briefly to the so-called 'confession-inscriptions' the authors of which laboured under the strong sensation of divine om-

---

[3] For Vovelle and Febvre cf. Dunand, art. cit.; D. Pikhaus, *Levensbeschouwing en Milieu in de Latijnse metrische inscripties* (Brussel 1978).

[4] 'Did the Greeks kneel before their Gods?' *BABesch* 49 (1974) 159-189.

nipotence (δύναμ(ε)ις) which punishes man for his sins and requires a confession of guilt. The question, of course, is whether this can be considered a normal component of Greek religiosity or rather an essentially Oriental phenomenon. I shall also touch in this context on the habit of praising (εὐλογεῖν) the deity in these inscriptions.

In view of a marked trend in the modern literature which I shall be treating directly, there is no getting away from the question of whether a link can be established between the dominant social structure and the 'colouring' or appearance of the affective relationship between god and worshipper in the various periods of that very long era known as Antiquity—a relationship which, in its most extreme form, was one of 'Ruler-Subject'.

II. 'Orthodoxy' and its gradations

The views of A. D. Nock and F. Bömer are seminal. Nock points out that in the Hellenistic-Roman period emphasis was placed on the concept of 'divine power', particularly evident in the formula which appears in countless votive inscriptions '(dedicated) in accordance with the command of the deity' (κατ'ἐπιταγήν, κατὰ πρόσταγμα or κέλευσιν): 'we may with reason connect these dedications "in accordance with the command of..." with that conception of *the gods as absolute rulers* which becomes prominent in Hellenistic times and finds expression in such titles as *kyrios, despotes, tyrannos*. The gods were assimilated to the *absolute monarchs* of the East'.[5] (my italics). Bömer observes that it is an un-Greek, Oriental trait if 'der Gott durch besondere Weisungen in seinen Kult und in das Leben des einzelnen eingreift. Daher geschehen auch Einzelheiten der täglichen Gottesverehrungen, ebenso wie die bedeutenden Ereignisse, etwa die Stiftung eines Kultes, häufig *kat' epitagēn (ex epitagēs, kata prostagma, ex iussu, imperio,* usw.) des Gottes. Die klassische griechische Religion kennt diese Uebung nicht. Die Ueberlieferung dieser Art begegnet im wesentlichen seit dem Hellenismus'.[6]

Both scholars associate this assumed change in religious sensibility with the obtrusion of Oriental deities and the rise of absolute rulers in the Hellenistic-Roman kingdoms. Classical Greek and Oriental conceptions of god are sharply distinguished from each other. An alteration in the

---

[5] A. D. Nock, *Essays on Religion and the Ancient World* (Oxford 1972) I, 47.
[6] F. Bömer, *Untersuchungen über die Religion der Sklaven in Griechenland und Rom* (4 volumes; Wiesbaden 1957-1963) vol. 3, 207/8.

organisation of society (the rise of autocrats) is reflected in an autocratic image of god coupled with a submissive behaviour towards the deity.

This hypothesis can only be properly 'falsified' if we have at our disposal an exhaustive collection of votive inscriptions, arranged chronologically and according to the type of deity or, better still, a *complete* Thesaurus Linguae Graecae on the basis of which we can study the above-mentioned key terms. Neither condition can be satisfied, despite—or should we perhaps say 'owing to?'—the fact that Graeco-Roman philology is a very ancient science. The result is, that we work by taking a number of soundings in the material, performed, the best we can, by consulting the indices of the Corpora and by reading the Bulletins Epigraphiques (1938 to the present day)[7] and the 25 volumes of the SEG.[8] This looks like a great deal, but it is far from being all there is.[9]

The positions which I wish to defend and which should be regarded as modifying the 'orthodox' position, are as follows:

1. Even before the Hellenistic-Roman period we can find traces, in Greek religiosity, of a close affective relationship between deity and worshipper, i.e. of a serving worshipper having the clear sense of depending on an imperious deity.

2. This relationship manifests itself, where *assisting* deities (e.g. Nymphs, Asclepius) are concerned, mainly, but not exclusively, in emergency situations.

3. This dependency is strengthened and disseminated in the Hellenistic-Roman period under Oriental influence and in connection with the rise of autocratic political systems.

---

[7] Annually appearing in the *Revue des Études Grecques*, by Jeanne and Louis Robert (abbreviated by us as *BE*). The Bulletins from 1938-1977 have recently been collected in eight volumes (Les Belles Lettres, Paris 1972-1979). Members of the Institut F. Courby in Lyon have produced indispensable Indices for the Bulletins from 1938-1973 (*Index du Bulletin Épigraphique 1938-1965*: les mots grecs 1972; les mots français, 1975; *Index du Bulletin Épigraphique 1966-1973*: les mots grecs; les mots français 1979). These are invaluable *instruments de travail* for those who want to have relevant information, drawn from epigraphical sources for terminological and thematic studies.

[8] *Supplementum Epigraphicum Graecum*, vol. I-XXV (Leiden 1923-1971). To be continued in Leiden under supervision of R. S. Stroud (Berkeley) and H. W. Pleket (Leiden), assisted by S. A. Aleshire (Austin, Texas) and W. Peeters (Louvain-Leiden). So far two volumes appeared: XXVI (1979); XXVII (1980).

[9] It is especially the information hidden in the large Corpora (*CIG, IG, TAM* and the various 'national(istic)' corpora) which is not easily accessible. *SEG* restricts itself to collecting new material, published in periodicals, Festschrifte and non-corpus monographs, and references to recent and relevant studies of old material.

a) *Strengthened*: the ever more frequent use of epithets like χύριος, δεσπότης; the omnipotence of the deity elaborated and celebrated ever more intensively; the believer as 'slave, servant of the deity'.

b) *Disseminated*: ever more deities worshipped as 'lord' or 'ruler'; this becomes what we might call a *structural* phenomenon, i.e. gods are conceived as rulers independently from the *incidental* emergency situation (see *supra* under 2).

4. Despite the increasing verticality in the relationship between deity and worshipper (see under 3) in the Greek religiosity of the votive inscriptions we hardly ever encounter references to a strong *awareness of sin* which leads the sinner to 'confession of sins' and thus to reconciliation with the wrathful, powerful deity. This last group of emotions (sin-divine wrath-punishment-confession-atonement) is to be found exclusively in the so-called Lydian-Phrygian 'confession-inscriptions' (see *supra* p. 153-4) and can be regarded as a contribution of Oriental religiosity.

III. *Ad fontes*

1. *Kneeling*

From the already quoted study by F. T. van Straten[10] it appears that, as early as in the fourth century B.C., believers in moments of personal distress knelt before the gods from whom they expected immediate help and whom they implored: Asclepius, Artemis, Heracles Pancrates (gods of healing), and the Eleusinian gods (the givers of personal fortune in many forms). In a text of the second century A.D., from the temple of Asclepius on the Insula Tiberina in Rome, we read that the blind Gaius was advised by the god to kneel (προσκυνῆσαι) in the temple and indeed got better after a few treatments.[11] In the Roman imperial period we find in Egypt—and therefore in a context of Oriental autocracy—countless so-called *proskynēma*—graffiti in which the worshipper begs the god for mercy on his knees.[12] If we were to base ourselves exclusively on these texts and only examine the *term* προσκυνεῖν/προσκύνημα, we could easily be misled to conclude that 'kneeling' was a late phenomenon which arose under Oriental

[10] Cf. note 4 above.

[11] W. Dittenberger, *Sylloge Inscriptionum Graecarum*³ (= *Syll.*³) no. 1173.

[12] Cf. A. J. Festugière, 'Les Proscynèmes de Philae', *REG* 83 (1970) 175-197; see also *Aegyptus* 51 (1971) 1-211.

influence. Bömer is obviously of this opinion when he approvingly quotes Wilamowitz: 'Knien ist orientalisch'.[13] But that this view is wrong requires no further proof after Van Straten's article.

In the second-century text of the Insula Tiberina mention is also made of the joy of the bystanders at the fact 'that the ἀρεταί (i.e. the miracles) of Asclepius have been made manifest'. As well as 'miraculous power' ἀρετή can also mean power (δύναμις) in general. We already come across this meaning in an Athenian votive inscription from the fourth century B.C. in which a certain Meneia says that she dedicated a stone to Athena 'after and because she saw the power/the miracle (ἀρετήν) of the goddess in a dream'.[14]

In moments of personal distress and in the ensuing personal relationship with the deity 'kneeling' and a sensibility for the miraculous power of the god(dess) constitute a constant feature over the centuries (4th century B.C.-2nd century A.D.) which is independent of the structure of society. Two points should, however, be added: 1st) the substitution of the term 'dynamis' for 'aretē' seems to be a post-classical phenomenon.[15] The obtrusion of the 'harder' term is eminently suitable to a time when earthly power becomes ever more hierarchical. But I shall be returning to the notion of power later (p. 178). 2nd) In the Hellenistic-Roman period there developed the custom of using personal experience of the miraculous, beneficial power of the deity as a starting-point for a description of the *universal* power of the same deity. The power is not simply experienced *incidentally* and personally but is described as a *structural* element. In the aretalogies of Isis and her companions—for that is what I have in mind—we no longer have a simple description of the individual experience but a glorification of divine omnipotence *in general*.[16] Is it purely by chance that this only comes to the fore in the cult of Oriental deities at a time of Hellenistic rulers and Roman emperors?

---

[13] Bömer, *op. cit.* (cf. note 6 above) vol. III, 207, note 2.

[14] Dittenberger, *Syll.*³, 1151; Y. Grandjean, *Une nouvelle arétalogie d'Isis à Maronée* (Leiden 1975) 2-7, cf. 2 note 7, en 5 note 19; F. T. van Straten, 'Daikrates' Dream. A votive relief from Kos, and some other *kat'onar* dedications', *BABesch* 51 (1976) 1-38, spec. 16. Cf. H. S. Versnel above p. 54 and note 219; F. T. van Straten above p. 77.

[15] Cf. van Straten, *art. cit.* (cf. note 14 above) 16 with note 226 (*arete/aretai*), 227 (*dynam(e)is*; with mainly post-classical material), 228, 231, 232.

[16] A. D. Nock, *op. cit.* (cf. note 5 above) 34-48; Y. Grandjean, *op. cit.* (cf. note 14 above) 6-7, with note 21.

2. *Commands*

In the present state of research we cannot do much else than to approve the orthodox view according to which votive inscriptions presented κατ' ἐπιταγήν ('at the command') of the deity date from the post-classical era. Nock's own material and Van Straten's list[17] point to this conclusion. But here too it is probable that what was expressed earlier, in changing formulas and at moments of personal need and religiosity, subsequently becomes automatic, a sort of Pavlovian reaction, under the influence of the increasing hierarchisation of political and religious life in general.

In *fourth-century* Athens we come across votive inscriptions for Asclepius presented 'because the god has commanded it' (τοῦ θεοῦ προστάξαντος).[18] In the cure inscriptions of Epidaurus mention is frequently made of the 'commands' of Asclepius (κέλεσθαι).[19] In a text from Oropus of the beginning of the third century B.C. the Jew Moschos (who was probably manumitted by his Greek master in the temple of Amphiaraus) tells us that he presented the stele 'after receiving the command from Amphiaraus and Hygieia in a dream' (προστάξαντος τοῦ θεοῦ). F. Bömer regards the conception of the 'unmittelbare Befehl der Gottheiten' as an un-Greek phenomenon. The Jew Moschos would consequently seem to have smuggled in an Oriental mentality.[20] I believe this is going too far. Although we are not dealing with a cure inscription, Amphiaraus and Hygieia were direct colleagues of Asclepius who used to give commands without having undergone any Semitic influence as early as in the fourth century.

The idea of power behind such 'commands' can be somewhat modified, however, when, in two other fourth-century inscriptions, we read of the divine 'advice' (ὑποθῆκαι, ὑποθημοσύναι) of Asclepius.[21] I cannot help feel-

---

[17] A. D. Nock, *op. cit.*, 45-46 (cf. P. Veyne, *Latomus* 24 (1965) 939, note 1); van Straten, art. cit. (cf. note 14 above) 24-25; cf. also M.-F. Baslez, *Recherches sur les conditions de pénétration et de diffusion des religions orientales à Délos* (Paris 1977) 37 and 118/19, who points out that the κατὰ πρόσταγμα-formula primarily pertains to Oriental and subsequently to Greek deities.

[18] *IG* II/III², 4410, 4969.

[19] R. Herzog, *Die Wunderheilungen von Epidauros* (Leipzig 1931) p. 10, L. 50; p. 28, L 31.

[20] Bömer, *op. cit.*, vol. II, 25-26; SEG XV, 293.

[21] *IG* II/III², 4355 and 4358. Cf. the use of the terms ἐφημοσύνη and ὑποθημοσύνη in Chr. Habicht, *Die Inschriften des Asklepieions* (A. v. Perg. VIII, 3, 1969) no. 131 (Roman Imperial period; ἐφημοσύναι of Paian, i.e. Apollo or Asklepios) and in M. Fränkel, *Die Inschriften von Pergamon* (A. v. Perg. VIII, 1, 1890) I, no. 14 (Hellenistic period: ὑποθημοσύναι of Pallas (for the latter text cf. W. Peek, in: *Studien zur Religion und Kultur Kleinasiens*, vol. 2, 1978, 700-701)). These examples show that the terms and the concomitant mentality of the

ing that what, in the classical period, is experienced *incidentally* (in *emergency situations*), and in a relatively mild form, as the deity's power of command, becomes structural and 'harder' in the post-classical era. By 'harder' I mean that the ubiquitous 'commands' of the deity must be seen in the context of the triumph of the conception of the omnipotence of the deity *tout court*.

3. Servant of the Deity

What is basically true of this entire paper is certainly true of this section: it should provide a stimulus for further research rather than a report of an *exhaustive* study. We can try to answer the question of to what extent the worshipper regards himself as the servant of his god by studying the terms ὑπουργός, λάτρις, ὑπηρέτης and δοῦλος τοῦ θεοῦ. Such a study will be preceded by certain observations concerning the words:

a) Θεραπευτής, Θεραπεύω, Θεράπων

Going through Bömer's volume[22] one cannot help feeling that these words often denote slaves or servile (slave-like) activities. When applied to free persons the context always seems to be either the cult of Asclepius or the worship of Oriental gods. An interesting parallel presents itself here with what we observed above about words denoting divine orders. In Epidaurus we find θεράποντες who were presumably slaves, but the interesting point is that 'θεράποντες sind nicht nur die Diener, sondern auch die Verehrer des Gottes, also die Adoranten, ohne dass damit etwas über ihre bürgerliche Stellung ausgesagt wird'.[23] Surely, it is significant that the term θεραπεία could denote both the worship of the suppliant and the service of the domestic servant. Perhaps, however, Bömer did not sufficiently emphasize the fact that, when these terms are used to indicate the worship of free people, it is, as we said above, in the cults of Asclepius and Oriental gods. In Pergamum θεραπευταί are on record in the Asklepieion and in the cult of Hygieia and other healing gods. In Ainos we meet a θεραπευτὴς τοῦ

---

classical period lingered on in later texts. At the same time (Zeus Soter) Asklepios is styled [x]όσμου παντ[όκρατορ] *apud* Habicht, *op. cit.*, no. 113 (c). We witness a combination of the *power*-ideology with the traditional 'mild' vocabulary of the divine advice in the same temple. But cf. W. Peek, *art. cit.*, 707-708 who argues that this is a dedication to Zeus.

[22] Cf. note 6 above; see vol. II, 126, 132, 170, 177; III, 46, 64, 92 ff., 151, 211; IV, 12, 16, 181.

[23] Bömer, *op. cit.*, vol. III, 64-65; we do not discuss literary metaphors like θεραπευταί ″Αρεως here; cf. *Studi E. Manni* (1979-1980), 1626, note 15.

φιλανθρώπου 'Ασκληπίου.[24] Aelius Aristides provides the psychological background to the epigraphical *therapeutai* of intense personal relations with Pergamene Asclepius. In moments of great personal distress the worshipper feels himself to be a servant of his deity.[25] This is true of any period in Antiquity. L. Robert has recently described this type of religiosity in the cult of Asclepius in late Roman Aigeai, as reflected in Philostratus' *Vita Sophistarum* (11,4). Significantly Apollonius styles himself a θεράπων (and ἑταῖρος) of Asclepius.[26] Θεραπευτής becomes a *structural* term to denote a structural attitude of subservience in the cults of Serapis, Isis, the Syrian Goddess, the Mother of the Gods.

In a recent inscription from Sardes[27] we read about the group of *neokoroi therapeutai* of Zeus Baradates (the Greek equivalent of Ahuramazda, a *Persian* god!!) who use to go into the adyton of the temple. L. Robert reminds us of the Persian neokoroi in the Ephesian cult of Artemis. In Ephesus the Persian word Megabyxos came to denote the neokorate: 'c'était un nom parlant. Devenu titre il proclamait *la dévotion totale du desservant* à la divinité' (my italics).[28] The entering of the adyton has its parallels in the *Egyptian* cults.[29] In this respect it is noticeable that, when M.-F. Baslez writes about humility in personal devotion on Delos, she refers to the cult of Serapis who wanted to have a temple on a refuse heap. In the cult of the latter we hear about *therapeutai*! It is only in Jewish inscriptions from Delos that the term ταπεινόω has been used explicitly in connection with θεραπευταί. The connotation of that word was too negative for it to be acceptable to Greeks, no matter how strongly hierarchical Hellenistic-Roman society was. Baslez refers for the phenomenon of intense self-humiliation to a passage in Plutarch's *On Superstition* (*par. 8*) where the context clearly points to Oriental cults, Jewish and otherwise.[30] *Therapeutes* was the mitigated Greek version of the rigid humility of Oriental worshippers to autocratic rulers and gods.

I tend to conclude from all this that terms which previously could be used to describe the mentality of people who were in urgent need of

---

[24] Cf. L. Robert, *Hellenica* VI, 10, note 3.

[25] Bömer, *op. cit.*, vol. III, 64, note 5; L. Robert, *CRAI* (1975) 319, note 41.

[26] *JS* (1973) 161-211, esp. 187; Bömer, *op. cit.*, vol. III, 64, note 5.

[27] *CRAI* (1975) 306-330, esp. 317-321.

[28] J.-L. Robert, *BE* (1968) no. 140 on p. 437-438.

[29] L. Robert, *CRAI* (1975) 319.

[30] M.-F. Baslez, *op. cit.* (cf. note 17 above) 304-305, with note 16; 192-197; for the connotation of ταπεινός cf. note 63.

medical help (Asclepius), in the post-classical world came to denote the 'total devotion' of worshippers in Oriental cults. The 'hierarchisation' of post-classical society is reflected in the increasing popularity of 'vertical' Oriental cults; the concomitant, structural mentality of humility expresses itself in the structural use of terms, previously used only incidentally in emergency cases.

b) Ὑπουργός

A text from the vicinity of Halicarnassus (2nd century B.C.) mentions a certain Apelles, son of Apollonius, who dedicates a relief to the *Anakes* ('Rulers') on which are represented Hermes, Achelous and three Nymphs.[31] Who these 'rulers' are is not known. The Nymphs were notoriously friendly, helpful goddesses with whom simple religious people often had an intimate relationship. We know, moreover, about their relationship with Asclepius. In Crete Achelous and the Nymphs were worshipped before Asclepius was introduced.[32] Whoever the *Anakes* were,[33] it is clear that, with the introduction of the Nymphs, a sphere of strictly personal religiosity is invoked; in such an atmosphere Apelles presents himself as the 'servant of the gods' (in my opinion, of the *Anakes*). 'Rulers' can probably ask for 'servants' although I am not aware that in the cult of these *Anakes* the worshipper presented himself as a 'servant'. For the time being I would conclude that the helpful, trusted Nymphs imposed his submissive role on Apelles; for it was clearly customary to kneel also before helpers like Asclepius and the Nymphs. Apelles, moreover, does not say that this relief was dedicated in an emergency situation. So we can probably regard his 'subservience' as the outcome of his personal religiosity. The use of ὑπουργός seems extremely rare. I know of two more examples; one pertains to a Christian who called himself the ὑπουργός of the designer of a mosaic in a Christian church in Thebes.[34] Clearly the term designated a subordinate worker in a Christian context. In the famous Dionysiac inscription from Tusculum (2nd cent. A.D.) we hear about a ὑπουργὸς καὶ σειληνοκόσμος, probably a 'servant' whose task it was to dress up the images of the Silenes in the mystery-cult of Dionysus. Though Bömer is

---

[31] *SEG* XVI, no. 648.
[32] Cf. van Straten, *art. cit.* (cf. note 14 above) 19.
[33] Cf. van Straten, *art. cit.*, 19 note 280.
[34] J.-L. Robert, *BE* (1968) no. 289.

probably right about 'die sakrale Tätigkeit' of this man,[35] we cannot say exactly why he was styled ὑπουργός of Dionysus. Let us, therefore, return to the Nymphs.

The religious mentality of Nymph worshippers emerges from texts in which νυμφόληπτοι are mentioned. We know, for example, about a certain Archedemos of Thera who did up a cave in Attica in c. 400 B.C., laid a garden for it and did everything as 'the man who was seized by the Nymphs' (ὁ νυμφόληπτος).[36] Another cave, in the mountains of Parnassus, has yielded an inscription by a woman who 'was seized as she listened to the Nymphs and Pan'.[37]

The number of texts is limited; we get the impression, particularly in the case of Archedemos, that the individuals concerned were somewhat eccentric. How small the 'degree of subservience' was appears, moreover, from a 4th-century text from Pharsalus[38] in which we encounter a certain Pantalkes who made a cave sanctuary on the inspiration of the Nymphs. Pantalkes dealt wholesale in gods, but Pan and the Nymphs come first, closely followed by Asclepius and his companions. The text is devoid of terms of subservience. On the contrary: joyfulness, high spirits and gratitude prevail. 'Go up, sacrifice to Pan, pray and delight (probably with culinary aspects: εὐφραίνεσθε);[39] here is the end of all misery, good will comes to you and strife will cease'.

Surely we are far from the idea of the deity 'keeping his worshipper(s) down' (κατέχων; cf. infra p. 177). In the literary sources the νυμφόληπτος occurs with two meanings: a) 'saisi de folie' ('taken by madness') and b) 'inspired by the nymphs'.[40] The former is clearly pejorative, while the latter does not seem to have links with cult-practice but is rather a literary metaphor.[41] Aristotle defines νυμφόληπτοι and θεόληπτοι as people who are ἐπιπνοίᾳ δαιμονίου τινὸς ὥσπερ ἐνθουσιάζοντες.[42] Divine inspiration in a cultic context is on record in a dedication from Maionia, in which a village 'κατ' ἐπίπνοιαν Διὸς Κιλλαμενήνου' dedicated statues of the mother of Mēn and of

---

[35] Cf. Bömer, op. cit. (cf. above note 6) vol III, 134-136.
[36] Cf. van Straten, art. cit., 19 with notes 264-268, and above p. 95.
[37] SEG III, no. 406.
[38] SEG I, no. 248.
[39] Cf. L. Robert, Hellenica X, 199-200.
[40] Mélanges Heurgon, vol. I, 1 ff.
[41] Cf. Y. Grandjean, Une nouvelle arétalogie d'Isis à Maronée (Leiden 1975) 38-43; L. Robert, Études Deliennes (BCH Suppl. I, 1973) 472 ff., esp. 476.
[42] Eth. Eud. 1214 a 5.

Mēn Tyrannos.[43] Similarly the priestesses of the goddess of Kastabala are said to have been 'possessed by θεία ἐπίπνοια'. Significantly the notion of 'possession' is expressed by a word related to κατέχω which is used in Maionian inscriptions to denote the grip of Mēn Tyrannos c.s. on entire villages.[44] The *nympholēptoi* from Attica, the Parnassus area and Pharsalus are a strongly mitigated predecessor of the divinely inspired worshippers of tyrannical, Oriental gods like Mēn Tyrannos and the goddess of Kastabala. By and large we can conclude that a mild form of 'subservience' may appear in the sphere of the intimate cult of very familiar gods, but that this subservience is a far cry from slavish submission and does not exclude a substantial element of joyfulness.

c) *Λάτρις*

We must now make a leap in time but not in mentality to a Coan funerary altar of the second/third century A.D. An eighty-three year old man, Chrysogonos, calles himself 'servant of the Nymphs' (λάτρις Νυμφῶν) and pronounces the following hedonistic words to passers-by from his tomb: 'enjoy another glass (πίνε) for you see what the end is'.[45] This takes us straight back to the realm of Pantalkes' cave. Λάτρις actually means the man who works for a wage (λατρεία = δουλεία ἐπὶ μισθῷ). From a sociological point of view, therefore, the word does not sound so good. Yet I do not think that we need appeal to the strictly hierarchical structure of the later imperial period in order to explain Chrysogonos' 'Selbstverständnis'. The old man belongs, rather, with those who appeared in the previous section (under ὑπουργός); he is an exponent of a permanent undercurrent of Greek personal religiosity.

In the classical period we encounter the term λατρεύω in an Athenian epigram (c. 300 B.C.) indicating the function of a priestess of Athena: 'a solemn disposition of fate brought me to the fine temple of the pure Pallas, and the heavy labour which I have fulfilled in the service of the goddess was not inglorious' (καὶ πόνον οὐκ ἀκλεᾶ τόνδε ἐλάτρευσα θεᾶι).[46] Here the term 'to serve' is connected smoothly with the glory which the priestess has attained for herself. We would appear, then, to be dealing with a descrip-

---

[43] E. Schwertheim, *MDAI* (I) 25 (1975) 358-365 (with J.-L. Robert, *BE*, 1976, no. 628).

[44] L. Robert, *La déesse de Hiérapolis Castabala (Cilicie)* (Paris 1964) 59-62 (κατακωχή, on p. 62).

[45] W. Peek, *Griechische Versinschriften*, vol. I, no. 378.

[46] *IG* II, 1378 (= Kaibel, *Epigrammata Graeca*, no. 850).

tion, couched in a somewhat difficult, poetic language, of the function of priestess of Pallas Athena, and indeed, the text was found on the Acropolis. Later we shall see that Euripides used the same verb in a very special manner, but for the time being I believe that we here find ourselves in the sphere of a public cult and that the indication of function is a literary embellishment without there being any question of 'personal subservience' in the sense of Apelles and Chrysogonos.

Euripides, as I said, played around with the term. In the *Phoenissae* the Phoenician women given as slaves to Apollo are described individually as 'servant of Phoibus' (Φοίβῳ λάτρις).[47] Since wage labour was regarded as being close to slavery it is not surprising that a temple slave should be called λάτρις (see the Suda definition above). What is still more interesting is that Ion, in the homonymous tragedy, is presented as a λατρεύων. In actual fact Ion is a temple slave, but he is described as a priest (line 326) and, more in general, as a noble free youth who has a very profound relationship with Apollo: 'oh that I may serve Phoebus for ever' (151; λατρεύων).[48]

Ion must have made a somewhat strange impression upon the Athenian auditorium; the worshipper of Apollo, whether he was an official or not, did not present himself in the public cult as a *servant*; the servants were the temple slaves, inferior staff, whose 'serving' was a function and quality of slaves. 'Sein (i.e. Ion's) Leben ist ein Erzeugnis dichterischer Verklärung, das der Wirklichkeit des griechischen Tempelalltags und dem normalen Glauben der Menschen des 5. Jahrhunderts (nicht) entspricht', writes Bömer quite correctly.[49] We must not overestimate the 'fermentative effect' of eminent literary products in surrounding society:[50] the serving Ion, who is formally a slave but who is essentially described as a free cult-

---

[47] Cf. Bömer, *op. cit.*, vol. III, 21.

[48] Cf. Bömer, *op. cit.*, vol. III, 44-47.

[49] Cf. Bömer, *op. cit.*, vol. III, 47-48.

[50] For the problem of whether, and, if so, to what extent one is allowed to generalize about the collective 'expérience vécue' on the basis of literary evidence cf. my remarks in the paper, mentioned above in note 2; cf. also A. Henrichs (cf. below note 94) 261 and P. Veyne, *Annuaire Collège de France* 76 (1976) 371: '.....un abîme mental séparait les dieux comme figures mythologiques et les dieux comme objets de la piété des fidèles'. It is interesting to notice that according to Veyne Lucretius and Epicurus, with their emphasis on the notions of retribution in the after-life and the resulting fear of death, reflect *the* 'sensibilité populaire', *the* 'attitudes vécues' of their contemporaries. However, if one studies these attitudes on the basis of D. Pikhaus' study of Latin funerary epigrams (cf. above note 3), one quickly realizes that less than 10% of these texts mentions the idea of retribution/reward in the after-life!

official and whose service to Apollo is very profound, long-lasting and sub-missive, hardly resembles the average priest in the public sanctuaries of Athens. Only—so much will I add to Bömer's appreciation—in the sphere of the personal religiosity of a very personal Nymph cult could the wor-shipper declare himself to be a servant, but even then without the almost ecstatic, submissive frame of mind of Ion.

We have a relevant and touching funerary epigram from Megalopolis (Roman imperial period) for the Isis priestess Dionysia.[51] The almighty (παντοκράτωρ) Isis made her her λάτρις in her fifteenth year; after 45 years of faithful service she summoned her λάτρις and πρόπολος to astral immor-tality.[52] In this public cult Dionysia, unlike the λάτρις of personal piety, was an exponent of Oriental religiosity which did not flourish purely by chance in a world of kings and emperors, of *honestiores* and *humiliores*. The kindred term λατρευτής ('worshipper, servant') appears, precisely, in the cult of Serapis or a similar deity, as we see in a damaged text from Ephesus (3rd century A.D.)[53] where, after the acclamation customary at that time and for that sort of god: 'Great is the name of the deity',[54] we read that a cult official has given new life to 'the association of subservient worship-pers' (τὸ συνέδριον τῶν λατρευτῶν). Λατρεία appears in a Jewish inscription from Argos in the sense of daily service to the god.[55] We come across λάτρις in a number of Christian texts with reference to the lowly, sub-missive worshippers of the god of the Christians.[56] The *incidental* designa-tion of the worshipper as 'servant' of the helping, friendly deity in the context of a profound personal religiosity and in emergency situations develops into a *structural* phenomenon in the cult of almighty Oriental deities in a markedly hierarchical period. The picture which the otherwise unknown provincial governor Plutarchus gives of himself and his religiosi-ty in an epigram from Samos (4th century A.D.) fits perfectly into this mentality.[57] He has recently been on a pilgrimage to the Ida caves of Zeus

[51] L. Vidman, *Sylloge Inscriptionum religionis Isiacae et Sarapiacae* (1969) no. 42.

[52] For the interpretation of interesting (but for the present study irrelevant) details of this text cf the references and discussion in J.-L. Robert, *BE* (1968) no. 265; (1969) no. 260.

[53] *SEG* XV, no. 710.

[54] Cf. L. Robert, *Hellenica* X, 86-88 and 299; H. S. Versnel, *Lampas* 9 (1976) 27 with note 67, and above notes 261 and 262.

[55] Cf. J. B. Frey, *Corpus Inscriptionum Judaicarum* I, no. 719, L. 7.

[56] Cf. *C(orpus) I(nscriptionum) G(raecarum)*, nos. 8721, 8752, 8804, 9355.

[57] Cf. L. Robert, *Hellenica* IV, 55-57. In L. Moretti, *IGUR*, no. 1191, a woman, born in Egypt and deceased in Rome is styled πάντων μὲν μακάρων ἀγνὴν λά[τριν]. Unfortunately the context is not very informative.

and now, in the Heraion of the Samos belonging to his province, asks
Hera 'the Almighty', (Παμβασιλεία) to preserve himself and his emperor.
Plutarchus calls himself the 'unimpeachable servant' (σὸν λάτριν ἁγνόν) of
the Almighty Hera. L. Robert pointed out that the emperor in question
must have been Julian the Apostate and that this very Julian displayed a
great devotion to Zeus Basileus. The use of λάτρις here would seem to me
to be a reflection of the subservience, deeply ingrained in the late Roman
Empire, both to emperor and to deity.

As λάτρις Dionysia—in contrast to the ὑπουργός Apelles and the old
Chrysogonos—led a life entirely devoted to Isis. Admittedly the idea of
divine election which crops up in her funerary epigram is not an exclusive-
ly Oriental notion. With reference to the formula 'a diis electa' (said of
Vestal priestesses) attested in Roman inscriptions of the third century
A.D. Nock rightly observes, however, that the conception 'is certainly in
line with much that we know from the *Hellenistic East*' (my italics).[58]
Nock's examples either concern Oriental gods or 'assisting' Greek deities
(Asclepius and Artemis) and come from the Hellenistic-Roman period. It
seems to me that the phenomenon of religious vocation in combination
with the λάτρις-motive testifies to the *accentuation* of the milder feelings of
dependency on the Nymphs and Asclepius in the personal religiosity of
the pre-Hellenistic era—an accentuation which arose under Oriental
influence and which was admirably suited to an autocratic society.

d) Ὑπηρέτης-Δοῦλος

Just as Dionysia presents herself *structurally* as the servant of the deity in
a public cult, so, too, the man (Marcus Antonius Glaucos) who names
himself 'servant (ὑπηρέτης) of the heavenly gods (θεῶν οὐρανίων)' in an
inscription from Melos of the first century A.D.[59] is a 'structural' servant.
Glaucos built a walled Sebasteion for Zeus Keraunios and the θεοὶ
οὐράνιοι[60]—a phenomenon, therefore, of symbiosis of emperor worship

---

[58] Cf. A. D. Nock, *Essays*, I, 255.

[59] *IG* XII, Suppl., no. 165.

[60] For θεοὶ (ἐπ)ουράνιοι cf. e.g. J.-L. Robert, *BE* (1966) no. 213, where the Roberts point
out that the epithet ἐπουράνιος is a normal pagan epithet, applied to pagan gods from Homer
to Nonnos. Nevertheless a chronological survey of the texts, which pertain to cultic reality,
would be useful in order to see whether the term is increasingly used in Hellenistic-Roman
times as a reflection of the changed structure of society and of the corresponding hierarchical
mentality. Cf. also L. Robert, *BCH* (1978) 437-451. For a θεὰ οὐράνια cf. F. T. van Straten's
contribution, supra p. 138.

and the worship of 'true' gods. I do not know, however, who the heavenly gods are, whether *the* heavenly gods collectively (cf. the cult of πάντες θεοί (all the gods)), or a specific set of heavenly gods. At all events the verticality contained in this term is such that Glaucos, who calls himself the 'common' priest of Zeus the God of Lightning, uses the term ὑπηρέτης for his relationship with the gods of the heavens. The awe for the οὐράνιος θεός is well illustrated by a text from Lesbos[61] in which a certain Zosimē dedicates an inscription to Zeus, θεὸς ὕπατος πανεπώπης (and to Pluto and Poseidon, *panasphaleioi*) because she has been saved 'by the providence of the heavenly god' (προνοίαις οὐρανίοιο θεοῦ). I suppose that οὐράνιος θεός refers back to the all-mighty Zeus 'who sees all things'. A Zeus πανδέρκης ('seeing everything') is on record in an oracle from Didyma (Roman Imperial Period). A votive altar from the same place mentions Poseidon Ἀσφάλειος.[62] Perhaps there is a connection between epithets like ὕπατος, πανεπώπης on the one hand and the conceptualization of οὐράνιος θεός. In Zosime's case personal misery and the hierarchical nature of city-life and of the Roman Empire at large may have led to the use of epithets which express the heavenly superiority of the god and implicitly the inferiority of the worshipper.[63] According to Kittel's Theol. Wörterbuch zum N.T. ὑπηρέτης is a free man who receives wages for his work. It is milder than the term 'slave'. Nevertheless it does refer in some cases to slaves, as, for example, in the case of ὑπηρέτης τῆς βουλῆς (servant of the Council).[64] It is like the connotation of λάτρις: wage labour functioned, to quote Cicero, 'loco servorum'.[65] Against this background we can understand how it was only with the increase of social hierarchisation that *free* men dubbed

---

[61] *IG* XII, Suppl. 30 (1st-2nd cent. A.D.). Cf. also the testimonia cited by H. S. Versnel above p. 29 and notes 111 f.

[62] Cf. L. Robert, *CRAI* (1968) 578-592; J.-L. Robert, *BE* (1967) no. 690; (1970) no. 416.

[63] It is precisely on Lesbos that an inscription (*IG* XII, 2, 58, B, 2-9; early 1st cent. A.D.) testifies to the 'verticality' existing between what was felt to be ταπεινότερα in *physis* and *tyche* (i.e. *inter alia* human beings) and those who acquired divine renown and possess θεῶν ὑπερόχ-ην καὶ κράτος. The context is the imperial cult. The text provides a striking illustration of the hierarchical view about the relation between this world and that of both gods and divine rulers. For humility in the context of Oriental cults (Dea Syria) cf. F. Kudlien, *art. cit.* (cf. note 135), 3, who also points out that the concept of *paradeigmatismos* ('Zurschaustellung'), on record in Ptolemaios' *Apotelesmata* III, 13 (= p. 154, 6-11, ed. Boll-Boer) and related to the 'show' of the ταπεινοί who humiliate themselves and confess their sins, belongs to Oriental religiosity.

[64] Cf. e.g. J.-L. Robert, *BE* (1956) no. 148.

[65] *De officiis* I, 150-151.

themselves in the cult with the term ὑπηρέτης. In the words of Bömer: 'Diese Entwicklungen sind nur dadurch möglich geworden dass Vorstellungen, die dem antiken Gottesdienst fremd waren, die klassischen Tätigkeiten verdrängten... Die aus dem Osten vordringenden Kulte verlangten den persönlichen Dienst, und dieser Dienst adelte die Menschen die ihn ausübten...'[66] The only marginal note I would make concerns Bömer's 'nur' and the categorical '*dem* antiken Gottesdienst'. Some preliminary work had already been performed in Greece in the sphere of personal religiosity.

The personal service which Bömer believes the Oriental deities demanded of their worshippers appears clearly in an inscription from Maionia (119 A.D.),[67] according to which the free[68] woman Trophime was 'called to service (ὑπηρεσία) by the deity' at a certain moment. Trophime did not listen, was punished with madness, but finally reported for service after doing penance and recovering. The deity in question—probably the local Mēn, well known to us from dozens of inscriptions—is described as a ruler who 'keeps down' the village (κατέχων). Scholars have indeed spoken of theocracy in this connection,[69] and in this particular context a free woman abases herself to acts of service, thereby using the same term as was used in the case of a slave dedicated elsewhere as a sacred slave (hierodoulē) 'so that she can serve the gods' (ὑπηρετεῖν).[70] In a recently discovered inscription[71] also from Maionia, we see that in the cult of an autocratic, dominant deity things came to such a pass that the religious activities of a free man are not only described by the term which also designates the behaviour of slaves dedicated to the deity (ὑπηρετεῖν) but actually by the word ἱερόδουλος. The man in question, Glycon (certain-

---

[66] Bömer, *op. cit.*, vol. III, 57 and 226. In L. Moretti, IGUR I, no. 108 (from Rome) one finds the ὑπηρέται of Zeus Helios Mithras Phanes who together with the ἱερεὺς καὶ πατήρ erect a dedication. One is not surprised by the occurrence of this title in the very hierarchical cult of Mithras. Cf. U. Bianchi (ed.), *Mysterium Mithrae* (EPRO 1979) 160-161 ('servi di dei'). Cf. also SEG XXVII, No. 369, L. 8/9.

[67] P. Herrmann, *Ergebnisse einer Reise in Nordost Lydien* (Denkschriften Österr. Akad. Wiss., Ph.-Hist. KL., Band 80) no. 18.

[68] Cf. Herrmann, *op. cit.*, 25, note 82.

[69] P. Herrmann, 'Men, Herr von Axiotta', in: *Studien zur Religion und Kultur Kleinasiens. Festschrift F. K. Dörner* (Leiden 1978) 415-424, esp. 421.

[70] Quoted by Herrmann, *op. cit.* (cf. above note 67) 25, note 82.

[71] G. Petzl, 'Vier Inschriften aus Lydien', in: *Festschrift F. K. Dörner* (cf. above note 69) 745-761, esp. 746-750. Petzl prefers to date the *hierodoulos* stage and the priesthood of the honorand *after* each other.

ly a free man since he has a patronymic)[72] is perhaps a priest of the deity, but is referred to further on in the text as 'his colleague-sacred slave' (τὸν συνιερόδουλον) by someone who does not have a patronymic, is thus probably a slave and calls himself 'the priest'. It is unnecessary to assume that the man honoured had once been a *hierodoulos* and subsequently rose to being a free man (priest). No, the text clearly indicates the simultaneousness of being free and ἱερόδουλος.

There is perhaps some supporting evidence for the simultaneousness of legal/juridical freedom and being a slave of the deity. In the cult of the Phrygian Apollo Lairbenos and Meter Leto, who are 'nur schwach gräzisierte Formen eines älteren einheimischen Götterpaares',[73] free people seem to dedicate their own children to the deities for purposes of temple-service. Scholars have assumed that these children were born from unions with slaves and that they were accordingly slaves themselves, but Bömer is surely right in believing that this assumption strains credulity and moreover that there is no question of sacred manumission here: 'Apollo Lairbenos herrscht wie ein orientalischer Fürst über seine Gläubigen, die seine δοῦλοι sind, *wenn sie auch bürgerlich als Freie gelten*'.[74] Free people can be δοῦλος of the god in a religious sense ('im religiösen Sinne').[75] In late Roman Macedonian Leukopetra, in the cult of the Μήτηρ Θεῶν Αὐτόχθων a certain Theodotē, styled εἱερόδουλος Μητρὸς Θεῶν Αὐτόχθονος, ἡ πρὶν Συμφόρου, gives a female slave and a 14-year old son of the latter to the deity on condition that they stay with the donor for the duration of her life.[76] The formula ἡ (or ὁ or οἱ) πρίν + gen. is on record in Macedonia in other cases which pertain to Αὐρήλιοι who, as G. Daux has recently shown, refer by the use of this formula to an earlier 'onomastic' situation (now Aurelius 'x'; previously 'x', son of 'y').[77] Although Theodotē is not an Aurelia, could we suppose that she was previously the daughter of Symphoros, who dedicated her to the Meter? Though slaves are known to have possessed slaves themselves, it is easier to explain the presence of two slaves by the assumption that Theodotē was the daughter

---

[72] Cf. J.-L. Robert, *BE* (1978) no. 435 on p. 472: 'On peut se demander aussi s'il ne s'agit pas d'un service volontaire de gens se consacrant sans réserve et *avec humilité* (italics are mine, H. W. P.) au service de la divinité et à l'intérieur du *doumos*'.

[73] Bömer, *op. cit.*, vol. II, 108.

[74] Ibidem, 110.

[75] Ibidem, 111.

[76] *SEG*, XXVII, 292.

[77] *SEG*, XXVII, 307, 308, 352.

of the free man Symphoros who gave her—or left her—the slaves. In a second text, 3 years later, a certain Aurelius Paramonos is said to have bought another slave from Theodotē.[78] In view of Glykon's *hierodouleia* it becomes attractive to suppose that Theodotē is an example of the daughter of a free man who devoted her life to the Mother-Goddess.

If this is too speculative, an alternative is presented by Bömer's discussion of the case of Stratō in a 3rd cent. A.D. inscription from Macedonian Edessa. Stratō conveys (χαταγράφω) a vine-yard to the goddess Ma; she calls herself δούλη θεᾶς. A. Cameron, followed by Bömer, feels that Stratō acted as a freedwoman: 'Um eine solche χαταγραφή durchführen zu können, muss Strato, obwohl sie sich eine δούλη θεᾶς nennt, bereits frei und darf sie nicht mehr Sklavin sein'.[79] If this is acceptable, we can visualize Theodotē also as originally being a slave of Symphoros who, after manumission (via dedication to the deity, a *normal* procedure in Greece), demonstrated the abnormal, un-Greek mentality of considering herself now the servant of the deity. Whatever the truth may be, Glykon, Theodotē and Stratō all seem to be people who, though legally free (free-born or manumitted) continue to call themselves slaves of the deity.[80] Bömer's words deserve to be quoted: 'Dass sich eine freie Person als δοῦλος θεοῦ = *servus dei* (oder gar *Dei*) fühlt oder bezeichnet, widerspricht dem antiken religiösen Empfinden diametral'.[81] This is confirmed by evidence about the Syrian mendicant friar Λούχιος, who, when he dedicates an altar to his Κυρία Atargatis, explicitly calls himself 'her slave' (δοῦλος αὐτῆς) and is sent on a mission by the deity (πεμφθεὶς ὑπὸ τῆς χυρίας Ἀταρχάτης): 'juristisch ist dieser Lukios sicher kein Sklave gewesen'.[82] Nock collected some parallels for the '*doulos*'-ship of the believer which all concern Oriental cults from the imperial period.[83] The words addressed to

---

[78] *SEG*, XXVII, 293.

[79] Bömer, *op. cit.*, vol. II, 89.

[80] I do not discuss a 2nd century A.D. inscription from Oinoanda (Bömer, *op. cit.*, vol. III, 106-107) because textual uncertainty prevents us from knowing whether a free man dedicated his slaves or his children to a Meter Oreia. Dedication of slaves to the deity with the intention not of manumitting them through that procedure but of turning them into *hierodouloi* who permanently work in the temple-area, of course is well-known: see e.g. J.-L. Robert, *BE* (1968) no. 358 (dedication of three *hierodouloi* to Anaeitis).

[81] Bömer, *op. cit.*, vol. II, 89.

[82] Cf. Bömer, *op. cit.*, vol. III, 106.

[83] A. D. Nock, *Essays*, I, 46, with note 92; cf. also the donkey into which Lucius was changed and who in the Greek novel is called the *doulos* of the deity whom he carried (A. Henrichs, *art. cit.* (see below note 94) 281). In G. Mihailov, *IG Bulg.* IV, 1941, one

Lucius in Apuleius' *Metamorphoses* (XI, 15), 'but when you begin to *serve* (*servire*) the goddess (Isis)' fit into this context perfectly. The Greek view was defined by Bömer as follows: 'Für den Griechen bedeutet die Berührung mit den Göttern Anerkennung einer höheren Macht und Beschränkung der persönlichen Freiheit, aber nicht gleich auch *douleia theou*'.[84] The acts of service of Dionysia and M. Antonius Glaucos reflect the verticality in both the religious and social relationships of their time. What we have is, as it were, an institutionalisation of incidental, earlier outbursts of personal religiosity, but people do not yet go quite as far as the true Orientals in calling themselves the slaves of the deity.

The relationship between deity and believer is also stressed in the Dionysia epigram by the epithet παντοχράτωρ (almighty) bestowed on Isis. This leads us to ask how far, in what period and with what intensity terms designating 'power' appear in cultic documents. We shall be concerned with words like παντοχράτωρ, (παμ)βασιλεύς (almighty king), χύριος (lord), δεσπότης (ruler), τύραννος, δύναμις (power, force) and kindred terms.

4. *Divine omnipotence*

a) *Παντοκράτωρ, (Παμ)βασιλεύς*

Pantokrator suits Isis perfectly. This Eastern goddess' omnipotence was praised to the skies in her so-called aretalogies. The editor of one such aretalogy, found recently in Maronea (Northern Greece), Y. Grandjean, talks rightly in his commentary of the 'omnipotence' and 'toute-puissance' of Isis and Serapis, and gives the necessary references for this thesis.[85] Παντοχράτωρ also typifies the Theos Hypsistos of the Jews and the God of the Christians.[86] We find it, too, in the (late) imperial period in Egyptian papyri as the epithet of Helios and a number of indigenous Egyptian deities.[87] Finally K. Keyssner traced the terms to the so-called Orphic

finds a son of Theodoulos who dedicates something to Theos Hypsistos. Though the latter is not to be identified with the God of the Jews, there might be a relation between this name and the connotation of the 'vertical' deity. In J.-L. Robert, *BE* (1972) no. 366 on p. 445 an Αὐρ. Θεόδουλος is on record in a *Christian* inscription.

[84] Bömer, *op. cit.*, III, 14; cf. also 89 ('dass sich eine freie Person als *doulos theou* = *servus dei* (oder gar *Dei*) fühlt oder bezeichnet, widerspricht dem antiken religiösen Empfinden diametral'); cf. also *ibidem*, 133-136.

[85] *Op. cit.* (cf. above note 14) 7 and 69.

[86] Cf. J.-L. Robert, *BE* (1965) no. 283; L. Robert, *Hellenica*, II, 155.

[87] Cf. A. D. Nock, *Essays*, vol. I, 383.

hymns of the late imperial period (2nd/3rd century).[88] It would seem clear
that we here have a designation of divine omnipotence which primarily
typifies Oriental gods and, in their wake, gods worshipped in late-Roman
Orphic groups. We shall see later (cf. *infra* p. 178) that notions of power,
like kneeling and other tokens of submission, were not an *exclusive* invention of the post-classical era; but we get the impression that it was precisely
in the Hellenistic-Roman period, in connection with the arrival of Oriental religiosity and autocratic rulers, that the power concept gained in intensity and was disseminated in the cultic reality of Greek religiosity. An
excellent example of this can be found in the funerary epigram of Salvius
Menas (Crete; 1st/2nd century A.D.).[89] The text concerns the cult of
Hermes in a cave in the Tallaion mountains and thus a form of personal
religiosity. Menas and his wife once forgot to bring their annual sacrifice
to Hermes; this omission resulted in the death of Mrs. Menas (*post hoc*,
propter hoc). The husband repented, improved his way of life and asked
finally: 'and you, almighty Eriounios (Παντοχράτωρ 'Εριούνιε) may you
keep this man alive so that he can honour your precinct for the whole of his
life'. The ubiquitous sense of divine omnipotence in this period is expressed in this votive inscription—which, incidentally, is purely Greek—by the
epithet Παντοχράτωρ, whereby the trusted Greek god Hermes 'under the
stress of emotion'[90] comes into line with the great, universally worshipped
'almighty ones'. Similarly, in a votive inscription from Cappadocia,
Hermes is both χύριος ('lord': see below) and σωτήρ ('saviour').[91] Παμ-
βασιλεύς/-εία (almighty king) appears in Christian inscriptions, as the
epithet of Hadrian and in the already mentioned Orphic hymns.[92] In the
fourth-century epigram of Plutarchus (see *supra* p. 165) we encountered it as
an epithet of Hera in the context of the 'subservience' of the worshipper.
Παμβασιλεία in this text can be put on the same level as παντοχράτωρ in
Menas' epigram.[93] In a text from Paros παμβασιλεία is applied to

[88] K. Keyssner, *Gottesvorstellung und Lebensauffassung im griechischen Hymnus* (1932) 31, 45.

[89] M. Guarducci, *Inscriptiones Creticae*, vol. II, par. XXVIII, 2; cf. P. Veyne, *Latomus* 24 (1965) 945, note 1.

[90] A. D. Nock, *Essays*, vol. I, 427, note 77.

[91] Id., vol. I, 75, note 99.

[92] G. Björck, *Der Fluch des Christen Sabinus* (Uppsala 1938) 102-103. It is perhaps not inap-
propriate to add here that in a graffito in one of the Ephesian 'Hanghäuser' the epithet παμβασίλεια is given to Rome, in a context of eternal *power*: 'Ρώμα ἡ παμβασίλεια, τὸ σὸν χράτος
οὔποτ' ὀλεῖται (*Die Inschriften von Ephesos, Repertorium*, vol. II, Bonn 1979, no. 599; cf. also
Anth. Palat. IX, 647 where the epithet is related to Rome's everlasting glory).

[93] Cf. also Bömer, *op. cit.*, vol. IV, 24 (*pampotnia Cybele*).

Persephone, but this may be due to the age-old idea that death rules supreme.[94]

A far more obvious product of the late (imperial) period is a text from Dacia where Hera Βασιλίσσα is mentioned.[95] The same applies to a votive inscription from an Attic cave where the dedicator, the Syrian Soaimos, suddenly speaks of the βασιλεῖς Πᾶνες (= royal Pan-gods).[96] We shall see later (cf. *infra* p. 175) that the traditional companions of Pan, the Nymphs, obtained the epithet κυρία (mistress) at the same time. In the Pantalkes epigram Pan is indeed invoked with the words 'oh ruler' (ὦ ἄναξ), but we should keep in mind that ἄναξ (and πότνια) 'seit dem frühen Epos fester Bestandteil der Dichtersprache waren',[97] i.e. that they were titles of address which persist throughout the centuries more or less as Homeric 'fossils'. In Pantalkes' poem Pan is also the patron of laughter, eating and drinking, in short of 'righteous daring' (ὕβριν δίκαιαν). Curiously enough when Pindar calls Pan a 'ruler' in a fragment of a hymn he produces the epic term μεδέων[98] and qualifies the lordship with a purely *geographical* term: 'lord *of Arcadia*'. This is clearly far more 'objective', more 'distant', than Soaimos' epithet βασιλεῖς, which is more expressive of the *personally* experienced majesty of Pan and his companions. The majesty of the god, which may well reflect the hierarchy of the imperial period just as much as the influence of Oriental religiosity, is splendidly expressed in a funerary inscription from Thessaly (3rd century A.D.) where 'the King, the greatest, almighty (παντοκράτορα) god, creator of everything, all gods and heroes and the mistress herself, 'Queen' ' are invoked as protectors of the tomb.[99]

[94] *IG* XII, 5, 310 quoted by L. Robert, *Hellenica* IV, 57, note 7; cf. also id., *CRAI* 1968, 584; A. D. Nock, *Essays*, vol. I, 75, note 97 (*despoina*: 'Queen of the underworld', quoted by A. Henrichs, 'Despoina Kybele: Ein Beitrag zur religiösen Namenkunde', *Harv. Studies Class. Phil.* 80 (1976) 253-286, esp. 259, note 16). Cf. Basileus, together with Neleus, as gods of the underworld in F. Sokolowski, *Lois sacrées des cités grecques* (1969) no. 14 (cf. RFIC (1978) 181), and a funerary pinax dedicated to Βασίλεια from Athens (IG II/III^2, 4645; 4th century B.C.).

[95] J.-L. Robert, *BE* (1961) no. 417.

[96] Cf. A. Wilhelm, *JOAI* 25 (1929) 54 ff.

[97] Cf. A. Henrichs, *art. cit.* (cf. above note 94) 255 note 7, and 263.

[98] Cf. A. Henrichs, *art. cit.*, 255.

[99] *IG*, IX, 2, 1201, quoted by Henrichs, *art. cit.*, 277, note 64. Cf. the expression τῷ τῶν ὅλων δεσπότῃ in a 6th cent. A. D. Christian papyrus (G. Björck, *op. cit.* (cf. above note 92) 81). The Thessalian inscription is certainly not Christian. However, the maker does seem to be influenced by trends which strongly focus upon the notion of religious power. After all the

Texts which simply mention *Basileus* and *Basilissa*, i.e. Mēn and the Mother goddess, bring us straight to the Oriental sphere of Asia Minor.[100] Elsewhere the same mother goddess is called 'queen of the cosmos' in the second/third century A.D. This text, like so many others, comes from Maionia where it was also customary to say that a deity (often Mēn) was 'king of the village', with all the theocratical implications of such a title.[101]

b) Κύριος, Δεσπότης, Τύραννος

As elsewhere, we tread here on ground which lies partly fallow and, where it does not lie fallow, is beset with pitfalls. I referred earlier to the fact that power concepts in the religious sector were not an exclusively post-classical affair. In classical Athens we encounter a healing god, Pankrates (all-mighty), in votive inscriptions. People even knelt before him; the conception of omnipotence clearly functioned in a sphere of personal distress and profound religiosity. Recent studies by Bömer and Henrichs[102] have submerged us with material containing cult epithets expressing 'power' like δεσπότης/δέσποινα, κύριος, τύραννος etc, but it is not always easy to spot their relevance for our subject.

Nevertheless we get the impression: 1st) that, as Henrichs observed,[103] the epithet δέσποινα was applied primarily to a group of deities originally connected with nature. We are dealing with the 'Mächte der beseelten Natur' which already wave their sceptre over Mediterranean man in the second millennium. Henrichs further concludes that 'diese Anrede primär in der religiösen Erfahrung einer vorliterarischen Religionsstufe wurzelt'. 2nd) that Homeric linguistic usage, itself rooted in a very autocratic period, had a fossilising effect in the sense that epithets like πότνια and

text dates from the late Roman Empire, during which the Oriental focus upon the powerful God runs parallel with similar Greek tendencies.

[100] S. Mitchell, *AS* 27 (1977) 89-90 (= *SEG*, XXVII, 851-852). In Miletus we have a dedication to Basileus (*Milet*, I, 7, p. 349, no. 285; late imperial period!). In Caunos we come across Βασιλεὺς ὁ θεός (J.-L. Robert, *BE* (1954) no. 274 (c); Imperial period!) The reader is referred to *P.W.*, vol. III, 82 ff. s.v. *Basileus* for some older examples of deities bearing the epithet βασιλεύς/βασιλίσσα: Apollo (healing God), Asclepius (cf. above p. 158 about Asclepius giving orders, already in classical times), Hera (late imperial period), Heracles (Italy; late imperial period; inscription by an *imperial* freedman). Cf. now also S. Şahin, *Katalog der antiken Inschriften des Museums von Iznik (Nikaia)* (1979), no. 43: dedication to Μὴν Βασιλεύς; Sahin refers to SEG VI, 79 (dedication Διὶ Βασιλικῷ; from the area between Dorylaion and Nakoleia in Phrygia).

[101] *SEG* IV, no. 645.

[102] Bömer, *op. cit.*, vol. III, 195-214; Henrichs, *art. cit.* (cf. above note 94).

[103] *Art. cit.*, 259-261.

ἄναξ/ἄνασσα[104] were automatically attached to certain gods without any deeper relationship of subservience being implied. 3rd) that in literary sources we are often confronted with somewhat distant, objective relationships. When Bömer refers to fifth-century expressions like 'Zeus, lord of all' (Ζεὺς ὁ πάντων κύριος: Pindar) and to gods characterised in literature as δεσπότης,[105] it is either a very general designation of power, in which there is no question of an affective personal relationship in a concrete cultic context, or the designation of a very specific power, which extends to more or less 'everything' (Olympus, the area or city, the temple, animals) but not to the individual worshipper. We may be able to connect this last aspect with the statement (sub 1st above) about that particular element of the power concept which was originally connected with nature. 4th) that the title δέσποινα/δεσπότης is rare in votive epigrams/inscriptions where a personal religiosity is very much present.[106] Most of Henrichs' examples come from the Anthologia Palatina and date from the Hellenistic-Roman era. Some concern the gods of the underworld. We saw in connection with Persephone Παμβασιλεία (cf. *supra* p. 173) that the main idea behind this was the omnipotence of death, which is always far more powerful than any mortal. The epithet expresses just as strongly, as it were, the fundamental and permanent impotence of man. When we look round at deities who can fulfil a helping, healing role (Nymphs, Asclepius, Ino) we immediately see that the first two do not appear in Henrichs' material (see note 58 of his article), though it must be added that the Nymphs only figure in certain passages in literature, and even then with an 'unengaged' geographical accentuation. For Ino, the nurse of Dionysus, we have a Thessalian funerary epigram in which this goddess of birth is invoked as δέσποινα and implored to extend her hands in blessing of house and property.[107] The atmosphere is substantially the same as that in the cult of the Athenian Pankrates.

In as far as it is possible to survey the material, we can say that it is only in the late Hellenistic-Roman period that we encounter votive inscriptions to the Nymphs and Asclepius in which the epithets κύριος and δεσπότης crop up regularly.[108] The term 'kyrios' was already at hand in the clas-

---

[104] Henrichs, *art. cit.*, 255, note 7, and 263.

[105] Bömer, *op. cit.*, vol. III, 210-213.

[106] Henrichs, *art. cit.*, 274, with note 58.

[107] Quoted by Henrichs, *art. cit.*, 274, note 58; cf. now also W. Peek, *Philologus* (1973) 66 ff. Cf. the remarks of L. Robert on the cult-epithet *Hyperdexios*, *Hellenica* X, 63-66 and 295-296.

[108] Cf. L. Robert, *RPh* (1959) 221-222.

sical period. Pindar used it, and in the late fourth century B.C. we come across the expression Τῷ κυρίῳ Ἅιδη in a fragment of the tragedian Sosiphanes.[109] Consequently I do not understand why Henrichs calls κυρία an 'unpoetisches Wort'.[110] Still less can we say that the term κύριος was not available for religious purposes in the classical era since it had not yet acquired the specific significance of 'lord'. The same goes for the frequent appearance of these words in votive inscriptions as was said about the κατ' ἐπιταγήν formula (cf. *supra* p. 158): the penetration of Eastern religiosity, combined with the rise of autocratic rulers, makes κύριος and δεσπότης into favourite epithets in votive inscriptions in general. In the wake of all this assisting deities like Asclepius and the Nymphs, who were formerly worshipped in a sphere of incidental submission, are now structurally provided with the epithets *par excellence* of the Hellenistic-Roman era.[111] A. D. Nock saw this clearly, as usual: 'Kyrios involves a notion of ownership and authority more concrete than that which is usually associated with the Greek Gods and exactly in accordance with Oriental precedent. Consequently we find in the Hellenistic Age, with the closer contact it caused with Eastern belief, a number of gods coming from Asia Minor, Syria and Egypt called 'lord' '.[112] To Nock's examples of κύριος and δέσποινα as epithets of Greek gods we should add Henrichs' material in addition to my own impression formulated above. Nor should we forget that the Oriental 'lord' notion was later immensely influential in the cult of purely Greek gods: what was previously incidental became structural.[113]

I do not believe that the term τύραννος functioned in the cultic reality of Greek religion. Versnel[114] has rightly pointed out that in the classical age certain gods were indeed furnished with the epithet τύραννος *in literary*

---

[109] Bömer, *op. cit.*, vol. III, 210; for Sosiphanes cf. Nauck, fragment 3.5.

[110] *Art. cit.*, 272.

[111] Cf. note 108.

[112] *Essays*, vol. I, 75.

[113] For κύριος cf. also Kittel, *Theol. Wörterbuch z. N.T.*, s.v., 1045 ff. In Kittel's view 'lordship' is not a basic characteristic of classical Greek deities. K. further points out, that the Greek gods were not conceptualized as creators versus mankind and world, but together with man were part of one and the same reality. (See on this subject P. A. Meijer, *infra* p. 225 ff.). In K's opinion this might have contributed to the fact, that in Greek religion the antithesis *kyrioi-douloi* did not play a role. This article purports to break through the cult of the generalising article 'the' ('*the* Greek Gods') and to show that in spite of the absence of the concept of the Creator, under the impact of Oriental cults and of changing social relations an increasing focus upon the lordship of gods and a sharpening of relations of subservience can be noticed.

[114] H. S. Versnel, *De Tyrannie verdrijven?* (Leiden 1978) 11, with notes 59-63.

sources. In the cases of Ares and Eros we are obviously dealing with a literary metaphor: the arbitrary fury of their dominion is suggested with a term by then strongly pejorative. With the Zeus of Greek tragedy we reach such heights of artistic awareness of god that, if we wish to speak of the Greek religiosity of cultic practice, we would be well advised to erect a firm partition between stage and temple/chapel. At the most I can join Bömer and others in talking of a sense of 'schlechthinnige Abhängigkeit' in classical Greece.[115] After all, the men of letters, with their exalted conception of god, must have appealed somehow to the hearts of their public. We have seen that in the temple individuals in the classical era kneel before, and all expect help from, an assisting deity. But Bömer was certainly also right when he observed that, in the temple religion of classical Greece, the feeling that man was the slave-like servant of a divine despot was absent. Man was no δοῦλος, the god no τύραννος.[116]

The latter first appears as a cult epithet in the post-classical era in the cult of Oriental deities or of orientalised Greek deities. Isis bears the epithet and so, above all, does the Mēn Tyrannos of Asia Minor; the late-Roman Orphic Hymns also use the epithet, while later Egyptian Jewish-Christian 'angehauchte' papyri are not averse to the word either.[117] Particularly in the case of Mēn the term tyrannos easily lends itself to incorporation in a global theocratic mentality. Mēn is 'king of the village', 'keeps the village down' (κατέχων).[118] We saw above (cf. *supra* p. 168) that this could bring the free man to ἱεροδουλεία. This god is almighty, he is 'der Herr des Leibes und der Seele dessen, der sein Knecht ist. Er ist der Herr des ganzen Menschen, aller seiner Taten, Sinne und Gedanken'.[119] In a recent publication P. Herrmann pointed out that here a 'Theokratie' is at stake whose 'Ausmass und Möglichkeiten...im 'geistlichen' Bereich... gerade durch die vielfältige Berichte der Sühninschriften beleuchtet (werden)'.[120] That 'geistliche' is important; it is definitely not necessary to think in terms of immense Oriental temple complexes with crowds of subservient ἱερόδουλοι.[121] The so-called atonement—or confession-inscriptions lead us to the numerous villages of Eastern Lydia and

---

[115] Bömer, *op. cit.*, vol. III, 213.
[116] *Ibidem.*
[117] Cf. Versnel, *op. cit.*, 11 (with the notes); Bömer, *op. cit.*, vol. III, 195-210.
[118] Cf. P. Herrmann, *art. cit.* (cf. above note 69).
[119] Bömer, *op. cit.*, vol. III, 206.
[120] *Art. cit.* (cf. above note 69), 421.
[121] Cf. Versnel, *op. cit.*, 28, note 69.

Phrygia where the average peasant and his wife know that they are the subjects of the local Mēn or Meter who 'keeps down' their village. The subjection of the worshipper is suitably attended by the feeling that he is always running the risk of committing (material and/or spiritual) *sins* and that the almighty god and/or goddess of his village will then mete out suitable punishments (in the shape of illness or worse).[122] This tension subsequently culminates in a confession of guilt, often induced by the god via his priests or dreams, and an eulogy of the power (δύναμις)[123] of the god(s) concerned. We thus read that the almighty Mother Goddess Leto first punishes a sinner with an ailment in his buttock and then performs a cure as the deity who makes ἐξ ἀδυνάτων δυνατά, i.e. who makes powerless (limbs) powerful again'.[124] In the background there certainly also lies the idea of the divine *power* which makes what is impossible possible. In another inscription from Lydia the same goddess is called the δυνατὴ θεός 'the deity who has power, who can do (everything)'.[125] It is high time to investigate more closely the term δύναμις (power) and related words.

c) *Δύναμις*

Already in 1926 A. D. Nock called our attention to the fact that in the Roman period the conception of 'divine power' adopted an ever more cen-

---

[122] Cf. F. Steinleitner, *Die Beicht in Zusammenhange mit der sakralen Rechtspflege in der Antike* (Leipzig 1913); cf. also Herrmann, *art. cit.* (cf. above note 69) 421 (with literature about the question whether or not the temple-authorities really administered justice in the villages). An up-to-date Corpus of all confession-inscriptions is a desideratum; after Steinleitner many new texts have been found. A comparative study of the religious mentality on record in these texts and of the evidence about guilt-feelings and confession of sins in Graeco-Roman religion at large is another desideratum.

[123] Cf. Steinleitner, Index s.v. *dynamis*.

[124] Steinleitner, *op. cit.*, no. 31. See on this expression also H. S. Versnel above p. 53 n. 218. In L. 5 St. read λοῦθρον = λύτρον ('ransom'). W. H. Buckler, *ABSA* 21 (1915) 172-173, no. 2, suggested γλουθ<ί>ον ('buttock'). A recent find, made by G. Petzl and myself in Kula (Maionia) in August 1977, shows that γλουθροῦν or γλουθρόν is the most probable reading (cf. H. W. Pleket, *Talanta* X (1980) 55-56 no. 13). Sappho depicts Aphrodite as a goddess who will use her power (δύναμις) to bring about a change in amorous feelings. A. Cameron, *HThR* (1939) 5 ff., compares this with the inscription mentioned in the text and esp. with the words ἐξ ἀδυνάτων δύνατα. This is not convincing. In Sappho's poems we do not have documents pertaining to genuine experience in a temple-cult (of Aphrodite); on the contrary, S.'s *dynamis* is an example of poetic phraseology on a par with the literary *mos* to call Eros a tyrannos. Aphrodite is the hypostatized passion which in the perception of poetical lovers can exert irresistible pressure upon her victims.

[125] *AJA* (1887) 348; cf. L. Robert, *Hellenica* X, 57, note 6. Cf. the words πάντα δυνατὴ γὰρ δόξα ὑψίστου θεοῦ in a *Jewish* apologetic treatise (cf. A. R. R. Sheppard in note 83 of his forthcoming article on 'Pagan Cults of Angels in Roman Asia Minor' in *Talanta* XII (1981).

tral place. His evidence consisted mainly in votive inscriptions to Oriental deities: Mithras, Sol Invictus, Isis and a number of gods from late Egyptian magical papyri and amulets.[126] We can now add an extensive amount of Lydian-Phrygian confession-inscriptions in which it is either said that the deity displayed his 'powers' (ἰδίας δυνάμεις) or that the believer publicly praised (εὐλογεῖν) the power of the deity after the cycle 'sin-punishment-repentance-recovery' in a text engraved on a stele (στηλογραφεῖν).[127]

Recently inscriptions have been found in Eastern Lydia in honour of 'the great Zeus of the twin oak' (thus a sort of tree deity; many oaks grew/grow in the area in question), whose δυνάμεις are invoked next to, and independently of, the deity in the opening of the text.[128] It is clear that the glorification of the 'power' of the deity, which originated from the Oriental cult of Meter and Mēn in Asia Minor, has been transferred to the cult of Greek gods in this area.[129] Nock had indeed already pointed out that, on a relief from the town of Thyatira in Western Anatolia, under the representation of lightning, there stands the text 'the power of Zeus, god of lightning'.[130] Not far from there, in the town of Saittai, we find Mēn characterised by the acclamation 'great is the Power of the immortal God', together with the slogans 'Great is the heavenly Mēn' and 'Unique is he as God in the heavens'.[131]

Both the Μέγας and the Εἷς acclamations flourished above all in the Roman period in the cult of Eastern deities (Serapis, Isis) and of colleagues from Asia Minor. The hierarchical structure of the imperial age explains why such slogans were also fashionable in acclamations to rulers and local magnates and benefactors.[132] The Oriental deities, who were hierarchical by nature, found in their worshippers a ground well prepared by the structure of society for the 'seed' of the ideology of power. Of course the word 'great' (μέγας) is not lacking in earlier Greek hymn literature: Euripides' creation of the great god Dionysus is all too familiar.

[126] *JHS* (1925) 84 ff. = *Essays*, vol. I, 34 ff.

[127] Cf. Steinleitner, *op. cit.* (cf. above note 122), Index s.v.; cf. also P. Herrmann, *op. cit.* (cf. above note 67) no. 21; *SEG*, IV, no. 647-648; Bömer, *op. cit.*, vol. II, 86.

[128] G. Petzl, 'Inschriften aus der Umgebung von Saittai (I)', *ZPE* 30 (1978) 250 ff. (with BE, 1979, nc. 434).

[129] Artemis also underwent Oriental influence and has been worshipped as Artemis Anaeitis (= the Persian Anahita) in this area.

[130] A. D. Nock, *Essays*, vol. I, 37, note 30.

[131] L. Robert, *Opera Minora Selecta*, I, 427, note 101.

[132] Cf. L. Robert, *Hellenica* X, 86-88 and 299; id., *La Carie*, II, 110 and in *BE* (1964) no. 252.

What we must realise, however, is that μέγας is late as a cultic epiclesis and should be distinguished from unengaged poetical *epitheta ornantia*.[133] Indeed, the devices of Euripides, which undoubtedly made a deep impression during the performance, did not necessarily affect every-day cult practice—and do not appear to have done so. 'Megas' acclamations as *cultic* practice are late. They belong to the Oriental gods and later to Greek deities orientalised in the hierarchical structure of society. We should also point out in passing that it is precisely in the astrological writings of the imperial period that the δυνάμ(ε)ις of the all-dominating stars is mentioned repeatedly.[134]

In comparison with the sphere I have just discussed of the awesome δυνάμ(ε)ις of great, punishing gods, the ideology of the so-called cure inscriptions of the Asclepieion of Epidaurus fades into nothingness. These texts are admittedly always about the sick but the illness is rarely regarded as a divine punishment.[135] In one episode an Athenian woman is said to have considered a number of the accounts of cures hanging in Epidaurus 'improbable and impossible' (ἀπίθανα καὶ ἀδύνατα). After this the god did

---

[133] Cf. H. S. Versnel, *Lampas* 9 (1976) 27, with the notes.

[134] Cf. L. Robert, *Entretiens F. Hardt*, vol. XIV (1967) 217. For the notion of δύναμις cf. also J.-L. Robert, *BE* (1944) no. 181 (Syria; 3rd cent. A.D.; theft of xoana from the temple of Zeus in Dmeir; followed by the manifestation of the *dynamis* of the God (Zeus Hypsistos)); (1955) no. 251 (Transjordania; 6th/7th cent. A.D.; Christian Inscription: Κύριε, ὁ θεὸς τῶν δυναμέων). Cf. also *ZPE* (1970) 63 (Θεοῦ δύναμι; Christian).

[135] Significantly enough O. Weinreich, *Antike Heilungswunder* (Giessen 1909) 120, with note 3, when talking about thoughts concerning disease as a consequence of punishment of a sin, has nothing to offer but a story from Aelianus (a *late* author!) pertaining to the cult of the *Egyptian* Serapis. F. Kudlien, 'Beichte und Heilung', *Medizinhistorisches Journal* 13 (1978) 1-14, esp. 5-6, mentions three examples from the Epidaurian *iamata* of people who confessed (2 × ὁμολογέω, 1 × δηλόω) their mistakes and subsequently were healed by the deity. First, the notion of 'sin' and punishment is implied rather than explicitly formulated. In two of the three cases the context is irrecoverable; in the third the 'sin' is conceived of as ἐξαπάτα (*SEG*, II, 58; XXVII, 41); verbs like χολάζω are absent. Second, irrespective of whether or not one interprets these instances as evidence for the existence of the 'sin-disease/punishment-confession-healing' mechanism one tends to agree with Kudlien when he refers to 'das geschlossene Schweigen aller übrigen Zeugnisse für den Asklepioskult und andere griechische Inkubationsheiligtümer' (p. 5). Kudlien regards these three Epidaurian cases as 'vereinzelte Fälle' (p. 6). I do not agree with him when he writes about Oriental influence or priestly dramatizing. There is no trace of Oriental religiosity in 4th century B.C. Epidaurus and if the priests wanted to dramatize the stories, they must have drawn upon recognizable feelings of the clientela of the sanctuary. My view is that in the context of the cult of a helping, healing deity we have here the first, hesitating and 'underdeveloped' signs of a mentality which in its institutionalized form and with much greater rigidity and harshness expresses itself in the cults of Oriental gods and of the Lydian-Phrygian Anaeitis and Mēn.

indeed heal the woman but on the condition that she dedicates a silver pig as a 'fee', in memory of her stupidity.[136] Asclepius is very mild and remains far removed from the tough, punishing gods of Asia Minor. In Epidaurus ἀδύνατα does not refer to the power glorification surrounding the Maionian gods. A further episode reports the scepticism of a male patient: the man had laughed at Asclepius' therapies and expressed doubts about Asclepius' real power (δύναμις); Asclepius then punished him for his presumption: the unfortunate mocker fell off his horse and was crippled. After the necessary prayers of supplication Asclepius finally cured him.[137]

Apart from the fact that this 'focus' on Asclepius' δύναμις only occurs once in the extensive series of accounts of cures, we can say that in this episode the power of the god was not explicitly reported and celebrated, but was only assumed, and that solely in the sphere of healing the sick and not in the general sense of the δυνάμ(ε)ις of Mēn or 'Zeus of the Oaks', for example. Asclepius' power is mentioned once and then only because someone mocked his very concrete power of healing. Asclepius does indeed inflict a punishment, but does not demand a confession of guilt[137a]—only prayers of supplication ('I shall not do it again: please make me better'). This single episode cannot be put on the same level as the accounts of the structural power of deities who are simply called δυνατός, who are, as it were, 'power'.

The institutionalization of divine power—an extension and intensification of the conception of omnipotence under the influence of the ubiquitous δύναμις notion—is on record in the inscription on a votive relief from the vicinity of Rethymnon (Crete; Roman imperial period). A certain Seteria depicted a large female breast on the stone and added the following words: 'Seteria dedicated this relief according to her vow to

---

[136] Cf. R. Herzog, op. cit. (cf. above note 19) p. 10, L. 34 ff.

[137] Ibidem, p. 22, L. 95 ff. Many centuries later the δύναμις of Asklepios is praised in the sanctuary in the Cilician city of Aigeai by Libanius and other intellectuals; cf. L. Robert, JS (1973) 191, note 6; but at the same time the god is φιλανθρωπότατος; he loves Aigeai which is θεοφιλής. We are not far away from the mentality of 4th century B.C. Epidauros. The self-consciousness of the members of the elite in 4th cent. A. D. Graeco-Roman cities was still large enough for them not to indulge into the habit of using institutionalized power-epithets and of behaving like subordinate, humiliated characters. Nevertheless it seems appropriate that it is precisely in the cult of Asklepios that Libanius c.s. used the word δύναμις. Cf. for a similar problem concerning the term θεραπευτής/θεράπων above p. 160, with note 26.

[137a] On the rareness of the concept of confession of guilt in Epidauros cf. Kudlien's article, mentioned in note 135 above.

Artemis Δυνατηρά'.[138] Artemis, who either filled the breast with milk for a
newborn baby or cured the baby itself or an inflammation of the breast, is
'(all) powerful'. In an earlier text from this same area Artemis is simply
εὐήχοος (hearing). The worshipper thanks the goddess for her life
(ἀναζῶσα) but there is no notion of power.[139] The idea of the 'listening,
hearing' deities is known to us from the classical period, while standard
cult epithets like εὐ-or ἐπήχοος come into their own above all in the post-
classical period.[140]

In classical Athens the notion of power occurs in the epithet of Heracles
Pankrates. Significantly enough this deity seems to be a 'heros
guérisseur'.[141] With this epithet we are in the realm of gods like Asclepius
who are known to have given commands to their worshippers, prepared in
their turn to humiliate themselves and to kneel (cf. *supra* p. 156-8). A deity
Pasikrata is on record in Ambrakia (Artemis Pasikrata), Thessalian
Demetrias and Macedonian Herakleia.[142] The editor of the Athenian
Pankrates—inscriptions adduces Pasikrata, thereby implying that the latter was also a healing deity and thus providing a parallel for the power
concept in the realm of Asclepius—like gods. Perhaps we should compare
Artemis Pasikrata from Ambrakia, worshipped by a woman, with Artemis
Dynatēra from Crete? Unfortunately, the interpretation of Pasikrata has
not been proved beyond doubt. Bömer calls the Heraclean Pasikrata, to
whom slaves are dedicated and who has *hierodouloi* at her disposition, 'eine
ungriechische Gottheit'.[143] The texts are late; consequently, if Bömer is
right, Macedonian Pasikrata is to be compared with the all-mighty Maionian deities with their *dynam(e)is*. N. D. Papahatzis seems to have related
the Thessalian Pasikrata with the cult of the funerary Aphrodite.[144] In that
case the cult of Pasikrata is to be connected with the well-known view

---

[138] M. Guarducci, *Inscriptiones Creticae*, vol. II, par. XII, no. 24.

[139] *Ibidem*, no. 23.

[140] F. T. van Straten, *BABesch*. 49 (1974) 184; O. Weinreich, *MDAI(A)*, 37 (1912) 1 ff.;
Index *BE*, s.v. ἐπήχοος; cf. also M.-F. Baslez, *op. cit.* (cf. above note 17) 294 ff., who points
to the frequency of this epithet in the cults of Oriental, orientalized Greek and more in
general of healing gods (or gods who bring σωτηρία: Asclepius, Demeter, Dioskouroi). From
the realm of the latter this phenomenon spreads over other cults, as indicated above. Cf. also
H. S. Versnel in his contribution to this book, p. 35 and note 137 (χύριος, σωτήρ, together
with ἐπήχοος).

[141] J.-L. Robert, *BE* (1959) no. 124.

[142] Id., *BE* (1965) no. 223; (1973) no. 253.

[143] Bömer, *op. cit.* (cf. above note 6) vol. II, 93.

[144] Cf. J.-L. Robert, *BE* (1965) no. 223.

about death ruling supremely over all mortals at all periods of antiquity. Besides the *dynamis* of Maionian deities and of Macedonian Pasikrata and the δυνατὴ θεός from Lydia we have a dedication to the *Theoi Megaloi* from Samothrace, who bear the epithets Θεοὶ Δυνατοί and Θεοὶ Ἰσχυρροί.[145] In an Orphic hymn they are called the εὐδύνατοι ἄνακτες. Ἄναξ, whether or not going back to old cult-practices, may have been a fossilized epithet by now.[146] The notion of divine power and force, as expressed by Δυνατοί and Ἰσχυρροί, however, is an institutionalization of previous and incidental awareness of the power of (healing) gods in situations of personal distress. The Δυνατοί are the divine counterpart of the social *potentes* (*honestiores*), and the divine colleagues of the stars, whose *dynamis* (or *dynameis*) is frequently praised in astrological treatises in the Roman empire. Finally *dynamis* of powerful gods has a very concrete parallel in the *dynamis* of a wealthy Late-Roman benefactor who is praised for having paid everything ἐξ οἰκείας δυνάμεως.[147] In view of what we said above about the word *therapeutēs* it is not irrelevant to note that these powerful Samothracian gods had their own 'Götterdiener' (Kabires, Kuretes etc.) who were called θεραπευταὶ τῶν ἱερῶν by Strabo.[148]

5. 'Advertisement' of the deity: eulogy (εὐλογία) and penance.

Returning to the Lydian-Phrygian inscriptions I should point out that G. Björck's theory according to which the confession-inscriptions are functionally comparable to the Epidaurus cure inscriptions is not very enlightening.[149] Björck emphasises the phenomenon of the glorification and advertisement of the deity, of the sinner humbling himself by doing *penance* and immortalising his *expressions of praise* on stone. I believe the 'sin and punishment' mechanism to be extremely unimportant in Epidaurus, as is the confession of guilt (cf. notes 135, 137ᵃ). The same applies to the above-mentioned (cf. *supra* p. 172) inscription of Salvius Menas. I admit that Menas thought in terms of a causal relationship; he suggests, perhaps out of extreme diplomacy, that negligence towards Hermes may indeed have caused the sudden death of his wife, but there is no trace of confession of guilt or of any term suggesting 'guilt' or 'sin'; nor are we entitled

[145] *IG*, XII, 8, 74 (2nd-3rd cent. A.D.).
[146] Cf. B. Hemberg, *Anax, Anassa und Anakes als Götternamen* (1955) 25.
[147] L. Robert, *Hellenica* III, 23-24 = *La Carie*, II, 110, no. 113.
[148] Bömer, *op. cit.* (cf. above note 6) vol. III, 151, with note 6.
[149] *Op. cit.* (cf. above note 92) 125 ff.

to describe Menas' epigram as a confession-inscription. Pantokrator Hermes is a milder spirit than the *dynamis*-filled Meter, Mēn or Zeus of the Lydian-Phrygian texts. Nor do I agree with A. D. Nock when he says that 'the whole is reminiscent of confession-inscriptions and of the aretalogy type in general'.[150] But let us return to Epidaurus. The accounts of cures are an implicit advertisement for Asclepius; in certain cure inscriptions from other Greek shrines it is even explicitly stated that the deity commanded what had happened and/or what had been dreamed to be written on a stele.[151] This does not detract from the fact that it is in the Lydian-Phrygian texts that στηλογραφεῖν becomes a standard technical term[152]—yet another institutionalization of what had certainly occurred before—and that this στηλογραφεῖν, furthermore, is directly related to the δυνάμ(ε)ις or the νέμεσις (punishment, revenge)[153] of the deity concerned. As for the feature of the 'praise of the deity' I feel that 'making propaganda' for the god's power and recording it, were admittedly on record in pagan inscriptions long before the Hellenistic period but that it was once again in the Lydian-Phrygian texts that an institutionalization of this feature took place by means of the term of *eulogia*. The question should be asked whether this is a pagan, Greek (and, if so, what we mean by 'Greek') or a non-Greek phenomenon, that is to say whether or not the habit of explicitly praising the god in this specific form is to be assigned to Oriental, i.e. Jewish influence.

Recently L. Robert has devoted some attention to this term. In 1964,[154] in a commentary on a new *confession-text* from Sardes, he wrote about the frequency of the use of *eulogia/eulogein* in 2nd cent. A.D. confession-texts from Maionia and stated: 'il (i.e. the term *eulogia/eulogein*) est original, ainsi d'ailleurs que les pratiques religieuses que reflêtent les documents de cette région'; furthermore he rejected Bickerman's view that '*eulogein* n'était pas un terme de la langue réligieuse grecque'. So in his view the term was part of Greek religious language; under 'Greek' he subsumed the *confession-texts*. Next to these the term also occurred in 'einer einfachen

---

[150] *Essays*, vol. I, 427, note 77.

[151] Cf. Bömer, *op. cit.*, vol. II, 25; Syll.³, 1172. Cf. H. S. Versnel above p. 54 f.

[152] Cf. Bömer, *op. cit.*, vol. II, 86.

[153] Cf. Herrmann, *op. cit.* (cf. above note 67) no. 18.

[154] *Nouvelles inscriptions de Sardes* (1964) 30, note 2; cf. also J.-L. Robert, *BE* (1965) no. 283; A. Th. Kraabel, 'Paganism and Judaism: the Sardes evidence', *Mélanges M. Simon* (1978) 13-33, esp. 25 ff.

Dankinschrift' (Herrmann)[155] and in two inscriptions from Egypt in which a Thracian Greek, named Aischrion, wrote: εὐλογῶ τὸν Εὔοδον θεόν, τὴν Εἶσιν respectively, i.e. 'I praise the god who shows the right way (Pan) and Isis'.[156] Robert did not elaborate his views about what 'grecque' stood for in the expression 'langue religieuse grecque'. He must have meant that within Greek civilization the wish to praise the deity and to formulate that in terms of *eulogia/eulogein* had developed autonomously, i.e. that is was not influenced by Jewish tradition. There was no comment, on the other hand, on the peculiar character of the Lydian confession-texts and on the fact that one of the Egyptian texts relates to Oriental Isis; there was in other words no comment on whether it really makes sense to subsume all this under the term 'Greek', as if the cults of Athena, Zeus e tutti quanti have more in common with the cult of Anaeitis and Mēn Tyrannos than the use of the Greek language.

In 1978, in a brilliant study on funerary imprecations[157] L. Robert sung his palinodia. Commenting upon the epitaph of the nobleman Fl. Amphicles from Chalcis, in which remarkable (almost literal) parallels with texts from Deuteronomium are to be found, and commenting in particular upon the expression εὐλογοῖτο ἐν παντὶ δήμῳ ('that he be praised among all people'), he opts for the view that both in the Egyptian inscriptions and in the Lydian texts Jewish influence may have been responsible for the choice of the word *eulogia*: 'Aujourd'hui je ne repousserais plus l'interprétation de E. Bickerman sur l'origine juive de la formule en Egypte, où les Juifs étaient si nombreux et actifs et ont laissé tant de traces dans la magie syncrétiste. Quant aux nombreux exemples de la Méonie que j'ai réunis et allégués, je n'exclus pas maintenant une influence du vocabulaire juif, tant les Juifs ont été nombreux et influents en Asie Mineure à l'époque impériale'.[158]

---

[155] P. Herrmann, *op. cit.* (cf. above note 67) nos. 39 and 43.

[156] Quoted by L. Robert, *op. cit.* (cf. above note 154) 30, note 2; *Euodos* often is identical with *Pan Euodos*, 'who shows the right way' (cf. Cl. Meillier, *REG* 88, 1975, 126, note 11). Is it perhaps significant that next to Jewish- and confession-inscriptions and texts relating to Isis, *eulogia* also is used in relation with a deity who of old helps his worshippers and appeals to their affections?; cf. also J.-L. Robert, *BE*, 1968, no. 382.

[157] *CRAI* (1978) 241-289, esp. 245-252.

[158] *Ibidem*, 249, note 47. Cf. the approach of A. R. R. Sheppard (see above note 125), who argues that some terms, used in pagan inscriptions concerning the cult of angels, were borrowed from Hellenised Jewish communities.

It is undoubtedly true that, statistically speaking, *eulogia/eulogein* are terms virtually monopolized by the Jewish language: in the Septuagint *eulogia* renders *beraka* ('Praise for the Lord') and in Jewish inscriptions the term is ubiquitous, both in the sense of 'Blessing to all of you' (*εὐλογία πᾶσιν*)[159] and in the direct sense of '*I praise the Lord*', 'Praise to the Lord'. Dictionaries and encyclopaedias emphasize that the word *eulogia* is a 'Semitismus',[160] i.e. is not to be understood from its pagan meaning. The *RAC*, in spite of its programmatic title, does not have one word on the term in non-Jewish/Christian sources. Fairness compels us to say that in the literary pagan sources *eulogia* is rarely used to convey the idea of praising the God. The word is only on record in poetic language with the meaning of 'having praise' for human institutions and beings.[161] The poetic solemnity of the word may have been an important factor in persuading the LXX-translators to choose this word instead of the more prosaic term *epainos* which, moreover, had been utterly secularized in civic documents.[162] Admittedly the latter word does occur in pagan Greek literature in the sense of 'praising the gods', but I feel that the overtones of the word must have been too 'civic', 'secular' for it to become attractive for people who wanted to praise their Jewish Lord.[163]

But there is still more to be said. *Eulogia* and *eulogein* do actually occur in Greek religious language, though not frequently. In Euripides' *Ion* it is Ion himself who 'praises his Lord Apollo'.[164] Now Ion is depicted as a combination of a temple-slave and a priest; he is conspicuous for his very intimate relationship with Apollo, which is characterized by terms denoting subservience (*λατρεύων*) and by *eulogein*. Above we quoted F. Bömer's words: 'Sein Leben ist ein Erzeugnis dichterischer Verklärung das der Wirklichkeit des griechischen Tempelalltags und dem normalen Glauben der Menschen des 5. Jahrhunderts nicht entspricht';[165] it should, however, be qualified by the comment that *latris/latreuōn* is also on record

---

[159] Cf. e.g. L. Robert, *Hellenica* XI-XII, 395.

[160] So in the *RAC* s.v. *Eulogia*; cf. also Kittel, *Theol. Wörterbuch z. N.T*, s.v.

[161] Cf. Kittel, s.v.; *Thesaurus Linguae Graecae*, s.v.; cf. also an example in a Rhodian epigram, J.-L. Robert, *BE* (1968) no. 382.

[162] I refer to the well-known *martyria/epainos* ideology in the numerous honorary decrees for 'Lokalpolitiker' and benefactors.

[163] Cf. H. S. Versnel in his contribution to this book 50; 59 ff.; cf. also F. T. van Straten, above p. 74 with note 45 (ambiguity of *epainein*).

[164] *Ion*, vs. 130 ff.

[165] Cf. above p. 164, with note 49.

in a few other texts, mostly in connection with the worship of Pan and the Nymphs, i.e. with intense private religiosity (see above p. 163-6).

Similarly *eulogia* is on record in at least one 3rd cent. B.C. inscription from Phokis (Elatea) in which a certain Eukleides is said to have ornamented the statue of Potnia Athēnaia with 'words of praise'.[166] Finally, I came across an example of *eulogia* in a funerary context from the 1st/2nd cent. A.D. from Tomi where the passer-by is asked to praise the deceased.[167] Admittedly, this does not relate to deities but the text shows that the word remained known in pagan circles; moreover, praise for the deceased is perhaps not too far removed from praise for divine beings or at least from the sacred in human life.

What are we to conclude on the basis of these admittedly rare examples? With due caution I suggest the following: 1) *Eulogia* occurs in at least two instances in an atmosphere of close personal religiosity. The a-typical Ion praises his God and, with considerably less signs of subservience, so does Eukleides. These examples are paralleled by texts in which in the same atmosphere worshippers of gods call themselves λάτρις, λατρεύων. 2) Would it not be possible to suggest that *eulogia* in the confession-(and thanks) inscriptions and in the Egyptian dedication to Isis is typical of the institutionalized subservience of Anaeitis-, Isis- and Jahwe-worshippers? In other words: Seeds, already sown in the pagan world and occasionally, i.e. in circumstances of intense private religiosity, not falling on barren soil, have come to full blossom in cults which are celebrated in honour of strongly vertical, Oriental Gods. If this is not wholly unacceptable we do not require the hypothesis that these worshippers borrowed the term *eulogia* from Jewish communities. The Anaeitis-worshippers may have chosen the term independently of, and basically for the same reason, as the Jews and their LXX-translators: it was *the* non-secularized Greek word for 'praise' and, moreover, a term which had been used in situations of great awe and respect for the god.

Both categories felt the requirement to coin a Greek expression for the need 'to praise the Lord' explicitly and regularly. For both categories this liturgical element is probably part of an Oriental heritage, Semitic (Jahwe) and Persian (Anaeitis). They expressed it, I repeat, *independently* with the term which was least secularized by the use in civic documents and which

---

[166] *IG* IX, 1, 131.

[167] *SEG*, XXIV, 1071. A systematic search for the term *eulogia* in Greek inscriptions may yield a richer harvest.

was known to have expressed feelings of subservience and awe in pagan religion. Incidentally, the same dilemma (*independent* development versus borrowing) presents itself in our assessment of certain fundamental aspects of Phrygian religion in the imperial period, as outlined by Robert in his CRAI-article.[168] In particular I refer to the cult of *Hosion* and *Dikaion*, of 'Sainteté' and 'Justice', sometimes even as angels. Justice played an important role in Jewish piety and the cult of angels was a well-known feature of Phrygian Christianity, e.g. in Kolossos. Robert describes the dilemma in his words on the role of Justice: 'ce qui témoigne d'un sentiment religieux profond, et qui peut *se comparer ou se rattacher* (Italics are mine, HWP) à la piété de cultes sémitiques et à celle des Juifs, où la Justice tient une si grande place'. In view of the general line followed in this article it is not surprising that I opt for 'se comparer' and for independent development in pagan Asia Minor. It is not improbable that in the 2nd century B.C. revolt of Aristoneikos the worship of Helios and/or Justice lurks behind the ideology of the Heliopolitai; it would be unwise to attribute this to Jewish influence.[169] If we consider *eulogia/eulogein* as a borrowing from Jewish synagogue-language—in Sardes the Americans actually discovered a synagogue!—we have also to face the fact that, to the best of my knowledge, there is no evidence for any other borrowing. There is no evidence for the representation of specific Jewish objects (menorah etc.) on the Lydian stelai or for specific Jewish theological doctrines and formulas. On the other hand it was Louis Robert himself who in a recent article[170] summarized what we know about Persian vestiges in Lydia and adjacent areas in Asia Minor. He explained a funerary imprecation: τὴν 'Ανατῖτιν τὴν ἀπὸ τοῦ ἱεροῦ ὕδατος κεχολωμένην ἕξει ('il encourra la colère d'Anaitis issue de l'Eau Sainte') by quotations from the Avesta showing that Anahita is 'une déesse de la nature et d'abord de façon éclatante, des eaux'.[171] Though I cannot claim to have read the whole of the three-volume French translation of the Avesta by J. Darmesteter, I did find the following: 'Nous te *louons*, O Ahurani, Eau d'Ahura; nous t'offrons bons sacrifices et bonnes prières, bonne offrande'.[172] I suggest that Persian

---

[168] *CRAI* (1978) 267-269.

[169] Cf. my remarks in *Tijdschrift voor Geschiedenis* 83 (1970) 83-86, esp. 86.

[170] *RN* (1976) 25-48.

[171] *Ibidem*, 44.

[172] J. Darmesteter, *Le Zend-Avesta* (1892-1893) (quoted by L. Robert, *art. cit.* (cf. note 170) 42, note 79) LXXVI.

influence coalesced with an undercurrent of pagan Greek religiosity in the non-Jewish *eulogia*-texts in Lydia. The ultimate root of the use of the formula 'I praise the God' is the feeling of dependence upon the deity, occasionally felt and expressed by Ion and Eukleides, and becoming a structural element in the cults of Isis and Anaeitis, Mēn Tyrannos and similar Oriental Gods.

The Jews were part of the latter tradition but they are not to be held responsible for the use of the word in non-Jewish circles.

IV. *Final chord*

There is at least one text in which most of our 'key' words and concepts appear, albeit not in combination, and which must be discussed. I refer to the expression of a very specific personal religiosity, viz. a curse inscription from the island of Amorgos (see Greek text above p. 32),[173] the dating of which is unfortunately uncertain. In the *editio princeps* the second century A.D. is suggested. Bömer opts for the first century A.D. and Zingerle for the second century B.C.;[174] the original editor's only argument was the circumstances in which the inscription was found: it came to light together with a third-century Jewish-Christian tablet. Zingerle pointed out that at least on one point (he means the formula 'to experience you as a merciful person': σοῦ εὐιλάτου τυχεῖν) the text is closely akin to Ptolemaic petitions. The script, especially the presence of many cursive letters, offers little hold. The argument of the original editor is perhaps the least weak. For my argument it makes little difference whether we opt for the 'late Hellenistic' or the 'Roman imperial' period. The story is soon told: with the assistance of all sorts of evil practices a certain Epaphroditus has persuaded the slaves of the author of the curse tablet to run away. In accordance with truly ancient usage the injured proprietor wishes the most terrible things on Epaphroditus—or rather, implores the goddess Demeter, whom we already know from other, Cnidian, curse tablets, to make sure that Epaphroditus gets his share of these things. Here I am exclusively concerned with the introductory formulas of the curse and with a

---

[173] Cf. Bömer, *op. cit.* vol. III, 207 and vol. IV, 136 f.

[174] Zingerle, *JOAI* 23 (1926) 67 ff. (with thanks to H. S. Versnel for the reference). In spite of the parallels in the Ptolemaeic petitions G. Björck, *op. cit.* (cf. above note 92), 129 ff., prefers a date in the Roman period, because there are more parallels for the *contents* of the Amorgos-tablet from that period; cf. now ZPE 41 (1981) 289-293 for a 2nd cent. B.C. oracle from Egypt with the εὐίλατος formula.

number of key concepts contained in them and here given in italics: '*Mistress* (κυρία) Demeter, *queen* (βασίλισσα), I, your suppliant, your *slave* (δοῦλός σου) *kneel* before you (προσπίπτω)... *Mistress* Demeter, I... seek refuge in you, *to participate in your mercy* (σοῦ εὐιλάτου τυχεῖν)... mistress Demeter, I beg you, *hear me* (ἐπάκουσον)'.

Bömer deals with this text in next to no time; he speaks of an 'ungriechische Demeter' and of 'eine bestimmte ungriechische religiöse Atmosphäre'. His arguments are: (a) Κυρία, βασίλισσα, are un-Greek terms of address; (b) kneeling is Oriental (cf. *supra* p. 156); (c) Εὐίλατος is a word from the realm of the Septuagint; (d) the term 'your slave' betrays an Oriental influence. What can we say about this in the light of the data collected and interpreted in this contribution?

Ad (a): in the so-called Attic curse tablets (*tabellae defixionum*; ever since the classical period) we may not find κύριος/α but we do find δεσπότης several times as the epithet of Hermes Chthonios, who is also invoked as κάτοχος ('he who keeps down the opponent of the curser');[175] in Cnidos itself, again on curse tablets we encounter Demeter as δέσποινα.[176] Henrichs pointed out (see *supra* p. 174 and note 94) that δέσποινα principally characterised a number of deities connected with nature. Athena too is invoked in prayer as Despoina.[177] It seems clear that already in the classical era deities could be invoked as 'rulers' by worshippers who prayed to them in times of personal distress. We have seen (cf. *supra* p. 175) that in the Hellenistic-Roman period objects of personal piety like the Nymphs and Asclepius were accorded the epithet κύριος (or δεσπότης). Βασίλισσα is the epithet *par excellence* of the Mother Goddess.[178] Henrichs mentions an 'Überlagerung eines (thebanischen) Meter-bzw. Demeterkultus durch den kleinasiatischen Kybelekult'[179] as early as in the fifth century B.C. in Greece itself (Thebes). All in all the two Cnidian titles of address of Demeter do not entitle us to conclude that we are in an un-Greek atmosphere. Κυρία may well contain an allusion to a Hellenistic-Roman custom by way of which the 'lord-ship' of gods becomes a structural phenomenon. In other words at the most Κυρία Βασίλισσα reflects the intensification and dissemination of the conception of omnipotence which

---

[175] Cf. Audollent, *Defixionum Tabellae* (1904) Index s.v.
[176] Cf. e.g. F. Steinleitner, *op. cit.* (cf. above note 122) 68, no. 42.
[177] Henrichs, *art. cit.* (see above note 94) 261 ff.
[178] Cf. note 100.
[179] *Art. cit.*, 256.

spread in the Hellenistic-Roman period in the context of hierarchical forms of society and obtrusive Oriental cults. In Cnidos this conception of omnipotence is contained in an originally Greek 'mistress'-title which appeared above all in the cases of gods of nature and the underworld.

Ad (b): Here we can be brief: we saw earlier (cf. *supra* p. 156) that 'kneeling' was by no means an exclusively Oriental custom; the Greek knelt in times of distress before the deity from whom he expected help; the kneeling curser of Amorgos was indeed in great distress and calls himself a suppliant. No Orientalisation is necessary to explain this kneeling.

Ad (c): Εὐίλατος ('merciful') appears not only in our text but also in an Attic text[180] from the Imperial period in which the Lycian slave Xanthos tells of the foundation (by himself) of a little sanctuary and cult in Attica of *Men Tyrannos* from Asia Minor. Xanthos pronounces the wish that 'the god be merciful to those who worship the deity in spiritual simplicity' (τοῖς θεραπεύουσιν ἁπλῇ τῇ ψύχῃ). The word also appears in several curse tablets from Cnidos where the curser wishes that the accursed should not find Demeter and Kore (or Pluto) εὐίλατος.[181] Bömer, following Wide, observes that the term 'in die sakrale Sphäre der Septuaginta gehört'.[182] Yet the question remains of whether, on the basis of all this, we can consider our text steeped in Oriental religiosity. In one of the Cnidian curse tablets we get the term (ἐξ) ομολογεῖν; in the Lydian-Phrygian confession-inscriptions this is *the* term used to designate the confession of guilt; ἐξαγορεύειν appears, with the same meaning, also in Cnidos.[183] In the Cnidian material, however, the curser hopes that the accursed whom he has 'dedicated to Demeter' will be induced by the goddess to come to the temple and there admit his misdeed. There is therefore no question of a worshipper who confesses his sin personally and by his own efforts in order to reconcile the deity and thus go on living in peace and quiet. Demeter must make the 'culprit's' life so bitter as to induce him to confess his misdemeanour and atone before the man who cursed him.

However this may be, we cannot solve the problem with a reference to Mēn Tyrannos and the Septuagint. It is even doubtful whether we can regard εὐίλατος as bridging the gap to the confession-inscriptions of Asia

---

[180] W. Dittenberger, *Syll.*³, no. 1042; cf. Bömer, *op. cit.*, vol. III, 198 ff.

[181] Steinleitner, *op. cit.* (cf. note 122), 68, no. 42; Bömer, *op. cit.*, vol. IV, 137, note 4; cf. also ZPE 41 (1981) 291/2.

[182] Bömer, *op. cit.*, vol. III, 207, note 3; vol. IV, 137, note 4; cf. also *ZPE* 41 (1981) 291-2.

[183] Cf. F. Steinleitner, *op. cit.*, Index s.v.

Minor. An extensive study of the vast 'corpus' of texts in which the deity is begged to be merciful (ἵλεως) is necessary in order to be able to catch the 'colour' of εὐίλατος in all its shades. We cannot provide such a study here. So much, however, is sure: ἵλεως and ἱλάσκεσθαι do indeed appear in purely Greek texts, both in the Hellenistic and in the Roman period.[184] As far as the 'colour' of εὐίλατος is concerned, we must for the time being let the matter rest.

Ad (d): 'your slave' is indeed extremely subservient. It is stronger than ὑπουργός and λάτρις. The question is what we should make of this predicate in *this* text from Amorgos: is it an intensification of the indications of subservience which we have already encountered in classical religion, in emergency situations and in an atmosphere of personal, affective religiosity, or should we agree with Bömer that ὁ δοῦλός σου is simply un-Greek and therefore Oriental?[185] I would opt for the first possibility. While the text is in some ways post-classical we can say that the change in the religious climate of that time (more κύριοι, δεσπόται, more δύναμις, more παντοκράτορες and kindred deities) has simply heightened the incidental classical subservience-in-very-personal-situations. Our incidental 'slave' of Demeter cannot be put on the same footing as the structural 'slave of Atargatis' (see *supra* p. 170 and notes 83 and 84). The latter was an Oriental, in the choice of his goddess and in his heart; I, at least, know of no priest in a Greek cult who calls himself the slave of his deity *as such*. Nevertheless we can conclude that elements did exist in the realm of Greek religiosity already in the classical era, seldom and cursorily though they may be attested, which acted as a sort of *praeparatio evangelica* for the common man whose head was not crammed with theological dogma, and facilitated the transition to a structurally subservient religion (Christianity). At all events Bömer's method, as applied to the text from Amorgos, is a little too facile.

[184] Cf. for ἱλέως-inscriptions (ἱλάσκομαι, ἱλαστήριον included) Index *BE*, s.v. ἱλέως etc.; L. Robert, *CRAI* (1968) 568 ff; cf. note 174 *in fine*.

[185] Bömer, *loc. cit.*; for private people (not priests) in Egypt calling themselves 'slave(s) of the deity' cf. now also ZPE 41 (1981) 291.

J. M. BREMER

GREEK HYMNS

In his paper contributed to this volume H. S. Versnel has discussed the many ways Greek and Roman women and men addressed themselves to their gods. They said their prayers loud and clear or whispered them, they proferred them on leaden tablets, wrote them on a piece of papyrus, cut them on stone or scratched them as graffiti on a simple anathema. But some prayers were also sung in the participation of cultic performances by either the entire community or by a chorus of performers. This type of prayers I call 'hymns'. Confining myself to Greek hymns, I present a threefold matter

— a discussion of the meaning of the word 'hymn' and its conventional structure;
— some remarks on the performance of hymns;
— a survey of the texts which have been transmitted to us, and an interpretation of some of them.

I. *'Hymn': the meaning of the word and the conventional structure*

A hymn is a sung prayer. Prayer is the more general concept, and singing does not necessarily belong to it.[1] Plato, reminiscing about the happy days when musical creativity was flourishing obediently within the old set of kinds (εἴδη), mentions the εὐχαὶ πρὸς θεούς, ὄνομα δὲ ὕμνοι ἐπεκαλοῦντο as the very first εἶδος ᾠδῆς.[2] Besides hymns proper (?) he distinguishes cultic songs in honour of Apollo (paeans) and Dionysus (dithyrambs). The general Attic usage seems to have been recorded by Pollux:[3] hymn, he says, is the generic term, under which several species, such as paean, dithyramb, prosodion etc. are classified.—Pindar uses the terms ὕμνος and ὑμνεῖν readily for 'songs', resp. 'the singing of songs' in which *mortals* are praised,[4] and passages like *Odyss.* 8, 429 and Aesch. *Agam.* 709 suggest

---

[1] In the index of A. Corlu's *Recherches sur les mots relatifs à l'idée de prière, d'Homère aux tragiques* (Paris 1966) the words ὕμνος and ὑμνεῖν do not occur.

[2] Plato, *Leges* III 700 b.

[3] Pollux, *Onomasticon* I 38.

[4] E.g. in *Olymp.* III 2 and *Pyth.* VI 7; it is interesting to see that Pindar himself in some cases qualifies the noun ὕμνος by the adjective ἐγκώμιος: so in *Pyth.* X 53 and *Nem.* VIII 50.

that the word ὕμνος itself does not convey more than the notion of 'sung text'.[5] But the specification 'a song directed to the *gods*' is fairly old: one finds it everywhere in the so-called *Homeric Hymns*. From the fourth century B.C. onwards the accepted distinction is ὕμνους θεοῖς καὶ ἐγκώμια τοῖς ἀγαθοῖς (sc. ἀνθρώποις, JMB).[6]

Aeschylus' implementation of the word ὕμνος several times[7] implies a special connotation, viz. of spell, enchantment, evocation. This semantic feature was made more explicit centuries later by Menander Rhetor[8] who introduced the term ὕμνος κλητικός: a song to invoke and to summon the gods. One finds a pregnant formula in Corlu's monograph on Greek words used for praying: 'L'appel du Dieu est une provocation à sa présence'.[9] This type of hymns is characterised by the occurrence of the imperative 'come' in one of its manifold variations: ἕρπε, ἐλθέ, δεῦρο, ἐπινίσεο, φάνηθι, μόλε.

As starting point for the discussion of the structure of a hymn there is Ausfeld's scheme:[10] invocatio—pars epica—precatio (although I find his second category not very suitable). The invocatio is an indispensable element: the simple utterance HELP is not yet a prayer; it has to be aimed at, or directed to, a divine person. This is realized by the invocation of the name of the god. As a hymn is a more formal and more elaborate kind of prayer, one can expect the invocation to be more elaborate in this case.

It is common knowledge that the Greeks gave many names and titles to their gods. In a playful Hellenistic poem[11] Artemis is presented as a small girl, sitting on her father's lap and asking for a special gift which will make

---

[5] In relation to our way of using the word 'text' for which the Romans are responsible (e.g. Quint. IX 4, 17) it is interesting to observe that Bacchylides (V 9) by his phrase ὑφάνας ὕμνον seems to etymologize the word ὕμνος as 'texture'; cp. also XVIII, 8. In his *Dictionn. Etym.* Chantraine warns: 'Cependant, ces formules n'autorisent pas à tirer ὕμνος du radical de ὑφή, ὑφαίνω (...) ce qui comporterait de grosses difficultés phonétiques'.

[6] Plato, *Resp.* X 607 a. Cp. Ammonius *De adfinium vocab. differ.* (ed. Nickau), 482: ὕμνος ἐγκωμίου διαφέρει· ὁ γὰρ ὕμνος ἐστὶ θεῶν, τὸ δὲ ἐγκώμιον ἀνθρώπων. On this relationship see also Versnel *supra* p. 56.

[7] In *Agam.* 1191, 1471 and *Eum.* 306, 331 (= 344) it refers to a song which is sung by demons and is dangerous for men; in *Choeph.* 475 and *Pers.* 620 it refers to a song sung by men by means of which they evoke chthonic powers.

[8] *Rhetores Graeci* (ed. Spengel) III 334.

[9] Corlu, *op. cit.* (cp. note 1), 72. People were very well aware of this aspect of religious song, cp. Euripides *Erechtheus* fr. 352 (Nauck) = fr. 41 (Austin): ὀλολύζετ', ὦ γυναῖκες, ὡς ἔλθῃ θεὰ χρυσῆν ἔχουσα Γοργόν' ἐπίκουρος πόλει.

[10] K. Ausfeld, De Graecorum precationibus quaestiones, *Jahrb. Class. Phil.* 28 (1903), 505 ff.

[11] Callimachus, *Hymn.* III 7.

her respectable as a divinity and on a par with her brother: δός μοι πολυω-
νυμίην. In his famous monograph Usener has endeavoured to explain this
πολυωνυμίη as part of a long tradition, going back to a much earlier, pre-
hellenistic period, when each one of the numerous so-called Sondergötter
was addressed with her/his specific name corresponding with her/his
specific function; in their mythopoetic power the Greeks ended up with a
relatively small group of gods, but conservatism (a quality inherent to
most forms of religion) caused them to keep most of the old names, and
they attributed them to their more personal gods as variant-names.[12]
Usener's theory is no longer generally used to explain all the names and
titles of the Greek gods; but even if one were to discard his diachronic
explanation of the facts, his theory still remains useful on the synchronic
level because one finds besides the 'proper names' of the gods often

a) alternative cult-names: e.g. Athena Pallas; Apollo Phoibos;
b) patro- or metronymica: Zeus Kronioon, Apollo Latoidas;
c) names of 'minor gods' who have merged with the 'major ones': Paian
   with Apollo, Hekate with Artemis, Enualios with Ares;
d) names indicating the habitual residence of the god: Aphrodite Kupris,
   Hera Argeia;
e) names indicating functions: Kourotrophos and Epipurgidia, both for
   Artemis;
f) epithets of which the original meaning and provenance is unclear and
   which have 'stuck' to the god as a result of their epic formularity:
   Hermes Eriounios, Athena Atrutone.

An ancient Greek who was formulating a prayer casu quo a hymn
searched for the names and titles that were appropriate to the occasion and
perhaps also the most effective; in this process of searching and formulating he—to quote Usener—'häuft die Beinamen und tut darin lieber
des Guten zu viel als dass man sich der Gefahr aussetzt das entscheidende
Wort zu übersehn'.[13] An expanded version or paraphrasing of (b), (d) and
(e) contributed most in uttering a solemn and impressive invocation. To
be on the safe side one could add 'with whatever name and after whatever
abode you are most pleased to be called'.[14]

[12] Usener, Götternamen (1896¹, Frankfurt 1948³).
[13] Usener, 336.
[14] Plato Cratylus 400 e: ὥσπερ ἐν ταῖς εὐχαῖς νόμος ἐστὶν ἡμῖν εὔχεσθαι οἵτινές τε καὶ ὁπόθεν
χαίρουσιν ὀνομαζόμενοι. Cp. Aesch. Agam. 160: there it is not a matter of attributes or epithets
but of the very name of the god. Cf. Versnel supra p. 14.

Between the invocation and the precatio there is very often an intermediary part in which the person who is praying points out to this specific god that she/he is the one who should help; this argumentation is normally found in one of the following forms:

1. *da quia dedi* (e.g. *Iliad* A 39-40: I have provided your sanctuary with a roof and have sacrificed fat thigh-parts to you);
2. *da ut dem* (*Iliad* K 292-294: I shall sacrifice to you a heifer with gilded horns);
3. *da quia dedisti* (*Iliad* Π 236-7: you have answered my prayers at an earlier occasion);
4. *da quia hoc dare tuum est* (Anacreon *PMG* 357: effortless and playful love is your speciality).

It is not so absurd that Ausfeld has categorized this intermediary part as *pars epica*, for there are quite a few cases in which variant (3) is used, and enlarged with narrative detail (compare e.g. *Iliad* K 285-290, Sappho fr. 1, 5-24). But there are many cases which do not readily belong to this category. One of the reasons for Ausfeld to decide on this category was the prominence of narrative in the so-called Homeric Hymns; these are, however, (although poems of respectable antiquity and making up quite an impressive corpus) only border-line cases of the corpus of the 'real' hymns used in ritual and cult. Therefore I prefer to use the three categories *invocation*, *argument*, and *petition*. [15]

A final remark about the 'argument': variant (3) is often combined with (4): the person who prays stresses the power, abilities and special privileges of the god, and the argument thus becomes a hymnic praise in itself, which serves both τὸ πρέπον and τὸ πιθανόν. [16]

---

[15] Zielinski had already replaced Ausfeld's category *pars epica* by one of his own: *sanctio*. As far as I was able to verify (I found his triad *invocatio-sanctio-precatio* quoted and discussed by G. Danielewicz, De elementis hymnicis in Sapphus Alcaei Anacreontis carminibus, *Eos* 52 (1974) 23-33 who refers to Zielinski's *Religia starzytnej Grecji* (Warzawa 1921), Zielinksi means by *sanctio* what I am trying to express by *argument*. In a similar vein R. M. Ogilvie writes on p. 30 of his *The Romans and their Gods* (London 1969): 'Prayer does not presume a favorable result; it recognizes that divine goodwill is the first requirement (....) it is a good *argument* (my italics, JMB), wherever possible, to advance reasons why a god should consider a request sympathetically'.

[16] The topics of hymnical praise have been set out in rhetorical treatises: Quint. 7, 7-8, and Alex. Rhetor in *Rhet. Graeci* (ed. Spengel) III 5-6. Stylistic features of hymns have been explored for the first time by E. Norden, *Agnostos Theos* (1912, Darmstadt 1974), 143-177. An inventory of the themes and phrases one usually finds in hymns has been made by K. Keyssner, *Gottesvorstellung und Lebensauffassung im griechischen Hymnus* (Stuttgart 1932).

The third part does not need a long discussion: most hymns contain a petition on behalf of the community: the god is asked to protect it against enemies, to give health and fertility to men, animals and crops etc. The odd idiosyncrasies observable in egoistic personal prayers are lacking here.

II. *Some remarks on the performance of hymns*

As basis of our discussion of how hymns were performed we can take a statement made by an author in late antiquity: ὁ κυρίως ὕμνος πρὸς κιθάραν ᾔδετο ἑστώτων.[17] We find a confirmation of this practice in the Cretan Hymn to the Kouros: 'μολπᾷ τάν τοι κρέκομεν πακτίσι μείξαντες ἅμ' αὐλοῖσιν καὶ στάντες ἀείδομεν τεὸν ἀμφὶ βωμὸν εὐερκῆ'.[18] This type of hymn performed at, or around, an altar, was called a παραβώμιον.[19] But it should be noticed that in other cases the hymn was sung while the performers approached the temple or the sanctuary and this seems the original way of singing the paean. This at least is suggested by the aetiological passage in *Hom. Hymn. Apollo* 514-518:

βάν ῥ' ἴμεν· ἦρχε δ' ἄρα σφιν ἄναξ Διὸς υἱὸς Ἀπόλλων
φόρμιγγ' ἐν χείρεσσιν ἔχων ἐρατὸν κιθαρίζων
καλὰ καὶ ὕψι βιβάς· οἱ δὲ ῥήσσοντες ἕποντο
Κρῆτες πρὸς Πυθὼ καὶ ἰηπαιήον' ἄειδον
οἷοί τε Κρητῶν παιήονες[20] οἷσί τε Μοῦσα
ἐν στήθεσσιν ἔθηκε θεὰ μελίγηρυν ἀοιδήν.

Because a paean was supposed to have an apotropaeic effect, it was raised when a Greek army or navy advanced upon the enemy.[21] The best-known case is of course Aesch. *Pers.* 388-394; and παιωνίζειν is a normal feature in Xenophon's battle-descriptions (I 8, 17 etc.). This specific aspect of approaching is prominent ih the word προσόδιον.[22] That this may

[17] Proclus *Chrest.* apud Photium *Bibl.* 320 b.

[18] See note 48.

[19] See the inscription quoted in note 35, line 8.

[20] G. Huxley, *GRBS* 16 (1975) 119-124, has argued that in line 518 the word παιήονες refers to the singers themselves. The name of the god contained in the invocation, 517, has become the name of the song and of those who sing it.

[21] A. Fairbanks, *A study of the Greek Paean* (Ithaca, New York 1900), 19-24. A complete list of all cases in which the singing of a battle paean is recorded is given by W. K. Pritchett in *Ancient Greek Military Practice* vol. I (Berkeley 1971) 106. Thucydides describes in V 69-70 the Spartan way of marching towards the enemy (military songs, flute-music) and gives a perfectly rational motivation for this practice: οὐ τοῦ θείου χάριν, ἀλλ' ἵνα ὁμαλῶς μετὰ ῥυθμοῦ βαίνοντες προσέλθοιεν καὶ μὴ διασπασθείη αὐτοῖς ἡ τάξις.

[22] The word is obviously already a technical term in Aristoph. *Aves* 853; in the inscription quoted in my note 34 the prosodion is distinguished from the paean.

include an aspect of dancing, is suggested by ῥήσσοντες in the Homeric Hymn; there are also other passages which refer to the dancing of a paean.[23] The dance is often performed by a small group of choreutai who are specially selected and trained for this purpose, although in other cases the whole community joined in the dance. Xenophon is evidently very pleased to inform us that his hero, king Agesilaus of Sparta, came home for the celebration of the Hyacinthia and ὅπου ἐτάχθη ὑπὸ τοῦ χοροποιοῦ τὸν παιᾶνα τῷ θεῷ συνεπετέλει and that after having gained a signal victory over the Argives.[24] The adults were anxious to train the young ones: in Arcadia the little boys had to memorize the words, tunes and steps of the ancestral paeans as soon as they could speak.[25]

It is perhaps no surprise that our evidence regarding Athens is most extensive. Each year dithyrambs were performed by men's and boys' choruses in honour of Apollo and Dionysus at the Thargelia and the Dionysia respectively (a dithyramb chorus counted fifty members). Every phyle presented two dithyrambs; in Aristotle's time for the Thargelia two phyles presented the dithyrambs in alternative years;[26] that means that each year fifteen hundred (1500) individuals were organized into choruses (tragic and comic choruses not included). Their training started at least a month before the actual celebration: during this period they were paid by the choregus, were exempted from other duties and underwent a strict musical and physical training programme. The ephebes did not engage in these choral performances; probably because it was felt to be more in accordance with the military nature of their duties that—when state festivals were performed—they escorted the processions (προπέμπειν), assisted at the sacrifices (θύειν) and added glamour to the occasion through military and athletic contests (ἀγωνίζειν).[27]

---

[23] Cp. the scholion to Apoll. Rhod. I 537; and Eur. *HF* 687: παιᾶνα Δηλιάδες ὑμνοῦσι, τὸν Λατοῦς γόνον εἱλίσσουσαι καλλίχοροι.

[24] Xenophon, *Vita Agesilai* II 17.

[25] Polybius IV 20, 8.

[26] The evidence for the Thargelia is presented by L. Deubner, *Attische Feste* (Berlin 1932, Darmstadt 1969) 198; for the Dionysia by A. Pickard-Cambridge, *The Dramatic Festivals of Athens* (Oxford 1968²) 74-77. There are the inscriptions in the *Fasti*, and the monuments set up by winning choregi; but far more revealing are two texts in which choregi defend their conduct as sponsor of dithyrambic choruses against accusers or assailants respectively, for the Thargelia Antiphon VI 11-13, for the Dionysia Demosth. XXI *passim*.

[27] Cp. C. Pelekidis, *Histoire de l'éphébie attique* (École Française d'Athènes, fasc. 13, Paris 1962), 211-256. There are two interesting exceptions: (a) *IG²* II-III 2086 (dated 163-164 A.D.), line 30 lists among the officials who were in charge of the ephebes a διδάσκαλος τῶν

There must have been many more festivals in Athens accompanied by hymn-singing, but besides the two mentioned in the previous paragraphs considerable evidence only exists for the Pythais.[28] This was an Athenian pélérinage to Delphi, sent out on special occasions and accompanied by a chorus of boys πυθαϊσταί παῖδες to sing the paean. Inscriptions prove the arrival and performance of a chorus of thirty-nine boys, trained by two choir-masters in 137 B.C. Ten years later there were no less than fifty boys, this time selected rather because of their noblesse and beauty than their musical abilities; for the paean to Apollo was performed by thirty-nine professionals (τεχνῖται) conducted by one choir-master. The Athenian authorities probably had good reasons to invest more money in this cultic performance.[29]

Concluding this survey of the singers in choral performances in or on behalf of Athens, one has to mention an entry in Pollux: in a list of officials, priests etc. at Eleusis, he includes ὑμνῳδοί and ὑμνητρίαι.[30]

It is doubtful whether ancestral, time-honoured hymns were performed at all these festivals. The evidence hardly allows any certainty in this matter,[31] but one may perhaps say that it is probable that at the Athenian

ἀσμάτων whose name was Στράτων Εὐνόμου Παιανιεύς. To the best of my knowledge this type of official is not recorded elsewhere in ephebic inscriptions of Athens. (b) In Heliodorus' novel (I 10, 13) a young man narrates Παναθηναίων τῶν μεγάλων ἀγομένων (...) ἐτύγχανον μὲν ἐφηβεύων, ᾄσας δὲ τὸν εἰωθότα παιᾶνα τῇ θεῷ κτλ. This novel is dated by M. v.d. Valk, *Mnemosyne* 9 (1941) 97-100, shortly after 351 A.D. In the Roman period the military aspects of the epheby moved so much to the background, that it was felt quite normal that they performed as a 'Jungmännerchor': cp. *IG*² II 1078, 29 (± 220 A.D.).

[28] *Fouilles de Delphes* III 2, 11 and 47. The hymns performed in the year 127 B.C. are found *ibidem*, nᵒˢ 137 and 138, with musical notation. For a discussion cp. G. Daux, *Delphes au IIe et Ier siècles avant notre ère* (Paris 1936) 564 ff.

[29] A very interesting case of a change the other way round, i.e. from a chorus of professional ὑμνῳδοί to a chorus of amateurs (in this case ephebes) admittedly for the sake of saving public expenditures, is found in Ephesus 44 A.D.: *Fouilles d'Ephèse* II 21, 53-63. In a later Ephesian inscription (Sokolowski, *Lois Sacrées des Cités Grecques, Suppl.*, Paris 1962, n. 121, 13-15) no details about singers or payment are given.

[30] Pollux, *Onomasticon* I 35.

[31] Because in the fourth century the authorities presiding over the festivals allowed choregi to present an 'old tragedy' or an 'old comedy' (attested from 386 and 339 B.C. respectively; for the evidence see Pick. Cambr., *Dram. Fest.*², 124), it is only logical to assume that 'old dithyrambs' were performed as well, although the evidence is scanty: *IG*² II 3055. On the other hand, we know several names of dithyrambic poets belonging to the second half of the fifth century and the first half of the fourth (Melanippides, Cinesias, Philoxenus, Timotheus); and choregic inscriptions bearing names of dithyrambic poets go well into the third century B.C. The evidence is presented and discussed in A. Pickard-Cambridge, *Dithyramb, Tragedy and Comedy*, 2nd ed. revised by T. B. L. Webster (Oxford 1962), 38-58.

Thargelia and Dionysia most of the dithyrambs were *new* compositions. At the Pythais of 127 B.C. the technitai performed a paean which was composed *ad hoc* by Limenius, the text and the musical notation were inscribed on a stone.[32] According to another inscription the Athenians honoured a Delian composer-poet Amphicles for writing a prosodion in honour of Leto and her children and training a chorus of Athenian boys to perform it at Delos in 165 B.C.[33] Unlike Limenius' composition Amphicles' prosodion has not been preserved; nor the prosodion, paean and hymn composed for the Delphic Theoxenia by the Athenian Cleochares, but they must have been of a surprisingly high standard, for the Delphian authorities decided in (±) 200 B.C. that the choirmaster of their sanctuary should henceforth make Cleochares' compositions part of the repertoire of the Theoxenia and perform them annually.[34]—By doing this the authorities presiding over the different festivals and celebrations took care that traditional and popular hymns kept their place and that antiquated material was replaced by new compositions from time to time.

One might be inclined to think that Athens, Delphi and Delos were in a very special sense places of cult, ritual and music. This view is of course correct, but—at least in the Hellenistic and Roman period—it seems to have been normal for city authorities everywhere to take much care of the religious traditions and more in particular of hymnody: in several cities choral societies existed, comparable with the local choral (or oratorio) societies in the Netherlands, and with the cathedral choirs in England: they were trained to sing the hymns properly and they performed them in honour of gods or deified men on the festival days according to the local religious calendar. I have collected examples of hymnic practice and will give them here without any pretension of covering the field completely.

The Ionian city Teos decided to honour the mother of king Eumenes II of Pergamum (197-160 B.C.). A boys' chorus had to sing a *parabomion*,

---

[32] Cp. I. U. Powell, *Collectanea Alexandrina* (Oxford 1925), 149-159.

[33] *Sylloge Inscr. Graec.*[3] 662: ἐπειδὴ(6) Ἀμφικλῆς, μουσικὸς καὶ μέλων (7) ποιητής ....(8).. προσόδιον γράψας(9)ἐμμελὲς εἰς τὴν πόλιν τούς τε(10)θεοὺς τοὺς τὴν νῆσον κατέχοντας..(12) ὕμνησεν, ἐδίδαξεν δὲ καὶ τοὺς τῶν(13) πολιτῶν παῖδας πρὸς λύραν τὸ(14) μέλος ἄιδειν ἀξίως τῆς τῶν θεῶν (15) τιμῆς καὶ τοῦ Ἀθηναίων δήμου κτλ.

[34] *Sylloge*[3] 450: ἐπειδὴ Κλε[οχ]άρης Βίωνος (3) Ἀθηναῖος, φυλῆς Ἀκαμαντίδος, δήμου Κικυννέως, ποιητὴς μέλων, ἐπιδαμήσας εἰς τὰν πόλιν, γέγραφε τῶι (4) θεῶι ποθόδιόν τε καὶ παιᾶνα καὶ ὕμνον, ὅπως ἄιδωντι οἱ παῖδες τᾶι θυσίαι τῶν Θεοξενίων· ἀγαθᾶι τύχαι· δεδόχθαι (5) τᾶι πόλει τὸμ μὲν χοροδιδάσκαλον τὸν κατ᾽ ἐνιαυτὸν γινόμενον διδάσκειν τοὺς παῖδας τό τε ποθόδιον καὶ τὸμ (6) παιᾶνα καὶ τὸν ὕμνον καὶ εἰσάγειν τοῖς Θεοξενίοις κτλ.

and a girls' chorus had to perform a dance and to sing a hymn in her honour.[35] In the same city a decree dating from the time of emperor Tiberius stated that on the days of the Dionysus-festival the ephebes were required to sing hymns at the opening of the temple doors.[36] That hymn-singing at this very moment was not an idiosyncrasy of the Dionysus-fans at Teos, is suggested by some lines in Callimachus' second hymn (6-8): the poet finds himself in front of Apollo's temple, and when he observes that the god is about to appear and that the doors open themselves,[37] he proclaims:

αὐτοὶ νῦν κατοχῆες ἀνακλίνασθε πυλάων,
αὐταὶ δὲ κληῖδες· ὁ γὰρ θεὸς οὐκέτι μακρήν·
οἱ δὲ νέοι μολπήν τε καὶ ἐς χορὸν ἐντύνασθε.

A glorious new temple was built for Artemis Leukophryene (207/206 B.C.) in Magnesia on the Maeander; the authorities decided that the old statue of the goddess, the ξόανον, should be carried with due ceremony to the new temple, and that in future this day was to be celebrated annually as the Εἰσιτήρια: it was expected of all women to go to the sacred precinct and of girls' choruses to sing hymns to Artemis.[38] In Megalopolis an altar was erected in honour of Philopoemen, the famous citizen who had become the leader of the Achaean Confederacy, 'the last of the Hellenes' (Plut. *Vita Philop.* 1, 7) after his death (183 B.C.), and the young men of the city were to praise him by singing encomia and hymns.[39]

[35] *Or. Graec. Inscr. Sel.* 309; corrected by L. Robert in *Étud. Anat.* 20(7): μετὰ τὸ συντελεσθῆναι τὰς κατευχὰς καὶ τὰς (8) σπονδὰς καὶ τὰς θυσίας, ἄισαι τοὺς ἐλευθέρους παῖδας παραβώμιον, (9) χορ]εῦσαι δὲ καὶ τὰς παρθένους τὰς ἐπιλεγείσας ὑπὸ τοῦ παιδονόμου, (10) καὶ ἄισαι ὕμνον.

[36] F. Sokolowski, *Lois Sacrées de l'Asie Mineure* (Paris 1955) 28: ὕμνους ἄιδεσθαι (8) καθ' ἑκά]στην ἡμέραν τοῦ προκαθηγεμ[όνος τῆς (9) πόλεω]ς θεοῦ Διονύσου ἐν τῆι ἀνοίξει τ[οῦ νεὼ ὑπὸ (10) τῶν ἐ]φήβων καὶ τοῦ ἱερέως τῶν παί[δων κτλ.

[37] Similar scenes (the doors open themselves, the pious community sings) are found in the Homeric Eiresione-song (Homer OCT, vol. V, p. 214), in the scene of the palace-miracle at Thebes (Eur. *Bacch.* 576-604), in Philostr. *Vit. Apoll.* VIII 30; cp. also Virgil *Aen.* VI 52 and III 92, with Servius *ad loc.* These and many other passages are discussed in Weinreich's monograph *Türöffnung* (etc.) = pp. 38-298 of his *Religionsgeschichtliche Studien* (Stuttgart 1968).

[38] Sokolowski, *op. cit.* 33 (= *Syll.*³ 695): τὴν δὲ ἡμέραν τήνδε ἀναδέδειχθαι εἰς τὸν ἀεὶ (25) χρόνον ἱεράν, προσαγορευομένην Ἰσιτήρια ... (26) .. γινέσθω δὲ καὶ γυναικῶν ἔξοδος εἰς τὸ ἱερὸν ... (28) .. συντελείτω δὲ ὁ νεωκόρος καὶ χοροὺς παρθένων αἰδουσῶν ὕμνους εἰς Ἄρτεμιν Λευκοφρυηνήν κτλ.

[39] Diodorus XXIX 18. The inscription containing this very decree has been found at Megalopolis: *Syll.*³ 624. It is all there: δέδοχθαι ταῖ (3) π]όλει τιμᾶσαι Φιλο[π]ο[ίμενα Κραύγιος

Details about the actual performance of hymns and the concomitant rituals are scanty. An inscription in Pergamum records in detail which payments—some in cash, other in natura—should be made to the ὑμνῳδοὶ θεοῦ Σεβαστοῦ (in casu: Hadrian) καὶ θεᾶς Ῥώμης; but not a word about the nature of their choral duties or the songs performed by them.[40] Another inscription[41] is more fit to activate our imagination: a certain Philopappianos, who fulfils in the city of Laodicea-on-the-Lycus the function of prophet of Apollo Pythios, records that he has gone to Klaros and that he has sung a hymn there in honour of Apollo Klarios assisted by a choir of boys and maidens. Present at the ceremony was the choirmaster who had done this job for the fifth time already; present, too, was an official with the fascinating title 'hymn-writer for life': the city-authorities must have feared that the gods had lost their taste for the traditional hymns, only continuous renewal of the repertoire was supposed to help! Follow the names of six boys and six girls.

I found the most elaborate details in an inscription[42] from Stratonicea (Caria), dated by Robert towards the end of the second century A.D. The council decides that every day Zeus Panamarus and Hecate should be honoured by a boys' chorus in the following way: thirty of them, of respectable parentage, should enter the bouleuterion where the statues of Zeus

---

(4) τ]ιμαῖς ἰσοθέοις ἀρε]τᾶς ἕνεκεν κτλ. .... (8) καὶ βωμὸν κα[τ]ασκευάξαι λευκόλιθον ὡς (9) κ]άλλιστον καὶ β[ουθυτεῖν κτλ. But the text is irrecoverable precisely there where the rites are prescribed; when it becomes legible again, it speaks about the distribution of meat and about contests.

[40] Prott & Ziehen, *Leges Graecorum Sacrae* (Leipzig 1886), 27 = *IGR* (Cagnat) IV 353. In the Roman period the name ὑμνῳδοί is often given to an official choir charged with regular singing of hymns in honour of the Roman emperor, or Roma and Augustus. Cp. *Inscr. Brit. Mus.* 192 and 371, 481 (Ephesus); 600 a 5 (Smyrna); 894, 13 (Halicarnassus); and *IGR* (Cagnat) I 562, 565, 1413 (Nicopolis on the Istros); IV 1398 and 1431 (again Smyrna); 1608 (Hypaepa).

[41] *IGR* (Cagnat) IV 1587: (1) Λαοδικέων πρὸς τῇ Λύκῳ (....) (9) Φιλοπαππιανὸς Βαλεριανὸς ὁ προφήτης Ἀπόλλωνος (10) Πυθίου, Κλαρίῳ Ἀπόλλωνι ὑμνήσας, τὰ τῶν (11) συνυμνησάντων παίδων καὶ παρθένων ὀνόματα (12) ἐχάραξε παρόντων αὐτῷ (τοῦ δεῖνα κτλ.) (13) καὶ Λουκίου Ἀστρανίου Βηρύλλου (14) τοῦ παιδονόμου τὸ εʹ, καὶ ὑμνογράφου διὰ βίου (15) Νηδυλλιανοῦ κτλ.

[42] Sokolowski, *op. cit.*, 69: (7) (...) ἔδοξε τῆι βουλῆι [αἱρεῖσθαι] νῦν ἐκ τῶν εὖ γεγονότων παῖδας τριάκον- (18) τα, οὕστινας καθ᾽ ἑκάστην ἡμέραν μετὰ τῶν δημοσίων παιδοφυλάκων [ἄξετ]αι ὁ παιδονό[μος ἐς τὸ β]ουλευτήριον λευχιμονοῦντας καὶ ἐστε- (9) φανωμένους θαλλοῦ, ἔχοντας δὲ μετὰ χῖρας ὁμοίως θαλλούς, οἵτινες συνπαρόντ[ων κα]ὶ κιθαριστοῦ καὶ κήρυκος ᾁσονται ὕμνον ὃν (10) ἂν συντάξῃ Σώανδρος Διομήδους ὁ γραμματεούς κτλ. (....) (15) (...) ἔτι δὲ καὶ τὸν καθ᾽ ἕκαστ[ον ἐνιαυτὸ]ν γεινόμενον ἱερέα τῆς Ἑκάτης καταλέ- (16) γειν ἐκ τῶν ἐν τῶι περιπολίωι τῆς θεοῦ καὶ τῶν σύνεγγυς παῖδας καθ᾽ ἕκαστον [ἐνιαυτὸν], καὶ αὐτοὺς ᾁσοντας τὸν συνήθη ὕ- (17) μνον τῆι θεῶι, καθὼς ἄνωθεν ἐγείνετο κτλ.

and Hecate had their place in a procession, dressed in white garments, wreathed, carrying young olive-shoots, accompanied by a herald and a lyre-player, and they should sing the hymn composed by a local poet (son of the secretary of the council). The text of the decree suggests that it is a novelty, or at least an innovation and expansion of an earlier ritual. The (possibly much older) cult of Hecate in the neighbouring Lagina should not be neglected, but the recruitment of the boys' chorus is here less careful (boys living either on the precincts or in the village will do), and it seems that they were not expected to sing every day; and the traditional hymn was probably judged to be good enough. So far our text from Stratonicea.

Although the evidence for the archaic and classical period is rather scanty, it is perhaps not too bold to conclude that in most Greek cities (Hellas, the islands and Asia Minor) hymn-singing in honour of both gods and deified men was a regular feature at religious festivals. The performance of these hymns may have been on occasion a matter for the whole community, but in the majority of cases it was set apart for a chorus of men or (more frequently) boys or girls. Only in the case of very special cults professional singers were kept on the pay-roll of the city.

III. *A survey of the remaining texts and some interpretations*

It is odd enough that we know relatively little about the texts of the hundreds (or perhaps better: thousands) of hymns, paeans, prosodia etc. which have been sung during all these centuries in so many places. As so often, Von Wilamowitz has summed up the situation in the plain-spoken statement: 'Die gottesdienstliche Poesie der alten Zeit ist verloren'.[43] This is probably due to the fact that in the crucial period—the third and second centuries B.C. when the Alexandrian scholars made up the corpus of what they thought to be 'classical Greek literature'—the ancient cult-songs were thought of as not sufficiently interesting, or too unsophisticated, or downright of no literary value. Be it as it may: it is on record that in the fifth century B.C. some of the very greatest of the then living poets composed poetry-cum-music for cultic purposes. Simonides was probably the most famous composer of dithyrambs; if one is allowed to believe what two epigrams say (for the text see D. L. Page, *Epigr. Gr.* XXVII and XXVIII)

---

[43] Ulr. von Wilamowitz-Moellendorf, *Griechische Verskunst* (Berlin 1921, repr. Darmstadt 1962) 242.

he obtained at least 56 (!) victories with his dithyrambs and one of them when he was already 80 years old. Aeschylus was asked by the Delphians to compose a paean for Apollo, but he answered: 'Tynnichus has made such an excellent one, that I am not going to risk my reputation: people value old and venerable statues more than new ones, don't they?'.[44] But in other cases he may have obliged the authorities by composing hymns or dithyrambs. Sophocles is known to have been actively engaged in introducing the Asclepius-cult in Athens[45] and to have composed a paean for the god.[46] But the Alexandrians thought it better not to include these *parerga* in their editions of the tragic poets. They *did*, however, accommodate in the 'Collected Poems of Pindar the Theban' one book of hymns, one of paeans, two of dithyrambs, two of prosodia; in his case at least there was an Alexandrian base for a sound tradition of the very best cult-poetry. But the professors and schoolmasters of late antiquity decided not to have this material copied for their students: it is only the epinicia which have come down to us via the medieval manuscripts. Fortunately a part of his book of paeans has been found in Oxyrhynchus: P. Oxyr. 841, a copy written in the second century A.D.[47] The sixth paean had been composed by Pindar for the Theoxenia (just as Cleochares' two and a half centuries later[34]): it is a splendid song with a long middle section (the term 'pars epica' is fully justified here) about Apollo, how the god had shown his irresistible power both before Troy and at Delphi itself.

Who ever wants to lay his hand on a Greek hymn (or paean etc.) that (a) can be securely dated to the archaic or classical (in the sense of prehellenistic) period, (b) has demonstrably been in practical use as (what we would call) a liturgical text, and (c) the text of which is tolerably complete, will indeed have serious problems and he will probably join Von Wilamowitz' sweeping statement. But the situation is not all that bad:

---

[44] Porphyrius *De abstin*. (ed. Nauck), II 18. The fame of Tynnichus' paean is confirmed by Plato *Ion* 534 d. Both testimonia are found in Page, *Poet. Mel. Gr.* 707.

[45] *Etymol. Magnum* s.v. Δεξίων; and the confused report in the *Vita Sophoclis* (in the OCT volume of Soph., § 11).

[46] Philostr. *Vita Apoll. Tyan.*, III 17: ὁ παιὰν ὁ τοῦ Σοφοκλέους ὃν Ἀθήνησι τῷ Ἀσκληπίῳ ᾄδουσιν. An inscription has been found with the title and the first words of this paean: *IG²* II 4510, as edited by J. Oliver in *Hesperia* 5 (1936) 112-113: (1) Σοφοκλέους [παι]άν(2)[Φλεγύα] κούρα περιώνυμε, μᾶτερ ἀλεξιπόνοιο θεοῦ(3) [.....].ς ἀκειρεκόμα, σέ[θ]εν ἄρξομαι [ὕμ]νον ἐγερσιβόαν (5) [...] συρίγμασι μιγνύ[μεν]ον (6)[...] Κεκροπιδῶν [ἐπ]ιτάρροθον (7)[...] μόλοις κτλ.

[47] They are presented most carefully in vol. II (fr. 52a-k) of the Teubner edition of Pindar by Snell & Maehler; an extensive commentary on the second and sixth paean has been given by S. L. Radt (Amsterdam 1958).

there is a handful of extant texts belonging to the period before Alexander the Great. I shall present them here summarily.

1. The Cretan Hymn to the Kouros. I immediately admit that there is one major gap in the text and that the text is known to us from a stone on which it has been engraved in the second or third century A.D. The text itself, however, has probably been composed in the fourth century B.C., and might well be the product of a religious mentality which is much older and belongs to the second millennium B.C.[48]

'Ιὼ μέγιστε Κοῦρε, χαῖρέ μοι, Κρόνειε,
πανκρατὲς γάνους, βέβακες δαιμόνων ἀγώμενος.
Δίκταν ἐς ἐνιαυτὸν ἕρπε καὶ γέγαθι μολπᾶ ⟨ι⟩,

Str. 1	τάν τοι κρέκομεν πακτίσι μείξαντες ἅμ' αὐλοῖσιν καὶ στάντες ἀείδομεν τεὸν ἀμφὶ βωμὸν εὐερκῆ.	'Ιὼ μέγιστε κτλ.
Str. 2	ἔνθα γάρ σε παῖδ' ἄμβροτον ἀσπί[δεσσι Κούρητες πὰρ 'Ρέας λαβόντες πόδα κ[υκλῶντες ἀπέκρυψαν.	'Ιὼ μέγιστε κτλ.
Str. 3	[–◡ ⏑◡ –◡ ⏑◡ –◡ ⏑◡ ––⏑] [–◡ ⏑◡ –◡ ⏑◡ –◡τᾶ]ς καλᾶς 'Αῶς.	'Ιὼ μέγιστε κτλ.
Str. 4	"Ωραι δὲ ? β]ρύον κατῆτος καὶ βροτὸς Δίκα κατῆχε καὶ πάντα δι]ῆπε ζώ ⟨ι⟩ ' ἁ φίλολβος Εἰρήνα.	'Ιὼ μέγιστε κτλ.
Str. 5	ἁ[μῶν δὲ θόρ' ἐς ποί]μνια καὶ θόρ' εὔποχ' ἐ[ς μῆλα κὲς λάϊ]α καρπῶν θόρε κὲς τελεσ[φόρος οἴκος.	'Ιὼ μέγιστε κτλ.
Str. 6	θόρε κὲς] πόληας ἁμῶν, θόρε κὲς ποντο(π)όρος νᾶας, θόρε κὲς ν[έος πο]λείτας, θόρε κὲς Θέμιν κλ[ηνάν.	'Ιὼ μέγιστε κτλ.

'O most mighty, Thou, Kouros son of Kronos, with absolute power over γάνος, be greeted. Thou art gone taking the lead of the δαίμονες. Come to Dirke at this anniversary day, and hear with gladness our music

---

[48] The text printed here is essentially the text as published by M. Guarducci in (a) *Inscr. Cret.* III 2, with some minor corrections as proposed by herself in (b) her contribution to the Festschrift for Doro Levi *Antichita Cretesi* (Catania 1974), II 36-37; in (c) her last presentation of the same hymn (in her manual *Epigrafia Greca* Roma 1978, IV 128) she has maintained these corrections. About the antiquity of the hymn and its religious mentality I refer to what Guarducci says: 'Protagonista dell' inno è un giovane dio antichissimo (forse preellenico) della natura rinascente, che i Greci dell' età arcaica identificarono con Zeus figlio di Crono'. (b, 33); in (c, 126) she contents herself with saying that the composition of this poetic text belongs to the 4th century B.C., 'attingendo con grande probabilità a un modello ancora più antico'. Von Wilamowitz (*GV*, 502) had ascribed the text to a poet of the 5th cent. B.C.

(str. 1) which we weave for you with our harps, mixing it with flutes; we sing it standing around your well-walled altar, o most mighty etc. (str. 2) for here it was that the Kouretes took Thee, immortal child, from Rhea, and hid Thee, dancing with their shields around you, o most mighty etc. (str. 3).. of the fair Dawn, o most mighty etc. (str. 4). The seasons were plentiful every year, and Justice ruled over mortals; and Peace governed all creatures, together with prosperity, o most mighty etc. (str. 5) Leap in our flocks and leap in the fleecy sheep; and in the fields of crops leap, and in the houses that they may come to fulfilment, o most mighty etc. (str. 6) and leap in our cities, too, and in the sea-faring ships; and leap in the young men of our cities, too, and spring in famous Themis'.

For detailed comment I refer the reader to the relevant publications;[49] I confine myself to some 'hymnological' annotations. The refrain is invocation and petition all in one: the first stanza situates the chorus; stanzas 2-3-4 present the argument, one of the form *da quia dedisti*: because *then* the birth of the young god introduced an era of peace, fertility and justice,[50] the god is beseeched to come and to confer the same benefits *now*. Stanzas 5 and 6 contain this imperative COME in an unexpected way. In his comm. to Hesiod's *Erga* 2, M. L. West had noted: 'When gods are called to the speaker's presence, the implication is that they do not operate from a distance. But this does not apply to all gods. Zeus, for example, is never invited to approach; he sees and acts from where he is'. The conclusion is justified that this θόρε is an indication of a very early stage of Greek, if not pre-hellenic, religious sentiment. This god, who is supposed to leap, to mount as a bull does, is evidently not the father of gods and men, the cloud-gatherer and Olympic supergod, but a young god who—probably in connexion with (subordination to?) a Mother-goddess—has absolute power (παγκρατής) over vegetation, fertility and the 'brightness and splendour' that accompany them.

2.   With the second text we find ourselves in a very different atmosphere, but it is nonetheless a text with a cultic function, although not

---

[49] Inter alia: W. K. C. Guthrie, *The Greeks and their Gods* (London 1950; I refer to the paperback edition Boston 1955) 45-51. M. L. West, The Dictaean Hymn to the Kouros, *JHS* 85 (1965) 149-159. In these discussions it has not been mentioned that the Knossos tablet KN Fp 1,2 contains a dedication (of a quantity of olive-oil) to di-we di-ka-ta-jo Διϝεῖ Δικταίῳ.

[50] I am making a dangerous simplification here: in the fourth stanza it is Dike, in the sixth it is Themis!

in official sense. At a sacrificial meal, when the portions of meat had been consumed, the libations and drinking that followed were accompanied by a paean;[51] in much the same way domestic celebrations, too, ended in libations and singing of the paean.[52] This paean-singing was often followed by the singing of so-called skolia: πρῶτον μὲν ἦδον ᾠδὴν τοῦ θεοῦ κοινῶς ἅπαντες μιᾷ φωνῇ παιανίζοντες, δεύτερον δ' ἐφεξῆς ἑκάστῳ μυρσίνης παραδιδομένης (..), ἐπὶ δὲ τούτῳ λύρας περιφερομένης ὁ μὲν πεπαιδευμένος ἐλάμβανε καὶ ἦδεν ἁρμοζόμενος, τῶν δὲ ἀμούσων οὐ προσιεμένων σκόλιον ὠνομάσθη κτλ.[53]

These skolia must have covered a whole range of subjects; at first songs with a religious atmosphere similar to the paean and ending up with songs in the mood of hilarity common to those who have drunk a good many cups of wine. The following skolion can be placed midway between the extremes:

ὦ Πάν, 'Αρκαδίας μεδέων κλεεννᾶς,
ὀρχηστὰ βρομίαις ὀπαδὲ νύμφαις,
γελάσειας, ὦ Πάν, ἐπ' ἐμαῖς
εὔφροσι ταῖσδ' ἀοιδαῖς κεχαρημένος.[54]

'O Thou Pan, who reignest over famous Arkadia, dancing companion[55] of the Dionysiac Nymphs, I pray Thee that thou may laugh at these merry songs of mine, having taken Thy pleasure in them'. In all its simplicity this poem is perfectly identifiable as a mini-hymn: line 1 contains the invocation, (name, domain over which the god reigns); line 2 the argument (type: *da quia hoc dare tuum*): Pan is the merry companion of wine-plus-water; line 3 and 4 the petition: the god is invited to come and to heighten the joyfulness of this symposion with his 'panic hilarity'.

3. With the Paean Erythraeus we are on quite different ground. In Erythrae on the coast of Ionia an inscription has been found, engraved ±

---

[51] *Iliad* A 470-473, Theognis 777-779, Xenoph. *Anab.* VI 1,4-5.

[52] Plato *Symp.* 176 a, Xenoph. *Symp.* II 1.

[53] Plutarch *Quaest. Conviv.* I, 1 (= *Mor.* 615 B 7). Cp. Fairbanks, *op. cit.* (see my note 21) 56-59.

[54] All skolia are to be found in Page, *PMG*, 884-909; the skolion in honour of Pan is no. 887. An enlightening discussion of them has been given by C. M. Bowra in *Greek Lyric Poetry* (Oxford 1962²) 372-397. In line 4 of the Pan-skolion I follow the reading proposed by von Wilamowitz.

[55] This mythical image of Pan dancing with the nymphs is, of course, derived from what every Greek could see for himself when he was travelling in the Greek countryside: a he-goat prancing over a waterfall. In the (probably contemporary!) nineteenth Homeric Hymn the same image is brilliantly worked out (1-11, 19-26).

370 B.C. with an elaborate 'lex sacra'; those who had come to the local
sanctuary of Apollo and Asclepius for reasons of health and healing were
to sleep in the sanctuary; the next day they were to sacrifice and to sing
paeans to Apollo and Asclepius; the stone preserves the text of two paeans;
only the second text is legible.[56] This must have been quite a famous
paean; copies of it, similarly engraved on stones, have been found in
Egypt (at Ptolemaïs, first cent. A.D.), in Macedonia (at Dion, second
cent. A.D.) and in Athens (third cent. A.D.)

> Παιᾶνα κλυτό]μητιν ἀείσατε
> κοῦροι Λατοΐδαν Ἕκ]ατον
>   ἰὲ Παιάν,
> ὃς μέγα χάρ[μα βροτοῖσ]ιν ἐγείνατο
> 5 μιχθεὶς ἐμ φι[λότητι Κορ]ωνίδι
> ἐν γᾶι τᾶι Φλεγυείαι,
> [ἰὴ Παι]άν, Ἀσκληπιὸν
> δαίμονα κλεινό[τατ]ον,
>   ἰὲ Παιάν·
> 10 [το]ῦ δὲ καὶ ἐξεγένοντο Μαχάων
> καὶ Πο[δα]λείριος ἠδ᾽Ἰασώ,
>   ἰὲ Παιάν,
> Αἴγλα [τ'] εὀῶπις Πανάκειά τε
> Ἠπιόνας παῖδες σὺν ἀγακλυτῶι
> 15 εὀαγεῖ Ὑγιείαι·
> ἰὴ Παιάν, Ἀσκληπιὸν
> δαίμονα κλεινότατον,
>   ἰὲ Παιάν.
> χαῖρέ μοι, ἵλαος δ' ἐπινίσεο
> 20 τὰν ἀμὰν πόλιν εὐρύχορον,
>   ἰὲ Παιάν,
> 22 δὸς δ' ἡμᾶς χαίροντας ὁρᾶν φάος
> ἀελίου δοκίμους σὺν ἀγακλυτῶι
> εὀαγεῖ Ὑγιείαι·
> 25 ἰὴ Παιάν, Ἀσκληπιὸν
> δαίμονα κλεινότατον
>   ἰὲ Παιάν.

[56] Information about the Paean of Erythrae is found in the apparatus of Page, *PMG* 934;
and in Sokolowski, op. cit. (see my note 36), no. 24. It has also been presented in the *In-
schrifte von Erythrai und Klazomenai*, edd. Engelmann & Merkelbach (Bonn 1973), II 205.—
I give here Page's text.

'Boys, sing the praises of Paian renowned for his wisdom, the sovereign son of Leto—IE PAIAN—who begot a mighty joy for mortals by sleeping lovingly with Koronis in the land of Phlegyas: IE PAIAN ASKLEPIOS MOST FAMOUS GOD IE PAIAN—from him are born Machaon and Podaleirios and Iaso—IE PAIAN—and fair-faced Aigla and Panakeia: all of them, together with radiant Hygieia, children of him and Epione—IE PAIAN ASKLEPIOS MOST FAMOUS GOD IE PAIAN—be greeted and come graciously to our city with its broad dancing-places—IE PAIAN—and grant that we may joyfully see the light of the sun, being fit in the company of radiant Hygieia—IE PAIAN ASKLEPIOS MOST FAMOUS GOD IE PAIAN'.

Some remarks: κοῦροι in line 2 probably refers to a local chorus of Sängerknaben; the pilgrims could follow the text on the stone and join in the singing as well as they were able, at least the recurring exclamations. Ἀσκλήπιον in line 7 places Asklepios as the object of ἐγείνατο; this accusative is repeated further on but as an exclamation (the god is spoken of in the third person throughout lines 1-18). Mythology here is subordinated to religion and faith: it is surprising to see how the story of Asklepios' birth from Koronis with its ominous overtones as we know it from Pindar's third *Pythian*, is here reduced to the most simple record: Apollo fathered him, and Koronis, Phleguas' daughter, was his mother. The main point is that the birth of this new god means joy for mortals: χάρμα βροτοῖσιν. Apart from the two Homeric names, all other names of the Asklepian family have some meaning: Iaso = Cure, Aigla = Radiance, Panakeia = Complete Healing; Epione's name refers to the homeric formula ἤπια φάρμακα, and of course Hygieia = radiant Health herself. This whole catalogue serves a double purpose, that of situating the god in his happy family and thus honouring him, and also that of enumerating the effects of the god's medical powers, and thus presenting the argument in this hymnic prayer. At the end (19-20) the hymn appears to be 'cletic': in the petition they beseech the god to come and visit their city. The implication of this 'visit' is spelled out clearly in 22-23: that they may live in health and happiness thereafter.[57]

Texts like this were sung with deep emotion, expressing either appeal and entreaty or relief and thankfulness, in the Asclepieia at Trikka,

---

[57] On the stone found in Ptolemais a stanza had been added at the end: 'Give everlasting water to the Nile, prosperity to our town and glory to all of Egypt'.

Epidaurus, Pergamum, Kos and in many other sanctuaries.[58] There are even indications that some places had a kind of 'hours', i.e. a daily routine of songs to be sung at fixed hours of the day. At Epidaurus two big stones have been found[59] bearing hymnical texts; on the first, hymns in honour of (a) all gods together, (b) Pan, (c) the Mother of the Gods, and on the latter, hymns in honour of (d) Hygieia, (e) Asclepius and (f) Athena. Texts (a), and (f) are very mutilated; texts (b) and (c) can be read and interpreted, but (b) is probably a fairly late composition, and (c) presents quite a few problems of its own.[60] I shall therefore discuss only (d), the song to Hygieia; it is highly probable that over its text the stone bore the indication ὥρᾳ πρώτῃ; it is quite certain that over text (e) ὥρᾳ τρίτῃ is written. Consequently it is possible that these stones together formed a 'breviary-on-stone' for daily worship.

4.   To turn now to the paean to Hygieia. It has been found not only here at Epidaurus, but also on a stone elsewhere[61] of much later date; it has been preserved in the manuscript tradition of Athenaeus; and there are four authors, all of them from the second to third cent. A.D., who refer to it or quote from it.[62] Lucian calls it τὸ γνωριμότατον ἐκεῖνο καὶ πᾶσι διὰ στόματος. It is said to have been composed by Ariphron of Sikyon, who is otherwise known to us as a lyrical poet (choregic inscription IG^2 II-III 3092, dated circa 400 B.C.).

    Athen. XV 701 F-702 B

       τὸν εἰς τὴν Ὑγίειαν παιᾶνα ᾄσας τὸν ποιηθέντα ὑπὸ
       Ἀρίφρονος τοῦ Σικυωνίου τόνδε·

[58] 'Sein von dort (= Epidaurus, JMB) aus seit dem 5/4. Jh. einsetzender Siegeslauf überzog die Oikumene with einem Netz von fast einem halben Tausend Kultfilialen'. W. Fauth in *Kleine Pauly* s.v. Asklepios, 647.

[59] *IG* IV² 1. The authoritative discussion of this group of texts has been given by P. Maas, *Epidaurische Hymnen* (Halle 1933).

[60] W. J. W. Koster has given a detailed interpretation of this Meter-hymn in *Meded. Kon. Ned. Akad. afd. Lett.*, N.R. 25 (1962) 4; cp. also M. L. West in *CQ* 20 (1970) 212-215.

[61] In Kassel, Germany, probably third cent. A.D. Evidently this massive stone has been taken as a precious talisman: it is reasonable to suppose that Greek-speaking soldiers of the Roman army had carried it all the way to their garrison-city. It can not have been a paean fit for singing the last minute before the attack!

[62] I refer again to Page, *PMG* for the text and further information about the two inscriptions and the literary tradition: this time it is no. 813. In his *Der Glaube der Hellenen* (the second edition of which has been reprinted in Darmstadt 1959) 221 n. 2 Von Wilamowitz suggests that Ariphron's paean had been composed at the same time and for the same occasion as Sophocles' (comp. my note 46).

Ὑγίεια βροτοῖσι πρεσβίστα μακάρων, μετὰ σεῦ
ναίοιμι τὸ λειπόμενον βιοτᾶς, σὺ δὲ μοι πρόφρων ξυνείης·
εἰ γὰρ τις ἢ πλούτου χάρις ἢ τεχέων
ἢ τᾶς ἰσοδαίμονος ἀνθρώποις βασιληΐδος ἀρχᾶς ἢ πόθων
5   οὓς κρυφίοις Ἀφροδίτας ἕρχεσιν θηρεύομεν,
ἢ εἴ τις ἄλλα θεόθεν ἀνθρώποισι τέρψις ἢ πόνων
ἀμπνοὰ πέφανται,
μετὰ σεῖο, μάκαιρ’ Ὑγίεια,
τέθαλε καὶ λάμπει Χαρίτων ὀάροις·
10 σέθεν δὲ χωρὶς οὔτις εὐδαίμων ἔφυ.

'Health, of all gods most honoured by mortals, grant that I may dwell in
thy company for the rest of my life and that thou remainest with me in thy
graciousness. For *if* there is a possibility for man to enjoy wealth or
children or royal power—a thing which makes man to be as a god—or
love—after which we chase with the stealthy nets of Aphrodite—, or if by
the favour of the gods any other delight or at least any relief from misery
has been revealed, then this (joy or delight) blossoms and shines with the
song of the Graces only when thou art with us, blessed Health: no man is
blessed without thee'. Compared with the Paean from Erythrae,
Ariphron's stands out as a far better poem thanks to the subtlety of its
rhythm and phrasing, and the suggestive catalogue of the 'values of life'.
Rhythm: the anapests provide a dignified and pleasing 'overture' (1-2);
the dactylo-epitrites (3-9) present the delights of life: first in rolling
hemiepè, then working towards a climax in cretics, closed by πέφανται;
8-10 repeat the anapestic invocation and give the final blessing, first in an
xexD line, then in a more down-to-earth iambic trimeter containing mortal wisdom in a proverbial form. The thematic structure of the hymn as
such corresponds with this rhythmic articulation; 1-2 contain it all: invocation, compact argument, petition; lines 3-10 develop this argument and at
the same time express devout praise. One could suppose it to be a personal
poem because of this poetic refinement; but the testimonia referred to
earlier prove that it was in general use both in official cult and in domestic
religion.[63]

After having presented these few specimens of ancient cult-poetry I am
obliged—before I can end my paper with a brief indication as to how the

[63] In Athenaeus 701 f-702 the singing of this paean is the equivalent of a prayer at the end
of a meal.

composition and performance of pagan Greek hymns petered out in the fourth century A.D.—to explain why I have not discussed important groups of poems which *prima facie* seem to come under the heading 'Greek hymns'.

First of all, when I stated that there is no corpus of hymnic poetry which has come down to us by medieval manuscripts, this was not absolutely correct: at some moment in time one can no longer pinpoint[64] but which must have been some time between the ninth and the twelfth century A.D. a Byzantine scholar collected in one volume four groups of hymns which had never been in actual use in Greek cults: (1) the Homeric Hymns, relatively short poems in epic fashion, probably used by rhapsodes as preludes for their recitals of Homeric poems,[65] (2) the hymns written by Callimachus (products of high literary culture and scholarship, but very esoteric—a cult-hymn is never meant to be enjoyed by the learned 'happy few'—, (3) hymns composed by Proclus, a Neoplatonic philosopher and mystic in the fifth century A.D., and (4) the so-called Orphic Hymns (they might have been used in the cult of an 'Orphic community' in Asia Minor, third or fourth century A.D.[66]). This book of hymns, although of paramount importance for Greek literature, especially its parts (1) and (2), need not detain us long here.

Far more important for our purpose are the hymns which are found in Attic drama, both tragedy and comedy. It cannot be fortuitous that especially in the parodos of tragedy and in the parabasis of comedy the chorus sings songs to one god, or a group of gods, in perfect hymnic

---

[64] The history of the tradition of the 'Book of Hymns' is discussed by Pfeiffer in his edition of Callimachus, vol. II (Oxford 1951), 1v ff.

[65] Lesky, *Gesch. der griech. Lit.* (Bern 1963²) 104: 'Wolf hat den richtigen Schluss gezogen dass diese Hymnen den Rhapsoden als Vorspiel für ihre epischen Rezitationen dienten'. This hypothesis has been worked out by H. Koller in a paper 'Das kitharodische Proömion', *Philologus* 100 (1956) 159-206. One might object that the Hymns to Demeter and Apollo seem to have some relation to official cult, in so far as they contain aetiologies of the mysteries of Eleusis, the festival in honour of Apollo at Delos and the Pythian oracle at Delphi respectively. In the most recent treatment of one of these hymns, the Hymn to Demeter (Oxford 1974) N. Richardson (p. 12) considers the possibility that this hymn 'may have been used in later times for various purposes and recited at festivals of initiation (...) There is however nothing to indicate that it was originally intended for such a use, and the analogy of other Homeric hymns with their reference to poetic contests (...) suggests that it was originally composed for recitation at a public festival, and perhaps for a traditional epic contest'.

[66] So Lesky, *op. cit.* (see previous note), 867.

style.[67] One might even be tempted to state that these texts were used in cult: were these festivals not organized in honour of Dionysus and celebrated in his precinct with the priest of Dionysus 'in the chair'? Even so this would be incorrect, because these hymns are integrated into the theatrical performance. If one analyses why the poet has given this particular type of text to the chorus at this particular point in the stage action, one finds that he has used the hymnic formulary and subordinated it to what he was aiming at with his tragic or comic action: the poetic intention has made the cultic convention serve a non-cultic purpose. But anyone who wants to study in depth the hymnic poetry of the Greeks as poetry has to go to, and will be fascinated by, these hymns bedded into drama.[68]

The same phenomenon is found in other literary genres: poets using the form of the hymn, hallowed by tradition, for specific poetic purposes. In epic there are (besides the Homeric Hymns mentioned above) the long hymnic address to Hecate in Hesiod *Theog.* 410-449 and his proems to both *Erga* and *Theog.* In lyric poetry Sappho 1, Alcaeus 34 and Anacreon 357 (*PMG*) are prominent examples; in elegy Theognis 773-782, in Pindar's epinicia *Olymp.* 14. Callimachus' hymns have already been referred to. Even philosophers took to writing hymnic poetry when they wanted to convey thoughts and sentiments that prose was unfit to express: Aristotle's paean in honour of Hermias and Aretè,[69] Cleanthes' hymn to Zeus.[70]

A final remark, again an apology for my omitting an important group of hymns here. Any historian of religion knows that compared with the few texts of ancient cult-hymns the harvest from the Hellenistic and Roman period is rich. Why did I not choose these hymns for a discussion? There are several answers to that question. First, their considerable number makes it impossible to present them all. Second, the hymns or aretalogies devoted to Sarapis and Isis present so many special problems that only

[67] Aesch. *Septem* 87-180, *Agam.* 160-183; Soph. *OT* 158-167; Eur. *Bacch.* 72-169; Aristoph. *Eq.* 551-564 and 581-594, *Thesm.* 312-326, 969-1000, 1136-1159. Cp. E. Fraenkel, *Philologus* 86 (1931) 3-11 = *Kleine Beiträge zur klass. Phil.* (Roma 1964) 355-363.

[68] There is H. Meyer's monograph *Hymnische Stilelemente in der frühgriech. Dichtung* (Würzburg 1933); and Keyssner's (see my note 16).

[69] His paean has been sung during many years in the domestic cult of the Lyceum. It is discussed from a viewpoint of biography and philosophy by W. Jaeger, *Aristotle* (Oxford 1962) 105-123, and a viewpoint of literary criticism by Bowra, *Problems in Greek Poetry* (Oxford 1953) 138-150; cp. also D. Wormell in *YCS* 5 (1935) 55-93.

[70] Discussed by G. Zuntz in *HSCP* 63 (1958) 289-328, and by A. W. James in *Antichton* 6 (1972) 28-33.

someone who has more than a superficial knowledge of Egyptian religion is qualified to discuss them.[71] Third, of the group of hymns which Powell has collected so conveniently in his *Collectanea Alexandrina,*[72] Philodamos' paean to Dionysos has recently been dealt with in great detail by Brian Rainer[73] especially in comparison with Aristonoos' paean; the hymns which have been engraved together with their musical notation, have also had a good deal of attention already; the paeans of Isyllos and Makedonios are derivative and modelled upon the paean of Erythrae. And last but not least there is Douris' paean for Demetrius Poliorketes. Enough of this apology: the attentive reader will have observed for himself that in this way I have managed (a rhetorical *praeteritio*) to give my survey of Greek hymns some semblance of completeness.

The importance of hymns for cult and religion in ancient Greece was very well seen by Julian the Apostate. In 363 A.D., the year in which he was to die, he wrote a letter[74] to a certain Theodorus appointing him inspector-general for all sanctuaries in Asia Minor. In a long series of orders and recommendations which cover not only the preservation of temples but also the moral standards of the pagan clergy he insists upon the duty of priests not to read any frivolous poetry (Archilochus, Hipponax) nor erotic prose novels; they should abstain from agnostic philosophers like Epicurus or Pyrrho, and study rather the teaching of religious men like Pythagoras and Plato. And he concludes this part of his letter by pointing out which kind of texts they ought to read above all others, yes even to learn completely by heart: hymns, hymns, hymns (Budé, *Lettres*, Tome I, p. 169-170).

> Ἀκμάνθανειν χρὴ τοὺς ὕμνους τῶν θεῶν· εἰσὶ δὲ οὗτοι
> 25   πολλοὶ μὲν καὶ καλοὶ πεποιημένοι παλαιοῖς καὶ νέοις·
> οὐ μὴν ἀλλ' ἐκείνους πειρατέον ἐπίστασθαι τοὺς ἐν τοῖς
> ἱεροῖς ᾀδομένους· οἱ πλεῖστοι γὰρ ὑπ' αὐτῶν τῶν θεῶν
> ἱκετευθέντων ἐδόθησαν, ὀλίγοι δέ τινες ἐποιήθησαν καὶ

---

[71] Cp. A. J. Festugière, *Etudes de religion grecque et hellénistique* (Paris 1972) 138-163, and the inaugural address by H. S. Versnel (Leiden 1978) *De Tyrannie Verdrijven?*

[72] I. U. Powell, *Collectanea Alexandrina* (Oxford 1925) 132-175.

[73] B. L. Rainer, *Philodamus' Paean to Dionysus* (diss. Univ. of Illinois), Ann Arbor Xerox Univ. Microfilms 1975).

[74] *L'empereur Julien*, ed. J. Bidez, vol. I² *Lettres*, no. 89. That he appointed Theodorus appears from this sentence: τί οὖν ἐστι ὃ φημί σοι νῦν ἐπιτρέπειν; ἄρχειν τῶν περὶ τὴν Ἀσίαν ἱερῶν ἁπάντων ἐπισκοπουμένῳ τοὺς καθ' ἑκάστην πόλιν ἱερέας καὶ ἀπονέμοντι τὸ πρέπον ἑκάστῳ. The quotation in the text of my paper is taken from pp. 169 and 171.

παρὰ ἀνθρώπων, ὑπὸ πνεύματος ἐνθέου καὶ ψυχῆς ἀβάτου
1 τοῖς κακοῖς ἐπὶ τῇ τῶν θεῶν τιμῇ συγκείμενοι.

Ταῦτά γε ἄξιον ἐπιτηδεύειν, καὶ εὔχεσθαι πολλάκις
τοῖς θεοῖς ἰδίᾳ καὶ δημοσίᾳ, μάλιστα μὲν τρὶς τῆς ἡμέ-
ρας, εἰ δὲ μή, πάντως ὄρθρου τε καὶ δείλης·

Julian speaks here with all his authority of pontifex maximus.[75] Our treasure of hymns, he says, contains a great many beautiful specimens of great antiquity and also many hymns composed by poets of more recent periods. It may not be possible to learn them all by heart, but one should at any rate try to be familiar with those which are regularly sung in the sanctuaries. The majority of these hymns have been given to us by the gods themselves, some of them have been written by men, it is true, but then under divine inspiration: the soul of poets who composed such hymns to the honour of the gods was untouched by evil. It is worthwhile to devote one's energy to this matter, and to pray frequently to the gods (apparently using these hymns) in private as well as in public worship; three times a day was best; failing that, at dawn and in the late afternoon at any rate (= 'Mattins' and 'Evensong' in the Church of England). There is another letter[76] in which the emperor orders the prefect of Egypt to give considerable attention (and funds) to sacred music. A chorus consisting of a hundred boys, selected out of noble families, should be in constant training; they should be fed and dressed with all possible care.

Evidently Julian cherished the hope that he could go on reorganizing and reviving the old cults; the hymns were to be an important element in this revival. He did not know he was to die himself in the same year, nor could he possibly know that shortly after his death Ambrosius would become bishop of Milan and (somewhat later) Synesius bishop of Cyrene—two men who stood at the beginning of the long tradition of Christian hymnody. Sanctuaries and boys' choruses would remain; but instead of the 'diesseitige, lebensfreudige' hymns of the ancient Greeks in which mortals prayed their gods to come and give them fertility, peace, to join their merry feasts and to keep them in, or to restore them to, good health, new songs were going to be performed in which pious communities proclaimed that their politeuma was in heaven: they marked their distance from this world and longed for the unseen, for immortality and a new αἰών.

[75] In his enthusiasm for hymns and in his rejection of frivolous literature Julian shows himself a follower of Plato, cp. *Rep.* X 607 a.

[76] *Ibid.* no. 109, pp. 186 and 188.

P. A. MEIJER

PHILOSOPHERS, INTELLECTUALS AND
RELIGION IN HELLAS

I. *Atheism*

1. *Introduction, problems*

Whenever he arrived in a town Dicaiarchus, the admiral of Philip V of Macedonia, used to set up an altar to Godlessness and Transgression of the Law: ἀσέβεια and παρανομία.[1] He even sacrificed on it himself.[2] To the intense pleasure and gratification of the 'believers' this defiant behaviour was punished by the gods in an unequivocal manner: they had the religious miscreant who had dared to provoke them die a martyr's death, and although he was not executed because of his irreligiousness, the hand of god was clear enough. The same sense of relief must have attended another case of provocation, that of the poet Cinesias and his 'rotary' the so-called 'kakodaimonistai', who used to dine on ἡμέραι ἀποφράδες, which was regarded as an insult to the gods.[3] This was a sensational affair, comparable to Sainte-Beuve's Good Friday dinners.[4] Lysias[5] reports with malicious glee that many members of the 'dining club' died prematurely, of what I take to be excessive consumption of alcohol or an increase of cholesterin with doleful consequences. He tells us with deep satisfaction that Cinesias himself was stricken by a chronic malady which was worse than death. This illness and the rapid demise of the club members must

---

[1] This paper has grown from what was originally a lecture delivered during a summer-course of the Vereniging Classici Nederland, august 1977. So for brevity's sake I had to limit my subject to the classical period, including Theophrastus. The section on *deisidaimonia* in Plutarch was added as a natural complement of Theophrastus' views on this notion.

[2] Polybios, *Histories*, XVIII, 54. See also P. Decharme, *La critique des traditions religieuses chez les grecs* (Paris 1904, Brussels 1966) 176. Though clearly out of date, this work can nevertheless be consulted fruitfully for its treasures of knowledge. Not without importance is also A. B. Drachmann, *Atheism in pagan Antiquity* (London 1922).

[3] G. Morrow, *Plato's Cretan city, A Historical Interpretation of the Laws* (Princeton 1960) 451. For Cinesias, W. K. C. Guthrie, *A History of Greek Philosophy* (Cambridge 1969) III 245, cf. E. R. Dodds, *The Greeks and the Irrational* (Oxford 1950) 188 ff.

[4] P. Decharme, *La critique* 135, 136.

[5] Lysias, fr. 73 (*Athen.* 12, 155 E).

have fully gratified the sense of self righteousness of the orthodox. I do not know of many examples in Antiquity of such an aggressive atheism attended by a missionary enthusiasm (if the word missionary is appropriate in this context). We also, of course, have the case of the Hermacopides and—an isolated episode—the parodies of the mysteries (also at a dinner!) which has been attributed to Alcibiades and his companions.[6] I[7] do not believe that it would be going too far to see in all this an essentially intellectual objective, an aggressively experimental attitude or a desire to show up the gods' incapacity of repression, if not simply to deprive them of their existence.

That type of atheism which was not actively provocative in practice but which limited itself to words (Θεοὺς μὴ νομίζειν[8]) and did not infringe upon the external forms of religion, appears, from Plato's *Apologia* (26 D E) to have been of considerable significance among younger men in Socrates' time. Atheism was certainly widespread even in Plato's own days—or so we read in the *Laws*. We are all familiar with Plato's tirade against the godless in the tenth book (884 A ff.). He there spits the fire of piety at:

a) those who deny the existence of the gods.

b) those who do not deny the existence of the gods but deny that the gods care about men.

c) those who accept the existence of the gods and acknowledge their care for men, but who believe that one can 'bribe' them with sacrifices and prayers.[9]

Atheism is here classed as ἀσέβεια, which is therefore not only applicable to those who wish to deprive the gods of their existence, but also to those who merely deny the providential care (πρόνοια) of the deities and to those who believe that sacrifice and prayer can achieve the forgiveness of sins. My main reason for citing this passage is to show how widespread the

[6] See Dodds, *The Greeks* 191-202 (cf. Thuc., *Hist.* VI, 27 and 60). Diagoras should be mentioned here, who took pride in the fact that he once used a statue of Heracles as fuel preparing his meal without being the worse for it, while passing the roguish remark: You just accomplished your thirteenth work, Heracles! (F. Jacoby, *Diagoras ὁ ἄθεος* (Berlin 1960) 26 and 6, A 10).

[7] To K. J. Dover this seems too far fetched: K. J. Dover, 'The freedom of the intellectual in Greek Society', *Talanta* 7 (1976) 26.

[8] θεοὺς μὴ νομίζειν means either not sticking to the usual cult or disbelieving the existence of the gods, W. Fahr, Θεοὺς νομίζειν. *Zum Problem der Anfänge des Atheismus bei den Griechen* (Hildesheim 1969) 158 ff.

[9] See W. de Mahieu, 'La doctrine des athées au Xe livre des Lois de Platon', *Revue belge de Philologie et d'Histoire* 1963 (41) 5 e.v. and 1964 (42) 16 e.v.

denial of god was. Plato's aggressivity on the subject is proof enough. He is particularly concerned with 'youths' with intellectual or semi-intellectual persuasions.[10] We can thus probably conclude that atheism found wide acceptance in intellectual circles. These intellectuals could help themselves more or less freely to the fruits from the orchards of science (Sophistry), philosophy and poetry in order to build up their vision of life. Curiously enough atheism had no success amongst *philosophers* (the categories of philosophers and intellectuals are therefore by no means identical); they were obviously not interested in the denial of the existence of the gods. One of the main points of this paper is to describe the background of this lack of interest, since the acceptance or rejection of atheism was to be largely decisive for people's attitude towards religion and religious practice.

We come across few philosophers on the list(s) of 'classical' atheists.[11] We find, for example, Diagoras of Melos, Prodicus of Ceos, Critias the Athenian, of whom Plato was a grand-nephew, Theodorus of Cyrene (also called ἄθεος), Anaxagoras of Clazomenae (sporadically) and Euhemerus (of Messene?). But Euhemerus brings us to a far later period, as does Theodorus, and their doctrines cannot be considered characteristic of the time with which we are now dealing. So the only philosopher who remains is Anaxagoras; the others mentioned on the list are Sophists like Prodicus, Sophist-like figures such as Critias, or Utopians like Euhemerus, known for his 'euhemerism'.[12] This gives us food for thought, and is at least in accordance with what I said about the propagation of atheism in intellectual circles and the lack of it amongst philosophers. Even Anaxagoras did not teach any atheistic precepts; at the most people took objection to some of his views.

It is interesting to consider how the atheist *par excellence*, Diagoras of Melos, came to be an atheist.[13] The misfortunes that often afflict the righteous and the success which frequently smiles on the wicked led him to criticize the rule of the gods and to deny their existence. Personal experiences may also have embittered him: we hear of a loan which was

---

[10] Their thoughts were nourished by prosewriters and poets (such as Critias, about whom more later) *Laws* 890A.

[11] W. K. C. Guthrie, *A History*, III, 236 and Fahr, Θεοὺς 236.

[12] About Euhemerus, H. F. van der Meer, *Euhemerus van Messene* (Amsterdam 1949) and F. Jacoby, *R.E.*, VI, col. 952-972.

[13] Guthrie, *A History* III, 235, cf. F. Jacoby, *Diagoras* 26 and Fahr, Θεοὺς 89 e.v.

never repaid.[14] There is little sign of a philosophical background.[15] What is certain is that Diagoras was accused of impiety, and was outlawed. Was it the fear of prosecution that made the philosophers wary of atheistic concepts—and that despite the fact that the philosopher was usually unscrupulously bold, of a boldness which bordered on *hybris*, whenever he reflected on anything?

2. *The attitude towards cult and atheism in Athens*

We know that to behave contemptuously or carelessly towards the cult was not without its dangers in Athens.[16] We are acquainted with some appalling examples of severe punishments for infringers of the cultic rules. One of several: the hierophant of Eleusis, Archias, offered a blood sacrifice on a day on which the offering should have been a basket of fruit and the sacrificer a priestess. Ps-Demosthenes reports that he was executed.[17] Transgressions against the cult or in the sphere of religion were strongly resented. The penalties meted out on the occasion of the Hermacopides trial and the violation of the mysteries were heavy.[18] Yet there is also another side to the matter. A man like Cinesias was not prosecuted, anymore than was Aristodemus, the dwarf (was he compensating for something?), who publicly stated that he did not believe in the gods and that he couldn't care less about the cult. This may have been because he was converted by Socrates in the *Memorabilia*,[19] which makes the whole business a littel fishy since the conversion takes place too easily and is submitted to too uncritically, as in so many tales of conversion. The behaviour of the public prosecutor also seems somewhat erratic, but we have to bear in mind that there was no *public* prosecutor at all, since accusations had to be handed in by individuals—hence the arbitrary strategy against atheism.

[14] Jacoby, *Diagoras* 5 (A3 and A4).

[15] Guthrie here shows less hesitation than Jacoby who is doubtful, but who is after all willing to accept the possibility of Diagoras not being a philosopher at all. For Jacoby his consideration that theology was part of philosophy, which I am inclined to doubt, was highly important. But to my mind Protagoras remarks about the gods had no philosophical character. After all, the sophists in their activities bordered upon philosophy or were just outside it, cf. P. A. Meijer, 'Kleine geschiedenis van het begrip ''Niets'' in de antieke wijsbegeerte' in: D. M. Bakker ed., *Reflexies* (Amsterdam 1968) 241.

[16] E. Derenne, *Les procès d'impiété, intentés aux philosophes à Athènes au Vme et au IVme siècles avant J.-C.* (Liège 1930) 10, 11.

[17] Ps-Demosthenes, *adv. Neaeran*, 116 ff, cf. Derenne, *Les procès* 10, 11.

[18] Dover, *Freedom* 26.

[19] Xenophon, *Memorabilia* I, 4, 2 ff.

Could one indulge with impunity in *theoretical* attacks on religion and the gods? No, says Gigon.[20] He claims that, strictly speaking, no attacks of this description took place. This may indeed have been true, but the agnostic theories of Protagoras ('I can neither say that the gods exist or that they do not exist, nor what their appearance is like etc.' fr. 4 *DK*) must have caused a stir, to say the least, and Critias and Prodicus (about whom more later) were hardly beating about the bush and must also have had an unsettling effect on the cult. Reports of the prosecution of these men, especially of Prodicus and Protagoras, do indeed reach us from Antiquity. But, as K. J. Dover, that master of the *ars dubitandi*,[21] wrote in his article on intellectual freedom, we should at least have some doubts about the trials for impiety of Anaxagoras, Protagoras, Prodicus and Euripides. According to Dover all that is sure is the trial and outlawry of Diagoras and the trial and condemnation of Socrates. It may not have been advisable to fill one's doctrine with atheistic ideas since these were not appreciated in Athens by the man in the street and invited prosecution, but the risk was not that great either. Finally, it was also necessary to find prosecutors who were prepared to act in a particular case. It can hardly have been fear of trials which inhibited the philosophers in their attitude towards the existence of the gods and religion. Even the Sophists did not let this restrain them. Other factors must also have been at play which withheld the philosophers from thinking atheistically.

The first thing we should do is to form an idea of the attitude of the most critical pre-Socratic philosophers, since this takes us outside Athens where we hear nothing of trials. Furthermore, we can investigate how far they dared and wished to go in their criticism. In the case of many thinkers before Socrates we either do not know whether they had special views on the subject or we know for sure that they were favourably inclined to the traditional set of gods and religion, sometimes even that they used religion for the formation of their own theories. We encounter a goddess, Dikè(?) at essential moments in Parmenides' poem supporting his opinions and doctrines.[22] I shall therefore be discussing two figures: Xenophanes is, as it were, pining to take part in the discussion, and Heraclitus, too, must be allowed to have his say.

[20] O. Gigon, 'Die Theologie der Vorsokratiker', in: *Entretiens sur l'Antiquité classique* I (Vandœuvres-Genève, 1954) 129.
[21] Dover, *Freedom* 25 ff, esp. 47.
[22] Parmenides, fr. 8, 14, see also 37 and 60 (*DK*).

3. *Two pre-Socratic thinkers on religion*

Xenophanes' remarks have the effect of a stone thrown into the middle of a pond, causing ripples to spread to the very edge. We come across the influence of his thought again and again.

Owing to limited space I shall sum up Xenophanes' theological thought as follows:

1. His criticism is based on his reaction against the ethically somewhat rancid gods of Homer and Hesiod (fr. 11 and fr. 12 *DK*), a criticism derived from what I can only call a decency criterion. It is unseemly if gods do the things which are unseemly for men, a sort of ethical *via remotionis*.

2. He is able to explain, with great psychological sophistication, how man reached his (anthropomorphic) image of god—a projection theory (see also the theriomorphic fr. 15, and fr. 16). In this he is an opponent of image worship.

3. In contrast to the all too anthropomorphic character of the traditional gods, he emphasizes the 'Ganz Andere' of his supergod, which leads to a positive[23] image of the deity, signifying a revolution in the development of religious thought.

4. This image of god is characterized by

a) the character of pure νόος (fr. 24: god sees all over, thinks all over, and hears all over (οὖλος ὁρᾷ, οὖλος δὲ νοεῖ, οὖλος δέ τ᾽ ἀκούει),

b) the unbridgeable gap between this god and everything else (fr. 23) in structure and thought,

c) immense power, which is fully and purely noetic. In other words the god rules everything through the force of his spirit.

5. Xenophanes provides a severe criticism of the myths.

6. He does all he can to bring the everyday forms of religious practice onto a higher level.

Criticism of the myths and the exaltation of prayer and hymn are contained in fr. 1, the symposium elegy, which is of religious-historical impor-

---

[23] I cannot agree with the latest tendency as to Xenophanes as to deny that he had a positive theology. Xenophanes' thoughts would have to be explained merely as reaction provoked by the morally not exactly edifying theological views of Homer and Hesiod, and nothing more, see D. Babut, 'Xenophane critique des poètes', *l'Antiquité classique* 43 (19-74). To my mind a deity who is said to be pure eye, pure mind and pure ear—however inconsistent this may be—is a novelty in its own right. The importance of such exaggerated theses à la Babut lies in the illustration of Xenophanes' ties with the thinking of his predecessors, and it sheds more light on the connections with the past.

tance. Here is a part of this elegy in a working translation (in the preceding passage the preparations for a splendid feast are described (fr. 1)):

> Joyful men should first hymn the god with pious words and pure
> thoughts
> and after libations and prayer for the strength to act
> righteously—for this is our immediate task—
> it is no act of recklessness to drink as much as you can take and
> still get
> home without an attendant, at least if you are not too old.
> Then you must praise the man who, after drinking, discusses noble
> things with which his memory inspires him, and that table compa-
> nion who talks of boldness,
> not the battles of Titans and Giants
> or those of Centaurs, inventions of a former generation, or turbulent
> civil broils, things with nothing good in them, but we must always
> be heedful of the good name of the gods.[24]

We are struck by the following:

1. the myths, or at least some of them, are rejected with great contempt as the inventions of a former generation: πλάσματα τῶν προτέρων. They are, of course, not ethical enough; even after-dinner conversation is too good for them! Or, from the perspective of Antiquity, I should say: *particularly* after-dinner conversation.

2. the important forms of religious experience, hymn, prayer and sacrifice (libation offering), are not rejected but are raised to a higher level. The hymn must have a 'pure' content. The word 'pure' (καθαρός) is perhaps the most characteristic as far as we are concerned. Prayer, too, is attended by a nobler intention. But we shall be returning to that later.

All these ideas of Xenophanes are connected with a decency criterion and the consequent purification of the concept of god, rather than with natural philosophical considerations, which only play a limited part. Xenophanes does not go much further than declaring the goddess Iris a coloured cloud (fr. 32) and saying of the gods in general that they are not made of water and earth like humans (fr. 14 and fr. 29).

---

[24] For a useful discussion (with references to the literature concerned), see Babut, *Xenophane critique des poètes* 93 ff.

So religion as such is not rejected, any more than it is by Heraclitus, whose natural philosophy is far more elaborate than that of Xenophanes and pervades his entire doctrine. This also appears from the fact that an all-penetrating and all-dominating fire takes its place in the shape of Zeus—if that, at least, is how we can interpret fr. 32 (*DK*): the one Wise is willing and unwilling to be called by the name of Zeus. Heraclitus physicalizes the concept of god momentarily by elevating the *archè* to a deity. But his philosophy encroaches on the concept of god elsewhere too: god is present in his fundamental precept, the *coincidentia oppositorum*. God is day and night, summer and winter, war and peace (fr. 67), and, on the basis of this precept, he criticizes others, like Hesiod, who let the day be born of the night without realizing that they are one and the same thing (fr. 57). It is also on the basis of this same precept that he regards the existing forms of religion: he is thus prepared to sanction the Dionysiac procession and the song to the phallus (fr. 15) because the faithful actually—even if unknowingly—confess the unity of Dionysus (life) and Hades (death), although they violate the decency criterion. Outside the religious ambience this must all have been regarded as particularly un-civilized and impudent. Heraclitus, then, does acknowledge the decency criterion in a certain sense, but it is sometimes cancelled out by the *coincidentia oppositorum* principle. The decency criterion is indeed applicable to the mysteries since, according to him, these are celebrated in an unholy fashion (fr. 14). He makes a similar complaint about purification rites with blood, which he regards as being the same as 'purifying' oneself with mud, something for which he seems to have had a strong distaste.

As far as prayer is concerned he makes a very aggressive remark (fr. 5). Men pray to idols as if they were bragging to the temples without realising who gods and heroes are. Heraclitus is not averse to praying in itself, but his complaint is aimed at the obtuse idea that the images are gods. What is at stake is the *direction* of the prayer, which must be to the gods themselves. Otherwise the suppliant is just as pointlessly occupied as the bragger who gossips to the temple without approaching the lord of the temple. The Greek word λεσχηνεύεσθαι means 'talk in the club'—and here we can detect a criticism of the content of the prayers, which Heraclitus obviously did not regard as sufficiently exalted. He also demands of the sacrificer the same purity for which he searches in prayer. According to fr. 69 there are two sorts of sacrifice, the entirely material sacrifice of the man in the street and those of men who are internally pure and clean, as can occur

sporadically in the case of an individual. It would thus seem that the
sacrifice is acceptable in certain cases, *provided* the sacrificer is pure and
clean, an idea which, if it really did originate with Heraclitus,[25] was very
influential, as we shall see.

That even Heraclitus did not always base his criticism solely on his
philosophy and that he also had other criteria is perfectly clear from what
has just been said. All this has nothing whatsoever to do with atheism;
there is an element of cathartic criticism whose object is profundity, not
demolition. In what follows I wish to show that in the whole of Greek
thought there was a factor which, to put it mildly, hardly encouraged the
development of atheistic ideas: the *relatively low status* of the gods.

4. *An obstacle to atheism*

I shall start with the following somewhat unsubtle, and in no way exhaustive, definition of what a god was for a Greek: a being who surpassed
him in

1. length of life: immortality
2. comfort and joy
3. knowledge of what takes place behind the scenes of life
4. power over nature and human life.

The deity, therefore, is *not* primarily a *deus creator*. God is not the *Creator*
of this world. We do not find this Jewish-Christian concept until Socrates
and Plato, and even when we do find it in Plato it is in a completely different perspective. The creator of this world is a craftsman (Demiurge),
not an engineer. The example of the cosmos precedes him; the Ideas and
even the 'matter' (ἐκμαγεῖον) come first. This is a clearly defined difference
from the Jewish-Christian Creator.[26] Plato's God works with available
matter after a model;[27] Jahwe creates out of himself. The other gods in
Plato have even less to do with creation.

---

[25] See M. Marcovich, *Eraclito Frammenti, introduzione, traduzione e commento* (Florence 1978)
358. This work is as far as I can see now the latest commentary on Heraclitus.

[26] See L. Tarán, 'The creation myth in Plato's Timaeus', in *Essays in Ancient Greek
Philosophy* ed. by G. P. Anton and G. L. Kustas (Albany 1971), 391 and 407, n. 162. It is not
opportune here to ask questions about a so called mythical character of the Demiurg and its
consequences as to the existence of this Demiurg. In Xenophon, *Mem.* I. 4, we find the
famous teleological views on god who made the world so perfectly: by not placing a human
soul in a bovine body and so on, see my *Socratisch Schimmenspel, Socrates' plaats in de Griekse
wijsbegeerte* (Amsterdam 1974) 109. But the idea of an excellent composition of the world in
Xenophon does not seem to me sufficient to be detrimental to what is said in the text.

[27] But see C. J. de Vogel, 'Het christelijk scheppingsbeginsel en de antieke wijsbegeerte',
Tijds. v. Filosofie 15 (1953) 409-423, see also note 91.

Heraclitus already provides us with an exemplary description of the deity in fr. 30 (*DK*): 'This world (order), which is the same for all, was neither made by one of the gods nor by one of men, but always was, always is and ever shall be a fire that lives for all eternity, with measures kindling, and measures going out'.

The ordering *archè*-principle, fire, constitutes for Heraclitus what I would call the *ontic prius*, i.e. that principle or those principles which *precede* all else either cosmogonically or cosmologically. Heraclitus' *ontic prius* comes before the deity who, in fr. 30, is mentioned in one breath and in the same slightly humiliating category as man and who gets such a modest place assigned to him. God is more than man (fr. 83), but he is in no way Creator. Even if Heraclitus calls Zeus the one Wise in fr. 32 and perhaps means that fire can be called Zeus in a certain sense, thereby momentarily physicalizing the concept of god and placing it on the same level as the *ontic prius*, this does not mean that fire becomes a Creator of matter: at best it remains an ordering principle. The *ontic prius* itself is not created for the Greeks. It is simply there; it merely predominates and comes first. The gods follow. At the most the concept of god can reside in the *ontic prius*, but there is still no question of a Creator. Even if the world is explained entirely materialistically that does not entail the disappearance of the concept of god. There is still room for the traditional gods: superior beings (see point 4) can indeed continue to exist. They are sometimes extremely useful for theory (Parmenides and Empedocles). To us 'moderns' atheism is above all a denial of the divine deed of creation, particularly of the material aspect of the world. In Jewish-Christian thought God stands or falls with his work of creation. If this reality can be explained materialistically and God is made superfluous as creator, there is a good reason for doubting his existence. In this connection it is interesting to observe that Bishop Berkeley, the famous eighteenth-century philosopher, a remarkable man who oscillated between elevated speculations and banal expositions about tar-water, put the concept of substance and especially its material aspect outside our powers of perception... in order to combat *atheism* (!).[28] If we

---

[28] *The Works of George Berkeley, Bishop of Cloyne*, ed. by A. A. Luc and T. E. Jessop (London 1948) II, 168; 'If the principles, which I endeavour to propagate are admitted for true, the consequences which I think evidently flow from thence, are that atheism and scepticism will be utterly destroyed, etc.', compare also 257: 'But laying aside matter and corporeal causes, and admitting only the efficiency of an all perfect mind, are not all the effects of Nature easy and intelligible?'

deny the knowableness of matter, we remove the basis of any materialistic atheistic explanation, at least according to the bishop. This is typical of the eighteenth century and later—but not of the sixth or fifth century B.C. A purely materialistic explanation does not affect the fact that—as we said—superbeings can exist who are better off than we are, beings, therefore, who are simply χρείττονες. The example of Democritus[29] is particularly illustrative in this case. If anyone opened the way for atheistic thinking he did so with the doctrine of atoms. Nevertheless he accepted the existence of superbeings who were actually in contradiction with the doctrine of atoms or could hardly be reconciled with it, and he accepted those objections into the bargain rather than give up the idea of 'god' altogether—and this despite his penetrating insight that religion must have arisen out of fear! He even prayed to the good powers that he might meet them.

So there was clearly a major factor which was to the disadvantage of atheism: it was not necessary to choose between God and matter. A man like Anaxagoras, who was a very materialistically orientated thinker— even his νοῦς is intellectual *matter*—did not wish to be an atheist; such a thing did not so much as enter his horizon. Everyone more or less agrees about this. I do not feel the need, as did Jaeger, Deichgraeber and Babut, to requisition the idea that the νοῦς was regarded as a god by him. He never says so anywhere himself.[30] Such a feat was reserved for Diogenes of Apollonia, who turned the νοῦς into ἀήρ, thus elevating it into a deity (fr. 5 *DK*). In this way the concept of god is simply adapted to the materialistic theory by being physicalized, and a certain aspect of reality is declared superior so that there is no conflict between matter in its best form and god. The *ontic prius* and the deity come here very close to one another, closer than we shall find again in Greek philosophy for many years to come. Even Heraclitus had perhaps dared to tread this same path: the physicalization of the deity.[31] The possibility of overlapping in Diogenes is given credence by the equivalence of the ἀήρ, the *optimum* of the *ontic prius*, and νόησις, the power of perception and thought, so central to Diogenes' doctrine. This concept of the νόησις seems to me to be an adaptation of

---

[29] For Democritus Babut, *La religion des philosophes grecs* (Paris 1974) 47. This little work is a very clear and instructive introduction with a useful bibliography.

[30] Cf. Babut, *La religion* 43. The word αὐτοχρατές (fr. 12 *DK*) is held to be an indication, since it is characteristic of the style of a hymn. But this fact does not imply that it is to be understood in a religious sense in Anaxagoras too!

Xenophanes' thought god (οὖλος δὲ νοεῖ). In this νόησις we find a per-sonalized element which makes it perfectly suitable to call the ἀήρ: θεός.

These thinkers are consequently far from throwing the concept of god and the existence of the gods overboard. Nor would this have been in anyone's interest. As long as the deity is typified by his superiority over man and as long as he is not a creator there is not the slightest danger—unless, that is, there are offensive consequences which were not intended as such, like the materialization of bodies believed to be gods: the sun, the moon, the stars. When Anaxagoras regards the moon as a piece of stone and the meteorite which fell in Aigospotamoi in 467 as evidence for his view that the heavenly bodies whirl round the earth and are therefore allied to it, he strikes at the heart of the average man who started his day with a prayer to the Sun and the Moon and ended it with one.[32] Socrates, too, keeps his distance from Anaxagoras' ideas in his defence in Plato.[33] He does not wish to be accused of atheism. Indeed, he is not an atheist—quite the contrary. But the fact remains that the natural philosophers had no atheistic intentions. We see this confirmed by the Stoa. If ever there was a materialistic current of thought in Antiquity, it was that of the Stoa. But despite the fact that according to the Stoics fire is the first principle and all else comes from it and is carried along by it, the Stoa is full of religious feeling. That is why it is such a distortion of hindsight to say that ancient atheism is a by-product of philosophy and goes hand in hand with the development of materialism. H. Ley,[34] a Marxist historian of philosophy, thinks along these lines. He sees materialism coming to the fore and religious views set aside even in Thales. Ley thus displays a fundamental lack of understanding of the fact that the Greeks did not need to choose between matter and god. Antiquity cannot be appraised from an eighteenth-century, or, later, from a Marxist, point of view. If we try to do so we see an atheist made in our own image, not in that of the Ancients.

[31] See p. 225.

[32] *Symp.* 220 D with R. G. Bury's commentary *ad locum*, *The Symposion of Plato* (Cambridge 1909 and reprints) 162. Important is *Laws* 887 E. See also A. J. Festugière, *La révélation d'Hermès Trismégiste* (Paris 1954) IV, 245, note 3.

[33] *Apology* 26 D with Burnets commentary, *Plato's Euthyphro Apology of Socrates and Crito* (Oxford, 1924) and reprints, 111. We do not stand in the need of an impiety-trial against Anaxagoras (Dover can have it, *Freedom* 28) to know that his ideas were *thought of* as atheistic. Plato's Socrates may be called in as a witness.

[34] H. Ley, *Geschichte der Aufklärung und des Atheismus* (Berlin 1966), I, 39, 179. See also Fahr, Θεοὺς 171.

The type of religious consciousness which developed from Greek philosophy can on no account be seen as atheism or as paving the way for it.

If atheism did *not* develop from philosophy, we are inevitably faced with
the question of *what* its origin actually was. I shall try to give a suitable
answer to this question in the next section.

5. *The origin of atheism*

In my opinion atheism has a completely different source: it comes, I
believe, from the historiography founded by Hecataeus of Miletus which
had an enormous influence on Sophistry. We can certainly go as far as to
say that Hecataeus regarded his own means of approaching the trade of
the historian as far superior to that of his predecessors—and he does not
hide his light under a bushel. Fr. 1 (Jacoby) of his *Genealogies* runs as
follows: 'I write this as it appears to be true to me. For the tales of the
Hellenes are many and absurd; that at least is my impression'. What does
he mean by 'absurd'? He probably means the supernatural element of
the mythological tale, the only form of history available. He confronts
the mythical story with his new criterion, the (pseudo)probable. Thus
Cerberus becomes a snake which was frequently in the vicinity of
Taenarum and which bit numerous people to death (biting is typical of a
dog), sending them to Hades. Hercules killed the snake and brought it to
Eurystheus (fr. 27 Jacoby).[35] The foremost representatives of this line of
thought perform truly remarkable feats in their treatment of myths. In
c. 490 Hellanicus provides the following specimen: when Achilles fights
with the river-god Scamander this simply means that he gets into trouble
with the rising water of the river.[36] In such a way is the mythical element
turned into secular history.

Ever since Xenophanes—there he is again!—there exists an obvious interest in the so-called 'first inventors' (πρῶτος εὑρετής).[37] It looks as though
fr. 18 of Xenophanes played a role of some significance in this development. It runs: 'the gods have not revealed all things to men from the
beginning, but as time goes by they find better ones'. 'Finding', in this

---

[35] Advisable is here a continuous consultation of W. Nestle, *Vom Mythos zum Logos*
(Stuttgart 1940, here 135), be it not without some caution. He is inclined to build up a
theory on disputed details.

[36] Cf. Nestle, *Mythos* 144.

[37] A. Kleingünther, Πρῶτος Εὑρετής. *Geschichte einer Fragestellung* (Leipzig 1933).

culturally optimistic fragment, is the invention of new things.[38] That Xenophanes was interested in this is also evident in fr. 4, where he ascribes the invention of money to the Lydians.

Hecataeus, too, displays a considerable interest in inventors. According to him, for example, it is not Cadmus who is the inventor or transmitter of writing, but Danaus (from Egypt).[39] He may have brought the Liburnian ship back to Liburnus (but this reposes on a felicitous conjecture).[40] We also find a special interest in 'inventors' in someone like Hellanicus, according to whom Deucalion was the founder of religion. Here the lines meet: the πρῶτος εὑρετής-theory links up with the rationalizing attitude to myths. Again we are closer to home. What we want is a person (or persons) who can be considered responsible for the origin of religion without having to appeal to mythological figures like Deucalion. Well, Prodicus of Ceos is the person who provides them. Men had so much respect, indeed, ardent admiration, for agriculture and its products which made their lives possible, that they accorded divine veneration to the so-called ὠφελοῦντα and τρέφοντα, elevating bread into Demeter, wine into Dionysus, water into Poseidon and fire into Hephaestus (fr. 5 DK). If we read fr. 5 in a certain way (in my opinion the right one) the inventors (εὑρόντας) of the ὠφελοῦντα also participate in this apotheosis.[41] Prodicus mercilessly interprets the gods as products of human exaltation, which in fact implies their abolition. That the 'first inventors' should also get their share in this process of deification fits into the tradition which starts with Xenophanes and runs through Hecataeus.[42] This form of interpretation earned Prodicus a place

---

[38] ἐφευρίσκειν in Pindar too means to invent (Pyth. XII, 7): the art Pallas invented. Cf. E. R. Dodds, The Ancient Concept of Progress, and other Essays on Greek Literature and Belief (Oxford 1973) 4.

[39] Nestle, Mythos 138.

[40] Nestle, Mythos 138. A happy conjecture, not mentioned as such by Nestle.

[41] See Guthrie, A History, III, 238 ff., against this M. Untersteiner, The Sophists (Oxford 1954) 211.

[42] This line of development is—I think—extremely important for the understanding of the growth of atheism. The rationalizing method of the mytho-historiographers calls out for an explanation of the beginning of history and the place of the gods in it. Fahr, Θεοὺς 86, sticks to the opinion that atheistic thinking should be explained from a growing insight in the antithesis nomos-physis. People broke away from the less and less satisfying tradition, putting their institutions, religion among them, to the test. Arbitrariness of gods and contradictions in beliefs and cults led to the idea that 'die Götter von Menschen geschaffen seien'. This was were the sophists came in (so Plato's opinion in Laws 889 E). Once one perceives the development from mytho-historians towards the sophists one realises the possibility of showing—as has been done too concisely in the text—how the development really took place.

in the ranks of the atheists and the honour of being sentenced to death by
the Athenians, although it seems perfectly possible from the suggestions of
K. J. Dover, whom I have already had occasion to mention, that atheism
never actually entailed such an honourable martyrdom (even the cup of
poison).[43]

Religion and its origins were tackled with particular cynicism by
Critias, the famous tyrant of 403, who formed a notorious couple of
villains with his partner Charicles. Men, or so he has the sly Sisyphus say
in the homonymous play, introduced a penal code in the time of social
chaos which prevailed at the beginning of history. Unfortunately the law
did indeed punish public transgressions, but it was powerless against what
men concocted in private. An intelligent man with a profound intuition
then introduced fear of the gods amongst men so that the wicked should be
afraid, even when they did, said or thought something evil in secret. He
therefore brought in the idea of an immortal god who listens and sees with
his mind, and who is superior in his powers of thought, a being with a
strong sense of injustice, endowed with a divine nature, who will hear all
that is said by mortals and discover all that is done by them: the 'big-
brother-is-watching-you-*theos*'. A highly refined psychologist, Critias put
the deity in a position to supply both fear—thunder and lightning—and
blessings—warmth and rain (we are pursued by conjectures: here (fr. 25
line 30 *DK*) ὀνήσεις for πονήσεις, cf. lines 35 and 36). This cunning devil
from a primeval period surrounded men with a cordon of fear and with
such violent terrors that his words provided the deity with a splendid
dwelling and extinguished lawlessness.

Old Xenophanes would have rubbed his eyes had he read the cynical
distortion of his image of god in what I can only call the 'atheist
manifesto'. This divine police inspector is called νόῳ τ'ἀκούων καὶ βλέπων.
Anyone acquainted with Xenophanes can easily detect an echo of fr. 23
οὖλος ὁρᾷ, οὖλος δὲ νοεῖ, οὖλος δέ τ'ἀκούει and not like Diogenes Laertius
(IX, 19) μὴ μέντοι ἀναπνεῖν. Even the emphasis on the deity's superior
powers of thought (lines 18 and 23) is reminiscent of Xenophanes' fr. 23

Fahr can only postulate on basically general grounds a beginning of atheism with the
sophists. But the antithesis *nomos-physis* can only lead to scepticism or agnosticism (Protagoras fr. 4 *DK*), not directly to so exact a theory of historizing mark on the basis of the
πρῶτος εὑρετής-concept as we can offer in our text.

[43] Dover, *Freedom* 41: his position as a martyr is a very weak one.

and 24. Xenophanes' attempt at purification, used to fabricate a police god!

As far as his theory is concerned Critias is methodically fully in line with his predecessors; this is a πρῶτος εὑρετής-theory *in optima forma*. His interest in inventions and inventors is extensively attested elsewhere in his work.[44] His (anonymous) inventor of religion, however, is a politician, like himself. Instead of an agricultural explanation, as in Prodicus, we get a political one. Critias' account of religion as an historical event (albeit difficult to date) is therefore something like the conclusion of the rationalizing-historicizing method which has here all but reached its limits (only Euhemerus may have gone further):[45] religion as the cynical invention of a sly-boots. Cynicism is apparent above all in the efficiency with which fear (thunder and lightning) and blessing (warmth and gentle dew) are exploited. Cynical, indeed, but we must not forget that a 'noble lie' is here being used for a noble purpose: repression of lawlessness which cannot even be repressed by law. Readers of Plato's *Republic* will recall that Plato, too, applies a noble lie in his ideal state (415 A ff). He seems to have copied the procedure of his illustrious relative, for Plato suggests that one must impress a noble and useful lie on the citizens: the myth of those born of the earth, one with gold, the other with silver, the third with iron and bronze in his heart, a myth whose object was to keep men within their social status, within their rank: the myth of pennies which can never turn into shillings and of shillings which can never turn into pounds. This does indeed cast light on Plato's attitude towards religion: religion is particularly useful for keeping people quiet and drugging them spiritually. I shall

---

[44] He had an omnivorous sociological interest (fr. 2 *DK*): the κότταβος (from Sicily), the θρόνος (from Thessaly), the letters (from Phoenicia). He breathed live into the old elegy, on political motives, see G. Patzer, 'Der Tyrann Kritias und die Sophistik', *Studia Platonica, Festschrift H. Gündert* ed. K. Döring and W. Kullmann (Amsterdam 1974) 6 ff. The data just mentioned are taken from an elegy. Compare also fr. 21, where a person is said to be the first to discover a *logos*. Καινίζειν is the specific term, synonymous with ἐφευρίσκειν, see above note 38, but with special emphasis on the new, the original, καινός so characteristic of the sophists.

[45] By his explanation of the gods as princes who exerted themselves to be honoured as gods. The initiative does not lie with the believers (as in the case of Prodicus) or with the lawgivers (Critias) but with a man himself, who hoped deification would pay. Everything is done to attract attention-King Zeus wanders about the world to found tempels. This is how his universality is explained (e.g. Zeus Ammon). Eventually he retires from the world to a mountain and hardly appears again. There he entertains ... inventors! and gives them great honours, Van der Meer, *Euhemerus* 30, 31. The essence of euhemerism is not deification of men (as already is found probably in Prodicus, compare 229) but in selfdeification of men.

say more about this later, however. We get the impression that Plato had wanted to be a sort of Critias, or at least that he admired his great-uncle.

It is interesting, incidentally, as well as slightly awkward, to have to add that the Sisyphus play (a piece for reading?) was also attributed to Euripides in Antiquity. But Von Wilamowitz has salvaged it for Critias, and this has been accepted more or less universally.[46]

I am glad to have here been able to give a picture of Critias and to have produced, little by little, the portrait of the intellectual of the Classical period. He was no philosopher in the strict sense of the word. He took ideas from philosophers, and particularly from the Sophists. He had a wide range of interests. We might call him a sociologist of culture, for his interest in this domain was broad. He was also a poet, the author of elegies, and a playwright. Above all he had chosen what the intellectual of those days tended to choose as a 'career': he was a politician and an unscrupulous one at that, as hundreds of dead citizens can (no longer) witness.

It looks as though people of that sort regarded the goings-on of the cult with contempt. They could find enough theories to support their convictions. From Sophistry—which was no more than a marginal aspect of philosophy—they could learn to think atheistically; from philosophy they could adopt a philosophical substructure (the theorems of Anaxagoras, for example). That is what Plato is also really describing in *Laws* X.

But the philosophers themselves remained religiously inclined and many were attached, some with the object of criticizing and purifying it, to traditional religion and those of its forms which their fellow citizens practised in everyday life. That is why we must imagine not only Socrates, but also Plato or Theophrastus, praying with raised hands. What did they think of prayer and cultic sacrifice? These are the problems to which I shall now turn.

II. *The philosophers' prayer*

1. *Xenophanes and Heraclitus*

Here too we must begin our discussion with the critical giant Xenophanes.[47] Here again, he has produced critical-reformatory works of

---

[46] Guthrie, *A History* III, 303, n. 1.
[47] See p. 221.

stature. As far as I know his devotional instructions in the symposium elegy are a religious innovation. The average Greek prayer (often in the form of a hymn) has a structure which can be defined as follows:[48] 1 *invocatio*, 2 *pars epica* (reason for obtaining a favourable response) 3 *preces* (the actual question or desire). As far as the first two sections are concerned, they usually played a very limited part for the philosophers. In Plato, for example, the gods are generally only invoked by name. Merits which fall under 2 are not emphasized, so that all we can say at this point is that Cleanthes' prayer-hymn is an exception.[49] In Xenophanes' devotional instructions we are, of course, simply dealing with section 3: the supplication. His reforms are only aimed at the content of this supplication. But this is unique: we must pray to God (probably Zeus, maybe Zeus Soter)[50] for the power to act righteously, τὰ δίκαια δύνασθαι πρήσσειν. This is perhaps the most altruistic devotional instruction which we find amongst the Greeks. Righteousness is directed to one's neighbour and the (political) community, for a righteous man observes the customs or the laws prescribed by the community so that he be just and good.[51] There is no trace of the whines of *Gebetsegoismus*, the supplication for favours or things of purely personal interest. This same desire to be of use to one's fellow men also appears in line 23, Xenophanes' appeal only to discuss noble matters after drinking a large glass of wine, and in the conviction which we encounter in the sport-elegy (fr. 2) that he has provided εὐνομίη for men, a good order which ensures that bread is in the pantry and provisions are in the store-house (fr. 2, 19).

---

[48] See above p. 2.

[49] The hymn of Cleanthes (*S.V.F.* I, 537) contains a great number of significant epithets (vs 1 and vs 32) in celebration of the merits of Zeus. This feature belongs to hymnical style (but see Festugière, *La révélation* III, 315). The relation of God's might with respect to human fate in the Stoic system is crystallized to such an extent that glorification of the divine qualities and merits does make sense.

[50] Guthrie (*A History* I, 375, cf. E. des Places, *La religion grecque* (Paris 1969) 141, note 21) has Dionysus in mind, which seems very unlikely to me. The contents of the prayer, the ability to act righteously, is not an appropriate thing one would ask Dionysus. We had better think of Zeus or more exactly of Zeus Soter (who according to H. Sjövall, *Zeus im altgriechischen Hauskult* (Lund 1931) 90, 'stets als der eigentliche Gott des Symposions betrachtet wurde'). Perhaps in this quality Zeus may have been called also ἐφέστιοσ., *ibidem*, 116. Guthrie's remark that the symposium elegy has nothing to do with serious theology misses the mark.

[51] The socio-political aspect of righteousness is stressed by C. M. Bowra, *Problems in Greek Poetry* (Oxford 1953) 7, 8, see below note 94.

We can surely assume that here too Xenophanes' novel concept of god lay in the background.[52] One cannot reach the supergod of fr. 23-26 with the current prayers. It would seem likely that this new form of religious thought also extended to the other deities whom Xenophanes does not discard, particularly to the god of the elegy, as emerges from the fact that the hymns to this deity must not include any unseemly thoughts. This god (Zeus and, by extension, also possibly the supergod) is certainly not guilty of the ἀθεμίστια ἔργα of fr. 12, but observes what is customary among men and certainly helps those who pray to him for the strength to behave righteously. That is different to the prayer of the rhapsodist in the Homeric hymns XV, 9 and XX, 8: give ἀρετή and ὄλβος, which Bowra, perhaps wrongly,[53] assumes to have been the background of Xenophanes' devotional instruction. But we have now again come back to *Gebetsegoismus*. In Xenophanes, at all events, we have a revolution in the attitude to prayer in the sense that he shifts our attention from narrow self-interest to the community and our neighbour.

The purification of devotional life touches, as we saw, on a different point in Heraclitus, the direction of the prayer.[54] We must not think that the images of gods represent something essential, or rather, we must indeed think that they represent something—the deity who is elevated far above the image which, in the best of cases, can only be an indication. Thus is image worship rejected, in the cutting terms typical of Heraclitus.

We know next to nothing about views of prayer after Heraclitus. The turning point for our knowledge of the attitude of philosophers towards prayer is the appearance on the scene of Socrates.

2. *Socrates*

According to H. Schmidt's useful work *Veteres philosophi quomodo iudicaverint de precibus*[55] Socrates prayed a great deal: *multum precabatur*. This affirmation is based on a passage in the *Oeconomicus* (V, 19, 20) where

[52] James H. Lesher argues that divination does not fit in with Xenophanes' own (positive) theology ('Xenophanes' "scepticism" ', *Phronesis* 23 (1978)). I agree. For it seems to me a case corresponding to the purification of prayer. I totally disagree with Lesher's attempt to use this rejection by Xenophanes of divination as a basis for the explanation of fr. 34.

[53] Bowra, *Problems* 7. The hymns Bowra refers to, present great difficulties in dating, see J. Humbert, *Homère Hymnes*, (Budé, Paris 1951) 200, 216.

[54] See above 223.

[55] H. Schmidt, *Veteres philosophi quomodo iudicaverint de precibus* (Giessen 1907) not very much appreciated by Festugière, *La révélation* II, 322 note 2.

Socrates claims that we must pray for the help and support of the gods at every opportunity. Now, the *Oeconomicus* is a suspect source since the landed nobleman Xenophon puts his own pedestrian views on house-keeping in Socrates' mouth. I myself have doubts about whether we should see in Socrates a diligent and frequent practitioner of prayer. For we know his devotional 'doctrine' from the *Memorabilia* I, 3, 1-4., also by Xenophon. It is not impossible that this devotional doctrine made it superfluous to pray much. What is curious in this context is the fact that remarkably few prayers are said in Plato's early dialogues.

The prayers which Plato has handed down to us—or should we say presented to us?—appear above all in the dialogues from his middle period and the last phase. This might suggest that the prayer frequency of the 'true' Socrates was not very high. That his devotional doctrine may have made excessive praying superfluous could appear from the *Memorabilia* I, 3, 1-4, where we read that the gods—in accordance with the traditional view—see the back side or, if we prefer, the upper side of things and events in their omniscience (already in Xenophanes fr. 24 and Alcmaeon fr. 1). To pray for something concrete could be completely wrong: it might lead to disaster. Consequently Socrates politely preferred to leave it up to the deity to decide what was good for him—a conviction also connected to his view of good, into which I cannot go any deeper here.[56]

At this point we could talk of ennobled *Gebetsegoismus*: only the gods know what is really good for someone. Should we, according to Socrates' line of thought, pray for this ἁπλῶς ἀγαθά every time? Is it really necessary for someone who possesses (or thinks he possesses) a 'hot line' to the deity via the *daimonion* and who is always alerted when he is about to do something wrong or something that might not work out well? This is one side of the matter. The other side is that Socrates did indeed direct prayers, just like the other Greeks. When he comes into motion after his twenty-four-hour trance in Potideia he directs a prayer to Helios, a perfectly normal Greek devotional practice, judging from the *Laws*.[57]

By simply leaving the prayer blank Socrates had an enormous influence (if, that is, he was not a 'disciple' of Pythagoras on this point, to whom the same practice has also been attributed).[58] We find it in Plato and later, in a

---

[56] Cf. my *Socratisch Schimmenspel*, 185.

[57] See note 32.

[58] See C. J. de Vogel, *Pythagoras and early Pythagoreanism* (Assen 1966) 271, text 36 (Diod. X, 9, 7-8). It is not unlikely either that Socrates was inspired by a Spartan habit of praying,

Middle Stoic like Posidonius: εὔξεται τε, φασίν, ὁ σοφὸς αὐτὰ ἀγαθὰ παρὰ τῶν θεῶν.[59]

Plato puts various prayers in Socrates' mouth, as well as various hints at prayer which go hardly further than the intention, as, for example, in *Phaedo* 117 C: 'Well (says Socrates to the man who gives him the poison), I think that praying to the god is lawful and necessary so that the passage thence (to Hades) may be successful. Therefore I pray: may it be so'.

The most famous prayer which Plato ascribes to Socrates (in the literal sense of the word) is the Pan prayer at the end of the *Phaedrus*.[60] It is definitely worth emphasizing this prayer for a moment since it gives a good impression of the difficulties we are faced with in interpreting Socratic prayers in Plato (279 B C): ῏Ω φίλε Πάν τε καὶ ἄλλοι ὅσοι τῇδε θεοί, δοίητέ μοι καλῷ γενέσθαι τἄνδοθεν· ἔξωθεν δὲ ὅσα ἔχω, τοῖς ἐντὸς εἶναί μοι φίλια. πλούσιον δὲ νομίζοιμι τὸν σοφόν· τὸ δὲ χρυσοῦ πλῆθος εἴη μοι ὅσον μήτε φέρειν μήτε ἄγειν δύναιτο ἄλλος ἢ ὁ σώφρων.

Here follows a working translation, with no pretensions:

> 'Beloved Pan and all other gods living here, will you please grant that I become "beautiful" within and that all that I have without be in accordance with what I have within. And may I consider the wise man rich and have that much gold which only can bear and carry with him ... the wise man!'

The invocation of Pan and other gods residing in the locality should not surprise us. They had already inspired Socrates earlier (and this is not reported without irony (262 D, 263 D)) in this dialogue which, as we know, is set in the open country outside Athens, the domain of Pan and the Nymphs. It is pointless to offer, as B. D. Jackson does,[61] another explanation for the invocation of Pan.[62] In *Cratylus* (408 B) Pan is called a son of Hermes because the *logos*, invented by Hermes, reveals all (πᾶν). Pan,

---

see the apocryphal *Alcibiades* II. This remarkable dialogue, devoted to prayer, contains many examples of prayers for things that will only be harmful for the person who prays (parents praying for children who only will be a source of woe to them). In this dialogue Socrates refers to the Spartan habit of simply praying for the good and the beautiful (148 C).

[59] Schmidt, *Veteres* 25.

[60] The longest prayer is the Eros prayer (*Phaedrus* 257 A B, see B. Darrell Jackson, 'The prayers of Socrates', *Phronesis* 16 (1971) 24.

[61] Jackson, *Prayers* 28.

[62] The irony of Pan and the Nymphs as a source of inspiration of a rhetorically underdeveloped Socrates has totally escaped the attention of T. Rosenmeyer, 'Plato's prayer to Pan', *Hermes* 19 (1938) 36, 37. He even makes of Pan the *logopoios* proper.

therefore, fits perfectly into a dialogue on speech. Apart from the fact that the first explanation is conclusive, we can object that the second suggests that Socrates could not normally pray to gods since he had to have a special connection with the god whom he invoked. We have already seen Socrates praying to Helios, although we do not know what he said. The rural scene at the close of *Phaedrus* is a perfectly satisfactory explanation in this case.

The prayer also raises a few further difficulties. We could connect the beauty of what is within with openness to Ideas, and especially to the Idea of the Beautiful, of which *Phaedrus* provides such a splendid myth (that of the soul chariot). For E. Bickel, in his article 'Platonisches Gebetsleben',[63] this Pan prayer is the 'Mustergebet' of the Academy since it exposes the threefold ideal of Plato and his school

1. inner beauty
2. outer beauty, i.e. a good physical development
3. the possession of a reasonable amount of money, something to which Plato was not averse.

What is unfortunate is that Bickel should interpret ἔξωθεν ὅσα δὲ ἔχω as 'der äussere Mensch', so as to include the gymnastic ideal. When applied to Socrates himself the result is absurd. According to everyone who talks about him (Xenophon in his *Symposium* and Alcibiades in Plato's *Symposium*),[64] Socrates was notoriously ugly; even his body was anything but well-formed: he himself pokes fun at his belly. The prayer 'may all that I have without be in accordance with what I have within, i.e. beautiful', sounds ridiculous coming from Socrates' thick lips. But Bickel does not wish to involve Socrates' outer beauty in the explanation, he only wants to interpret the phrase as the expression of the gymnastic ideal of the Academy (with an appeal to *Republic* 403 C). Neither did it escape W. Kranz[65] that Socrates was not particularly good-looking; according to him Socrates meant that friendship and harmony must exist between that which is without and that which is within, and that there should be no

---

[63] E. Bickel, 'Platonisches Gebetsleben', *Archiv f. Gesch. d. Phil.* 21 (1908) 543. According to R. Hackforth, *Plato's Phaedrus* (Cambridge 1952) 168, 169, this prayer has nothing to do with the preceding part of the dialogue: it gives the floor to the authentic Socrates, which is—as I think—a regular misinterpretation, as will become clear from our treatment of this matter.

[64] See my *Socratisch Schimmenspel* 18.

[65] W. Kranz, 'Platonica I', *Philologus* 94 (1941) 322, 323.

strife between the two. But what that can have meant in Socrates' case escapes me.[66]

We must obviously interpret ἔξωθεν δὲ ὅσα ἔχω in another manner, probably as (external) possessions, commodities, money. Then the word 'rich' would not seem so odd in the passage. In that case the linking would be as follows: inner beauty must be in harmony with outer properties, which must also be 'beautiful': but 'beauty' applied to property entails another form of beauty, namely the beauty of moderation. This beauty resides in a relatively small amount of earthly means, as much as a wise and sensible man can, and wishes to, take with him—and that will not be excessive.

In addition to the scholars[67] who take the prayer for money or gold literally there are exegetes who will not admit of finances or suchlike.[68] 'That much gold' is thus an ironical metaphor for spiritual wealth, spiritual gold. And one can never have enough of that. Terms like φέρειν and ἄγειν come into their own. Ἄγειν even suggests a means of transport since φέρειν, bear oneself, is not sufficient. We can take φέρειν καὶ ἄγειν in the recurrent sense of 'plundering', although ἄγειν usually comes first in this case. But if ἔξωθεν δὲ ὅσα ἔχω refers to property precisely because of the contrast with πλούσιον, then the spiritualization of 'that much' must be considered less likely. Socrates' remark that this is only a 'moderate prayer' (μετρίως ηὖκται) and Phaedrus' reaction to it, with the Pythagorean κοινὰ τὰ τῶν φιλῶν, which applies above all to property, are so many signals that we should take the term χρυσοῦ πλῆθος literally. All the emphasis then falls on ... ὁ σώφρων. In that case the sentence contains an anticlimax, first the dramatic ὅσον-ἄλλος then, as anticlimax: ... the σώφρων does not need that much. We must indeed regard the σοφός as truly rich: true wealth is wisdom. The σώφρων does not need much concrete wealth. Here we can detect an allusion to a remark made by Phaedrus at the beginning of the dialogue. He would prefer to succeed in learning Lysias' speech by heart than to earn much gold (228 A), and that was a considerable concession for the financially bankrupt Phaedrus

---

[66] I fail to see Rosenmeyer's interpretation according to which the prayer has to do with communication of the Academy with the outsiders.

[67] P. Friedländer, *Platon* (Berlin 1954) II, 502, 503; H. Leisegang, *RE*, XX 2, 2478-9; E. des Places, *La religion* 245; G. J. de Vries, *A Commentary on the Phaedrus of Plato* (Amsterdam 1969) 266.

[68] Rosenmeyer, *Plato's prayer* 38; W. Kranz, *Platonica* I, 332.

(Lysias XIX, 15). In this prayer Socrates teaches Phaedrus that he must seek inner wealth (through the Idea of beauty, for example), not concrete wealth, and still less the tinsel of orators like Lysias—in keeping with the entire argument of the final section of the *Phaedrus*.

At the same time the prayer is an object lesson in rhetoric. Stylistically it is somewhat extravagant and rhetorically artificial. Rhetorical, certainly, is the attractive opposition τἄνδοθεν (with a prim crasis), later taken up by τοῖς ἐντός, with ἔξωθεν. And then the word φίλια 'in accordance with'! Besides, the φέρειν and ἄγειν are a little too grandiloquent for a mere possession of gold. The combination is used elsewhere (*Laws* 817 A), in an *elevated style*, to characterise tragedians. The construction ὅσον μήτε ... μήτε ... ἄλλον ἤ is also not entirely unpremeditated. What is rhetorically impressive is the ὁ σώφρων at the end. Admittedly all important words are at the beginning or the end of a sentence, as Kranz saw. Plato does indeed give a 'Mustergebet', but in a different sense to the one suggested by Bickel. In keeping with the dialogue, which is about rhetoric, Plato offers a specimen of it at the end: a well organized prayer. That suited him perfectly. We must not forget that the *Phaedrus* is a positive dialogue, not an aporetic one, so that Plato cannot allow it to end in philosophical helplessness. The myth which Plato liked to put at the end to conclude positive dialogues (cf. *Gorgias*, *Phaedo* and *Republic*) had already been used.

That this was no authentic Socratic prayer is something we can easily grant to Bickel and Kranz. What is at stake is not praying for goodness *tout court*. Besides, the prayer is too materialistic for the notoriously poor Socrates, who even prided himself on his indigence, and is anyhow too stylised.[69] So I also think it misleading to discuss this prayer to Pan under the heading 'prayers of Socrates'.

Jackson, moreover, comes to the following conclusions in this well-organised and informative article:[70]

1. the purpose of Socrates' prayers in Plato is to make the dialogues more lively.

2. they serve to give emphasis (the prayer is used as a support) in the development of difficult ideas.

3. they defend Socrates against anyone who might dare to accuse him of ἀσέβεια.

---

[69] *Apol.* 23 C, see also Xenophon, *Mem.* I, 3, 3.

[70] Jackson, 'Prayers', 70.

This last point is debatable, even unacceptable, on the basis of what Jackson himself brings on the carpet, viz. that these prayers are *not* to be found in the early dialogues where it would have been appropriate to defend Socrates in this way. It looks as though Socrates' prayers for an unspecified good were useless as a defence—even the pious Xenophon is miraculously brief on this point. Only later, when all that Socrates had said and thought in the course of time, and through the many dialogues in his name had become somewhat faded, could prayer be produced as a stylistic device.. Or did Plato himself have a greater interest in drawing people's attention to prayer: was he himself becoming a little more pious?

3.   *Plato's view of prayer, his devotional experience*

If we wish to define Plato's attitude towards prayer on the basis of what has been said hitherto, of the prayers provided in the dialogues which have been discussed so far, we must admit that their content is relatively meagre and perhaps somewhat impersonal. This is also the opinion of W. J. Verdenius in his paper 'Platons Gottesbegriff'.[71] Prayer is used in support of a discussion or in the presentation of a difficult idea.[72]

What I want to show in this section is that Plato took prayer essentially very seriously, and that we can even speak of a profound devotional experience, certainly in the last phase of his life. We must here draw on *Laws*, where he no longer tries to vindicate the stringent ideal of the normativity of Ideas for the life of the state and declares the deity the measure of all things in a very typical variant on Protagoras' adage (*Laws* 716 C). The only means of binding people's conscience is still religion as far as he is concerned.[73] Hence also his uncommonly violent polemic with the atheists and the ungodly of different shades. This desire to give men a dominant norm, placed far above them, is stated with the utmost clarity: 'Truly the tirade against the atheists has been made in somewhat vehement terms in our desire to triumph over the wicked. But, Clinias, our desire for triumph was due to our fear lest these people, if they gained the upper hand in an argument, should think they could do more or less anything they liked' (*Laws* 907 B).

---

[71] W. J. Verdenius, 'Platons Gottesbegriff' in *Entretiens sur l'Antiquité classique* I (Genève 1952) 241 ff.

[72] *Timaeus* 27 B D, 48 D E, see Jacksons's survey, 'Prayers' 15, 16.

[73] E. Sandvoss, 'Asebeia und Atheismus im klassischen Zeitalter der griechischen Polis', *Saeculum* 19 (1968) 323.

The punishment he recommends is shutting them up in a 'think camp' (σωφρονιστήριον) or an isolated prison, (δεσμωτήριον) according to how obstinate their atheism is (*Laws* 909 A B).[74] In Plato we still encounter the need for a means of repression (cf. Critias), a norm of censorship, and moral constraint via the gods and religion. But it must be added that he *himself* fully believes in the gods, even in the Olympian ones. There is a passage in *Timaeus* (40 D, 41 A) where mention is made of the generation of a second group of deities (the Olympian ones) beside the astral gods, the heavenly bodies, which became of increasing importance for Plato. Timaeus excuses himself by saying that we cannot prove anything or know anything about the traditional gods, as we can about the stars. We can only rely on what their children have said about them—and they should know! This last remark has been regarded as an example of irony, for which Socrates and Plato are so famous.[75] But the fact that these gods should be clearly involved in the address to the gods held by the Demiurge and that they play such an important role in the *Laws*, where they are taken perfectly seriously, should put us on our guard.[76] We must beware of playing the astral gods off against the Olympian ones.[77] Funnily enough, again in the attack on the wretched atheists, the opponent automatically lets himself be persuaded *en passant* about the existence of the Olympian gods by the proof of the existence of astral gods, and Apollo and Helios have a single temple ascribed to them in the *Laws* (*Laws* 945 E). Nor must we draw a distinction between these two groups. Plato cannot do without the Olympians because they have various areas of life commended to their special care in *Laws*. We might wonder whether Plato used them *pour besoin de la cause* and whether he himself retained a mental reservation, but this is most unlikely in view of what I have just said.

If Plato *really* believed in the Olympians his attitude to sacrifice and prayer must also be a source of evidence. Well, Plato has written some

---

[74] E. Sandvoss, *ibidem* 327, draws attention to the humanizing of the penal system in Plato's *Laws* as compared to the Athenian procedure, to which Socrates fell a victim 1) differentiation of crimes (we may add: better foundation of the charges), 2) medicinal explanation (atheism as a disease), 3) introduction of a house of correction (σωφρονιστήριον as an answer to Aristophanes' φροντιστήριον). True, Plato wanted to be more lenient than the Athenians, but it remains a matter of doubt whether a house of correction or isolation is more humane than the death penalty with the possibility of escape by voluntary banishment.

[75] F. M. Cornford, *Plato's Cosmology* (London 1937) 139.

[76] See Babut, *La religion* 94 and G. Morrow, *Plato's Cretan city* 444, 445.

[77] For astrolatry, E. des Places, *La religion grecque* 255 ff.

very fine things about prayer in the *Laws*, things which do not suggest the slightest reservation. He says emphatically that the good, i.e. the sensible and righteous man must consort with the gods by way of sacrifice, *prayer* and votive offerings, in short by way of the entire service dedicated to the deities (*Laws* 716 C ff.). Prayer in Plato is again a *Bittgebet* (*Laws* 801 A), while the prayer for forgiveness[78] virtually never appears:[79] his object is never to repair evil which has been committed. Prayer may well be a supplication for something we desire, but with this limitation: we can really only pray for what is beautiful and righteous (*Laws* 687 D E). This can be summed up in the prayer for understanding—νοῦς—in order, I should add, to be able to make the right supplication. In Plato prayer can also be of intercession. A father will join his prayer to that of his child, but only when he is asking for something good. Otherwise the father will pray for the contrary.

In the parents-children relationship in Plato we see a highly refined form of devotional altruism. As far as the *granting of prayer* is concerned the prayer of the aged father or mother, grandfather or grandmother, can achieve a great deal. God does not often refuse such suppliants. Even their imprecations are uncommonly powerful: the negative prayer of intercession. Plato speaks appropriately and touchingly about the most powerful image, the greatest jewel in the house—an aged father or mother. Aged parents, or grandparents, are a gift from god (ἑρμαῖον 932 A ff.), a godsend.[80] I even find moving the addition: 'and if they depart in their youth they will be much missed'. Plato's involvement with this devotional relationship may have been due to the fact that he himself lost his father, Ariston, in his youth, and obviously felt this to be a profound loss and missed him deeply. The words spoken in the death scene in *Phaedo*[81] also come to mind: 'we felt ourselves robbed of a father'. Plato clearly sought a father figure in Socrates, as did many of his friends. I do not believe that I

---

[78] What we find in Plato, is first of all the 'Bittgebet'. Only once do we come across a prayer for forgiveness, the Eros prayer, in which forgiveness is asked for what was wrong in the argument (*Phaedrus* 257 B). Jackson, *Prayers* 26, thinks that this kind of prayer was not appropriate for Plato.

[79] We do find this in Socrates' conversation with his son Lamprocles, which I consider as one of the most touching pieces in Xenophon (*Mem.* II, 2, 1, see my *Socratisch Schimmenspel* 289, 290).

[80] Plato offers this thought twice within a few lines and in hardly varied terms: this thought was obviously very precious to him; *Laws* 931 A and 932 A.

[81] *Phaedo* 116 A, see my *Socratisch Schimmenspel* 289, 290.

am very far wrong in saying that it is precisely in the touching phrase 'if they depart in their youth they will be much missed' that Plato's personal involvement in prayer and its power emerges most clearly. Someone who speaks so emotionally about prayer obviously took it seriously and experienced it profoundly. For him it was more than a formal duty; it was an activity which could move his heart. Where his attitude to the parents-children relationship is concerned we detect in him a devotional altruism—of the parents for their child—which I, for one, find impressive. Or is this rather a highly sophisticated form of *Gebetsegoismus*?

There is one other problem to which we should now turn. According to some scholars we can, indeed we must, call the Intelligible and the highest, the Idea of the Good, 'god'. A vehement champion of this view, initially at least, was Prof. C. J. de Vogel who, in an sharp article,[82] expressed herself rather harshly about those scholars who disagreed with her. She later reached a considerably more moderate position.[83] In her book *Plato, de filosoof van het Transcendente* she goes no further than to say that we must simply call the highest principle, Good, 'divine' in Plato and that Plato perhaps intentionally avoided the term 'god' as an honorific title for the Good in order to steer clear of a disrespectful and unsuitable personification. W. J. Verdenius[84] too claims that the Idea of the Good is the highest deity for Plato and that we can indeed call Ideas 'god'—and this despite the fact that Plato himself never designates Ideas (not even the Idea of the Good) with the name 'god', or even suggests that we might.[85] Verdenius appeals to the predicative meaning of the word 'god' for the Greeks. It only refers—and Verdenius cites Von Wilamowitz—to an instance which is of 'überragende Bedeutung'.[86] That is why we can call the Ideas 'gods'.

I do not share this view for, as I see the problem, we cannot get away from the question of why *prayers* are not directed to Ideas in Plato.

---

[82] C. J. de Vogel, *Philosophia*, I *Studies in greek philosophy* (Assen 1970) 219.

[83] C. J. de Vogel, *Plato, de filosoof van het transcendente* (Baarn 1968) 150, 151 in the section: 'what did Plato call God'?

[84] Verdenius, 'Gottesbegriff', 242-246. In E. des Places, *La religion grecque*, 235, note 35 we find a series of scholars of the same opinion. See especially P. J. G. M. van Litsenburg, *God en het goddelijke in de dialogen van Plato* (Nimweguen, 1955) 102-180, who presents a 'tour d'horizon'.

[85] For *Tim.* 37 C τῶν ἀιδίων θεῶν γεγονὸσ ἄγαλμα see Van Litsenburg, *God en het goddelijke* 70.

[86] Verdenius, 'Gottesbegriff' 243; Von Wilamowitz, *Der Glaube der Hellenen* (Berlin 1931) 1932, I, 18.

Verdenius[87] has an answer to this too: prayer in Plato is so impersonal. Prayers are actually aimed at the Ideas, but they are aimed indirectly. Because the Ideas are so impersonal—the more impersonal the higher the deity—we cannot address our prayers to them directly. In my opinion the fact that we cannot pray to Ideas is an argument against their deification. They are not gods. They are part of the *ontic prius* in this world. Here again we come up against the deep division in Greek thought which we already encountered in Heraclitus.

The possibility of identifying the *ontic prius* with the deity in the style of Diogenes of Apollonia—of identifying, in other words, the highest Idea with the highest god—obviously did not attract Plato, probably because the deity is not high enough for this identification. Plato is clearly too attached to the personal element in the term 'god' for him to call the Idea god.[88] This personal element does not lend itself to an *ontic prius*.[89] We are here confronted with what we might regard as a paradox: the word 'god' is too 'low' for the Idea, as we see in *Phaedrus* 249 C, where Plato explains that the deity is god because he always consorts with Ideas which obviously represent a higher order. Equally paradoxical is the fact that the concept θεῖος, which can certainly be applied to the Ideas, is higher than θεός. The description of Ideas as θεῖος does not make them into gods; J. van Camp and P. Canart[90] conclude: 'θεῖος ne met pas les formes au rang des dieux'. Θεῖος in antithesis to ἀνθρώπινος is a hyperbolic metaphor in normal linguistic usage with the connotation 'superior', 'of the highest order'. Hence the suitability of this word to express the superiority of the Ideas without entailing a divine status. Thus θεῖος is 'higher' than θεός.

Not only do the Ideas come first and belong to the *ontic prius*, but so does matter[91] in its basic form (ἐκμαγεῖον), which Aristotle, *mutatis mutandis*, was

---

[87] Verdenius, 'Gottesbegriff' 270, Von Wilamowitz, *Glaube* II, 254: '.. beten kann gewiss kein Mensch zu diesem Gotte'.

[88] G. M. A. Grube, *Plato's thought* (London 1935 and reprints), ch. V, 'the Gods', makes very useful reading as to the relation of the Idea of Good and God. Apart from that Plato did much for the purification of the notion of god (*Rep.* II 379 A ff; cf. Van Litsenburg, *God en het goddelijke* 8 ff.).

[89] Van Litsenburg, *ibidem* 195. This personal element is fully acknowledged now by C. J. de Vogel, *Plato* 151.

[90] J. van Camp et P. Canart, *Le sens du mot θεῖος chez Platon* (Leuven 1965) 416.

[91] It may be tempting to follow C. J. de Vogel, *Scheppingsbeginsel* 413 ff. who adheres to the opinion that there is no question in the *Timaeus* of pre-existent matter in the form of the four elements. But this point of view would not be easy to accept because of *Timaeus* 53 A B.

later to call πρώτη ὕλη. The gods take second place (the Demiurge) or third (the Olympians); they are still superbeings, even for Plato, but are conceived personally and are consequently prepared to hear man when he prays and ready to accept his sacrifice when it is offered to them. If we confront the Idea with the sacrifice the absurdity of the deifying hypothesis is still more striking. The direction of a prayer to an Idea could still be a possibility, as could the eulogy by way of a hymn, although there is no mention of either in Plato, but offering sacrifices to the Idea seems quite impossible, although it was perfectly normal to do so to a god.

At this point the way seems to have been paved for the next subject, the philosophers and sacrifice. I shall restrict myself to the views of Plato and, above all, to the ideas of Theophrastus, in whose theory of sacrifice a number of lines meet. His doctrine marks the culmination of concepts of sacrifice in the Classical period.

III. Sacrifice

1. Plato and sacrifice

We now approach the essence of the term εὐσέβεια: piety, as it is frequently translated, from σέβεσθαι, to venerate, to behave in the right manner towards the gods.[92] This is the virtue which embraces man's dealings

---

Besides, in the *Timaeus* there appears the ἐκμαγεῖον (50 C), in my opinion a pre-existent form of matter (against which De Vogel, *ibidem* 415, 416).

'Εκμαγεῖον means literally a matter on which impressions can be made: eg wax. This basic form of matter is prior to the Demiurg. He works with it. The origin of *this* matter is as dark and mysterious as the basic elements of Parmenides' Doxa, Fire and Night. They did not come into existence by positing by men, least of all by a logically false positing such as Mansfeld suggests (J. Mansfeld, *Die Offenbarung des Parmenides und die menschliche Welt* (Assen 1964) 215). According to him a false logical procedure is to be held responsible for the existence of the two forms. Once in existence by the miracle of this procedure they are used by the goddess to be dynamically worked on. So that we end up in a hopeless vicious circle in my opinion; men create the elements, by means of which they are to be created themselves by the goddess. In their mysterious origin the elements in Parmenides are much akin to Plato's ἐκμαγεῖον. The logical procedure is purely a matter of epistemology, in which the forms Fire and Night are apriori given. We may add that in Plato too (*Republic* 597 B) we come across the thought of God as Creator of the Ideas (*ontic prius*). But this may be called a sidetrack of Plato's thought, as appears from the *Timaeus*, which provides the main line. In the *Republic* Plato wanted this thought because of his criticism of painting and dramatic art. Plato often wanders far from the main road of his thought. In the *Republic* we even meet the Idea(!) of Evil, a time-bomb beneath the whole platonic system. The relation between the *ontic prius* and the gods is once more illustrated by the epicurean philosophy: the gods of Epicurus would not have had the slightest notion of the world, had this world not been prior to them (cf. J. M. Rist, *Epicurus, an Introduction* (Cambridge 1972) 148).

[92] E. des Places, *La religion grecque* 371, with literature.

with the gods. Since prayer is always a prayer of supplication, there is
rarely an element of true veneration in it. True veneration only comes into
its own in the offering of τιμή. Together with the hymn, in so far as it is not
a prayer, sacrifice is the only thing we can 'return'. Here we automatically
think of the *Euthyphro*, which is about piety, ὅσιον, a word which can in
many respects be regarded as synonymous with εὐσεβής. As we know, the
theses of Euthyphro are systematically demolished right from the beginning of the dialogue, according to the familiar Platonic procedure—even
the view (15 A) that we must offer the gods τιμή and γέρας. For Socrates
(Plato) asks Euthyphro: what do we have which we did not first get from
the gods? And yet it appears from the *Laws*, for example, that Plato
himself sees the sacrifice as the best means of giving expression to veneration, and considers it of the utmost importance.

To start with I should emphasize that we must assess the term εὐσέβεια
properly: it is not, anyhow in the Classical period, total devotion or
dedication to the divine. As Ps-Aristotle[93] says, it is a department or complement of righteousness, which regulates our behaviour towards those to
whom we owe something, although righteousness sometimes also displays
the tendency to become synonymous with virtue in so far as the righteous
man must satisfy the laws established by society.[94] This aspect found its
concrete shape in Aristotle in so-called general justice, as opposed to
particular justice. When it comes to definition, however, righteousness is
regarded as the correct line of conduct towards one's neighbour, with
εὐσέβεια as a complement.[95] It is thus the εὐσέβεια which regulates our
cultic debts towards the gods. If we fully appreciate this value of the word,
we can see why in the Stoa, for example, from which we would indeed expect great 'piety' or devotion, the word εὐσέβεια is not accorded the honour

[93] Ps. Aristoteles, Περὶ ἀρετῶν καὶ κακιῶν, 1250 b22: πρώτη τῶν δικαιοσυνῶν—ἡ εὐσέβεια—πρὸς τοὺς θεούς, εἶτα πρὸς δαίμονας κτλ.
[94] Righteousness turns out to be almost synonymous with moral goodness, unrighteousness with dito badness, see *Gorgias* 507 A B and *Rep.* 407 A ff. Righteousness in Xenophanes is of this type, see note 51.
[95] *Euthyphro* 12 E. This word develops the tendency to become of a wider sense. Often it is more than just veneration in the right way (see D. Kaufmann-Bühler, 'Eusebeia', 994, 995 in *Reallexikon für Antike und Christentum* 6, Stuttgart 1966) although it must be admitted that veneration according to what formally can be asked, is still the main thing (Kaufmann-Bühler, *ibidem*, 991 and see also Dodds' remark: 'The Greeks were apt to think of piety as a contractual relation rather than a state of mind', *Plato Gorgias* (Oxford 1959) 336 *ad Gorgias* 507 B 2).

of signifying it. Even amongst the Stoics it is only a part of righteousness: the giving to everyone—even to the deity—his due.[96]

In this same light it becomes clear why Theophrastus' work Περὶ Εὐσεβείας 'On Piety', which I will be returning to later, seems to deal particularly with sacrifice.

I have already referred to sacrifice in Heraclitus who—and this is particularly relevant, since he seems to have been the first to do so—dwelt on the necessity of sacrifice springing from a pure 'conscience'. Socrates—to make a necessary jump—could be seen sacrificing regularly, according to Xenophon (Xen. Mem. I, 3, 3). He too laid emphasis on the inner condition and disposition of the sacrificer. The gods obtain the greatest pleasure from the sacrifices of the most pious. The satisfaction of the gods and their cult leads to mantic recommendations about life in general (Xen. Mem. I, 4, 18). The value of the sacrifice is not determined by its size, since the sacrifice of the rich is of no more value than the modest sacrifice paid for with modest means. It would be ethically monstrous if the gods derived more gratification from the large sacrifices of evildoers than from the small ones of the pious. The special link with the deity, of which Socrates possessed the prerogative, the daimonion, did not inspire him with an attitude towards sacrificial practice different to the traditional one. That he was not averse to the blood sacrifice either can be deduced from his last words: 'sacrifice a cock to Asclepius' (Phaedo 118 A). According to tradition the blood sacrifice was indeed rejected by the Pythagoreans[97]—a rejection first attested in Empedocles, who appears to have been influenced by Pythagoras on this point. In the time of peace under Aphrodite, he says in the 128th fragment (DK), fruit was offered and the altars were not dripping with the blood of sacrificial animals. Defilement by bloodshed is, for him, the origin of all misery for the psyche which was originally divine.

Our best source of knowledge of Plato's spirituality of sacrifice is Laws 716 C-717 A, a passage to which I have already referred earlier.

The basis of Plato's thought is here the 'becoming like god'. The most famous passage in this connection is Theaetetus 176 B, where Socrates maintains that evil will always exist since it is the indestructible pendant of good. It is therefore better to escape (ἐνθένδε ἐκεῖσε) from earth upwards (φυγή). This φυγή is the famous doctrine of the ὁμοίωσις θεῷ κατὰ τὸ

---

[96] Chrysippus' definition, see M. Pohlenz, Die Stoa (Göttingen 1948) I, 126; II, 72.
[97] C. J. de Vogel, Pythagoras 271.

δυνατόν. What does the ὁμοίωσις contain? According to Mrs. C. J. de
Vogel[98] it contains the 'becoming like god' as the intelligible, behind
which lurks the view that Ideas are also god. But this interpretation seems
implausible if we keep in mind that no doctrine of Ideas is to be detected in
the *Theaetetus* (W. D. Ross[99]) and that in this dialogue we find, in so many
words, what the ὁμοίωσις contains: becoming righteous and pious μετὰ
φρονήσεως. Here discernment is not the vision of Ideas or anything like
that, but the 'inferior' awareness of what is righteous. This interpretation
can be supported by Plato's remark that nobody shall ever be more similar
to the deity than he who is most righteous.[100] Righteousness is the path to
the ὁμοίωσις. In the *Laws* this is specifically stated. We must become like
gods where judiciousness and also righteousness are concerned, although
this concept is worded in a somewhat veiled manner but not unclearly.[101]
Admittedly in the *Republic* (500 A-501 A) to become divine means yielding
to speculations about the Ideas, but we will have to accept that there is also
a way of observing the greatest righteousness in order to climb up to the
gods and reach our ultimate destination, existence on a star (*Timaeus* 42
B). The couplet ἐνθένδε ἐκεῖσε in the *Theaetetus* seems to allude to this too. I
believe the urge to escape from this world to be one of the deepest incen-
tives of Plato's activity as a philosopher: he had a profound aversion to the
perishable. No one who is aware that righteousness also contains a complement of the gods will be surprised that Plato underlines the necessity of
giving the correct sacrifice in the *Laws*, immediately after the statement
that we must be godlike in judiciousness—which implies righteousness.

---

[98] C. J. de Vogel, *Philosophia* I 220.

[99] W. D. Ross, *Plato's Theory of Ideas* (Oxford 1951 and reprints), 101.

[100] The expression μετὰ φρονήσεως cannot therefore save De Vogel's position, still maintained in her 'Plato', 159, viz. that becoming like god in the *Theaetetus* has to do with the
vision of the Ideas. In *Philosophia* I, 220, indeed, she uses ὁμοίωσις in the *Theaetetus* as an
argument in favour of the thesis that the intelligible is god, because the term μετὰ φρονήσεως
which we find continually in the company of the ὁμοίωσις and is mentioned in one breath
with it, would point to the Ideas. Our explanation shows that already in the *Theaetetus*
becoming like god is merely a matter of being righteous and that accordingly μετὰ φρονήσεως
is not at all to be explained 'intelligibly'. Conclusive seems to me that in the *Laws* (906 B)
μετὰ φρονήσεως is mentioned in one breath with the rescuing force of righteousness and
σωφροσύνη, whereas no trace of intelligibility is found in this type of μετὰ φρονήσεως in the
Laws.

[101] In *Laws* 716 D ff. Plato starts out from σωφροσύνη, but righteousness is undoubtedly
implied (compare *Laws* 906 A), because ὁ μὴ σώφρων is called at the same time ἄδικος, see
H. Merki, ΟΜΟΙΩΣΙΣ ΘΕΩΙ. *Von der platonischen Angleichung an Gott zur Gottähnlichkeit bei
Gregor von Nyssa* (Freiburg in der Schweiz 1952) 5.

He also adds an interesting note: we must sacrifice with a pure soul (καθαρὸς.....τὴν ψυχήν). Otherwise the sacrifice is not accepted and there is no possibility of success. The success of the sacrifice is apparent in the contribution to the *eudaemonia* which the gods can provide. This is ambivalent: on the one hand the sacrifice is a proof of veneration; on the other it supports the prayer of supplication (for here, 716 D, the prayer is meant as a request for *eudaemonia*), as we also find elsewhere in the *Laws* (801 A)—two aspects which I regard as being in conflict with each other.

Perhaps it is still less possible for sacrifice than for prayer to make up for evil deeds (717 A). Plato was rigidly consistent on this point after the *Republic* (364 B C). The gods do not accept anything from someone unrighteous: neither sacrifice nor prayer nor initiation into the mysteries can avail the guilty man (see also *Laws* 905 D). If Plato had had to abandon this idea, his work would have lost its religious grip.

How seriously Plato took not only prayer but also sacrifice is something we can learn from a pericope in the *Laws*. The aged, almost eighty-year-old author reaches back to a strongly emotional experience, an impression from his childhood. He appeals to the atheists by referring to the unforgettable manner in which their parents behaved when bringing sacrifices, when praying for themselves and their children. These parents did not pray (or sacrifice we may add) to *non-existent* gods, but to real, truly existing ones (*Laws* 887 D E). The zeal of the parents together with the righteousness of their care for their children would be wasted on non-existent gods: so gods do indeed exist—a sort of emotional syllogism.

We can conclude that Plato, like Socrates, still had a traditional attitude towards the cult, but an attitude which was relatively pure. The most radical innovation was perhaps Plato's measures for the restriction of votive offerings, which were also a part of the service in honour of the gods (*Laws* 955 E ff.). Aristotle remains outside the picture since he never, or hardly ever, devoted special attention to sacrifice and prayer—at least in what has remained of his works.[102] The only reason for mentioning him is his ambivalent, perhaps somewhat hypocritical attitude towards popular forms of religion. In the *Metaphysica* (1074 b 5) he expresses himself with a certain arrogance about the traditions which serve to convince the people and to place them in a state of dependency, while, in his will, he himself is

---

[102] Of Περὶ εὐχῶν only one fragment is found in W. D. Ross, *Aristotelis Fragmenta selecta* (Oxford 1955) 57.

busy redeeming a vow with images of gods (cf. Diogenes Laertius V 16). Aristotle's disciple Theophrastus, on the other hand, takes the cult very seriously indeed and displays a completely different attitude to that of his master. It is to him that the following section will be devoted.

2. Theophrastus and sacrifice

a) The object of the sacrifice

Theophrastus' work Περὶ Εὐσεβείας was exhumed by Jacob Bernays in the last century from Porphyry's De Abstinentia, one of those typical nineteenth-century philological feats.[103] It has been published more recently in a (slightly) extended form by W. Pötscher, from whose edition I shall be quoting. Theophrastus' main theme is his aversion to blood sacrifice in the tradition of Pythagoras and Empedocles,[104] whom he quotes enthusiastically (fr. 12, l(ine) 8, ed. Pötscher). This aversion on Theophrastus' part is based on the οἰχειότης,[105] the relationship between man and beast. The animal soul and the human soul have the same first principles, as well as the same affections, (πάθη) as he says in fr. 20 in fine. Theophrastus gives a variety of arguments for rescuing the animal from being sacrificed—without, however, being a vegetarian, as E. des Places, for example, claims.[106] Here follows a limited selection of these arguments:

1. It is unjust to damage something or someone for the benefit of so sacred a matter as sacrifice (fr. 7, l. 14). We must not rob a living being of its life on the pain of violating piety. Such a life is more valuable than that of plants, whose fruits should indeed be used for sacrifices: plants themselves cast off their fruit.

2. If it is not permissible to sacrifice useful animals, may we not offer animals which are useless or wild and damaging? No, for although we do not commit a crime by killing them,[107] we would be giving the gods

---

[103] J. Bernays, Theophrastos' Schrift über die Frommigkeit (Berlin 1860). W. Pötscher, Theophrastos 'Peri Eusebeias', griechischer Text, herausgegeben, übersetzt und eingeleitet (Leyden 1964).

[104] p. 247.

[105] The οἰχειότης, the kinship of plants, animals, men and gods is naturally something other than the stoic selfrealisation οἰχείωσις. See W. Pötscher, Strukturprobleme der aristotelischen und theophrastischen Gottesvorstellung (Leyden 1970) 139.

[106] E. des Places, La religion grecque 13, see also the following note.

[107] Here I seem to hear a sound not completely in harmony with vegetarianism. Killing animals is allowed, but only in the case of nocuous animals and they may obviously be eaten. I am not the only one to hear this sound, Pötscher, Strukturprobleme 125.

something which is essentially bad. That is just as wrong as the sacrifice of a mutilated animal. The offering of such beasts would be an insult (fr. 12, l. 33).

3. Humans are only interested in pleasure: useful animals, which cannot be eaten, like donkeys and elephants, are never sacrificed, not to mention useless ones like snakes (fr. 12, l. 66 ff.)! From this we see that what human beings like about sacrifices is the edible part which they reserve for themselves, so that their norm of εὐσεβές or ἀσεβές is the principle of profit (fr. 6, l. 15). Theophrastus' accusation of consumer selfishness is not unjustified. The economy of the sacrifice to the *ouranioi* is a striking feature amongst the Greeks: only the inedible portions were sacrificed, while the meat returned to the sacrificer. The Greeks had cunningly ordered matters according to consumer economics, and therefore did far better than those who let their meadows be grazed by untouchable sacred cows. Even in Hesiod we find a theomythical reflection of this phenomenon which aroused the amazement of the Greeks. We only have to think of Prometheus' sacrifice (*Theogonia* 533 ff.).[108]

Theophrastus' theory also reveals the object which did *indeed* come into consideration at sacrifices:

1. The entire history of evolution (fr. 2) shows that even in the earliest time (in Egypt) people began to sacrifice herbs and grass-like plants. Fires in honour of the visible gods of the heavens were fed with roots and leaves because fire resembled them most. The Greek word θύειν derives, according to Theophrastus, from θυμίασις (θυμιᾶν), which means smoke, so we learn from etymology (a much exploited means of seeing through primeval situations ever since Hecataeus) that the sacrifice originated from burning and that the blood offering was totally unknown, animals only having appeared on the scene much later (after the trees). Sacrifices of perfumes (myrrh, cinnamon, incense and saphron) were introduced with some difficulty, as we see from the name which the first generation of sacrificers gave to this innovation: curses, ἀρώματα, from ἀράσθαι, by which their present name should be explained (an incorrect etymology).

---

[108] Hesiod tells us how Prometheus prepared two sacrifices: 1) meat and fat intestines packed up in a bovine stomach. 2) meatless, bare bones packed up in fat. Although Zeus saw through the disguise, he chose the latter sacrifice—flying into a rage! In this peculiar way their economical manner of sacrificing was explained by the Greeks themselves. According to K. Meuli and E. des Places old motives from hunting times were at the back of this behaviour, see E. des Places, *La religion grecque* 138.

In a further stage of evolution come the trees. Their leaves and fruit were offered. When the noble fruits of the fields were discovered, first grains of corn were sacrificed and later, with the invention of mills, meal. When men discovered oil and wine new sacrificial material became available. It therefore appears from the whole development that originally plant-like materials were offered and that the animal sacrifice must be of a later date. We here have a very interesting combination: on the one hand an optimistic vision of the development of nature and culture which, in view of the interest in inventions, appears to be orientated towards development sketches in the manner of Prodicus and Critias (which actually go back to the interest of the historiographers in inventions and first inventors);[109] and, on the other, something which was just as typically Greek: a pessimistic outlook on development, particularly religious development. Things become ever nastier: the simple fruits of the soil come into competition with the blood sacrifice—a phenomenon of religious degeneration.

Pötscher[110] tries to explain the obviously normative aspect of early religion with the doctrine of *dynamis* and *energeia*, but this holds out little chance of success since even Aristotle, for example, teaches the inferiority of what is a mere disposition and the superiority of what develops: *energeia* is preferred to *dynamis* (*Met.* 1094 b 1 ff.). Theophrastus thinks in terms of religious degeneration, as do Hesiod, Empedocles and the Stoa.[111] This has nothing to do with the doctrine of *dynamis* and *energeia*.

---

[109] See p. 228.

[110] Pötscher, *Strukturprobleme* 114, see also his edition of *Peri Eusebeias* 125, 126.

[111] In Dicaiarchus too, who was a peripatetic as well, a mixture of optimism as to technical progress and pessimistic preference for primeval times is to be found. In Theophrastus the pessimism is centred on religion. This preference for primeval times is not found in Aristotle, the master of both. So Dodds is right to observe that their pessimistic views on their contemporary situation 'surely would have surprised their master', *Progress* 17, see also L. Edelstein, *The idea of Progress in classical antiquity* (Baltimore 1967) 134, 135. Theophrastus' preference for primeval times seems understandable to me. The bloody practice of sacrificing of his day did not suit his ideal of continuous piety. To think that the situation in earlier times was better (with Hesiod: Golden Age) and Empedocles (fr. 128 *DK*), is rather an obvious conclusion. Culturo-technical progress can be observed without making an ideal out of it, as the historiographers and sophists did. Their cultural optimism produces the impression of being a substitute for religion. From a religious point of view, obviously the most important to Theophrastus, there is progress too, but in the wrong direction: deterioration of religious feelings and practices. What is most surprising, after all, is Theophrastus adopting the idea of evolution in nature.

2. The gods provide for us and give us the chance of living decently (νομίμως) on the fruits of the land (fr. 7, l. 9).

3. They also help us to raise crops, especially the gods of the heaven (fr. 19, l. 9). There is a magnificent form of cooperation between gods and men. The gods contribute to the fruits which we ourselves have sowed and planted (fr. 7, l. 32). Man himself invests trouble and effort in agricultural products, so that they are particularly suitable as sacrificial gifts: the gods thus get a cake made not of their *own*, but of *our*, dough. In this manner even Plato's Socrates in the *Euthyphro* gets an answer.

How did man get round to offering blood sacrifices? Such a thing is the inevitable result of times of famine. In the absence of fruit people offered an animal or a man, since they were reduced to eating animals or even to cannibalism. Sometimes, too, there were misfortunes with beasts which became the cause of certain sacrificial rites. Here Theophrastus shows himself to be an expert sociologist of sacrifice (fr. 3 *in fine*, fr. 6).

b) *The attitude of the sacrificer and the mode of the sacrifice*

Not only did Theophrastus reflect theoretically on the object of the sacrifice, but the demands made on the disposition of the sacrificer (fr. 7, l. 35 and 45) and its consequences for the mode of the sacrifice also interested him. In the style of Plato he requires the sacrificer to have purity of psyche, and in the manner of Socrates he requires him to make a small sacrifice, not because of ultimate lack of money but because the size of the sacrifice is of no importance. What is at stake is the intention. We must sacrifice frequently but little, a small quantity of the daily meal (fr. 9, l. 13), a custom which already appears in Homer (Odysseus and his mates in the cave of Polyphemus first sacrificed some cheese before feasting on Polyphemus' own quality cheeses).[112] Only then is continuous piety attained—the συνεχὴς εὐσέβεια—Theophrastus' ideal. It is above all the continuity which expresses the deepest veneration for the deity as benefactor (not as 'creator'!). This veneration leaves no room for the contractual element so characteristic of Greek religious feelings. Theophrastus himself specifically states that veneration must not resemble a 'gift on a contractual basis', but that it must express the respect which we show, for example, by making way for a superior (fr. 8 *in fine*).

For Theophrastus sacrifice is just as much an expression of respect as of thanks, and finally it can also be a supplication for something good (χρεία

---

[112] Sjövall, *Zeus* 89.

ἀγαθῶν)—which always comes last with him. Theophrastus is not very selfish (fr. 12, 1. 42). The small sacrifices of one's own meal, in other words of the voluntary fruits of the soil, are best suited to give shape to continuous piety, i.e. the continuous respect for our benefactors and betters. Large sacrifices are a bane and have completely distorted the religious perspective (fr. 8): hecatombs appal the deity. Olympias, Alexander's mother, once sacrificed a thousand oxen, an exorbitant amount which could only result in a swarm of evil (ἑσμὸς κακῶν), viz. incorrect veneration of the deity (δεισιδαιμονία) and wantonness (τρυφή). Besides, it makes way for the idea that gods can be bribed with sacrifices: an unrighteous man must not count on the fact that an evil deed once performed can then be bought off. And indeed, we cannot expect this effect from a couple of mere cakes or pieces of fruit, Theophrastus' sacrificial material. Theophrastus is well aware of the relativity of the sacrifice: the gods have no need whatsoever of our sacrifices. Moreover, how can we teach temperance to the young if they are led to believe that the gods are carousing in luxury and consume enormous meals of quite unappetizing proportions (fr. 8)? The gods look more to the ἦθος of the sacrificers than to the πλῆθος of the sacrifices (fr. 7, *in fine*).

These are all views which can be understood in the tradition of the fathers, viz. the philosophical fathers. In Theophrastus' doctrine of sacrifice, with continuous piety at its heart, such ideas obtained a certain culmination, a certain perfection. Now, however, we must turn to something completely new and very special in the history of sacrifice, and the question is whether Theophrastus understood and sensed its scope, or in any case the sensation it would create. We read (fr. 8, 1. 18): the gods look at the inner disposition (ἦθος[113]) of the sacrificer, which is still Socratic and Platonic, but the greatest sacrifice is to think correctly (ἡ ὀρθὴ διάληψις) about the gods themselves and the sacrificial situation (my interpretation of πράγματα). The best sacrifice is a pure mind (νοῦς καθαρός) and an unemotional soul (ψυχὴ ἀπαθής). This also implies (οἰκεῖον[114]) that one

[113] It is most surprising, that the advanced point of view of the above mentioned *Alcibiades* II (see note 58) is also that the gods pay more attention to the ψυχή than to the presumptuousness of the sacrifice (149 E, 150 A).

[114] To my view what is most important both in νοῦς καθαρός and in ψυχὴ ἀπαθής is the approach and the intention, as will be further explained in the text. The term οἰκεῖον to me means here 'in harmony with' (the preceding). καί I think means 'hence'. Pötscher, as a result of his interpretation, assumes three objects of sacrifice 1) a pure mind, 2) a soul without passions, 3) apart from these, it is suitable to offer modest sacrifices: the crops. It

must offer modest (μετρίων) sacrifices, not by the way (παρέργως) but with full abandonment (σὺν πάσῃ προθυμίᾳ). And this indeed is a new set of ideas: the immolation of a νοῦς καθαρός and a ψυχὴ ἀπαθής.

What we should understand by a pure mind and a passionless soul is not immediately evident. Babut's statement[115] that we must sacrifice 'thus' in an 'esprit de pureté' does not solve any problems. For what we must make clear is exactly what the *sacrifice* of the mind means. We read in the same context that the greatest sacrifice is a correct vision (ὀρθὴ διάληψις) of the gods and their position in religion (πράγματα), the sacrificial situation.

Are we going too far if we suppose that the pure mind is the bearer of the correct vision of the gods and religion? I do not think so. We are certainly not dealing with a form of devotional spirituality entailing the dedication of the spirit to the deity.[116] It is far more a question of having the right intellectual attitude and facing the consequences: making modest sacrifices as a sign of continuous piety. Theophrastus tries to imagine the situation of the gods as recipients of sacrifices. Only the right predisposition (ἦθος) on the basis of the correct convictions are of value to the gods, which implies that men's psyche should not be dragged along by their passions. Only then is the sacrifice acceptable.

How should we interpret ψυχὴ ἀπαθής, and particularly the word ἀπαθής? Let me proceed from the context. I have just said that the πολυτέλεια introduced a swarm of evil, certainly incorrect veneration of the deity (δεισιδαιμονία), perhaps excessive fear of the gods, wantonness, and the idea that the gods can be bribed by sacrifices. Δεισιδαιμονία and τρυφή in particular can be interpreted as πάθη. In this case the νοῦς is no longer pure and the psyche is dragged along (= is no longer ἀπαθής), so that all the proportions (of sacrifice) disappear. I believe that we must see ἀπαθής in connection with the καθαρός of the νοῦς. That also emerges elsewhere.

The concept 'pure' (καθαρός) is not applied to the mind in fr. 9 but to the soul and the ἦθος, the inner disposition. People think that they must go

---

seems beyond doubt that οἰκεῖον can be interpreted as 'suitable', as does Pötscher, *Struktur-probleme* 84. But to me it has here the sound of 'cognate', 'akin', 'in harmony with', as fits in well with Theophrastus' usage of this word elsewhere (fr. 12, 21, see note 105); so I translate 'implies'.

[115] Babut, *La religion* 132.

[116] In Diogenes the Cynic one could just think so. Veneration of the Gods is a working of the soul. But in fact this means no more than having just and appropriate thoughts about the Gods. Here too, devotion is not the point. Correct veneration is no more and no less than adopting the right thinking about the Gods, see Babut, *La religion*, 141.

to the sacrifice wearing a freshly washed robe on a freshly washed body, without their soul having been purified of evil (κακῶν). But the gods feel most kinship with what is divine in us, the soul. In the first place, therefore, we should purify the soul before we come into contact with them. But what are these κακά with which the soul can be afflicted? Is it unrighteousness and moral evil? I assume that this was not what Theophrastus had primarily in mind, for he begins to speak again in a tone of reproval of the presumptuousness of the sacrifice of the wicked. The sacrifice does not have to be valuable. The cleansing of the psyche and of the inner disposition thus fit again into a pure view of the sacrificial act: the small sacrifice of the meal. We get the impression that the νοῦς is con- tained in the psyche which is called most akin to god and is thus considered most representative of man. Consequently the word 'pure' can also be ap- plied to the psyche. Obviously νοῦς καθαρός and ψυχὴ ἀπαθής from fr. 8 also form a coherent whole, a mind which, by way of a correct vision, ensures that the soul does not let itself be dragged along by passion to incorrect sacrificial practices.

So Theophrastus certainly does not mean that the sacrifice of mind and soul should replace the sacrifice of any object whatsoever. That would mean the abolition of sacrificial practice—and there is no question of that! The new spirituality of sacrifice leads to the characteristic ideal of con- tinuous piety with its small but frequent sacrifices from the table—the final phase of the purification of the classical doctrine of sacrifice which already started, as we saw, in Homer. It was only later philosophers that were to abandon the practice of sacrifice. The Stoa does so in principle, on the one hand violating the principle but on the other readmitting it with the daily sacrificial practice—for the sake of the man in the street.[117]

Seneca gives a pure interpretation of the authentic Stoic point of view in fr. 123 (Haase): *non immolationibus et sanguine multo (deum) colendum; quae enim extrucidatione innocentium voluptas? (deus colendus est) mente pura honestoque proposito. Non templa illi in altitudinem saxis exstruenda sunt: in suo cuique con- secrandus est pectore (deus).*

God gets pleasure not from (blood) sacrifices—the idea of the fruits of the soil does not even occur to him—but from a *mens pura*, the νοῦς καθαρός of Theophrastus and from the good intention (*propositum*) of behaving according to Stoic principles. This *honestum propositum* looks like an echo of πάσῃ προθυμίᾳ, and it may be so, but it is certainly no synonym, for in πάσῃ προθυμίᾳ the dogmatic element to be found in the typical Stoic '*propositum*' is lacking. In Seneca, therefore, an evident transformation has taken place with respect to Theophrastus' view of the object to be sacrificed: not fruits but the mind. Here, however, I am transgressing the limits of the period I have undertaken to treat.

I do not believe, as I already said, that Theophrastus realized that his new ideas would be so important for others and would have a deep effect on their thought. We must not forget that the idea of sacrificing the νοῦς καθαρός and the ψυχὴ ἀπαθής only occupies a minor place in his work: it only appears once. The larger part is devoted to the sacrifice itself, the object and the means of sacrificing. For Theophrastus himself continuous piety is far more important. This would not be the first time that a thinker had not been fully aware of the most interesting and original element in his own work. We would like to hear him at greater length on questions like: what exactly is a νοῦς καθαρός, and what is ψυχὴ ἀπαθής?

There is one more point I would like to investigate, namely Pötscher's heroic efforts to connect the νοῦς καθαρός—with the Νοῦς as the highest god, the ψυχὴ ἀπαθής with the Ouranos and the (φαινόμενοι) οὐράνιοι θεοί (heavenly bodies), and the offering of modest sacrifices with the mythical deities[118] who are accepted by Theophrastus without further ado.[119] Such attempts have something attractive about them. If the mythical deities have πάθη, and according to Theophrastus they do indeed—or so says Pötscher[120] (just think of raging Zeus)—they cannot be connected with the offering of a ψυχὴ ἀπαθής, and still less with the sacrifice of a νοῦς καθαρός, which is reserved for the highest god: the Νοῦς.[121] Pötscher devotes a great deal of attention to the fact that in Theophrastus the heaven is called ἀπαθής, which means that heaven is bound to receive the sacrifice of a ψυχὴ ἀπαθής.[122] The difference between the three sorts of god does not emerge from Περὶ Εὐσεβείας, but is to be found elsewhere, in my opinion a weak point. Indeed, Pötscher's entire argument, to which a certain amount of erudition cannot be denied, must be wrong for the following reasons. In

---

[118] Pötscher, *Strukturprobleme* 83, 85, 95 (conclusion), see also W. Pötscher in the article 'Theophrastos' in '*Der Kleine Pauly, Lexikon der Antike* (Münich 1979) V, 724.

[119] Pötscher, *Strukturprobleme* 76.

[120] Pötscher, *Strukturprobleme* 94.

[121] Pötscher, *Strukturprobleme* 85, esp. 103.

[122] Pötscher, *Strukturprobleme* 80, esp. 90.

the first place the psyche is also called καθαρά (fr. 9, l. 5), so that the νοῦς does not have the monopoly of this predicate—something which hardly favours so sharp a distinction as Pötscher wishes to introduce.[123] In the second place the mythical deities and the heavenly gods are constantly lumped together in a 'Sammelplural', θεοί,[124] which seriously weakens the barriers. In Helios, moreover, we have a group and a name which overlap. In the third place there is no question of a Νοῦς as the highest god in Περὶ Εὐσεβείας (although there is indeed in Theophrastus' *Metaphysica* 7 b 23), and it seems unlikely that Theophrastus himself should make no mention of the connection between something so important as the νοῦς καθαρός and the highest god, Νοῦς, and should leave it up to his scholarly readers to discover this connection. Finally, the activity of the *entire* company of gods is comprised under a single name: assistance in agriculture (fr. 19),'which seems to entitle *all* gods to sacrifices of the fruits of the soil. Even the gods of the heavens benefit from them, although they are supposed—at least by Pötscher—simply to be venerated with ψυχὴ ἀπαθής. Fr. 19 tells us that the pious man expects to be received in heaven amongst the gods after his death, amongst the entire set of gods (τὸ σύμπαν γένος), of the οὐράνιοι, viz. amongst those whom we now see (on earth) and must venerate with the fruits of which they are the joint cause: τὸ σύμπαν γένος τῶν ἐν οὐρανῷ θεῶν, οὓς νῦν ὁρῶντας τιμᾶν δεῖ τούτοις, ὧν συναίτιοι ἡμῖν εἰσίν ...[125]

The clause 'whom we now see' refers to heavenly bodies and not to images of the gods. The *ouranioi* who, according to Pötscher's interpretation, should only be venerated with ψυχὴ ἀπαθής fall, in any case, under the category of those venerated with fruit, whereas the traditional deity Asclepius must be approached according to fr. 9 with a ψυχὴ καθαρά on entering his temple. This then, is no temple of an astral god, as we might have expected from Pötscher's arguments, but the temple of a 'mythical' god who must have derived pleasure from veneration with fruits of the soil. Pötscher's hypothesis must therefore be rejected; so nothing is to stand in the way of my own elucidation.

All that we have encountered in Theophrastus so far would appear to be the work of a man to whom the word εὐσεβής can be applied. We cannot

---

[123] But see Pötscher, *Strukturprobleme* 80 and 103.

[124] Pötscher, *Strukturprobleme* 101-106 thinks otherwise.

[125] Pötscher, *Strukturprobleme* 105 does not pay much attention to the implications of συναίτιοι.

deny that he has a deep feeling for purification. He is the most consequential purifier of the ancient sacrificial practice, a practice which he leaves substantially untouched. Yet this does not mean that he was a bigoted sanctimonious fanatic. In his *Characters*, and particularly in his sketch on the misplaced piety of the deisidaimon, Theophrastus pokes fun at the religious neurotic. This is a witty piece in which he disposes far more easily with a religious fanatic than someone like Plutarch who devoted his pastoral care to that very same man.

IV. Δεισιδαιμονία

1. *Theophrastus*

The *deisidaimon* is the man who thinks that the gods are determined to spite him and who can only protect himself with the utmost caution.[126] In his XVIth Character Theophrastus says that δεισιδαιμονία can easily be regarded as a sort of cowardice (δειλία). In Theophrastus δειλός[127] is also the man who sees dangers everywhere, who spots a pirate behind every headland and who asks, when the sea is rough, whether there is anyone who is not initiated. This same cowardice, now concentrated in the relationship with the gods, is the essence of Theophrastus' definition of the δεισιδαιμονία. The *deisidaimon* is someone who detects the hand of the gods in every event. He should not be called 'super*stitious*' but 'super*faithful*'. It is not that he believes in different things to anyone else, but that he experiences everything in a distorted perspective. When a mouse gnaws his bag of meal he goes to the Exegete to ask what he should do. If the Exegete tells him to take it to the cobbler's to be patched he takes no notice and makes a sacrifice to avert the danger. As if the Exegete were not one of the most scrupulous authorities in religious matters! Bion of Borysthenes observed wittily that we could only talk of a prodigy if the sack had eaten up the mouse.[128] And many other doings of the overwrought neurotic are reported. He rushes around apotropaeically with an olive sprig in his mouth and always feels threatened by defilement and pollution.

The word 'deisidaimon' only obtained its unfavourable meaning in a rather late period. For a pious man like Xenophon it is naturally

---

[126] For this notion: E. des Places, *La religion grecque* 369. Important are P. J. Koets, *Deisidaimonia* (Purmerend 1928); H. Bolkestein, *Theophrastos' Charakter der Deisidaimonia* (Giessen 1929), and D. Kaufmann-Bühler, *Eusebeia* 1016, 1017.

[127] Theophrastus, *Charakter* V, 2.

[128] Koets, *Deisidaimonia* 37.

favourable, just as it is for Aristotle who points out, in his *Politica* (V 1315 a 1), when discussing the stability of a tyranny, that it is as well for the tyrant to show himself to be extremely scrupulous in religious matters: here too the term *deisidaimon* is used. It continues to retain its favourable meaning throughout Antiquity, especially in inscriptions: fear of the gods was typical of the man in the street and continued to be so. I base myself here on data in the still cited dissertation of P. J. Koets.[129]

The word seems to have obtained its unfavourable meaning in Theophrastus' day, possibly in comedy. Theophrastus, then, was keeping up with the times when he wrote his sketch.

We should compare this negative concept δεισιδαιμονία with the positive concept εὐσέβεια, which is so penetratingly analyzed and described by Theophrastus. Since Pötscher's edition[130] we have a fragment (fr. 8) where the word δεισιδαιμονία appears twice. The introduction of πολυτέλεια produced a swarm of evil, δεισιδαιμονία and τρυφή, together with the idea that the gods can be bribed and that evil can be repaired through (large) sacrifices. The neurotic continuo is still absent, however. The δεισιδαιμονία simply refers to an exaggerated fear of the gods, but this fear only manifests itself in an incorrect attitude towards sacrifice. There is still no mention of δειλία and the word seems here to be the opposite of εὐσέβεια, knowing how to sacrifice the right thing. We do not know for sure if what we find in Theophrastus is the neat formula of the peripatetic triplet which we find in Stobaeus (*Ecl.* II, 147, 18):[131]

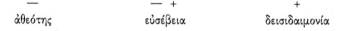

—	— +	+
ἀθεότης	εὐσέβεια	δεισιδαιμονία

In Aristotle himself we do not yet get it; indeed, that would have been impossible because the plus-term was not yet available: δεισιδαιμονία is still only used by him in a positive sense. In Theophrastus we do indeed get something like ἀθεότης. In the third fragment we read of people called ἄθεοι because they do not sacrifice, so we can draw up the following triplet according to the data in Περὶ Εὐσεβείας

—	— +	+
ἄθεοι	εὐσέβεια	δεισιδαιμονία

---

[129] Koets, *Deisidaimonia* 98.

[130] Pötscher, *Peri Eusebeias* 37 ff.

[131] Pötscher, *Strukturprobleme* 121, 123, thinks along this line, but he does not take the neurotic overtones and meaning of *deisidaimonia* into account.

The curious neurotic significance is still not to be found here since religious fear inspires, at best, excessively expensive sacrifices, but has no further scope of action. We can therefore conclude that the neurotic twist does not come from the analyses in Περὶ Εὐσεβείας but that this particular meaning was taken by Theophrastus from comedy. Even the mouse appears in comedy! An inverted relationship would also be conceivable, especially since, in the δεισιδαιμονία of the *Characters*, we actually encounter the pendant of the continuous εὐσέβεια of Περὶ Εὐσεβείας: viz. continuous fear. As a pendant, therefore, δεισιδαιμονία fits perfectly into Theophrastus' thought, and he may well have been the first man to give a neurotic bias to the word. The difference of genre, the comic *Character* as opposed to the serious analyses of Περὶ Εὐσεβείας may also have played a part. However this may be, *Plutarch* does *indeed* set out from the peripatetic triplet with a δεισιδαιμονία which can be interpreted neurotically.

2. *Plutarch*

The neat formula ἀθεότης-εὐσέβεια-δεισιδαιμονία is certainly the point of departure of Plutarch the pastor and pastoral worker in his early work Περὶ Δεισιδαιμονίας (171 F), where he gives a penetrating nosography. The sense of constant fear is strikingly described. The atheist says there is no god... and fends for himself. The *deisidaimon* says there are gods but they do not help us—on the contrary, they harm us.

Plutarch's remarks are of the greatest interest. A slave is indeed out of his master's reach at one point: he can even insist on being sold again (166 D). The man who is frightened of the sea need have no fear when he is at home. When slaves sleep they are no longer afraid of their master; but even in his dreams the *deisidaimon* is still afraid. For he fears the divine power under which he might succumb at any moment (166 E). There is no escape: robbers can resort to temples, but the *deisidaimon* is still more scared there than elsewhere, for the temple is the lair of the religious lion. Even death, a deliverance for so many, means, for the *deisidaimon*, transition to a world where everything is still worse (166 F).

Plutarch depicts the psychopathology of the *deisidaimon* in violent colours and in shrill tones. Within the peripatetic triplet he plays off the *deisidaimon* against the atheist, who puts up a better show than the religious neurotic (167 F ff.). The atheist who denies the existence of the gods is more endurable than the supertheist who suffers so much from the idea that the gods are βλαβεροί and λυπηροί, and that their specific activity consists in βλάπτειν instead of ὠφελεῖν (167 F ff.). According to Plutarch the *deisidaimon* is simply not clever enough to be an atheist (165 B and 167 E). He has a weak character and is paralysed by fear: think of the Jews who continued to celebrate the Sabbath as the enemy were setting up their ladders (169 D). And here we see Theophrastus' view returning: *deisidaimonia* is cowardice. Plutarch cannot have had a very favourable impression of the frightened 'superstitious' in Delphi. The anterooms were full of these people who wanted to bore the deity with their futilities. Hence, probably, his preference for the atheist. This preference may also have been connected with the fact that Plutarch was evidently drawing on a Cynical source, viz. a diatribe written by Bion of Borysthenes.[132] Bion was a notorious atheist who let the child of belief trickle out with the bath-water of *deisidaimonia*. Plutarch brought the *deisidaimon* and the atheist of Bion within the peripatetic triplet, and to think that he could have been so naïf as not to notice that he was introducing a preference for the atheist at the same time seems to me to be underestimating his intelligence.[133] Yet we must add that this choice was to give way in later works to an equally great aversion to *both* phenomena (*De Iside et Osiride* 355 D).[134]

So we see how views of atheism can change. Plato combats atheists with fire and sword: he even wants to lock them up. Plutarch explains them away, at least in comparison with the *deisidaimon* who is so stupid as not to let himself be talked out of his fear therapeutically by the philosopher and the statesman.

I now see that the circle is complete. According to the author of the *Dissoi Logoi* every argument must have a beginning, a middle and an end. According to Heraclitus the beginning and the end of a circle are the same thing. This is also true of my paper: it started and ends with atheism.

---

[132] G. Abernetty, *De Plutarchi qui fertur de superstitione libello* (Koningsbergen 1911) 89 ff.

[133] See H. Erbse, *Plutarchs Schrift* 'Περὶ Δεισιδαιμονίας, Hermes, 80 (1952) 300.

[134] H. Moellering, *Plutarch on superstition* (Boston 1963) 80, 81; see also J. Gwyn Griffiths, *Plutarch's De Iside et Osiride* (Cambridge 1970) 25, 26 and 291.

LIST OF ABBREVIATED TITLES OF BOOKS AND ARTICLES

D. Babut, *La religion* = *La religion des philosophes grecques* (Paris 1974).

C. M. Bowra, *Problems* = *Problems in greek Poetry* (Oxford 1953).

P. Decharme, *La critique* = *La critique des traditions religieuses chez les grecs* (Paris 1904, Brussels 1966).

E. Derenne, *Les procès* = *Les procès d'impiété, intentés aux philosophes à Athènes au Vme et au IVme siècles avant J.-C.* (Liège 1930).

E. R. Dodds, *The Greeks and the Irrational* (Oxford 1950).

——, *Progress*, = *The Ancient Concept of Progress and other Essays on Greek Literature and Belief* (Oxford 1973).

K. J. Dover, 'Freedom' = 'The Freedom of the Intellectual in Greek Society', *Talanta* 7 (1976).

W. Fahr, Θεοὺς = Θεοὺς νομίζειν. *Zum Problem der Anfänge des Atheismus bei den Griechen.* (Hildesheim 1969).

A. J. Festugière, *La révélation* = *La révélation d'Hermès Trismégiste* I-IV (Paris 1954).

W. K. C. Guthrie, *A History* = *A History of greek Philosophy* (Cambridge I, II, III, 1962 ff.).

B. Darrell Jackson, 'Prayers' = 'The prayers of Socrates', *Phronesis* 16 (1971).

F. Jacoby, *Diagoras* = *Diagoras ὁ ἄθεος* (Berlin 1960).

D. Kaufmann-Bühler, 'Eusebeia' = 'Eusebeia', in *Reallexikon für Antike und Christentum* 6 (Stuttgart 1966).

P. J. Koets, *Deisidaimonia* = *Deisidaimonia* (Purmerend 1928).

W. Kranz, 'Platonica' = 'Platonica I', *Philologus* 94 (1941).

P. J. M. G. van Litsenburg, *God en het goddelijke* = *God en het goddelijke in de dialogen van Plato* (Nijmegen 1955).

H. F. van der Meer, *Euhemerus* = *Euhemerus van Messene* (Amsterdam 1949).

P. A. Meijer, *Socratisch Schimmenspel* = *Socratisch Schimmenspel, Socrates' plaats in de griekse wijsbegeerte*, (Amsterdam 1974).

G. Morrow, *Plato's Cretan City* = *Plato's Cretan City, A Historical Interpretation of the Laws* (Princeton 1960).

W. Nestle, *Mythos* = *Vom Mythos zum Logos* (Stuttgart 1940).

E. des Places, *La religion grecque* = *La religion grecque, Dieux, cultes, rites et sentiment religieux dans la Grèce antique* (Paris 1969).

W. Pötscher, *Peri Eusebeias* = *Theophrastos Peri Eusebeias, griechischer Text, herausgegeben, übersetzt und eingeleitet* (Leyden 1964).

——, *Strukturprobleme* = *Strukturprobleme der aristotelischen und theophrastischen Gottesvorstellung* (Leyden 1970).

W. Schmidt, *Veteres* = *Veteres philosophi quomodo iudicaverint de precibus* (Giessen 1907).

H. Sjövall, *Zeus* = *Zeus im altgriechischen Hauskult* (Lund 1931).

W. J. Verdenius, 'Gottesbegriff' = 'Platons Gottesbegriff', in *Entretiens sur l'Antiquité classique* I (Genève 1952).

C. J. de Vogel, 'Scheppingsbegrip' = 'Het christelijk scheppingsbegrip en de antieke wijsbegeerte', *Tijds. v. Filosofie* 15 (1953) = *Theoria, studies over de griekse wijsbegeerte* (Assen 1967).

——, *Pythagoras* = *Pythagoras and early Pythagoreanism* (Assen 1966).

——, *Plato* = *Plato, de filosoof van het transcendente* (Baarn 1968).

——, *Philosophia I* = *Philosophia I, Studies in Greek Philosophy* (Assen 1970) (also in *Theoria*).

U. von Wilamowitz-Moellendorff, *Glaube* = *Der Glaube der Hellenen* I, (Berlin 1931, 1932).

INDEX I: NAMES AND SUBJECTS

INDEX II: GREEK AND LATIN WORDS

INDEX III: SOURCES

ANCIENT AUTHORS

INSCRIPTIONS

PAPYRI

1a

1b

1a-b. London, B.M. 1906. 12-15.1: Attic black-figured cup, height of frieze ca. 2 cm. By
courtesy of the Trustees of the British Museum.

2. Boston, M.F.A. 03.997: bronze statuette, height 20 cm. Courtesy Museum of Fine Arts. — 3. Athens, N.M. 1416: marble relief, height 45 cm. — 4. Athens, N.M. 6447: bronze statuette, height 28.8 cm. — 5. Athens, N.M. 6837: bronze shield, diameter 10.8 cm.

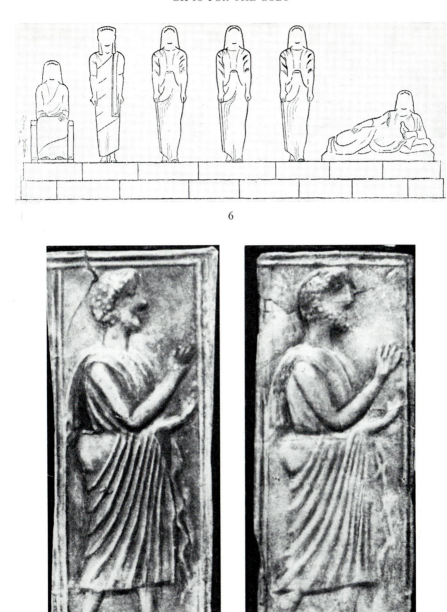

6

7

6. Marble group from the Heraion of Samos. — 7. Silver and bronze repoussé reliefs
from Mesembria.

8

9

8. Athens, N.M. 1431: marble relief, height 30 cm. — 9. Athens, N.M. 1408: marble
relief, height 25 cm.

10

11

12

10. Berlin, St.M. K91 (Inv. 723): marble relief, height 42 cm. Courtesy Staatliche Museen.
— 11. Delos, A 1858: bronze ears, height 10 cm. — 12. London, Wellcome Institute
Hist. Med. R 6665/1936: marble relief, width 38.5 cm. By courtesy of the Wellcome
Trustees.

13

14

13. Athens, N.M.: painted wooden pinax, height ca. 15 cm. — 14. Athens, N.M. 1395: marble relief, height 50 cm.

15

16

15. Paris, Louvre 752: marble relief, height 48 cm. Courtesy Musée du Louvre, photograph M. Chuzeville. — 16. Paris, Louvre 755: marble relief, height 49 cm. Courtesy Musée du Louvre, photograph M. Chuzeville.

17a

17b

17a-b. Istanbul, Mendel 836: marble stele, height 146 cm.

18

18. Athens, Akr.M. 581: marble relief, height 67 cm.

19a

19b

19a-b. Athens, N.M. 1335: marble relief, height 57 cm.

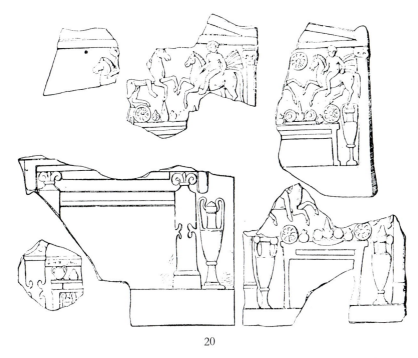

20

21

20. Taranto: fragments of terracotta reliefs. — 21. Tegea 132: marble relief, height 56 cm.

22

23

22. Athens, N.M. 4466: marble relief, height 70 cm. — 23. Athens, N.M. 2756: marble
relief, height 57 cm.

24

a

b

25   26

24. Athens, N.M. 6695: bronze statuette, height 7 cm. — 25a-b. Corinth: terracotta
models of *likna*, width ca. 9 cm. — 26. Marble stele from Ayazviran, height 88 cm.

27

27. Athens, N.M. 11036: terracotta pinax, height 44 cm.

28

29

30

28. Athens, N.M. 2723: marble relief, height 46 cm. — 29. London, B.M. 798: marble relief, height 34 cm. By courtesy of the Trustees of the British Museum. — 30. Syracuse 21186: Attic red-figured lekythos.

31

32   33

31. London, B.M. 2155: marble relief, height 52 cm. By courtesy of the Trustees of the British Museum. — 32. Athens, Akr.M. 577: marble relief, height 58 cm. — 33. Rhodos 14464: bronze wheel, diameter 7.4 cm.

34   35

36

34. Athens, N.M. Akr 739: fragment of Attic red-figured crater. — 35. Berlin F802: terracotta pinax (reverse), height 10.5 cm. — 36. Vari, relief in cave.

37

38

39

40

37. London, B.M. 252: bronze axe, length 16.5 cm. By courtesy of the Trustees of the British Museum. — 38. Berlin F831: terracotta pinax (reverse), height 10.5 cm. — 39. Athens, N.M. 1409: marble relief, height 34 cm. — 40. Bucarest L595: marble relief, height 41.5 cm.

41

42

41. Piraeus 405: marble relief, height 41 cm. — 42. Budapest and Vatican: marble relief, height 40 cm.

43

44

43. New York, M.M.A. 24.97.92: marble relief, height 26.7 cm. Courtesy Metropolitan Museum of Art. — 44. Nicosia, Cypr.M. 1935/B. 56: terracotta group, height ca. 9 cm. By courtesy of the Director of Antiquities and the Cyprus Museum.

45   46

45. Marble stele from Kula, height 66 cm. — 46. Marble stele from Köleköy, height 100 cm.

47

48

49

47. Brauron 5: marble relief. — 48. Marble stele from Phrygia. — 49. Modern Greek
picture of Hagios Modestos.

50

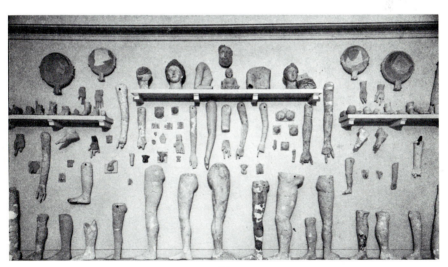

51

50. Athens, Akr.M. 7232: marble relief, height 16 cm. — 51. Corinth: terracotta votive offerings.

52. Athens, N.M. 3526: marble relief, height 73 cm. — 53. Athens, Epigr.M. 3224: marble relief. — 54. Marble stele from Gölde. — 55. Marble stele from Lydia Katakekaumene.

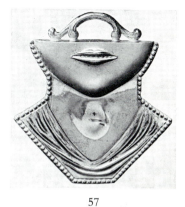

56

57

58

56. Athens, N.M. A11386: painted marble relief, height 19.3 cm. — 57. Modern Italian metal ex voto from Naples. — 58. Paros: marble plaque, height 13 cm.

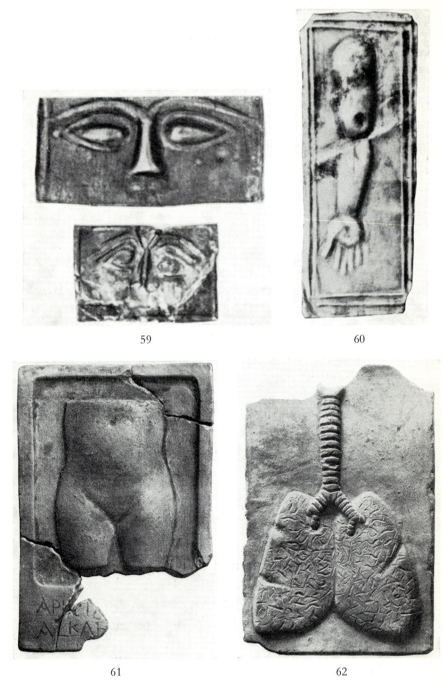

59

60

61

62

59-60. Metal repoussé reliefs from Mesembria. — 61-62. Terracotta reliefs from Kos (?),
height ca. 11 and ca. 12 cm.

63

64

63. Athens, N.M. 1821: marble relief. — 64. Terracotta relief from Kos (?), height ca. 12 cm.